STUDIES OF THE AMERICAS

edited by

Maxine Molyneux
Institute for the Study of the Americas
University of London
School of Advanced Study

Titles in this series are multidisciplinary studies of aspects of the societies of the hemisphere, particularly in the areas of politics, economics, history, anthropology, sociology, and the environment. The series covers a comparative perspective across the Americas, including Canada and the Caribbean as well as the United States and Latin America.

Titles in this series published by Palgrave Macmillan:

Cuba's Military 1990–2005: Revolutionary Soldiers during Counter-Revolutionary Times
   By Hal Klepak

The Judicialization of Politics in Latin America
   Edited by Rachel Sieder, Line Schjolden, and Alan Angell

Latin America: A New Interpretation
   By Laurence Whitehead

Appropriation as Practice: Art and Identity in Argentina
   By Arnd Schneider

America and Enlightenment Constitutionalism
   Edited by Gary L. McDowell and Johnathan O'Neill

Vargas and Brazil: New Perspectives
   Edited by Jens R. Hentschke

When Was Latin America Modern?
   Edited by Nicola Miller and Stephen Hart

Debating Cuban Exceptionalism
   Edited by Bert Hoffman and Laurence Whitehead

Caribbean Land and Development Revisited
   Edited by Jean Besson and Janet Momsen

Cultures of the Lusophone Black Atlantic
   Edited by Nancy Priscilla Naro, Roger Sansi-Roca, and David H. Treece

Democratization, Development, and Legality: Chile, 1831–1973
   By Julio Faundez

The Hispanic World and American Intellectual Life, 1820–1880
   By Iván Jaksić

The Role of Mexico's Plural in Latin American Literary and Political Culture: From Tlatelolco to the "Philanthropic Ogre"
   By John King

Faith and Impiety in Revolutionary Mexico
   Edited by Matthew Butler

Reinventing Modernity in Latin America: Intellectuals Imagine the Future, 1900–1930
   By Nicola Miller

The Republican Party and Immigration Politics: From Proposition 187 to George W. Bush
 By Andrew Wroe

The Political Economy of Hemispheric Integration: Responding to Globalization in the Americas
 Edited by Diego Sánchez-Ancochea and Kenneth C. Shadlen

Ronald Reagan and the 1980s: Perceptions, Policies, Legacies
 Edited by Cheryl Hudson and Gareth Davies

Wellbeing and Development in Peru: Local and Universal Views Confronted
 Edited by James Copestake

The Federal Nation: Perspectives on American Federalism
 Edited by Iwan W. Morgan and Philip J. Davies

Base Colonies in the Western Hemisphere, 1940–1967
 By Steven High

Beyond Neoliberalism in Latin America? Societies and Politics at the Crossroads
 Edited by John Burdick, Philip Oxhorn, and Kenneth M. Roberts

Visual Synergies in Fiction and Documentary Film from Latin America
 Edited by Miriam Haddu and Joanna Page

Cuban Medical Internationalism: Origins, Evolution, and Goals
 By John M. Kirk and H. Michael Erisman

Governance after Neoliberalism in Latin America
 Edited by Jean Grugel and Pía Riggirozzi

Modern Poetics and Hemispheric American Cultural Studies
 By Justin Read

Youth Violence in Latin America: Gangs and Juvenile Justice in Perspective
 Edited by Gareth A. Jones and Dennis Rodgers

The Origins of Mercosur
 By Gian Luca Gardini

Belize's Independence & Decolonization in Latin America: Guatemala, Britain, and the UN
 By Assad Shoman

Post-Colonial Trinidad: An Ethnographic Journal
 By Colin Clarke and Gillian Clarke

The Nitrate King: A Biography of "Colonel" John Thomas North
 By William Edmundson

Negotiating the Free Trade Area of the Americas
 By Zuleika Arashiro

History and Language in the Andes
 Edited by Paul Heggarty and Adrian J. Pearce

Cross-Border Migration among Latin Americans: European Perspectives and Beyond
 Edited by Cathy McIlwaine

Native American Adoption, Captivity, and Slavery in Changing Contexts
 Edited by Max Carocci and Stephanie Pratt

Native American Adoption, Captivity, and Slavery in Changing Contexts

Edited by
Max Carocci
Stephanie Pratt

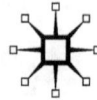

NATIVE AMERICAN ADOPTION, CAPTIVITY, AND SLAVERY IN CHANGING CONTEXTS
Copyright © Max Carocci and Stephanie Pratt, 2012.

All rights reserved.

First published in 2012 by
PALGRAVE MACMILLAN®
in the United States—a division of St. Martin's Press LLC,
175 Fifth Avenue, New York, NY 10010.

Where this book is distributed in the UK, Europe and the rest of the world, this is by Palgrave Macmillan, a division of Macmillan Publishers Limited, registered in England, company number 785998, of Houndmills, Basingstoke, Hampshire RG21 6XS.

Palgrave Macmillan is the global academic imprint of the above companies and has companies and representatives throughout the world.

Palgrave® and Macmillan® are registered trademarks in the United States, the United Kingdom, Europe and other countries.

ISBN: 978–0–230–11505–7

Library of Congress Cataloging-in-Publication Data

    Native American adoption, captivity, and slavery in changing contexts / edited by Max Carocci and Stephanie Pratt.
       p. cm.
    "Papers presented at the conference Adoption, Captivity and Slavery: Changing Meanings in Colonial North America that took place at the British Museum, in London on Feb 17th and 18th, 2008."
    Includes bibliographical references.
    ISBN 978–0–230–11505–7 (alk. paper)
    1. Indian slaves—North America—History. 2. Slave trade—North America—History. 3. Indian captivities—North America—History. 4. Adoption—North America—History. I. Carocci, Max. II. Pratt, Stephanie, 1958–

E59.S63N38 2011
973.04′97—dc23   2011020945

A catalogue record of the book is available from the British Library.

Design by Newgen Imaging Systems (P) Ltd., Chennai, India.

First edition: January 2012

Contents

List of Illustrations   vii

Preface   ix
J. C. H. King

Introduction: Contextualizing Native American Adoption,
Captivity, and Slavery   1
Max Carocci and Stephanie Pratt

Chapter 1
Ripe for Colonial Exploitation: Ancient Traditions of
Violence and Enmity as Preludes to the Indian Slave Trade   23
Marvin D. Jeter

Chapter 2
The Emergence of the Colonial South: Colonial Indian
Slaving, the Fall of the Precontact Mississippian World, and
the Emergence of a New Social Geography in the
American South, 1540–1730   47
Robbie Ethridge

Chapter 3
Southeastern Indian Polities of the Seventeenth Century:
Suggestions toward an Analytical Vocabulary   65
Eric E. Bowne

Chapter 4
From Captives to Kin: Indian Slavery and Changing Social
Identities on the Louisiana Colonial Frontier   79
Dayna Bowker Lee

Chapter 5
Capturing Captivity: Visual Imaginings of the English and
Powhatan Encounter Accompanying the Virginia Narratives
of John Smith and Ralph Hamor, 1612–1634   97
Stephanie Pratt

Chapter 6
Strategies of (Un)belonging: The Captivities of
John Smith, Olaudah Equiano, and John Marrant   117
Susan Castillo Street

Chapter 7
Captive or Captivated: Rethinking Encounters in
Early Colonial America   131
Patrick Minges

Chapter 8
A Christian Disposition: Religious Identity in the
Meeker Captivity Narrative   147
Brandi Denison

Chapter 9
Visual Representation as a Method of Discourse on
Captivity, Focused on Cynthia Ann Parker   167
Lin Holdridge

Epilogue
Reflections and Refractions from the Southwest
Borderlands   185
James F. Brooks

Notes on Contributors   197

Bibliography   201

Index   247

Illustrations

Figures

1.1 Locations of major archaeological cultures and tribes to mid-18th century. Map by Robbie Ethridge © reproduced with the author's permission.   24

1.2 *Pipe* Mississippian culture *ca.* 1200. The Putnam Dana McMillan Fund. Minneapolis Institute of Arts accession number: 2004.118.   35

2.1 The transformation of the Southern Indians, 1540–1715. Map by Robbie Ethridge. Reproduced courtesy of the University of North Carolina Press.   48

5.1 Detail, "Map of Virginia" engraved map (frontispiece) in John Smith's *Generall Historie of Virginia* (London, 1624; shelfmark G.7037). © The British Library.   105

5.2 *Tombe of the Weroans* watercolor drawing by John White, *ca.* 1590. © The Trustees of the British Museum, London.   106

5.3 *Their Idol called Kiwasa* engraving by Theodore de Bry, after John White, published in Theodore de Bry, *Grand Voyages*, Part I, London, 1590. © The British Library.   107

5.4 "Pocahontas deceitfully handed over to the English" engraving (plate 7) by Abelius after Georg Keller in Theodore de Bry and family, *Grand Voyages*, Part X (London, 1619). © The British Library.   109

5.5 "Various scenes in Virginia", engraved illustration (between p. 40 and 41) in John Smith's *Generall Historie of Virginia* (London, 1624; shelfmark G.7037). © The British Library. 111

5.6 "Smith saved from death by Pocahontas and religious ceremonies", copperplate engraving from Johann Ludwig Gottfriedt's *Newe Welt vnd americanische Historien* (Frankfurt: Bey denen Merianischen Erben, 1655). This is an abridged version of Theodore de Bry and Sons, Grand Voyages, Part XIII (London, 1634). © The Wisconsin Historical Society. WHi-23856. 113

9.1 Frances Slocum with her two daughters, George Winter, watercolor 1841. Courtesy of Tippecanoe County Historical Association, Lafayette, Indiana. 171

9.2 Cynthia Ann Parker, A. F. Corning, 1860 [Hacker]. Courtesy of Denver Public Library, Western History Collection, call no. X-32238. 179

9.3 Cynthia Ann Parker, photograph by William W. Bridgers. Courtesy of Degolyer Library, Southern Methodist University, Dallas, Texas Ag.2008.0005. 180

E.1 Reconstructed eighteenth-century fortified *placita* at Rancho de las Golondrinas, image courtesy of author. 186

E.2 *Cuarto de Cautivos* at Rancho de las Golondrinas. Image courtesy of author. 187

E.3 Martínez Hacienda, *cuarto de cautivos* in far corner of courtyard. Image courtesy of author. 189

E.4 Potsui'i Incised Jar from Puye village, New Mexico, *ca.* 1425–1525, courtesy New Mexico Laboratory of Anthropology, collection no. 20852/11. Puye LA47 Museum of Indian Arts and Culture/Laboratory of Anthropology, Department of Cultural Affairs. www.miaclab.org. Photography by David McNeece. 189

Table

4.1 Slaves counts in Natchitoches post French censuses   87

Preface

Here Max Carocci and Stephanie Pratt publish an exceptional group of essays from a groundbreaking conference held in 2008 at the British Museum, part of the *Atlantic Trade and Identity* season starting in 2007 which commemorated the 200th anniversary of the abolition of the slave trade. In what follows, they have taken the theme of captivity as an eloquent gateway into understanding the other parts of a complex of deeply embedded practices, which included slavery and enforced adoption in early North America. In an imperial context, the broad theme *Captives* (2002) was first brought to general attention by Linda Colley's work of the same title. In this volume the editors have focused again on Native American abduction, its consequences, and the hybrid narratives that both separate and join the story with broader histories. But complex histories, such as the colonial enslavement of Native Americans, Native American slavery, and the relationship of Native America and African America, seldom sit easily in either historical discourses or inside museums and their displays. And, in a sense, that is as it should be: these are not histories with which institutions and individuals should be comfortable. Further, the material evidence of complex stories seldom survives except in a few outstanding objects. One such item is the early eighteenth-century Virginia drum, which came with the foundation collection of the British Museum in 1753 labeled then as an "Indian" drum, although actually of Akan origin from coastal Ghana.[1] This was included in the British Museum's 2010 *History of the World* project. Another group of items are "warrior ties" or tumplines, made of vegetable fiber and used to hobble the captives of Native Americans as they walked into adoptive servitude. Similarly complex and also seldom mentioned are the relationships of African and Native Americans. In his autobiography *Colored People* (1995) Henry Louis Gates, Jr. speaks of his great-uncle Griff Brice as hunting and fishing as though he owned the woods, part of his West Virginia cultural inheritance as a Native American.[2]

All Gates's relations claimed Native American descent, "Negroes with green eyes" he calls them. Further Gates says that Griff's abilities as a hunter, and his rhiney or reddish color provided evidence of Native American ancestry for the Gates family. The close association of Native Americans with African Americans, in a complex and difficult relationship, has rarely been explored—witness the story of Chief Buffalo Child Lance, the silent screen actor, perhaps first introducing to the wider world this important reality through the life of a famous and tragic antihero. The editors' ambition, amply fulfilled here, is to bring together a cultural and anthropological understanding of Native American slavery, with a separate look through case studies at the visual and textual record. It is to be hoped that further research and scholarly publication will follow.

J. C. H. King,
Keeper of Anthropology
Department of Africa Oceania and the Americas
The British Museum

Notes

1. The drum of *fontomfrom* type is widely made and used in Ghana today, and was probably brought to America on a slave ship. There, it may have been used in the morning exercise of dancing the slaves.
2. Henry Louis Gates, Jr., Colored People (London: Penguin Books, 1995), 157.

Introduction: Contextualizing Native American Adoption, Captivity, and Slavery

Max Carocci and Stephanie Pratt

This book gathers together the majority of the papers presented at the conference "Adoption, Captivity and Slavery: Changing Meanings in Colonial North America" that took place at the British Museum in London on February 17 and 18, 2008. The conference was planned to fit in with the many national events that were organized to mark the anniversary of the abolition of the slave trade in Great Britain in 1807 and our intention was to mark these events with a fresh examination of the Anglo-American and indigenous context for slavery and its associated practices of captivity, forced labor, and adoption. As the conference organizers we felt that the timing for such an event seemed appropriate as this broader context would give us an opportunity to bring to public attention the largely unacknowledged history of Native American[1] enslavement taking place in a precontact situation at each other's hands, and later in the postcontact period, at the hands of British and other colonial powers.

The historical and interpretative framework known as the British Atlantic with its emphasis on a developing African slave trade was also a factor in directing our attention toward those areas of North America involved with the historical development of European and Indian slaving enterprises, such as the Mid-Atlantic states, French Louisiana, and parts of the Southwest. Most of the case studies under examination here address instances we recognize as slavery, adoption, and captivity that converged in interesting and unprecedented ways. The particularly rich cultural context engendered by these new historical predicaments enabled us to unpack the complexities articulated around these notions.

Programs of museums and academic institutions concerned with this anniversary showed that, contrary to the enormous coverage of the Atlantic middle passage, there was little or no reference to the pre-African origins of the slave trade in North America either in planned publications or in research symposia then taking place. The gap seemed especially puzzling given the well-documented British involvement in slaving campaigns against Native Americans decades before a systematic and formalized plantation system was instituted in North America through African forced labor at the beginning of the eighteenth century.

Current treatment of North American slavery in standard historical accounts tends to do away with Native Americans in a few sentences. The majority of recent studies of slavery in the Americas hardly mention the involvement of Native North Americans, and those who do, mostly concentrate on the indigenous populations of Mexico, the Caribbean, and southern regions (Davis 2006; Eltis, Lewis, and Sokoloff 2004; Heuman and Walkin 2003; Rawley 2005). From these books, we can gauge that the indigenous peoples of North America experienced some form of bondage under the Europeans, yet their experiences are generally represented as incidental or marginal to the larger narrative of North American history, so much so that in a recent essay historian Joyce Chaplin (2005) has aptly called this phenomenon the "captivity without the narrative." Indeed, a large part of past and present scholarship continues to prefer articulating North America's historical narratives around tales of Native American resistance to colonization, relegating Africans to being the only true victims of the cruel trade in human beings.

With this collection we want to challenge this popular view by focusing on the variety of ways in which Native Americans became victims, but also perpetrators, of slaving practices encouraged by the historical predicaments that followed from the colonial encounter. The general focus of this book is precisely the variety of instances of captivity, bondage, or kidnap of indigenous Americans and to a lesser extent Europeans and Africans that enable us to frame a Native American discourse about slavery and cognate notions. The case studies presented here show a multiplicity of permutations of the commonly held notion of slavery, which includes a variety of different ways of incorporating people into new social settings that cannot be adequately described with this term. In what follows it becomes clear that framing a discourse about slavery with reference to the Native American context is no simple endeavor due to these permutations, and the ways we can interpret the practice of slaving and other forms of social incorporation are often the result of intercultural exchanges that are generally described through the language of the colonizers. Native accounts that report their views on these issues are much less well known, understood, or uncovered and could be termed a "hidden history" for the general public. What we know of their experiences under slavery or captivity is at best conjectural, if not extremely patchy.

Although many American Indian slaves' names have reached us through historical documents (Ekberg 2007), unfortunately in most cases, they will probably remain only names (chapter four in this volume; Wedel 1973). With the exception of rare biographical details of unique individuals such as, for example, the Siouan Francisco de Chicora who described his lands to the Italian writer Pietro Martire d'Anghiera in the sixteenth century, the famous Patuxent, Tisquantum, who helped the Pilgrims in 1621, LaSalle's mysterious "Pana" slave, or Lamhatty, the escaped Towasa slave, who told his ordeal to the English in 1706, the few indigenous narratives that were retrieved cannot account for the extreme diversity of occurrences documented over a period of more than 400 years throughout the continent (Bushnell 1908; Minges 2004). With this book we try to achieve the difficult task of finding a common language with which we can bridge incommensurable systems of thought, politics, and cultural signification that converge in the experiences we now term "adoption," "captivity," and "slavery" as they were contingently negotiated between Native Americans, Africans, and Europeans (chapters six and seven in this volume).

As recently highlighted by several scholars, what renders the crosscultural translation of these notions even more problematic is the extreme malleability of the concept of slavery under different cultural predicaments and historical locations, from the western areas of the Northwest Coast, the Plateau, and California (Donald 1997; Hajda 2005; Heizer 1974; 1988; Mitchell 1984), through the Southwest (Brooks 2002), and the Texas/Mexico frontier (Barr 2007), to the Midwest (Ekberg 2007), the Northeast (Donald 1985; Rushforth 2003), and the Southeast (Ethridge and Shuck-Hall 2009; Gallay 2002; Perdue 1979; Santos-Granero 2009). This body of research has begun to trace the economic and cultural contours of a complex phenomenon that has in the extensively recorded trade in captives its most detectable permutation (Martin 1994; Mitchell 1984; Wiegers 1988). This collection's essays directly engage with this body of work through the presentation of new case studies that can expand it while asking questions that emerge from an interdisciplinary dialogue between distinct theories and methodologies derived from anthropology, history of art, literature, and archaeology. We wished that this exercise would challenge the analytical terms and categories used in these disciplines to frame the discussion of slavery and its cognate notions.

In addition, with regard to the concepts at the thematic center of this book, no one has yet attempted to bring together different perspectives on these issues that the present collection tries to champion through an examination of Native American case studies. Here each author individually explores specific aspects of these notions, while they collectively contribute to draw the outlines of very complex colonial scenarios in which ideas of adoption, captivity, and slavery emerge as historically contingent, culturally specific, multilayered, unstable, negotiable, and often mutually exclusive. This complexity is an invitation to radically rethink the theoretical parameters through which we interpret both current and past societies. As academia is currently moving toward theoretical, methodological, and analytical cross-fertilizations, this first attempt to examine in detail the ways in which seemingly discrete concepts can converge in complex formations has great potential for future theoretical and methodological developments across and beyond disciplinary boundaries.

Because of the complexity of the issues raised by this interdisciplinary approach at the London conference, we subsequently contemplated whether a widespread lack of engagement with the full experience of North American slavery and its associated practices of captivity and adoption didn't require a complete reassessment of the field as it had been understood up to this time. In other words, we reached the conclusion that without the addition of the American Indian contexts and experiences, a true picture of the history of slavery on the continent would not be possible.

Consequently, we posed as the principal aim of this book the examination of the phenomenon of Native American slavery through added analyses of instances of adoption and captivity because of the role these activities played not only in the contingent adjustments to new contexts required by the colonial encounter, but in the creation of the discursive, visual, and textual representations of these New World predicaments. Here specialists operating in the various disciplines tease out the meanings attributed to adoption, captivity, and slavery as instances of cross-cultural exchange in which novel forms of incorporation of humans in alien social settings generated new meanings. Their analyses can be used to build a more informed understanding of the interaction between beliefs, practices, and representations without which none of the historical dimensions of Native American slavery can be fully appreciated.

Examples of both the recorded and visual evidence relating to experiences of adoption, captivity, and slavery are here given equal significance because they can help us evaluate the intricate relationships between lived realities, their various perceptions, and textual and visual languages through which this knowledge was divulged. The book has therefore two main objectives: that of considering the analytical usefulness of categories that describe both experiences and representations, and that of generating more unexpected connections between academic fields generally kept separate.

What is more, the potential connections that can be drawn between the essays represented in this collection reach well beyond what may appear as a pure academic exercise. Now more than ever, a simultaneous examination of adoption, captivity, and slavery, framed from the perspective of indigenous Americans, has serious implications not only for a deeper insight into the history of the continent at large, but for the lives of contemporary people that occupy the geographical areas that today are labeled North America and the Caribbean. Indeed, such discussions can be fruitful in further expanding our comprehension of the current processes of identity formation, as well as inviting a wider evaluation of the historical bases at the root of the legal and political struggles of a substantial number of social constituencies that often fall between the cracks of polarized discourses about blackness and whiteness. These are notably nonfederally recognized Native American groups, Creole blacks, Black Indians seeking tribal citizenship, Métis (legally recognized Canadian ethnic group of French and indigenous descent), as well as Caribbean peoples whose indigenous ancestry has been obliterated by a discourse about racial purity and whose metaphorical power can be clearly detected in the existing racialized and polarized political idioms of the United States, Mexico, Canada, and elsewhere.

These and many other groups are the product of an intermingling of peoples that has its roots in slaving, captivity, barter, exchange, ransom, and other forms of human incorporation that frequently brought together peoples from very distant areas, especially between Africans coming from overseas territories and Native North Americans shipped to the Caribbean (e.g., Boissevain 1981; Covington 1967; Forbes 1993; Lauber 1979 [1913]; Morgan 1984; Peyser 1989/90), but also, extensively, between European colonists, adventurers, soldiers, and entrepreneurs and Africans, or Native Americans in North

America (Sayers, Burke, and Henry 2007; Usner 1992; chapters six and seven in this volume).

It has been finally proven that sending Native American captives as slaves to the Caribbean islands was a common procedure among all the colonial powers. With the available figures at hand Gallay (2002) calculated that the British alone sent to the West Indies more than 51,000 people before 1715 in what some have rightfully called a "middle passage in reverse" (Lauber 1913, p. 127, note 2; Nash 1974, p. 113; Wright 1981, p. 130). Accurate numbers coming from French, Spanish, and Dutch sources are still wanting. In addition, the present numbers do not account for the many captives who went unrecorded either because they died during forced marches to their destinations, or simply because they appear under European names without ethnic affiliation. The forced "diaspora" of Native Americans that was at the base of a colony-to-colony exchange system deployed by all European powers in North America continued well into the early eighteenth century, and in some areas like the Spanish borderlands, California, and Great Basin, into the nineteenth century (Heizer 1974; chapters eight and nine in this volume).

As growing numbers of African slaves entered into an evolving system of bondage, new forms of social interaction emerged in which the original irrelevance of racial differences recorded among Native Americans and Africans was turned on its head to become the basis of colonial discriminatory laws aimed at controlling increasingly mixed populations (chapter four in this volume). It is partially because of racial laws (such as those passed in Virginia's colonial legislation) and census miscounting that Native Americans gradually disappeared from the records of history as victims of slavery, serfdom, and other forms of bondage that today are most often associated with Africans.

The common perception that Indians never formed a substantial portion of North America's total slave population has, in part, its roots in the routine reclassification of Indians as blacks that began shortly after the British moved toward the establishment of a chattel model of slavery. This reclassification systematically wrote Native Americans out of the official records. As new racial classifications became more prominent in the systematic management of the colonial populations, nonwhite people slowly became "people of color," and by default became associated with the growing "black" population. The result of the correspondence between these racialized terms was the conflation of racial classification with geographic provenance that rendered coterminous the nouns "black" and "African" (Forbes 1983; 1993).

As some scholars have often remarked, the purposeful reclassification of Native Americans as "black" or "people of color" resulted in a "bureaucratic genocide" that today renders difficult the reconstruction of a widespread and prolonged history of Native American slavery, bondage, and serfdom (Herndon and Sekatau 1997). The bureaucratic erasure of Indians from the records of the history of slavery and other forms of bondage offers supporting evidence of the complexity of nonblack and white versions of history that have been trapped in a dualistic framework that has hampered the construction of a more realistic version of the lives of those who experienced the facts of slavery during colonial times.

The unprecedented level of interethnic relations occurring in colonial contexts is as important for a reassessment of issues of adoption, captivity, and slavery across ethnic classifications as are the large movements of peoples that occurred as a result of European governments' policies, their colonies' own economic development, and individual entrepreneurship. All this gave rise to a complex web of relocations, resettlements, barter of people, and involuntary migrations that crisscrossed the northern American hemisphere and the Caribbean area throughout the eighteenth century. Both large- and small-scale movements often led to the dissolution of ancient nations, and the creation of new social groupings that invite us to rethink entirely the notion of "extinction" of peoples. All this had a deep impact on ethnic and group identity as many of the Caribbean and North American enclaves such as the Westo (chapter three in this volume) emerged and then "disappeared" from the continent's geohistorical map during these turbulent times. As is evident from the essays in this collection, adoption practices became more widespread as colonial powers dissolved entire populations and shipped the remnants to overseas colonies. The rarely explored population dynamics referred to in this volume call attention to unexpected centers of human exchange around which developed distinct local and distant peripheries. This is a perspective that can potentially disrupt a conventional version of economic and political geography generally concerned with the history of the Atlantic slave trade.

It is on these premises that the authors of this collection have collectively acknowledged the need for an urgent reevaluation of both the visual records and the terms that frame the multiple forms of bondage, social incorporation, and human exchange occurring between different groups in North America's colonial period with the aim of augmenting and expanding an existing corpus of studies that, so far, has maintained separate the many Native American experiences and narratives of slavery, adoption, and captivity (Turner Strong 2002).

Framing the Field

The terms "captivity," "slavery," and "adoption" frequently recur in the specialized literature about Native American cultural practices, but also in the historical treatment of wars and interethnic relations. Such terms also surface in the conventionally romanticized stories of foreigners selected to become honorary members of Indian tribes, and feature in studies of hierarchically ordered societies that support evolutionist theories that explain the rise of cultural complexity. Instances of adoption and captivity populate the images of populist and propagandistic literature of the colonial period, and the lurid details of the sufferings of individuals in bondage have become a literary *genre* in its own right: the captivity narrative (chapters five, six, eight, and nine in this volume). Imagery of the brutal, violent, and "savage" Indian contained in captivity and adoption narratives created a strong stereotype within popular representations. The ubiquity of the scalping Indian image, for example, has overridden more nuanced analyses and interpretations of the contexts in which scalping practices found their meaning. Past scholarship has generally represented scalping as inhuman or extreme; current understanding of Native American belief systems is however reevaluating simplistic explanations of such practices.

These biased representations are the product of specific linguistic and philosophical histories that are shaped by the meanings given in Indo-European languages to notions that do not always correspond to evaluations found in Native American terminologies. Achieving the analytical clarity necessary for a deeper understanding of social and cultural realities that may appear universally similar despite differences in time and space, or pertaining to diametrically opposed epistemologies, is an arduous task because in a tumultuous era of transformations such as North America's colonial period a multiplicity of practices may have simultaneously lived side by side, perhaps overlapping, or even replacing, previously existing models of social integration operating among different linguistic groups.

Among the first scholars that examined the semantic mismatch between incommensurable categories presented by several North American cases was Almon Lauber who in his groundbreaking early twentieth-century *opera magna* about Indian slavery (1979 [1913]) defined the term "slavery" to which he juxtaposed the term "adoption" and the concept of "prisoner." With regard to this nomenclature, he eagerly pointed out that some misunderstanding may derive from the erroneous interpretation of colonial French and Spanish sources that report the widespread Native American practice of taking prisoners as synonymous with "slavery." He also referred to the term "adoption," which he says is often confused with the same concept (Lauber 1979, p. 25). What is most interesting about his juxtaposition of terms that in most European languages describe very different experiences is precisely that an in-depth reading of North American ethnology and history necessitates a clarification of the multiple ways in which these terms converge as is apparent from the contributions in this collection. Recorded ethnohistorical and ethnographic practices among Iroquoian and Siouan-speaking peoples, for example, show that the language of adoption was used to describe a variety of forms of social incorporation that not only set up roles and hierarchies among adopters and adoptees, but also fixed cosmic imbalances generated by the loss of tribal members (Beauchamp 1975 [1906]; Skinner 1915; Speck 1942; Starna and Watkins 1991; Traphagan 2008). Among several tribes, for example, ceremonial scalp adoption reveals how the vital forces contained in human hair could replace the loss of human life. As such, scalps legitimately functioned as virtual adoptees (Carocci 1999; forthcoming 2012).

As a working definition Lauber (1979) adopted a notion of slavery that, to paraphrase his words, referred to the general practice of eliciting labor from individuals who had no decision-making autonomy throughout their life (p. 26). Importantly, he also highlighted however that ideas of valor, prestige, personal power, and authority influenced locally based notions of captivity and adoption through a complex interplay of practices, values, and beliefs that differed between ethnic groups speaking very different languages from period to period.

Although it would be tempting to restrict a concept of "slavery" to the definition given by Lauber, we must also be aware that in a Native American context there exist other examples of un-free labor and conditions of bondage that do not require physical work and that, while not always institutionalized, nevertheless share some of the characteristics outlined in Lauber's definition. In a useful bibliography prepared by Russell Magnaghi (1998) we can detect a move toward a notion of slavery that is closer to the interpretation proposed here because he includes in it forms of bondage, captivity, and forced labor that elude any strict definition of slavery as can be seen by his addition of "evangelization" among the terms associated with coercion and lack of individual choice. In his bibliography Magnaghi included books and articles that concern roles based on forced labor such as the Spanish *repartimientos* and missions where Indians were congregated on the pretense of religious education, indigenous norms that limited the agency of some sections of the population, or instances of total dependency on what appears to be a master or an owner. While his exemplary compilation is undoubtedly useful, he omits forms of permanent bondage that did not entail forced labor, but that rather served ritual and symbolic functions, for example, among the precolonial Mississippian societies (chapter one in this volume, but also Santos-Granero 2009), the Cherokee, Iroquois, and Siouan Indians, or among the peoples of the Northwest Coast, to cite a few. Especially these latter forms cannot be assimilated to utilitarian versions of permanent un-free statuses in that they include religious and spiritual meanings alongside notions of prestige and social standing that hardly feature in general discussions of slavery. Moreover, the whole gamut of experiences encompassed under this nomenclature has a gendered aspect that ought to include forced marriages, concubinage, and prostitution imposed on Native women adopted, exchanged, or captured for ransom (chapters four and five in this volume).

As often happens in North American colonial predicaments, features such as forced labor conditions that are generally deemed best to describe a state of permanent slavery, cross-cut the differences generally drawn between captivity, slavery, and adoption to enter other realms of experience: for example, marriage (Barr 2005), or labor apprenticeship (Herndon and Sekatau 2003). But because these various experiences can either be temporary or permanent and they are multilayered, a straightforward application of the aforementioned notion of slavery is not always universally suitable.

Anthropologist Pauline Turner Strong (2002) has remarked that scholars until now worked almost independently on the issues covered by the terms originally juxtaposed by Lauber. Her review of the existing literature up to 2001 suggests that terms such as adoption, captivity, and slavery might *still* be viewed separately (p. 339). Her preference for words such as "incorporation" and "subordination" encourages us to think about alternative ways in which these different terms can satisfactorily express the complex scenarios presented by the many instances of exchange and the gradual assimilation of people between colonial-period Africans, Native Americans, and Europeans.

In a recent analysis of Native American female captivity among Spanish and French of the eighteenth century, historian Juliana Barr demonstrated that the almost infinite variability of forms of bondage experienced by these women can expand our understanding of slaving practices precisely because in them converge a multiplicity of meanings that exceed the categorical definition of slavery as a "chattel-oriented system of coerced labor" (Barr 2005, p. 46). Her argument, alongside James Brooks's convincing evidence is that, in the North American context, there is a fine line between kinship and slavery (chapter four in this volume, but also Brooks 2002), which shows the emergence of a novel way to approach the multifaceted nature of Native American practices of social incorporation.

This is the perspective shared by the contributors to this collection who have integrated in the treatment of their particular cases notions of bondage and coercion that encompass multiple experiences and accounts of slavery, captivity, and adoption in a fluid formation in which historically situated meanings converge in a seamless continuum bringing together the many peoples that interacted on the North American continent over more than 400 years.

Framing the Visual Field

Turner Strong's (2008) recent overview of the field of representation of Native American culture and art from a multidisciplinary perspective lends us the opportunity here to reevaluate such material for its contribution to the conceptual bases of the terminology of adoption, captivity, and slavery. Published studies of the visual representation of Native American peoples and their cultures in European art have greatly expanded the general approaches to be taken to the field of colonial image-making and its meaning (Bickham 2005; Feest 1967; Gaudio 2008; Honour 1975; Pratt 2005). However, as with the historical and anthropological situations, no single study has concentrated exclusively on the imagery of slavery, captivity, and adoption as cultural/intercultural phenomena that may be interrelated. Analyses have been made of the sixteenth-century illustrated accounts of travel to the Americas published by Theodor de Bry (*Historia Americae*, 1590–1634), some of which included images of the captivity and ritual incorporation practices to be found in certain Native American cultures of the South East and Brazilian Amazon areas during the early colonial era (Alexander 1976; Bucher 1981). The melding of image and text that structures the narratives included in European travel literature as a form of expression has been evaluated and theorized (Bucher 1981; Pratt 1992; particularly with respect to the cross-cultural encounter.

Studies of captivity narratives as a particularly American literary form often discuss the imagery that accompanies such accounts but none so far have fully explored in a synoptic history the visual representation of Native American captivity (chapter nine in this volume). U.S.-based art historians have built a substantial literature on the imaging of the American West, of which the Indian captivity is a major component (Hills 1973; Schimmel 1991) but this is the most dominant trope to be fully examined in the secondary literature and it is not often shown in light of other wartime or slaving practices that existed in conjunction with it.

It is unfortunate, in light of such existing studies, that more recent published histories of colonial contact, trade, and warfare often leave image-making and the processes embodied in visual representation unaccounted for and under-analyzed in contradistinction to the written texts recounting these activities (Gallay 2002; Starkey 1998). It is only very recently that an examination that integrates the production of Native American imagery within the wider field of visual culture of its particular historical era has appeared (Gaudio 2008). In addition, a number of anthropological studies address the ways that Native-produced material culture can also be mobilized to further account for a visual culture of slaving or captivity (Stephenson 2007; chapter one and epilogue in this volume). Many of these analyses address the ways that imagery concentrates and conceptualizes for its audiences some of the violent and warlike aspects of the Native American cultures that Europeans were contacting at this time. The problem of imagery as an irrefutable form of evidence has also left much relevant visual material out of the historical account, or has accepted it uncritically as anthropological or ethnographical data (Sturtevant 1976). Reference works such as some encyclopedias show images that are clearly relevant but underinterpreted and left as mute evidence (Keenan 1999). For the most part, visual imagery is deployed merely as illustrative matter in historical accounts of these practices and for want of visual analysis it has been rendered mute and unavailable to investigators as a means of further understanding and interpreting these phenomena as they were enacted in violent or other forms of social, bodily, or spiritual incorporation in Native American societies.

There exist only a handful of examples of colonial period image-making that focus in particular on the activities of Native American slaving, captivity, social incorporation, and the variety in these practices. The account of captivity written by Hans Staden (first published

1557, and reprinted in 1592 as *Americae tertia pars memorabile provinciae Brasiliae historiam contine[n]s, germanico primùm sermone scriptam àIoan[n]e Stadio..., nunc autem latinitate donatam à Teucrio Annaeo Priuato Colchanthe* [i.e., J.A. Lonicer] in Theodor de Bry's *Grand Voyages*) is one of the earliest attempts at a visual and narrative account of an individual's own captivity with indigenous Americans, in this case among the Tupi peoples of South America. Other examples emerged later from increased colonial exposure to Native American practices during the late seventeenth to early eighteenth centuries (de Batz 1735; La Page du Pratz 1758; Lafitau 1724; Lahontan 1703; Smith 1612 and 1624; Von Graffenreid 1711), several of which attempt to depict from either the viewpoint of the observer or from one's own perspective as victim scenes of individual instances of captivity, torture, and slavery. For instance, in an illustration to John Smith's *Generall Historie of Virginia*, 1624, one scene depicts Smith restraining a captive Indian man with what looks to be a narrow band or strap tied at one end around the Indian man's upper arm and attached to Smith's belt by the other end, described in script on the image as the Indian being "bindeth" by Smith (see figure 5.5 in this volume). On this occasion, the illustrator may have been told of this binding of a captive by Smith himself or was encouraged to represent the fact of captivity by such a method. Burden straps or warrior ties, to which this imagery might be likened, would enter the proto-ethnographic collections in Britain and Europe during a later period of contact but this later material evidence speaks retrospectively to what might be termed the "material fact" of Smith's representation of captivity.

Some of these visual accounts are a precious reminder that proof of slaving or adoption practices can also be found in the objects depicted in them. Ties used to bind prisoners and captives are a striking example of the necessity to recover material evidence to support textual and ethnographic analysis. These studies can complement more recent archaeological research that has revealed through the study of an object's particular design and typology interesting facts about adoption and slavery that support the extent of these practices in a variety of interethnic contexts well into the eighteenth century (Mrozowski 2010; Sayers, Burke, and Henry 2007; Silliman 2010).

In 1724 Father Joseph Francois Lafitau published his account of the cultural practices of the Iroquois/Hodenosaunee peoples with whom he had lived for a number of years at a Catholic Mission in Sault Saint-Louis (Caughnawaga), French Canada. The illustrations to his account contain a number of references to captivity, warfare, and social incorporation. In 1735 a French artist, Alexander de Batz (1685–1737), created a handful of watercolor paintings based on his experiences with the Illinois/Inoca Indians. The caption to one of these makes reference to captivity and possible social incorporation in the seated female figure labeled "Fox [Meskwaki Nation] female Indian captive," part of the larger image titled "Indians of several Nations bound for New Orleans 1735." In the painting, De Batz actually uses the word slave (*esclave*) rather than "captive" to identify his figure "but understands clearly that the *Inoca* notion of slavery was quite different than that of the Spanish, French, English, or later, Americans" (Stelle 2008). This painted drawing remains one of the singular instances of visual commentary about the complexities and visibilities of such practices that transcended racial and other societal boundaries. Very few historical or critical studies of the extent and range of this visually constructed material have been undertaken to date (Stephenson 2007; and Sturtevant 1978).

The Broader Context

The present reevaluation of the visual accounts and terms that describe experiences of slavery, captivity, and adoption that concern Native American indigenous groups during the colonial period reveals the forcefulness with which they and the experiences they described impacted upon social and cultural interactions between local and foreign populations. As a result, in our attempt to make sense of ambiguous relationships between the concepts, lived realities, and their representations we found it necessary to adopt a double perspective that took into consideration the interaction between the macro- and microlevels of analysis on an hemispheric scale. On a macrolevel, it was essential to include in our assessment historical and cultural dynamics that focused on both the centers and the peripheries of the Atlantic and North American worlds in which Native American slaving enterprises operated. A microdimension was equally important to uncover the multiplicity of connections between local events and these larger structural constraints, and how these were shaped by and simultaneously shaped people's lives and meanings in the real world.

In this volume we have concentrated on areas and case studies that most clearly show contrasting perspectives on social incorporation to enable a simultaneous comparison between ideas, practices, and representations across historical and geographical contexts. These cases selected here show the ways in which traditional cultural practices and ideas evolved and changed under the impact of the colonial experience. The unique situation created by the commodification of people brought with the introduction of structured and systematic slaving practices, especially in the eastern parts of North America, enabled us to tease out ruptures and continuities in Native American customs and beliefs and how they have been variously imagined and represented among Euro-American audiences.

If we were to draw a geopolitical map of the variety of practices associated with Native American enslavement, captivity, and adoption on the American continent during the period covered by the present essays (ca. A.D. 800–1879), we would see a sequence of shifts in the simultaneous overlapping of multiple centers and peripheries that developed around economic and political dynamics entertained along the North to South and West to East axes. As is slowly becoming clear from research concerned with local North American history published over the last twenty years, slaving networks covered, at different times, most if not all the North American continent from Mexico to Canada and from the Pacific to the Atlantic well after the United States decreed the abolition of the slave trade in the early nineteenth century. For much of the period between 1492 and the beginnings of the eighteenth century these networks also included what is now Mexico and much of the Caribbean islands as trade, communication, and exchange of ideas, people, and objects circulated in both directions between the Spanish, the British, the French, and the Dutch, in both their island and mainland domains (Elliott 2006; Wolf 1982; Wright 1981).

In the eastern United States the dramatic indigenous population decline following the introduction of Euroasiatic infectious diseases may have had a significant impact on the dissolution of the late Mississippian chiefdoms such as Cofitachequi in South Carolina, Coosa in Georgia, Apalachee in western Florida, Mabila in Alabama, Chicasa and Natchez in Mississippi, just to cite a few (chapter one in this volume; Kelton 2007). The subsequent establishment of European settlements in the areas left empty after the breakdown of such powerful polities was followed by a series of calculated strategies aimed at playing against each other the linguistically diverse descendants of Mississippian chiefdoms that regrouped in a variety of highly dynamic social and political formations between the early 1500 and the first decades of the eighteenth century (chapters two and three in this volume; Ethridge and Hudson 2002; Ethridge and Shuck-Hall 2009).

With the establishment of the fortress of St. Augustine on the Atlantic coast in 1565 began the Spanish missionary efforts over a large area of the southeast and the Florida peninsula. This happened twenty-three years after the royal decree signed by Charles V in 1542 that prohibited enslaving Indians in response to Spanish cruelty toward indigenous subjects of the Emperor and after several expeditions prepared to kidnap Native American inhabitants of the coastal areas to replenish the dwindling indigenous Caribbean labor force (Axtell 1997; Nash 1974; Wright 1981). In spite of this benevolence the missionary system proved to be a glorified system of forced labor as large numbers of Native North Americans worked incessantly to maintain roads, fields, and buildings for the Catholic Church and the crown. Once the Spanish were finally driven out of the territory of Florida, partially under the pressure of English slaving expeditions, Spanish priests were forced to flee to Cuba with large numbers of Timucua and Apalachee converts. The relocation of Catholic converts to the Caribbean is only one aspect of the resettlement of Native Americans to southern island provinces and the impact they had on the islands' populations. The French, the English, and the Dutch at different times shipped war prisoners and captives to their Caribbean properties showing that at least until the early eighteenth century the movement of human cargos occurred along the North–South axis and not only across the Atlantic. Although small numbers of Native American captives crossed the Atlantic to be sold in the ports of Seville, Morocco, and the rest of Europe, this trade does not constitute the rule but rather the exception (Habib 2008; Sturtevant 1993; Vaughan 2006). A compelling example concerning the extent of Native American captivity, adoption and incorporation practices across transcultural boundaries is found in a rare case of a child whose name appears on a tombstone from the early eighteenth century in Kent, England. Named on the tombstone as "John Panis," he died at age nine, having been a member of the aristocratic Pitt household, possibly as either a servant, or a playmate for his children. In a similar manner, the face of a young Cherokee or Choctaw male sitter who provided the Indian features to the support figures for the Townshend Monument in Westminster Abbey of 1761 designed by Robert Adam is also a tantalizing reminder that this young man also may have been a captive from one of the same areas discussed in this volume (Pratt 2005, p. 64).

    The checkerboard patterns of ad hoc political alliances that emerged in North America between the French, the Spanish, the Dutch, and the English and local indigenous groups for the control of land and resources solicited the emergence of an intricate network for the sale and barter of captives (chapters two–four in this volume) that by the early eighteenth century stretched as far west as New Mexico and as far north as the Great Lakes. Western captives traded across Texas reached the market towns of New Orleans, Natchitoches, Mobile, and Charlestown to be shipped to New England provinces and Caribbean outposts or to be used in local farmsteads and households.

Population dispersal, disease, and social realignment left large tracts of land empty to a burgeoning market economy that required manual labor in order to make it profitable. This market demand for inexhaustible human labor contributed to the reduction of the number of indigenous peoples available for work. This was the prelude to the importation of ever larger numbers of Africans to the continent during the late seventeenth and early eighteenth centuries. Despite this, it appears that in some states the number of Native American slaves almost equaled, and during some periods, outnumbered Africans. As of 1708 the Louisiana population comprised 122 soldiers and sailors, 77 settlers, and 80 Indian slaves (Usner 1995). In Rhode Island, a census of 1730 shows a total of 935 Europeans, 333 African slaves, and 233 Native American slaves. For the same year in the Carolina territory Native American slaves were 1,400, one-fourth of the total population (Wood 1988). Although a proper Native American slave trade ended with the second half of the eighteenth century, many scholars have remarked that slavery and other forms of bondage for many Native individuals, and especially for youngsters and women, continued under other forms that could not be detected under the appearance of benevolent humanitarianism or domestic life (Barr 2005; Herndon and Sekatau 2003; Sainsbury 1975; Silverman 2001).

During the eighteenth century, the growing numbers of African manual laborers, as some scholars have discussed, did not only depend on indigenous peoples' dwindling numbers. Indeed, since the very beginnings of French and English colonial enterprises in North America administrators became aware of the potential danger posed by keeping Native American slaves who could either run away or plot against the colonists, as demonstrated in the case of the insurrection organized by the escaped Native slave Sancousy in Louisiana (Usner 1989, p.108). Rebelliousness, recalcitrance, and the potential threat represented by the proximity of Native slaves' communities may have had a significant impact on colonial administrators' preference for Africans over Native Americans to work their fields (Wolf 1982, p. 202–203).

How the Participants Approached the Themes

The contributors to this book are concerned with the ways in which notions, images, and experiences of adoption, captivity, and slavery have been talked about and understood by both protagonists and commentators in the context of the study of North American histories and cultures. What brings them together is a firm focus on the empirical data, as well as textual and visual idioms that frame perceptions and representations of adoption, captivity, and slavery in a variety of intercultural settings.

Collectively the authors in this volume sketch a picture of large parts of the American continent that although may appear to be culturally, geographically, and historically disconnected from the point of view of the study of slavery and cognate notions of adoption, captivity, and bondage, are connected in that seamless continuum that we have come to understand in relation to ideas and experiences of incorporation of new members into alien social settings.

Several of the authors in this collection have highlighted the gendered aspect to issues of incorporation with nuanced detail (chapters four, five, and seven–nine). In the context of the seamless continuum proposed here, the juxtaposition of captivity accounts to other descriptions of incorporative practices renders ever more apparent the relevance of a gender dimension for an informed reading of perceptions and representations of the facts of captivity, adoption, and slavery. Minges, Bowker Lee, Holdridge, Denison, and Pratt challenge the canonical view of active and passive principles woven into the historical accounts and captivity narratives to reveal how the gender roles of women and men were not predetermined factors in the deployment of history. Many of the named and unnamed women and men in these accounts equally emerge as passive recipients or as active agents of both history and their own destinies. Despite distances in time and place, the Queen of Cofitachequi's alleged escape with an African slave discussed by Minges, the entrepreneurial Jean de La Grande Terre studied by Bowker Lee, and the resistance to reincorporation into Euro-American society of adoptee Cynthia Parker, the focus of Holdridge's essay, show different levels of negotiation of actors' positions as active historical agents that deal with harsh historical predicaments in their best interest. Pratt and Denison further reveal how implicit assumptions about gender underpinning both visual and textual representations crucially determine differences in perceptions of captivities, abductions, and social incorporation.

The juxtaposition of different modalities of representation collected here further invites us to reflect upon racial and ethnic meanings elicited in many of the accounts. Virtually all the authors contribute to outline the complexities of interethnic interactions engendered between distinct groups (Native American and not) both before (chapter one) and after the colonial encounters. Castillo Street and Minges, in particular, openly explore different aspects of interethnic encounters between Africans, Europeans, and Native Americans in the context of captivity, a theme that strongly emerges in the treatment of ethnic and cultural hybridization of individuals and groups also discussed by Bowne and Ethridge in the Southeast, Bowker Lee in Louisiana, and Holdridge in Oklahoma.

The book is divided into two main sections. One covers an archaeological, ethnohistorical and anthropological examination of the evidence relating to slavery and other cognate terms, and the other looks at the visual, iconographic, and textual representations of the ideas and notions underpinning the experiences of social incorporation. Essays gathered here follow a broadly chronological order that reflects the conference structure. What is more, the long historical spread and the geographical breadth in the scope of the book allows one to trace evolutions, continuities, and ruptures in the practices and notions intended for analysis.

Marvin Jeter sets the precolonial premises for a full discussion about the historical developments of the facts of slavery and social incorporation later examined by Robbie Ethridge, Eric Bowne, and Dayna Bowker Lee. Jeter's examination of Mississippian warfare and violence explains the progression from proto-historic forms of political aggression to historically documented slaving practices discussed in detail by Robbie Ethridge who delves into a detailed analysis of one Native group, the Chickasaw, who were pivotal in the slave trade with the English throughout the mid-eighteenth century. Eric Bowne, in turn, maps out the complex networks of slaving Indian groups such as the Westo and Occaneechi that emerged under the pressures of colonial demands for pelts and labor following the collapse of Mississippian chiefdoms and the introduction of market economies.

Dayna Bowker Lee presents instead the case of Native women bartered or married to Frenchmen in colonial Louisiana, and the consequences this had on the emergence of current ethnic groups in that region. Her discussion of slaving and captivity networks across the continent ties in with Brandi Denison's, Lin Holdridge's, and James Brooks's treatment of cases of captivity from western states. Bowker Lee explains how by the early eighteenth century Louisiana became an important doorway and sorting point for thousands of western and southwestern slaves and captives that eventually found their way to eastern colonial markets. These are the networks referred to by James Brooks in his essay, which crisscrossed the Great Basin, Southwest, and southern Plains at the center of Denison's and Holdridge's essays.

Brooks delineates the geographical contours of a complex system of precolonial barter and exchange that settlers exploited to their advantage for trading captives and slaves who ended up in colonial households. Significantly, he reveals that evidence for social incorporation was expressed by stylistic influences and borrowings found in material culture. This discussion not only reveals the extent of such networks, but suggests new possible avenues of research in material and visual analyses of the facts of slavery that are addressed by the essays in the section on visual and textual representations in this collection.

Here Stephanie Pratt, Susan Castillo Street, Patrick Minges, Brandi Denison, and Lin Holdridge look at particular case studies to tease out the complexities of the interplay between textual and visual representations and the lived experience.

Stephanie Pratt's analysis of the early visual accounts of Englishman John Smith's rescue at the hands of Pocahontas offers new insights into the discourses surrounding captivity, kidnap, adoption, and abduction that show how visual accounts can reveal something about the power differences and implicit meanings surrounding notions of captivity and adoption at the core of the colonial enterprise.

The three captivity narratives analyzed in Susan Castillo Street's essay, John Marrant, Ouladah Equiano, and John Smith, further invite a reassessment of the meanings associated with experiences of captivity and adoption conveyed through textual rhetoric.

Patrick Minges approaches the issue of Native American African interactions under conditions of bondage. His examination of recorded accounts of such unions becomes a reflection on the nature of ethnic identity under strenuous predicaments engendered by the colonial encounter.

Brandi Denison gives a detailed study of the Meeker Massacre, a captivity narrative that involves Ute Indians of the Great Basin in the late nineteenth century. She shows the discrepancy between captives' lived experiences and ideologically-led textual propaganda that makes apparent the gendered, functional aspect of captive capture in the broader schemes of colonial conquest that echoes Pratt's analysis of the very different treatment received by John White and Pocahontas during their respective captivities.

Lin Holdridge's visual and textual exploration of Cynthia Ann Parker's captivity and adoption into the Comanche tribe at the end of the nineteenth century finally reflects on the social construction of the notion of the "captive," one that uncompromisingly conveys a monolithic idea of the captives' experience that ill reflects the lived reality of many who found themselves struggling to adapt to the troubling and troubled predicaments engendered by incommensurable idioms of incorporation across ethnic boundaries.

James F. Brooks draws the book to a close with a discussion of Southwestern case studies that further highlight the complexities of cross-cultural exchanges presented in this section. The evidence he brings to support his arguments clearly shows the role that adoptions, captivities, and slaving practices had in the construction of historical contexts that, ultimately, had an everlasting impact on the ethnic, cultural, and social landscapes of North America.

Note

1. The term Native American will be used throughout this book to describe the indigenous peoples of North America. This is the official definition of the U.S. Census, but terms such as "American Indian," "Indian," "Native," and "indigenous" will be equally used by individual authors to refer to Native Americans in accordance with a more inclusive use of the definition.

Chapter 1

Ripe for Colonial Exploitation: Ancient Traditions of Violence and Enmity as Preludes to the Indian Slave Trade

Marvin D. Jeter

This chapter's perspectives are broad geographically and culturally, and centuries-deep in time, providing background contexts for later chapters dealing with more recent times and more restricted places and topics. It emphasizes my main areas of archaeological experience in the Lower Mississippi Valley (henceforth LMV), Southeast, and Midwest (figure 1.1), with comparative glances toward the Eastern Seaboard, and westward to the Plains and the Southwest.[1]

In America, members of the general public often ask archaeologists which Indian tribe's artifacts and other remains we are dealing with. Recent federal legislation about repatriation makes such questions more pertinent, but correlating such material "archaeological culture" data with ethnohistorically named groups defined in terms of ethnicity, language, and behavior is fraught with difficulties, as I found over the years (Jeter 1977, pp. 254–6; 1986; 2002; 2009; Jeter et al., 1990). Yet, some progress can be claimed, and a number of probable or possible connections will be suggested in this chapter.

Regardless of specific continuities, widespread ancient traditions of conflict and enmity made Native Americans ripe for exploitation by European colonialists using divide-and-conquer strategies and tactics. As in Africa and elsewhere, the colonial powers who intensified and "commodified" the trade in North American Indian slaves during the mid-seventeenth century took advantage of long-established habits and practices (cf. Bourdieu 1977) of warfare, raiding, and captive-taking (Cameron 2008).

Figure 1.1 Locations of major archaeological cultures and tribes to mid-18th century. Map by Robbie Ethridge © reproduced with the author's permission.

In addition to adoption or slavery (key themes of this volume), the unfortunate captives faced another possibility: death, in some regions preceded by truly horrible ritualized torture (Fox 2009, p. 73; Trigger 1990, pp. 58–63; Williamson 2007). Summarizing the early historic situation, anthropologist Alfred Kroeber (1939) famously wrote that Eastern U.S. Indian warfare was "insane, unending,…and yet…integrated into the whole fabric of Eastern culture" (p. 148). Kroeber's statement was based mainly on the ethnohistorical data at hand some seventy years ago, often referring to situations exacerbated by European contacts. Now, with much more archaeological and bio-anthropological (including forensic) data at hand, we can see that violence and warfare were deeply rooted in precontact times, indeed institutionalized and ritualized. This subject is ethically difficult, given the undeniably horrendous colonial and later Euroamerican treatment of Native Americans (not to mention modern "civilized" warfare), and claims about a lost Edenic past by revisionist Native writers (e.g., Deloria 1995; Means and Wolf 1995).

But alas, mostly male violence and some forms of warfare are essentially "cultural universals" in the long sweeps of history, anthropology, and prehistoric archaeology on all continents (D. Brown 1991, pp. 108–110; Keeley 1996). As Emerson (2007) has remarked, such romanticized and idealized visions actually "dehumanize" (I would say, "superhumanize") precontact Indians, creating "a false impression of 'otherness'" (p. 147). And numerous recent publications (e.g., Arkush and Allen 2006; Chacon and Dye 2007; Chacon and Mendoza 2005; Lekson 2002; Rice and LeBlanc 2001) effectively "refute the last shreds of illusions about a peaceful precontact past" (Arkush 2008, p. 560). However, there do appear to have been some regionally idyllic episodes, as will be noted later.

Culture-Historical Overview

North America has been occupied for over 12,000 years, first by roving Paleo-Indian hunters and gatherers (Anderson and Sassaman 1996; Haynes 2002). After 5000 B.C., some Eastern U.S. Archaic groups domesticated native plant species on a modest scale (B. Smith 2007) and began living for months in favored locations. Around this time, "skeletons with grievous wounds first become reasonably common" (Milner 2007, p. 191). Late Archaic sites, dating after 3000 B.C., have produced evidence of widespread intermittent violence (Claassen 2005; Monsforth 2007; M. O. Smith 1997), continuing into later times and perhaps becoming a factor in major migrations (Whyte 2007).

During the Woodland period (*ca.* 500 B.C.–1000 A.D.), semisedentary lifestyles became more common, with more elaborate ritual life (Anderson and Mainfort 2002). Middle Woodland (*ca.* 100 B.C.–500 A.D.), "Hopewellian" cultures flourished in the Midwest and elsewhere (including the Marksville culture of the LMV), participating in a very widespread exchange network, suggestive of generally prosperous and peaceable conditions (Milner 2007, pp. 192–3). However, there is some evidence for occasional "predatory" violence, perhaps symbolized by polished wolf jawbones that were probably worn ritually by shamans (Seeman 2007).

Over much of the East, populations and violence increased during the Late Woodland period, which has also been called the "Woodland conflict" period (Morse and Morse 1983, pp. 181 ff). The adoption of the bow and arrow around 600 A.D. (all dates henceforth are A.D.)

probably indicates both the need for more efficient hunting technology and escalating intersocietal violence (Nassaney and Pyle 1999). At several sites of the Troyville culture (*ca.* 400–700) in the southern LMV, unusual face-down burials have been found (Jeter et al. 1989, p. 151). Their meaning is uncertain, but possible explanations include internal social deviance (alleged witchcraft in times of stress?) or disposal of enemies. Arrow points of types common in parts of Arkansas *ca.* 600–1000, made on Arkansas stone materials, have been found with headless burials in Mississippi (Brookes 2003, pp. 7–8, 94; Connaway 2003, p. 25).

However, it was in later prehistoric times, the main focus of this chapter, that violence and warfare really increased over the East. Some Late Woodland tribal societies, fueled by intensifying agriculture (featuring native Eastern crops more than still-incipient maize; Lopinot 1997; 2003) and competing for arable land, gave rise to chiefdoms after 900 or 1000. This began what is called the Mississippi (or Mississippian) culture period in the Mississippi Valley (Jeter et al. 1989, pp. 171–220; Morse and Morse 1983, pp. 201–301; Phillips 1970, pp. 923–54; Phillips, Ford, and Griffin 1951), much of the Southeast (B. Smith 1986; Steponaitis 1986) and Midwest (Bareis and Porter 1984; Fortier, Emerson, and McElrath 2006).[2]

The earliest chiefdoms appeared along the Central Mississippi Valley in the American Bottom region opposite modern St. Louis, and in the northern LMV below the Ohio-Mississippi juncture (Bareis and Porter 1984; Morse and Morse 1983, pp. 201 ff, figure 10.1).[3] Chiefdom sociopolitical organization spread up major tributaries of the Mississippi and especially down the LMV, then beyond the Mississippian culture regions in the 1000s. By the 1100s, it had reached the Gulf Coastal Plain from western Louisiana to eastern Florida, into eastern Georgia and Tennessee, and the central Ohio Valley; by the 1200s, it extended along the Atlantic Seaboard from central Florida to the Carolinas (Anderson 1999, figure 15.5). In the process, non-Mississippian chiefdoms had developed among the Caddoans of the Trans-Mississippi South and the Plum Bayou–Coles Creek–Plaquemine peoples of the southern LMV. Mississippian-influenced tribal cultures included the Oneota of the upper Midwest and Fort Ancient in the central Ohio Valley; varied remnant Late Woodland tribes were in more remote regions (Milner 2007, pp. 187 ff, figure 9.1).

On almost all fronts, the expansion of sociopolitical complexity was accompanied by escalating violence. The chiefly societies were inherently unstable, either cycling back and forth with simpler tribal organization (Anderson 1996a; 1996b) or with chiefly power alternating between dispersion among single-mound centers and concentration at multimound centers (Blitz 1999; Blitz and Lorenz 2006; Pauketat 2003, pp. 42–3). Also, climatic fluctuations may have had significant effects on their preindustrial subsistence bases. Roughly in chronological order, several important developments can be identified, as follows:

- By 1050, the great Cahokia site became dominant in the American Bottom, with ample evidence of social hierarchy and violence.
- Related sites, probably including colonies, soon spread into the hinterlands; some sites were fortified, and evidence of violence abounds.
- By the 1200s, other major centers were developing to the south; arguably, the so-called classic Southern Cult iconography began at Cahokia around 1250 and spread beyond.
- By 1300 or 1350, Cahokia was essentially abandoned, but the major southern centers were flourishing.
- But after 1400, they declined too; most were abandoned by 1450. And, apparently due to warfare, a very large "Vacant Quarter" opened up around the Ohio-Mississippi juncture.
- By 1500, new warring chiefdoms had appeared, most notably along the northern LMV in and near northeast Arkansas; that is the situation documented by the first European expedition into the Southeastern interior, that of Hernando de Soto in the early 1540s.

The remainder of this chapter will examine these late prehistoric developments more closely, and will then focus on some related situations in protohistoric and early historic times.

Cahokia

By 1050,[4] the greatest Mississippian center of all had formed at the Cahokia site.[5] It eventually featured more than one hundred mounds, including the largest mound north of Mesoamerica, circles of wooden posts (so-called woodhenges; Hall 2004, pp. 98–99, figure 9; Pauketat and Emerson 1997, p. 14, figure 1.6), and a "truly monumental" bastioned palisade (rebuilt several times) around the major "elite" precinct (Emerson 2007, p. 137; Emerson and Pauketat 2002; Hall 2004, figure 6; Iseminger et al. 1990; Milner 1998; Pauketat and Emerson 1997; Trubitt 2003). A remarkable relatively early burial in

Mound 72 focused on an individual male on a blanket of thousands of shell beads, with a huge trove of exotic artifacts including sheets of copper and mica, some four hundred arrowheads (probably originally in quivers), nineteen "chunky stones," and apparent retainer burials of several beheaded or "behanded" males and a group of more than fifty young women (Fowler 1974, pp. 20–2, figure 6; 1975; Fowler et al. 1999).

Earlier views of Cahokia as an "urban" center of a large prehistoric state (Fowler 1974, 1975; O'Brien 1991) were downplayed in the 1990s by "minimalists" (Milner 1998; Muller 1997). But during the past decade, modified views of its "city" status and ideological-behavioral dominance have emerged, suggesting that a "Big Bang" of sociopolitical and economic change occurred relatively briefly, around 1050 (Emerson 2002; Pauketat 1997; 2002; 2004; 2007). In discussing an apparently forced colonization of the low, loess-blanketed uplands just east of Cahokia by multicultural, lower-class farmers at about that time, Pauketat (2003) explicitly compared the displacement of African slaves in the American South, and suggested that such resettlements of subject populations were an integral part of Cahokia's formation (p. 57). This intrusive farming effort reached a peak around 1100, then declined rapidly. The uplands were virtually abandoned by about 1150, and where the people went is "uncertain" (p. 50).[6]

At Cahokia itself, population peaked, perhaps at 10,000–15,000 people, before 1100, decreased by about half by 1150, and declined more slowly during the next century (Pauketat 2003, pp. 45–48, figure 5). Palisade construction started relatively late, after 1150, and intensified after 1200, possibly marking a change from "corporate" leadership emphasizing collective community action in mound construction and related ceremonies to "network" strategies promoting warrior-class prestige (Trubitt 2003, pp. 149–51, 160–2). In a recent study of Cahokia's demise, Emerson (2002) suggested that it collapsed abruptly (with another "bang," as it were) by 1300 (pp. 136–9); it was virtually abandoned by 1350 (Benson et al. 2009; Fortier, Emerson, and McElrath 2006, p. 197).

Northward and Eastward Expansion, Interaction, and Conflict

Mississippian culture spread in all directions by migrations or diffusion, influencing or impacting other cultures in the process. After an extensive review of regional and areal literature, Milner et al. (1991)

concluded: "There can be little doubt that intergroup aggression was an important fact of life in many parts of prehistoric eastern North America, especially during the millennium preceding European contact...consistent with the widespread occurrence of palisaded villages and...Mississippian artwork featuring war-related themes" (pp. 593–5). Mississippian cultures are indeed well known for evidence of warfare (Milner 1999; 2007), especially in probable "frontier" or peripheral situations, and for violent themes in iconography (Dye 2004; 2007; Emerson 2007), which will be summarized later.

Northward expansion up the Mississippi Valley produced palisaded villages in Iowa and adjacent southern Wisconsin, dating *ca*. 1050-1150, that have yielded both Late Woodland and Mississippian ceramics, plus "hybrid" forms, that may represent the work of captives (Theler and Boszhardt 2006, pp. 459–60). This process also involved tributary valleys such as that of the Illinois River, where Mississippians, apparently from (or closely related to those of) the American Bottom, made an initial intrusion before 1100 into the territories of Late Woodland peoples (Conrad 1991, p. 124). Some burials show evidence of death by imbedded arrowheads; one included four headless men, a possible "retainer sacrifice"; another had apparently been scalped, but sites are not fortified and the Mississippians may have been generally welcome (pp. 128–32, figure 6.4; Poehls 1944). However, extensive excavations at Orendorf, one of a cluster of slightly later "temple town" mound sites in the central Illinois Valley, indicate that it flourished under hostile conditions in the 1200s, while Cahokian influence was dwindling. At least one of its precincts, including over ninety structures, had a bastioned palisade that was expanded twice, but the settlement was eventually burned (Conrad 1991, pp. 132–41, figure 6.5). Its adversaries may have included other Mississippians, as evidenced by some arrow point types found "in fatal context" (Conrad 1991, p. 140).

Farther north, an unusual southeast Wisconsin site was given its misnomer "Aztalan" by nineteenth-century antiquarians who thought it was a colony of mythical "Mound-Builders" from Mexico who were unrelated to Eastern U.S. Indians. Instead, it was probably a colony of Cahokia, established around 1100 as another intrusion into Late Woodland territory and abandoned after 1250 (Goldstein and Richards 1991; Price et al. 2007, p. 527). It also had a central precinct surrounded by palisades with bastions (Price et al. 2007, figure 2). Isotopic analyses of human bones indicated that there were a number of "foreigners" at Aztalan, and some of the foreign isotopic values indeed matched those for bones found at Cahokia (pp. 531–6).

Meanwhile, northwest of Cahokia, some Late Woodland societies had evolved into the Oneota culture after 1150 (Theler and Boszhardt 2006, pp. 460, 463), and expanded southward, meeting resistance from resident Mississippians. The Norris Farms site in the central Illinois Valley was an Oneota cemetery, dating from the late 1200s into the 1300s (Santure et al. 1990). A thorough analysis of 243 burials from it found that 43 had died violently; 14 of those had been scalped (as indicated by patterns of multiple unhealed stone-tool cut marks across foreheads near the hairline and elsewhere on the skull), 3 others had apparently survived scalping, and 11 had been decapitated, suggesting "chronic warfare" (Milner and Smith 1990, pp. 144–8, figure 11.11; Milner et al. 1991, pp. 583ff, figures 1–3). By the late 1300s and early 1400s, with Cahokia defunct, the major connections of this region's remaining Mississippians were with others far to the south, near the Ohio-Mississippi juncture; "dramatic social and political instability" was apparent, and Oneota "migrants" were moving in from the north (Conrad 1991, pp. 149–53).

Interactions between Cahokians and societies to the north had not all been hostile. In addition to the diffusion of agricultural plants and practices, Mississippian material culture spread widely. Ramey Incised and other Cahokian pottery has been found in Oneota sites well to the north, northwest, and west (up the Mississippi and Missouri drainages), and Oneota imitations of these styles are also known in this territory; Cahokians also extracted stone and mineral resources from the north (Hall 1991, pp. 11–13, figure 1.4; Kelly 1991, pp. 63ff, figures 4.2–4.5, table 4.2).

An interesting comparative perspective comes from the Fisher site, near Chicago; it dates from 1225 to 1300. Near its center was a mass burial pit, and other burials were found in two mounds nearby. Evidence of violent death included skulls showing proof of blunt-weapon trauma and cut-marks from scalping, indicative of "repeated, small-scale raids and ambushes... occasionally punctuated by larger, devastating attacks" (Strezewski 2006, p. 264, figures 1–5). Regionally, there was a no-man's-land between Fisher and Cahokian-Mississippian sites to the southwest, and Oneota sites to the west and northwest (pp. 269–72).

Eastward, after 1100 the Ohio Valley saw the rise of palisaded Mississippian mound centers such as Kincaid in southern Illinois (Butler 1991; Muller 1986) and Angel in southern Indiana (Hilgeman 2000), both of which declined by 1450; plus the less complex but longer-lasting non-Mississippian Fort Ancient culture in the Kentucky-Ohio-West Virginia borderlands (Drooker 1997; Griffin 1943). Still farther to the northeast, proto-Iroquoian culture was developing; its origins are debatable, but it is generally agreed that palisaded villages of warring agriculturalists, living in bark-covered longhouses and probably organized as matrilineal tribes, had appeared by 1300, if not earlier (Martin 2008, pp. 444, 452).

The Lower Mississippi Valley and Southeast

A more extensive, longer-lasting expansion of Mississippian material culture, practices, and possibly people in some cases took place to the south and southeast. The resident southern peoples, being more populous and sociopolitically complex than their northern Late Woodland contemporaries, may have been less susceptible to migratory intrusions, but quite receptive to Mississippian techno-economic infrastructure, modes of sociopolitical organization, and at least in some cases, the ideology of violence (Anderson 1997, pp. 267-8). For example, at the early Caddoan Crenshaw site (*ca.* 1000–1100) in southwest Arkansas, clusters of human skulls, totaling more than 200, have been found, as well as clusters of detached human mandibles, totaling at least 216, though it is uncertain as to whether these represent trophies or some unusual local mortuary program (Schambach 1996, pp. 39–40, figures 5.5–5.7).

Apparently mainly by peaceful means (see the next section), Mississippian culture spread down the LMV, to below the Arkansas-Louisiana state line, at a rate of about 100 kilometers (or sixty miles) per century between 1000 and 1500 (Jeter 2003a, p. 184; Jeter et al. 1989, pp. 171ff, figures 15–21; Morse and Morse 1983, pp. 201ff, figures 10.1, 11.1, 12.1; cf. Phillips 1970, p. 940). Items of Cahokian material culture also traveled south, mainly around 1200. Some Ramey Incised and other Cahokian pottery, and stone materials, spread into the Lower Yazoo Basin of western Mississippi (Brain 1989, pp. 117–22; Williams and Brain 1983, pp. 375–6, 408–14) and the Tensas Basin of northeast Louisiana (Wells and Weinstein 2007). Southeast Arkansas has produced several such items, most notably a remarkable (unfortunately, looted) female figurine pipe, made of "Missouri flint clay," probably from a Cahokian workshop (Reilly 2004, figure 1; cf. Emerson et al. 2002). Similar artifacts are known from the American Bottom, Spiro on the Arkansas River in eastern Oklahoma, various Southeastern sites (Reilly 2004, figures 13, 15–18, 20, 22–23), and Caddoan sites (Emerson and Girard 2004).

A more rapid and violent "hopscotch" intrusion into the Late Woodland Southeast, probably involving migrations, by 1100 saw the rise of rather isolated Mississippian polities around major, often palisaded, mound centers (Jenkins 2009, pp. 198–214, figures 9–11; Pauketat 2007, p. 112). These included Moundville in western Alabama (Steponaitis 1983), Etowah in northwest Georgia (King 2003), and Macon Plateau in south-central Georgia (Hally and Williams 1994). Chiefdoms also arose along the Chattahoochee River (Blitz and Lorenz 2006), the northwest Florida Gulf Coast (Marrinan and White 2007), the Savannah River (Anderson 1994), and elsewhere in the Southeastern interior, the Appalachian margins, and along the Atlantic Seaboard (Anderson 1999, figure 15.5). Again, some of these agriculturalists erected palisades and engaged in escalating violence (Dye and King 2006; Jacobi 2007; Marceaux and Dye 2007; Milner 2007; Ross-Stallings 2007).

At about the same time, the Spiro site emerged at the western edge of the Southeast culture area. Long regarded as a "Caddoan" center (J. Brown 1984; 1996), Spiro has been reinterpreted (correctly in my estimation) as a Mississippian outpost, linked to Cahokia and other Mississippi Valley centers, which set up its own *entrepots*, exchanging prestige goods to Caddoans for valuables such as *bois d'arc* bows, and also trading these bows to Plains tribes for bison products (Schambach 1993, 1999, pp. 169–75, figure 8.2).[7]

Giving Peace a Chance?

Concluding a review of recent books on prehistoric warfare and violence, Arkush (2008) wistfully expressed a desire for "glimpses of peace….a different way of living, with its own distinctive signatures and practices" and "a new kind of work: the archaeology of peace" (p. 564). In contrast to the foregoing examples of mayhem, we may have such a glimpse in the LMV.[8]

From the Plum Bayou culture (*ca.* 600s–1100) of central to eastern Arkansas to the related Coles Creek culture (*ca.* 700–1200) on both sides of the Mississippi to the south, the archaeological record is one of dispersed hamlets and farmsteads, and a few small villages, around local to regional mound centers, but lacking nucleated villages and apparently without palisaded settlements. Burials generally lack grave goods, and evidence for violence is equivocal (Jeter et al. 1989, pp. 161–70). Plum Bayou culture featured the major "Toltec" (another misnomer) mound center (Rolingson 1998), but it was probably more like a cathedral than a fortress. A recent study of several "cultural element" distributions suggested that a "relatively permeable transition zone" rather than a well-defined boundary, connected Plum Bayou peoples with Coles Creek groups, "perhaps facilitated by linguistic relationships" (Jeter and Scott 2008).

Summarizing Coles Creek culture, Williams and Brain (1983) remarked impressionistically that it "exudes self-confidence and comfort" (pp. 405–408). They noted that in any given region and time, "multiple [mound] centers" appeared to be "the nuclei of relatively equal and autonomous sociocultural units" that were "in close contact with each other" resulting in "a remarkable degree of...homogeneity for the entire Coles Creek area."

Occupying most of the same regions and many of the same sites, variously influenced by Mississippian contacts, the successor Plaquemine culture (*ca.* 1200–1500s) added significantly to the mounds early on, but continued the dispersed settlement pattern (Brain 1989; Jeter 2007, pp. 161-7; Jeter et al. 1989, pp. 205–20). A recent edited volume on Plaquemine archaeology (Rees and Livingood 2007) includes no mention of palisades, and only passing references to warfare elsewhere. There are some hints of incipient social ranking in mound versus nonmound burials, the latter including specialized cemetery sites, possibly indicating ancestral veneration. Grave goods, including a few ceramic pipes (Jeter 2007, pp. 181–2) that might indicate the beginnings of calumet-like peace ceremonies, are more common, but "elite" burials are so far lacking. Williams and Brain (1983) referred to the period *ca.* 1200–1400 as a time of "ecumene" and cultural florescence (pp. 412–14).

Cultural-ecological factors may have underlain this situation. Maize agriculture caught on, and became significant, later in the southern LMV than in the Midwest. The abundant wild food resources and milder climate of this "Sportsman's Paradise" (the longtime Louisiana motto) reduced the "overwintering problem," permitting resistance to intensified agriculture and warfare over land and stored crops (Jeter 2003a, pp. 184–6; Kidder 2007, p. 205). This recalls the reference to early "corporate" versus later "network" leadership at Cahokia, or Colin Renfrew's (1974) similar distinction between "group-oriented" and "individualizing" chiefdoms. In the southern LMV, perhaps such a shift was not made until terminal prehistoric or protohistoric times.

The "Southern Cult" and Violence

Three Southeastern sites, Spiro, Moundville, and Etowah (all in frontier or enclave situations), have long been famous as centers of the "Southeastern Ceremonial Complex" (Waring and Holder 1945; cf. Galloway 1989; Hamilton 1952; Howard 1968; King 2007a; Phillips and Brown 1978). Jon Muller, who has led the way in defining and dating different Cult styles and motifs, prefers "Southern Cult," at least for the core of often-violent subject matter (Muller 1989, pp. 13ff; 2007, p. 16) and that usage is followed here.

Several researchers have recently suggested that the Cult's roots can be traced back to the American Bottom region, where they say the early "Braden style" first appeared as Cahokia was in decline during the mid-1200s (Kelly et al. 2007; King 2007a; 2007b).[9] Although Cult materials have been found north of Cahokia, for example, in the central Illinois Valley (Conrad 1991, pp. 140, 143, 145, 155), they are best known in the South, and the putatively later "Craig" style, named after the Craig Mound at Spiro, probably developed there (J. Brown 2007b; 2007c; Phillips and Brown 1978).[10] However, Cult items are generally quite rare in the Arcadian southern LMV (pp. 202–206).

Significant Cult imagery emphasizes "prowess in fighting," the "importance of weaponry," and "political domination" (J. Brown 2002, p. 31). Less commonly, the losers are portrayed, as in the "kneeling prisoner" or "bound captive" stone pipes of the LMV (figure 1.2; cf. Dye 2004, figures 8 and 9). There are also scenes showing victorious warriors clubbing captives (Emerson 2007, figure 6.2) battling with large weapons, or using them to kill or decapitate victims; also, "ceremonial" polished-stone monolithic axes or celts and very large flaked-stone knives or "maces" have been found (Dye 2004, figures 10–11, 16–20, 27–29; Marceaux and Dye 2007, figures 9.1–9.4).

Remarkable Cult artifacts, often engraved Gulf Coast shells, or *repoussé* plates made of cold-hammered native copper, typically show a winged (often raptorial bird-beaked and -tailed) dancing warrior with a ceremonial weapon in one hand, and a human head in the other; plus some other key motifs (J. Brown 2007a, pp. 77ff, figures 4.1, 4.2; Phillips and Brown 1978, pp. 185ff). They include a "forked eye" outline, probably derived from an awe-inspiring predator, the peregrine falcon. In addition to the major centers, smaller sites such as Lake Jackson in northwest Florida (Jones 1982; Scarry 2007) and Mangum, a Plaquemine cemetery in southwest Mississippi (Cotter 1952), have produced such plates.

Often shown hanging from the "birdman" dancer's belt is a breechclout-like device that has been called the "bellows-shaped apron" due to formal resemblance to a blacksmith's bellows. James A. Brown (2007b) has suggested that this is in fact something quite different, a stylized image of a "sacred scalp," and that it changed through

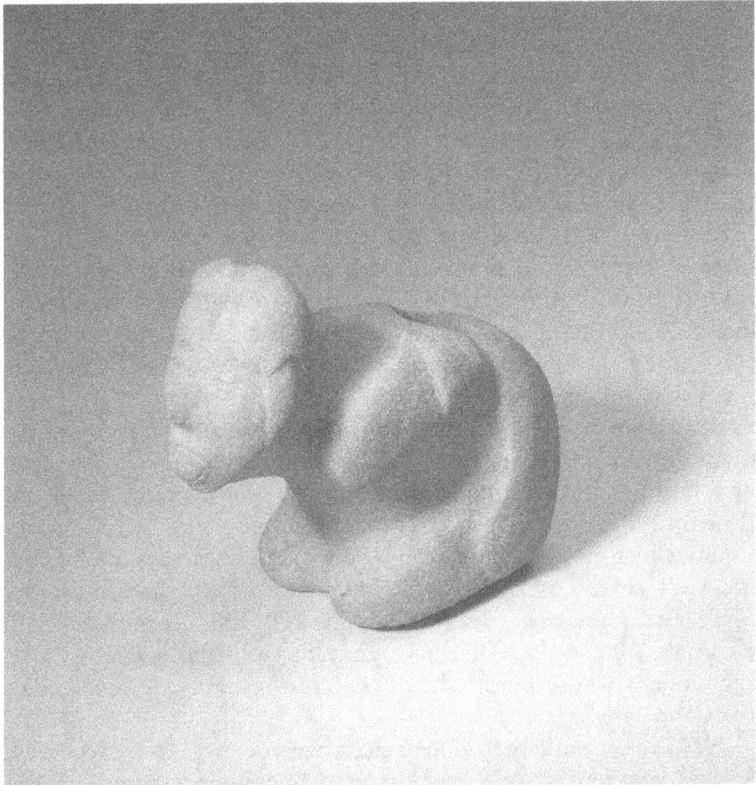

Figure 1.2 *Pipe* Mississippian culture, *ca*. 1200. The Putnam Dana McMillan Fund. Minneapolis Institute of Arts accession number: 2004.118.

time, beginning in the 1200s with a "Braden" version covered by lines representing human hair (pp. 41ff).[11] Brown's (figure 3.1) sequence shows those hair lines becoming sparser and more abstract through time, and suggests that by the 1400s the shape had slimmed down, from the "bellows" outline to one he calls "carrot-shaped," though retaining the "sacred scalp" implication. The same shapes also occur as hair patterns on Late Mississippian "head pots" found in and near northeast Arkansas (Cherry 2009, figures 32 and 203–205), providing independent support for Brown's interpretation.

The study of Cult iconography inevitably leads into such questions of meaning. For the prehistoric Indians, these images must have had rich, multilayered associations, but much has been lost or is arguable. Lacking written records, we are left with various kinds of interpretations. For decades, archaeologists (e.g., Muller 1966, 1989) have been borrowing analytical concepts from Western art history, and making (or claiming) some progress. But as Muller (2007) cautions, it is uncertain "just whose meaning emerges in *our* analyses of the artistic representations of people who have been dead for hundreds of years" (pp. 24–5). Some (e.g., Hall 1989; cf. Brown and Dye 2007; Knight et al. 2001; Lankford 2007a, 2007b; Reilly 2007) suggest that these images deal with myths, including motifs of death and resurrection, and deities, perhaps even astronomical constellations, more (or rather) than mundane, earthly situations. They probably did have other-worldly aspects, but they certainly were created in man's image. And as has been seen, there is ample circumstantial evidence that during those times, some very earthly, all-too-human violence was also going on.

Several analysts have proposed interpretations based on Indian myths recorded (in some cases, as late as the early twentieth century) by folklorists and anthropologists, but this involves more problems. Brown (2007a) readily concedes that there are a number of discontinuities in time (over 500 years), space, and culture (Cahokia and the Cult centers versus historic Indians in distant locations) (pp. 57ff). But some (e.g., Hall 2004, pp. 100–103; Kehoe 2007; cf. J. Brown 2007a, pp. 93ff) have gone further, and suggested that the Siouans whose myths they cite were the direct descendants of the Cahokians.[12]

However, it was largely due to chance whose myths were recorded. Such themes must have been widespread among many ethnic and linguistic groups (Hudson 1976, pp. 120ff; Jeter 2009, pp. 376, 385–6), just as Cahokian artifactual influence spread widely (as noted earlier). The late prehistoric southward ventures of outlying Oneota peoples into the American Bottom after the demise of Cahokia might well have inspired legendary claims of ancestral Siouan connections to the formerly great mound center.[13]

Green (2001) has independently suggested that the Chiwere Siouans were likely descended from sociopolitically simpler non-Mississippians. With significant relevance to one of this volume's main themes, he suggested that their prehistoric ancestors were influenced by the dominant Cahokian-Mississippian ideology and mythology, through ceremonies of *adoption*, establishing fictive kinship. He noted that Chiwere ethnohistory and the archaeology of probable proto-Chiwere Oneota (or Late Woodland) sites does not reflect the sociopolitical complexity implied by the oft-cited Winnebago (Ho-Chunk) and other Chiwere mythology. Previously, a similar argument from a linguistic (lexical) perspective had concluded that Siouan speakers were probably "peripheral to the complexities of Mississippian developments" (Mochon 1972, p. 502).

Terminal Prehistoric and Protohistoric Developments

After 1300, Cahokia was virtually abandoned (Emerson 2002), but the major southern centers were flourishing. By about 1400, they declined too; most were abandoned by 1450 (J. Brown 1996; King 2003; Steponaitis 1986). And apparently due to warfare, in the former Mississippian heartland along the valleys near the Ohio-Mississippi juncture, a very large "Vacant Quarter" opened up around 1450 (Williams 1990) and remained essentially unoccupied into the 1500s (Cobb and Butler 2002). The famous "headpots" of this period in northeast Arkansas and southeast Missouri may represent war trophies or deceased kinspeople (Cherry 2009). Who were the groups surrounding the "Vacant Quarter" on the eve of European contacts, warring with and avoiding each other?

To the northwest, the Oneota archaeological culture is mainly correlated with the Chiwere Siouans (Green 1995; 2001; Griffin 1937; 1960). To the north were probably Algonquian-speakers, including the Illini.[14] To the northeast, the Fort Ancient culture could have been at least partly Algonquian-speakers (Griffin 1943) or multiethnic (Essenpreis 1978). Some of them, or near neighbors, may have been another Siouan subdivision, Dhegiha, as discussed later. South and southwest of the "Vacant Quarter," in the northern LMV, were Mississippian chiefdoms, some of them "paramount" chiefdoms, also to be discussed shortly. Other Mississippians, probably mostly Muskogeans, were east of the Mississippi.

LMV archaeologists generally refer to a "Protohistoric Period" with rounded-off beginning and ending dates of 1500 and 1700 (Dye 1986). It is usually subdivided into our beloved Early, Middle, and Late subperiods, with the breaks at 1541 (first Spanish contact) and 1673 (first French contact). Contacts in the greater Southeast were earlier, most notably by the Spanish as they began to explore Florida.

An especially poignant example, connecting the Southeastern and Southwestern situations, is the case of Alvar Nuñez Cabeza de Vaca, one of the survivors of an expedition's 1528 west Florida shipwreck. They walked and fought their way to northwest Florida, and built rafts to sail the coast to Mexico, but were swept into the Gulf by the Mississippi's current, then hit by storms, and marooned on the Texas coast. They were enslaved by local Indians and put to arduous tasks, and most of his companions died. He and three others, including a "Moorish" slave named Esteban, escaped and became traders between mutually hostile tribes of the coastal and inland zones, and he developed a reputation as a shaman-healer. Escaping again, they entered the Southwest, visiting Indians in what is now New Mexico and possibly Arizona before making their way to Mexico in 1536 (Reséndez 2007).

Their story inspired the 1539 expedition of Fray Marcos de Niza, guided by Esteban until he was killed by Puebloan (Zuni?) Indians (Hammond 1956), and the 1540–1542 *entrada* of Francisco Vázquez de Coronado. The latter reached northern New Mexico pueblos and eventually the Plains proto-Wichita "Quivira" of central Kansas, again reporting hostile relations among Indian groups. By then, roving Apacheans had reached both of these culture areas, raiding more settled tribes, and dealing in captives (Vehik 2002; 2006).

Meanwhile, the Hernando de Soto *entrada* blundered through the greater Southeast from 1539 to 1543. There have been two major efforts to establish the Spaniards' course, first by John Swanton (1939), without much archaeological data to help him. The other, by Charles Hudson (1984; 1993), began in the 1980s, when the archaeological data bases, and dates, were much better. The two reconstructions have some similarities, but significant differences, especially west of the Mississippi. The Swanton version had de Soto going into Louisiana. Hudson's route keeps him well to the north, in Arkansas, which agrees with the distributions of appropriate Spanish artifacts, archaeological sites, and Indian population concentrations, as now known (Young and Hoffman 1993; cf. Galloway 1997).

Research on the *entrada* has revealed much about the Indian groups encountered. But, there are serious problems in trying to mesh archaeological data with ethnohistorical data, because of "dimensional contrasts" (Jeter 2002, pp. 177–80, table 1). The dimension of *space* is basic in archaeology, which can control it accurately and precisely, but the ethnohistorical documents are vague at best. However, archaeological control of *time* is weak, due to the infamous "plus or minus" factor of decades, whereas the de Soto accounts often pin down events to the day and hour. With regard to *culture*, archaeologists emphasize materials, like artifacts, and an "etic" social-scientific point of view (Harris 1979, pp. 32ff). However, the de Soto documents were based on observations of Indian behavior, which (along with the Indians' "emic" meanings) were filtered through the "emic" viewpoints of observers who were not anthropologists.

Further complicating matters, LMV researchers must deal with two rather different ethnohistories, Spanish and French, from widely separated parts of the Protohistoric period. The Spanish documents only cover three years; most of the specific names they used for Indian groups, settlements, or territories did not survive into historic times. The dense populations of "paramount chiefdoms" they described in and near northeast Arkansas did not survive either. The long Middle Protohistoric subperiod has been called the "Protohistoric Dark Ages" (Dye 1986, p. xii; Jeter 2002, p. 183). During this 130-year span with no European visits, there were major changes among the Indians: population decimations and movements, perhaps due to European diseases or "epic" droughts (Jeter 2007, pp. 193–4). As a result, when the French arrived the cultural landscape was very different. Northeast Arkansas was virtually deserted, but there were still major Indian settlements along the Lower Arkansas Valley.

Many of the specific Indian group names the French recorded have survived, but the problem has been connecting them to the rather different names recorded earlier by the Spanish. Recently, a new approach used Hudson's locations for the various Indian settlements named in the 1540s de Soto accounts, and for the first time, combined them with Swanton's linguistic affiliations for names of places and peoples (Jeter 2002, pp. 206–13). This resulted in coherent geographic clusters, leading to a new view of linguistic group locations and historical processes shortly before and after European contact (figure 2).

Some had suggested that the Quapaw were already in Arkansas, but there are no Siouan names in the de Soto accounts (Rankin 1993). Instead, from northeast to west-central Arkansas, the names are most likely Tunican. Others had suggested that the Tunican homeland had been in northwest Mississippi (Brain 1989), or even far west in the Oklahoma-Arkansas borderlands (Schambach 1999). The new scenario places the Tunican homeland along a lengthy segment of a trail, along the southeastern Ozark margin, that could have linked Cahokia and Spiro prehistorically, perhaps establishing the tradition from which Tunicans emerged as major traders in historic times, farther down the LMV. It also agrees with some oral traditions (Jeter 2002, pp. 206–209; 2009).

Another surprise was that the names in central to southeast Arkansas, and on into adjacent Mississippi, were uniformly Natchezan, just as they were farther down the Mississippi Valley. The latter was expected near the home of the historic Natchez Indians, but the northern distribution had been overlooked, although some oral traditions of much larger aboriginal territory support this. The new scenario calls these people "Northern Natchezans" (Jeter 2002, pp. 206–11). The de Soto accounts document some Indian intertribal enmity, violence, and captive-taking, especially in northeast Arkansas; this may have involved Tunicans against Northern Natchezans. There are also hints of Indians enslaving other Indians, even cutting the tendons of their legs to prevent escapes, but these are only from the least reliable chronicler, Garcilaso de la Vega (Jeter 2009; cf. Dowling 1997; Henige 1997).[15]

What happened next, between 1543 and 1673? A breakthrough resulted from late-1980s research at a site with a rather British-sounding name: Goldsmith Oliver, on the Arkansas River at Little Rock (Jeter et al. 1990). On the basis of existing literature, a Quapaw site from the 1700s, producing French trade goods, had been expected. But when the glass beads and tubular brass beads were analyzed, they turned out to be most probably Spanish-derived, dating around 1600, in the middle of our "Dark Ages" (M. T. Smith 1990). There were no Europeans anywhere near Arkansas then. The most likely source, about 1,000 miles away, was the Spanish mission system around St. Augustine, Florida, and from there, down-the-line, Indian-to-Indian trade.[16]

This new insight forced a reinterpretation of related sites along the lower Arkansas Valley, as not historic 1700s Quapaw, but Middle Protohistoric, early 1600s, pre-Quapaw. Several of these sites have produced similar glass and brass beads, as has one in northwest Mississippi, near the mouth of the Arkansas, coincidentally called the Oliver site.[17] This has more recently been supported by the finding of what probably *is* an early to middle 1700s Quapaw and French site; it has produced a rather different Indian artifact assemblage (House 2002).

Shatter Zone Shock Waves

So, when did the Quapaw come to Arkansas, from where, and why? In the new scenario (Jeter 2002), this at last involves the LMV with the Northeastern and Eastern Seaboard slaving "shatter zone" (Ethridge and Shuck-Hall 2009) and its first shock waves along the Mississippi (Jeter 2009). First, the Dutch armed the League Iroquois with improved flintlocks in the 1640s. These "Five Nations" began raiding their neighbors, killing some captives, and adopting or enslaving others. They overwhelmed the Hurons by 1651 and the Neutrals in 1653, driving both groups westward; and defeated the Erie by 1656

(Snow 2007, p. 154). The Erie moved far south, becoming known as the Westo in western Virginia, and eventually arrived on the middle Savannah River in Georgia, living in northern-style bark-covered longhouses (Bowne, 2005).

The next dominos to fall, as it were, probably included the proto-Dhegiha Siouans. They may well have been the "Eastern Fort Ancient" archaeological culture's peoples, who lived in elongated structures, probably covered with bark (Hanson 1966, pp. 7–13, 177, figures 3–4; 1975, pp. 14–18, figures 9, 13, 14, table 1) and whose record ends in the mid-seventeenth century (Holmes 1994, pp. 95–6), or nearby peoples (Jeter 2002, pp. 213ff, figure 3; 2009). Around 1660, these Siouans fled down the Ohio; from its mouth the Osage went up the Mississippi-Missouri drainage to southwest Missouri, where they lived in non-regional bark-covered longhouses. The Omaha or "Upstream People" continued up the Missouri to the Nebraska borderlands, and lacking appropriate trees, adopted a Plains earth-lodge house style. The Quapaw or "Downstream People" went down the Mississippi to the locality around the Arkansas-Mississippi juncture, living in regionally unprecedented bark-covered longhouses, soon to be encountered in this "homeland" by the French.[18]

This agrees with several oral traditions, including one that en route, the Quapaw defeated a Tunican remnant in northeast Arkansas. It also matches the 1673 Marquette map, showing Quapaw villages around the Arkansas-Mississippi river juncture, and Tunicans still up the Arkansas Valley. By then, the Northern Natchezans, probably including the Taensa, had already moved down the Mississippi toward their southerly kin, to be accommodated or "adopted" (I. Brown 1985, pp. 16, 190; cf. Barnett 2007; Jeter 2009) and "discovered" by La Salle in 1682.[19]

Marquette's party was shadowed by armed Iroquois; he heard from the Quapaw and others that there was also warfare and raiding going on to the south, so he turned back and returned to Canada. La Salle's follow-up expedition to the Mississippi's mouth found more evidence of violence, decapitations of enemies, and slavery (Jeter 2009). Meanwhile, the English in South Carolina had founded Charles Town (Charleston) in 1670, dispersed the Westo in 1680 (Bowne 2005), and looked farther west, arming the Chickasaw. By 1685 if not earlier, along with long-resident LMV groups, the Quapaw in their new refuge were once again "under the guns" of Indian slavers (Ethridge 2009b; chapter two in this volume; Johnson et al. 2008, pp. 3–8).

Historically Contingent Postscripts

There is a significant amount of historical contingency involved here. The Dutch had begun their Eighty Years' War with Spain in 1568. By 1610 they were doing well and colonizing productive warmer climes around the world; founding northerly New Amsterdam in 1625 was almost an afterthought. By the 1640s, they were clearly winning the war on many fronts (Boxer 1965, pp. 332–4), and their English rivals were distracted by revolution and civil war at home; that was the context of their arming the Iroquois to exploit the interior's resources and peoples.

The Iroquois had been engaged by French Canadian allies of their Indian enemies as early as the 1530s. According to oral tradition, their famous "League" was formed to stop endemic intratribal hostilities and unite the members against other tribes. The time is a matter of dispute, but is generally believed to have been in the late 1500s. They did not have close encounters with the French and Dutch until shortly after 1600. The Iroquois suffered population losses of around 60 percent in a 1634 smallpox epidemic, and more in later outbreaks, so by the 1640s they were highly motivated to take captives and adopt some of them; indeed, they apparently maintained their population by this means. Iroquois ideologies emphasizing revenge and prestige through violence probably intensified the situation (Snow 2007, pp. 150–9). The Iroquois apparently did not participate significantly in the Euroamerican slave economy, but their new adoptees sometimes brought in their own grudges against more distant peoples and inspired attacks against them (Fox 2009, pp. 72–5).

Iroquois trade with the Dutch, mainly involving furs, boomed only briefly. In 1664 the English took New Amsterdam and began turning it into New York (Boxer 1965, p. 335). And the next year, the Second Anglo-Dutch War broke out, famously chronicled from the English side in the diaries of Samuel Pepys (Tomalin 2002). This left the English as the major Indian slave exploiters in the East in the late 1600s and early 1700s, via their Indian clients such as the Westo and Chickasaw, as seen in chapters two and three in this volume.

With Euroamerican expansion of the fur trade and slaving, the "shatter zone" moved westward in the later 1600s and 1700s (Esarey 2003; Jeter 2009). As French influence spread out from the Mississippi Valley onto the Plains, groups such as the Osage and Wichita became involved (Barr 2005; DuVal 2006).[20] Meanwhile, from obscure and unpromising beginnings in the Great Basin, the Comanches had emerged through the Rockies onto the western Plains by the early

1500s, then expanded southward and eastward, obtaining Spanish horses and breeding them. By the 1700s, they had displaced Apaches and others, and established a vast "empire" in the southern Plains, eastern margins of the Southwest, and adjacent Mexico, based on raiding and obtaining captives (see chapter nine and epilogue in this volume) as slaves or for ransom; their reign endured well into the 1800s (Hamalainen 2008, pp. 18–180, 250–9).

Eventually, with American frontier expansion, these and other Native Americans were subdued and faced with death, captivity, displacement via removal to reservations, or often-ambiguous "adoption" via U.S. policies of assimilation (Hinsley 1981, pp. 287–8). Aspects of some of their old militaristic traditions have been transmuted into valorous participation in America's twentieth- and twenty-first-century wars, and survive locally to regionally in institutions such as "warrior societies" with their own symbolic ceremonial regalia and rituals.

Notes

I thank Max Carocci, Stephanie Pratt, and the British Museum staff for organizing and hosting the February 2008 conference that resulted in this and the other chapters in this volume. Robbie Ethridge of "the great university at Oxford" (Mississippi!) was instrumental in arranging my participation. Tom Green, director of the Arkansas Archeological Survey, provided support in general, and specifically with most of my travel expenses. My dear wife Charlotte Copeland and her daughter Sandi (herself a paleoanthropologist) accompanied me on the trip. We thank our British friends and hosts, Di and Geoff Timms, and Sarah and John Foster. The trip also permitted one last brief visit with our oldest British friends, Joyce and Ian Papworth, both of whom died a few months later; this effort is dedicated to their memories.

1. The anthropological approach taken here begins with the archaeologically congenial "infrastructures" of cultural-ecological material conditions of subsistence production and population reproduction, relating these to "structures" of sociopolitical organizations and "superstructures" of belief systems, ideologies, and symbolic performances, all within contexts of changing physical, biological, and sociocultural environments (Harris 1979). This may provide a useful counterpoint to other chapters' emphases on meanings.
2. I am using the well-established "chiefdom" term for these relatively complex societies, despite recent opposition to it (Pauketat 2007; cf. Jeter 2003b, pp. 114–15). Labels for stages in this process are contested. In the 1980s, an "Emergent Mississippian period" (*ca*. 900–1050) was inserted between Late Woodland and full-blown Mississippian (Kelly

et al. 1984). Recently, its "Mississippian" nature has been questioned, and "Terminal Late Woodland" suggested instead (Fortier and McElrath 2002; Fortier, Emerson, and McElrath 2006, pp. 191–5). About the same time, the pithouse-pueblo transition, and associated sociopolitical changes, were occurring in the Southwest (Plog 1974; see also note 5).

3. For me, as for geologists (Saucier 1974) and many archaeologists (Phillips 1970; Williams and Brain 1983), the LMV is the broad alluvial plain extending from the Ohio-Mississippi juncture to the Gulf of Mexico, and the Central Mississippi Valley (CMV) is the narrower Mississippi Valley between the Illinois and Ohio junctures. Some others (following Morse and Morse 1983) call the CMV the segment between the Ohio and Arkansas junctures, but for me, that is the northern LMV (Jeter 2002).

4. Here and for related Mississippian sites in nearby regions, I am using the recently recalibrated American Bottom chronology of Fortier, Emerson, and McElrath (2006, figure 3).

5. There are several interesting Southeast-Southwest parallels, possibly correlated with climatic changes (Benson et al. 2009; Jeter 2003b; 2007, pp. 189–91; Lekson 2002; Neitzel 1999). Both areas saw early cultural florescences, tinged by violence, in major northern centers: Cahokia and Chaco (fl. *ca.* 900–1125; Lekson 2002; 2006). In both, major later developments took place to the south. There were populous Classic Hohokam sites (*ca.* 1150–1350s) in southern Arizona, and a great center called Paquimé or Casas Grandes (*ca.* 1250–1500?) in Chihuahua, Mexico; again, warfare was important (Lekson 2002; Ravesloot and Spoerl 1989; Schaafsma 2007a; 2007b; Wallace and Doelle 2001; Wilcox et al. 2001).

6. The "Big Bang" of development at Cahokia took place within "one of the wettest fifty-year periods during the last millennium" but subsequent "persistent" and "severe" droughts may have caused the abandonment of the nearby upland farms and triggered the palisade construction at Cahokia itself (Benson et al. 2009). Perhaps some of the upland farmers relocated northward to regions such as the Illinois Valley.

7. Meanwhile, on the Plains, societies were also becoming more complex, accompanied by increasing interaction, including trade and violence, especially after 1200 (Vehik 2002).

8. Arkush (2008, p. 564) distinguished between "two kinds of peace." One, which she called "state-imposed," featured top-down domination and pacification, and may be represented on the Mississippian prestate level by what Pauketat (2004, p. 124; 2007, pp. 124, 155–6) has called "Pax Cahokiana," *ca.* 1050–1200. For Arkush, the other kind of peace, a sort of coexistence among equals, was "more remarkable." It might be exemplified by the southern LMV non-Mississippians discussed here.

9. Braden is a small eastern Oklahoma community near Spiro, where the style was named.
10. However, Jeffrey Brain, who had previously argued for a beginning after 1400 (Brain and Phillips 1996; Williams and Brain 1983, pp. 342, 416–19), has recently reiterated that position (Brain 2008).
11. The February 2008 conference that led to this book featured a poster that showed, hanging from a pole, scalps with long hair, one of them somewhat resembling the "bellows-shaped apron" in shape.
12. Muller (2007) has compared such attempts to the story of a drunk who loses his car keys off in the dark, but looks for them under a streetlamp, because "the light is better" (p. 23).
13. Similarly, some Navajo origin stories (Warburton and Begay 2005, pp. 533–6) claim ancestral connections to a number of "Anasazi" or Ancestral Pueblo sites that are generally regarded by archaeologists and some other Indians as predating the Athapaskan migration into the Southwest, or not related to the Navajo or other Athapaskans. Other examples of such "symbolic appropriation" of archaeological sites are known (e.g., Gnecco and Hernández 2008; see also McGhee 2008).
14. Perhaps Algonquians should be given some consideration as possible descendants of the Cahokians. Esarey (2003) has called attention to a later role of the Illini, starting in the late 1660s, as slavers of Plains Indians to their west, selling them to Ottawa middle-men who sold them to French Canadians.
15. John Connaway (2005, personal communication) reports a late prehistoric (*ca.* 1000) burial from northwest Mississippi with evidence in the form of partially healed cut-marks, indicating that the Achilles tendon had been cut with a stone knife and the unfortunate individual had lived for some time after that.
16. Another fascinating possible source, not much farther away, is the Spanish colonial occupation that began in 1599 on the Upper Rio Grande in New Mexico. In fact, the governor, Don Juan de Oñate, led a hopeful expedition out onto the Plains in 1601, to a "Great Settlement" that was probably a proto-Wichita site group on the Arkansas River in southeast Kansas (Vehik 2006, pp. 211–12). Distributing trade goods there would have halved the distance to the Goldsmith Oliver site, downstream all the way (see also the next note). However, our most diagnostic European glass bead type has not yet been reported from New Mexico or Kansas.
17. The Oliver site in northwest Mississippi has also produced European beads similar to those from Goldsmith Oliver and other Lower Arkansas Valley sites, plus over 100 tiny disk beads made of turquoise or similar minerals, almost certainly from the Southwest (Connaway in press).
18. This "Very Late Dhegiha Migration" suggestion, along with my complementary "Tunicans and Northern Natchezans" scenario, has found

some acceptance (DuVal 2006, pp. 3, 67–8, 265–66; cf. Barnett 2007, p. 14; Hudson 2002, pp. xxx–xxxi) and has not yet been seriously challenged.

19. The "Mississippian" archaeological assemblage of the Taensa in northeast Louisiana had surprised earlier researchers who expected a Plaquemine-derived complex like that of the Natchez proper (Phillips 1970, p. 945). My scenario proposes that the Taensa were originally Northern Natchezans in eastern Arkansas or adjacent Mississippi, and their artifact assemblage had been "Mississippianized" by southward diffusion (and perhaps some immigration) before they moved well to the south.

20. DuVal (2006) sees the Arkansas Valley as, in effect, the center of the universe for its inhabitants, emphasizing the Quapaw and the Osage, and to some extent the Quivira-Wichita on the Plains (cf. Vehik 2006) as "agents." However, the Euro-Americans also had "agency," backed up by superior technology and other advantages (Diamond 1997).

Chapter 2

The Emergence of the Colonial South: Colonial Indian Slaving, the Fall of the Precontact Mississippian World, and the Emergence of a New Social Geography in the American South, 1540–1730

Robbie Ethridge

Two hundred years after Europeans invaded what is now the American South, the precontact Mississippian world of the Native peoples was in collapse. This collapse was not sudden; it took almost 200 years to run its course. We now know that many of the Indian societies of the eighteenth-century South, the ones with which we are most familiar and whose descendants are recognized today—the Creeks, the Cherokees, the Chickasaws, the Choctaws, the Catawbas, and so on, formed out of the collapse of Mississippian chiefdoms such as Coosa, Mabila, Pacaha, Chicaza, Cofitachequi, and others that existed in the sixteenth century (figure 2.1).

If we are to comprehensively understand the full transformation of the Mississippian world, what is needed is an interpretive framework against which each instance of collapse and reformation can be placed. I have begun to offer such a framework, one that has come to be known as the "Mississippian shatter zone" (Ethridge 2006, pp. 207–18; 2009a). The Mississippian shatter zone, as I have defined it elsewhere, was a large region of instability in eastern North America that existed from the late sixteenth through the early eighteenth centuries and that was created by the combined conditions of the destabilization of Native polities by their engagements with Spanish conquistadors; the internal political weaknesses of Native polities; the introduction of Old World pathogens; and the inauguration of a nascent capitalist economic system by Europeans through

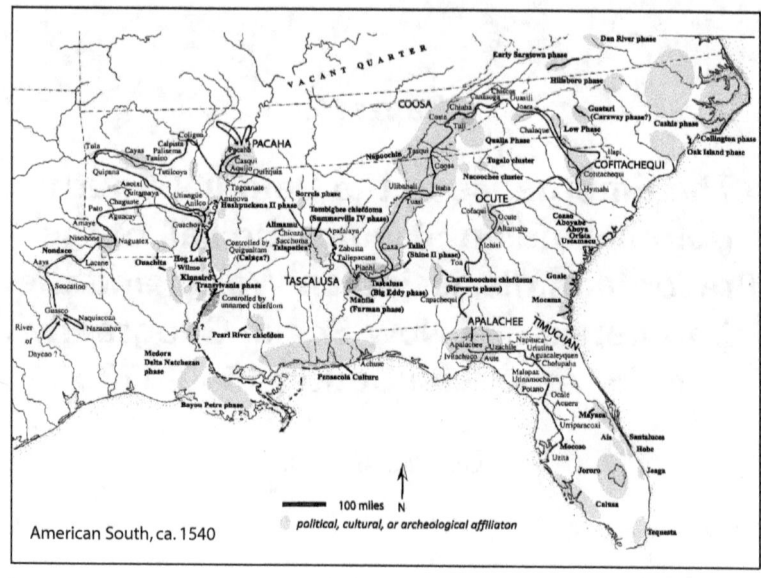
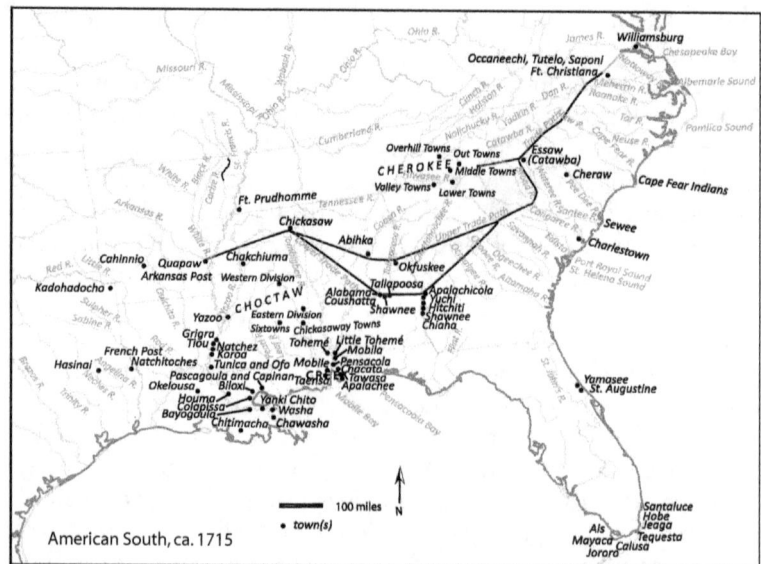

Figure 2.1 The transformation of the Southern Indians, 1540–1715. Map by Robbie Ethridge. Reproduced courtesy of the University of North Carolina Press.

a commercial trade in Indian slaves (Hudson, 2002, pp. xxii–xxxvi). Drawing on a few examples, this essay sketches some of the dramatic changes in the geopolitics of the American South in the 150 years after European contact.

"Mississippian" is the name archaeologists use to designate the time period between roughly 900 and 1700 C.E., during which Southern Native peoples were organized into a particular kind of political organization termed the "chiefdom." Chiefdoms are ranked political orders with basically two ranks—elite and nonelite lineages. During the Mississippian period, the elite lineages, from which a chief or "mico" was drawn, represented a centralized authority and controlled much of chiefdom life. However, archaeologists believe that these dynasties were fragile and susceptible to usurpation by pretenders to power at the least signs of weakness. Geographically, Mississippian chiefdoms typically had a central town with impressive public architecture for the elite such as the flat-topped earthen temple mounds found today at Moundville; smaller mound towns and farming villages were situated across the countryside. Southern chiefdoms were fairly small, running about fifty kilometers along a river valley, and they were based on a corn agricultural economy. However, chiefdoms sometimes merged to form larger political units that archaeologists now call "complex and paramount chiefdoms," although the ties binding such chiefdoms appear to have been quite tenuous. Over the 600-year history of the Mississippian way of life, many chiefdoms rose and fell.[1]

The first Europeans to witness the full scope of the Mississippian world and leave written descriptions of it were Hernando de Soto and his army. Landing in present-day Tampa, Florida, in 1539, de Soto's expedition explored the Southern heartland for the next four years, but failed in its objective of establishing a colony in North America. At the time of de Soto's *entrada*, there were dozens of chiefdoms in the South, many of which de Soto and his army encountered (Hudson 1997; 2005). Simple and complex chiefdoms existed side by side, and in at least one case in northwest Georgia, de Soto encountered a powerful chief named Coosa who had built an alliance of several chiefdoms into a paramount chiefdom that spanned from present-day eastern Tennessee to northern Georgia and eastern Alabama (Smith 2000).

Most scholars agree that the presence of de Soto and his large army had profound effects on many of the Mississippian polities through which they passed such as that of Coosa. The paramountcy of Coosa seems to have faltered for a few decades after its encounter with de

Soto. Coosa recovered somewhat, and then, sometime around 1560, it went into steep decline. People abandoned the mound centers and many began a long migration south, eventually settling in central Alabama in the late seventeenth century where they fused with a local population to become the Abihkas. Archaeologists propose that Coosa's decline occurred because of the introduction of Old World diseases by the Spanish expedition and a subsequent extreme loss of life (pp. 96–121). I would argue, however, that Coosa, as a paramount chiefdom, would have been one of the most unstable political entities in the Mississippian world and it could have fallen for any number of reasons, including the instability brought on by de Soto's long march through and pillaging of the entire province (Ethridge 2010, pp. 60–88).[2]

De Soto and his men came as a conquering army, and in the cases of those chiefdoms that saw intense action, the direct military assault of the Spanish may have precipitated their collapse. This was probably the case at the chiefdoms of Napituca in northern Florida, Anlico in Arkansas, and Tascalusa in Alabama (Hudson 1997, pp. 110–15, 238–49, 266–74, 336–8). In the case of Tascalusa, the people of Tascalusa and their allies in Mabila waged a surprise attack against de Soto in the battle of Mabila. Although they succeeded in pushing de Soto out of the region, they suffered heavy losses in the battle. The chiefdom of Tascalusa still existed in 1561, when Tristán de Luna's men came into central Alabama, but it was greatly reduced from its former power. Fifteen years after their encounter with Luna, the people of Tascalusa quit building mounds and central towns in favor of smaller, compact towns. They also moved slightly north, to the confluence of the Coosa and Tallapoosa rivers. Likewise, at Mabila, which was located on the central Alabama River, people left the province. Some migrated northeast to join those citizens of the former Tascalusa; some moved south, to the Gulf area, where they joined the Mobilians. In addition, the people in the adjacent chiefdom of Apafalaya on the Black Warrior River also fell on hard times. Apafalaya did not participate in the battle of Mabila and de Soto only briefly passed through the chiefdom although he may have killed their mico while there. It looks as though Apafalaya went into decline simply because the polity could not withstand the regional instability all around. Many of the people joined those at the confluence of the Coosa and Tallapoosa. These groups, some of the descendants of the former chiefdoms of Tascalusa, Mabila, and Apafalaya, would form the core of the Alabama Indians of the late seventeenth and eighteenth centuries (Biedma 1993, pp. 232–6; Elvas 1993, pp. 94–106;

Ethridge 2010, pp. 60–88; Jenkins 2009; Priestly 1928, vol. 2, p. 291; Rangel 1993, pp. 285–97; Regnier 2001).

Another neighboring chiefdom to the east of Tascalusa also went through some dramatic changes after their encounter with de Soto. At the time, Talisi was allied with Coosa, but the mico of Tascalusa was courting the chiefdom to join him as he made a bid for a paramountcy. It is unknown whether or not Talisi participated in the battle of Mabila, but clearly the regional instability in the aftermath of de Soto had an effect on the polity. By 1600 they had also quit building mounds, but they stayed in their homelands and became a fairly stable polity. The towns of Talisi—Kulumi, Atasi, and Tukabatchee—would comprise the core of the seventeenth-century province known as Tallapoosa, which would become one of the nuclei of the eighteenth-century Upper Creeks (Biedma 1993, p. 232; Elvas 1993, pp. 94–5; Ethridge 2010, pp. 69–71; Jenkins 2009; Knight 1994, pp. 373–92; Rangel 1993, pp. 285–8; Waselkov and Smith 2000, pp. 242–64).

There was another significant emigration from central Alabama into the lower Chattahoochee River valley. Sometime between 1500 and 1585, a group of people from Tascalusa had established a town in Talisi, known today as the Ebert Canebrake site. It looks as though some of this group continued to move east, eventually settling on the lower Chattahoochee. Unfortunately, we do not know whether this move was before or after the battle at Mabila. Once on the Chattahoochee, these immigrants established a chiefdom with two town sites with mounds, one on either side of the river at present-day Columbus, Georgia. These two sites, undoubtedly, are the original sites of the towns known historically as Cussetah and Coweta (Jenkins 2009, pp. 227–36).

This immigration profoundly affected the local chiefdoms on the Chattahoochee as archaeologists report a dramatic reduction in the number of sites. They interpret this to mean that either these local people were incorporated into the new chiefdom or suffered some kind of population loss either from disease or military confrontation. Even so, they continued to live side by side with the newcomers. Archaeologists also believe that the newcomers spoke a Muskhogean language and that the local people spoke Hitichi. By 1630 or before, the two peoples would merge into one multilingual polity, known as Apalachicola (Blitz and Lorenz 2006, pp. 70–2; Jenkins 2009, pp. 227–36; Knight 1994, pp. 383–4; Worth 2000, pp. 269, 271–2, 274).[3] Apalachicola would later become the core nucleus for the Lower Creeks. Given the historical relatedness among the people of the Chattahoochee, the lower Tallapoosa, and the upper Alabama, it should not be too surprising that by the eighteenth century all of these groups would fuse into the Creek Confederacy (Jenkins, 2009; Knight, 1994).

Certainly the most spectacular chiefdoms that de Soto encountered were those of the lower Mississippi River valley. Between present-day Memphis and the confluence of the Arkansas River stood numerous large, rich, organized, and thickly populated chiefdoms. Their names, Quizquiz, Casqui, Pacaha, Utiangue, Anlico, Guachoya, Aminoya, and so on, are largely lost to us today—no wonder, since these polities disappeared soon after the Spanish expedition left their river banks. When the French expeditions paddled down the lower Mississippi 130 years later, they found instead only a few Illinois settlements and four Quapaw towns. Both groups had most likely arrived only a few decades earlier. The only lower valley chiefdom left standing in the late seventeenth century was Natchez, the much reduced polity of the famously bellicose and prosperous Quigualtam, whose impressive navy had chased the survivors of de Soto's expedition down the Mississippi River as they retreated to Mexico (Biedma 1993, pp. 238–46; Elvas 1993, pp. 111–58; Ethridge 2010, pp. 116–48; Jolliett and Marquette 1917, pp. 254–6; Joutel 1998, pp. 255–67; La Salle 2003; Minet 1987, pp. 45–50; Rangel 1993, pp. 299–306; Tonti 1846, p. 60; 1898, pp. 77–81).

The collapse of the Mississippi valley chiefdoms and the virtual abandonment of much of the central river meander zone is one of the greatest historic puzzles of the American South. We still do not have a good sense of why these chiefdoms fell, or about where the people went afterward. For now, it looks as though some of the people migrated west, up the Arkansas and Red rivers where they joined local Caddoan-speaking chiefdoms. Some may have moved south to the confluence of the Yazoo River where they reestablished a small chiefdom later known as Tunica. Some undoubtedly joined the Natchez as the historic records clearly indicate that the Natchez took in many refugees in the seventeenth century. Some continued further south, past the Tunica and the Natchez, and settled along the mouth of the Mississippi. Here they did not reconstitute their chiefdoms, but either joined other small nonchiefdom groups or maintained some degree of social and political independence. The Gulf coast groups would become known as the *petites nations* in the eighteenth century (Brain 1978; Brown 1982, pp. 177–9; Ethridge 2010, pp. 116–48; Mainfort 2001; Ramenofsky 1987; Smith 2002, pp. 17–18).[4]

From the de Soto records, we know that the lower valley chiefdoms were in a state of shifting alliances. De Soto was directly involved in the political and military jockeying between Guachoya and Anlico, and Casqui and Pacaha, and it is likely that de Soto's presence upset the balance of power in the region. Still, it is puzzling as to why these power struggles could bring down *all* of these impressive chiefdoms. Archaeologist Ann Ramenofsky (1987) has proposed that high losses from introduced disease precipitated the collapse and abandonment of the lower Mississippi valley. As is well known, one of the major impacts of European contact was the introduction of Old World diseases. Until recently, scholars attributed much to the changes in Native life after contact with diseases and a so-called demographic collapse, or crippling and quick loss of life. Now, however, scholars acknowledge that the loss of life was not a sudden collapse, but rather a continuous drain of population over a hundred or more years through serial disease episodes. They also acknowledge that the subsequent changes in Native life were not solely due to disease, but also to contributing factors such as slaving, internecine warfare, dropping fertility rates, violent colonial strategies such as genocide, and general cultural and social malaise from colonial oppression (Alchon 2003; Baker and Kealhofer 1996; Galloway 1995, pp. 134–41, 159–63; Hutchinson 2007; Milner 1980; Perttula 1992, pp. 148–82; 2002; Ramenofsky 1987, pp. 174–76; Ramenofsky and Galloway 1997; Smith 1987, pp. 129–47; 2000, pp. 112–21; 2002; Snow and Lamphear 1988; Stojanowski 2004; Thornton 1987; Worth 1998, vol. 2, pp. 1–37).

Disease episodes certainly and continually tore at Mississippian life, but it was the introduction of the capitalist economy through the colonial Indian slave trade *combined* with disease and the instability brought about by the Spanish explorations that shattered the Mississippian world. Although Spain had established St. Augustine and a vigorous mission system in Spanish Florida as early as 1565, the Spanish did not run their regime along capitalist lines. Rather it was the Dutch, the French, and the English that ushered in the new global economy. By the early 1620s, the Dutch, the English, and the French had established what Alan Gallay has called "beachheads of empire" along the Atlantic seaboard and opened a trade in slaves, guns, and furs, and each lost no time in recruiting Native allies and traders. This set in motion an intensive intra-Indian competition for access to the European trade across the present-day northeastern and mid-Atlantic states, which resulted in much intra-Indian conflict and hostility. The result, in some cases, was the emergence of what I have termed "militaristic slaving societies." These were Indian societies that gained control of the trade, and "through their slave raiding, spread internecine warfare and created widespread dislocation, migration, amalgamation, and, in some cases, extinction of Native peoples"

(Ethridge 2006, pp. 208–209).[5] The first generation of militaristic slaving societies were groups particularly poised to link to the new economy—groups such as the Iroquois of New York; the Westos; a group of Erie and Neutrals who, fleeing the Iroquois, migrated first to Virginia and then to Georgia; and the Occaneechis of North Carolina, a local, well-organized group who moved to where the Trade Path crossed the James River to take advantage of the new trade opportunities opening in Jamestown. These three groups, and perhaps unidentified others, were key agents in the creation and expansion of the Mississippian shatter zone through a relentless raiding of their Indian neighbors for slaves.

Iroquois slaving campaigns had serious repercussions throughout the eastern woodlands. Many northeastern groups fled to the Great Lakes region where they formed new groups such as the Wyandots, and forced local groups such as the Sioux to flee to the Plains; some moved south, into the present-day mid-Atlantic States (Richter 1992, pp. 60–6; White 1991, pp. 11–13). By the mid-1600s, Iroquois raiders were moving into the lower midwest by way of the Ohio and Mississippi river valleys, and archaeologists believe that the eastern Ohio valley was largely depopulated by the mid-1600s because of Iroquois raiding (Drooker 2002, pp. 118–24; Pollack 2004, pp. 188–90). In fact, the Quapaw who the French explorers encountered on the Arkansas River in the 1680s may have been one group in an exodus of people speaking Dehiga Siouan from the Ohio valley at this time (Duval 2003, pp. 67–8; Hoffman 1990, pp. 213–19; Jeter 2002, pp. 213–19; 2009, pp. 373–5; Sabo 2000, pp. 185–6). Archaeologists also suspect that many refugees from Iroquois raiding migrated west into present-day Michigan, Ohio, and Illinois, where they settled in unpopulated areas, joined local populations, or displaced them (Drooker 2002, p. 233; Smith 2002, pp. 3–21). Archaeologists believe that the Illinois on the Mississippi River were feeling the repercussions of this widespread instability decades before direct contact with Europeans (Easery 2007; Mazrim and Esarey 2007). I have recently argued that the chiefdoms of the lower Mississippi valley felt shockwaves emanating from Iroquoia and that this contributed to their collapse (Ethridge 2010, pp. 116–48).

The contributors to a recent volume edited by myself and Sheri Shuck-Hall (2009) document the depopulation of, and multiple migrations by various Native Southern groups that resulted from Westo and Occaneechi predations between 1640 and 1682. The Atlantic coastal chiefdoms of Guale and Mocama, which had been incorporated into the Spanish Mission system of Florida, were the first to suffer from

Indian slaving (Worth 2007, pp. 9, 36, 40, 45). As early as 1661, the Westos and perhaps others were raiding the Georgia and South Carolina coast for Indian slaves to sell to Jamestown traders. This also marked the beginning of an almost twenty-five-year retreat into Spanish Florida for the Guale and Mocama. By 1684, all of the Guale and Mocama who had not been enslaved or joined other groups had moved south, away from the Georgia coast leaving the entire coastline void of people (pp. 15–18; Saunders 2000, p. 50). Westo and Occaneechi aggressions also can account for the disappearance of the chiefdoms of the lower Piedmont such as Cofitachequi (Gallay 2002, pp. 51–2; Hudson et al., 2008). When de Soto came through in 1540, Cofitachequi was a large, well-organized paramount chiefdom (Biedma 1993, p. 229; Elvas 1993, pp. 85–6; Hudson 1997, pp. 187–90; 2005; Rangel 1993, pp. 278–90). For reasons unknown, twenty-seven years later, when the Spaniard Juan Pardo encountered Cofitachequi in 1567, the polity was still intact, but clearly it was being eclipsed by the nearby polity of Joara. Still, Cofitachequi was in existence as a polity as late as 1670, when the English slaver Henry Woodward passed through on his way to the Westos. Soon after, however, Cofitachequi and the other Piedmont chiefdoms of Joara, Guatari, Otari, Yssa, and Olamico began to fall apart, most likely due to Westo and Occaneechi slaving. Some survivors congregated in a previously abandoned section of the Wateree river valley where they soon coalesced into the Catawba; others took up a migratory existence near the Carolina colony where they became known as "settlement Indians" (Beck 2009; Fitts and Heath 2009).

Other lower Piedmont chiefdoms also fell. The archaeological record on the Cherokee-speaking polities is too incomplete to reconstruct with any certainty their history during this tumultuous time, except to say that they quit building mounds and moved their towns slightly southwest. The Coosada chiefdom on the Tennessee River broke apart, with some migrating southwest to join the polities on the Alabama and Chattahoochee rivers. The chiefdom of Ocute in central Georgia, likewise, broke apart around this time, undoubtedly due to its proximity to the Westos who moved to the Savannah River around 1660. Many of the Ocute survivors moved to the coastal areas that had been abandoned by the Guale and Mocama where they coalesced with others into the Yamasee Indians. Some moved west, where they joined those groups on the Chattahoochee (Beck 2009; Bowne 2000; 2005, pp. 89–105; 2009; Davis 2002, p. 144; Ethridge 2010, pp. 149–93; Fitts and Heath 2009; Jenkins 2009; Meyers 2009; Schroedl 2002, pp. 212–13; Shuck-Hall 2009;

Smith 2002, pp. 3–21; Ward and Davis 1993, p. 430; Williams 1994; Worth 2009).

The first signs of these militaristic slaving societies having outlived their usefulness to English trade interests occurred by around 1680, and a series of European and Indian wars ensued. The Occaneechis were diminished in 1676 in Bacon's Rebellion; the Westos were destroyed in 1682 by a group of Shawnee mercenaries in the pay of Carolina traders; the Iroquois were seriously reduced by their wars with Europeans and Indians and by 1686 they began their long retreat into New York and Canada. With the monopolies of the militaristic slaving societies broken, the interior Natives whom the monopolies had blocked from the trade for decades joined with European traders, and we see the emergence of a second generation of militaristic Indian slaving societies. The result, as Alan Gallay (2002) so aptly wrote, was a "frenzy of slaving" in the lower South (p. 130).

After the Occaneechis were dislodged, the Tuscaroras became the prevailing middlemen in the southern Piedmont.[6] The Cherokees began slaving throughout the southwestern Appalachians and Piedmont (Gallay 2002, pp. 319–22). Archaeologist Brett Riggs (forthcoming) recently characterized the early colonial Yuchis as mobile, militaristic slavers. The newly formed Yamasees soon stepped into the breach created with the destruction of the Westos and began slaving far and wide (Jennings 2009; Kelton 2009; Worth, 2009). Between 1685 and 1698, the Abihkas, Alabamas, Tallapoosas, and Apalachicolas also began intense slaving campaigns (Boyd 1936; 1949; Boyd, Smith, and Griffin 1951; McDowell 1992; Nairne 1988; Woodward 1911). The Chickasaws too became militarized slavers.

Most scholars agree that direct contact between the Chickasaws and Europeans, and the consequent participation in the European trade system did not occur until sometime between 1685 and 1690. However, there is growing evidence that they may have been involved before then. For example, there are some indications that between 1670 and 1690 the people of the lower Mississippi River valley had access to European trade goods and that they were in great turmoil (Ethridge and Shuck-Hall 2009; Jolliett and Marquette 1917, pp. 227–80; Joutel 1846, pp. 85–193; Tonti 1846, pp. 82–3). In 1682, La Salle met a small group of Chickasaws near present-day Memphis, and they told him they were several days' travel from their towns. The La Salle accounts, although not containing much information on this encounter, indicate that the Chickasaws probably were not yet armed with European guns, that they ranged far and wide, and that they had free access to the Mississippi River (Jolliet and Marquette

1917, pp. 227–80; Joutel 1846, pp. 85–193; Stubbs 1982). Just four years later in 1686, in an effort to locate La Salle's remaining men, Henri de Tonti traveled down the Mississippi from Illinois. Tonti's accounts are much more complete, and his description of the Indian groups of the lower Mississippi valley indicates much turmoil, with many being assailed from European-armed eastern groups and with those around the confluence of the Yazoo River complaining specifically about gun-toting Chickasaw raiders who traveled to their towns via the Yazoo basin (Galloway 1995, p. 175; d'Iberville 1981, p. 89; Tonti 1846; 1898).

We must begin to reconcile the fact that Charles Town traders were not among the Chickasaw until 1685 with the documentary evidence that suggests European goods had already circulated this far west and that the Chickasaws were well-honed raiders by 1686. Therefore, we must consider the possibility that the Chickasaws had become involved in the European trade, either directly or indirectly, before their contact with Charles Town traders. One source for these goods may have been through an intra-Indian exchange network through which Spanish goods moved into the Southeast from Spanish Florida (Waselkov 1989a). Another source may have come from the West. In a close examination of the late-seventeenth to early eighteenth-century ethnohistoric evidence, David W. Morgan (1997) concludes that the Caddos along the Red, Arkansas, and Missouri Rivers owned European (Spanish) goods and horses (but most likely not guns) as early as 1680 (pp. 108–109). Whether or not these goods ended up in Chickasaw hands is uncertain, although Morgan points out a possible 1687 reference to Chickasaws raiding in Caddo country (p. 102).

There is also the possibility that Chickasaws became engaged in the trade before 1685 through contacts with Indian middlemen, European traders from the Atlantic seaboard, or through the notorious *coureurs de bois*. The *coureurs de bois* (commonly translated as "adventurers" or "trappers") were independent Canadian traders who were scattered throughout the Midwest and mid-South, usually living in Indian villages (Lauber 2002, pp. 75–8; Nairne 1988, p. 37; Rowland and Sanders 1929, pp. 25, 32, 81; see also Podruchny 2006; and Woods 1980). The *coureurs de bois* certainly could have provided the Chickasaws with European-manufactured items, if only on a small scale, and, although they are historically known as fur traders, the documents clearly indicate that they also traded in slaves. There are also some indications that the Chickasaws may have been making long-distance trade journeys to points north and northeast. As is well known, the Indians of North America had far-flung trade networks prehistorically and historically (Tanner 1989, pp. 6–20; 2002). The French documents from Canada indicate much north-south movement of Indians and there are several accounts of northern Indians in and around Chickasaw towns and Chickasaws in and around the Ohio River valley and points northeast (see especially Archives des Colonies, Séries C11). Some Chickasaws may have established trade relations with English slavers in the mid-Atlantic, as they regularly traveled up the Ohio River valleys to points northeast (d'Iberville 1981, pp. 174–5). In addition, by the 1670s, Virginia traders were crossing the Appalachians and regularly trading with Shawnees and other Indians along the Ohio River, and documents indicate that these traders made contacts to the west with the Illinois and to the south with the Chickasaws (Alchon 2003, pp. 138–9; Ethridge 2010, pp. 149–93; Gallay 2002, pp. 103–104; Lauber 2002, pp. 62–118; Rushforth 2003, pp. 777–808). The governor of French Louisiana, Pierre le Moyne d'Iberville (1981), in 1699, noted that some Chickasaws had built a town on the Ohio River, although he does not indicate when they settled in the town or why they did so (p. 174). The Chickasaws could also have been trading with French trading houses around the Great Lakes, as the Canadian and Louisiana documents indicate southern Indians moving freely that far north (Ethridge 2009b, pp. 254–5; d'Iberville 1981, p. 175; see also Archives des Colonies, Séries C11 and C13).

Trading with Indian middlemen is also a likely way in which the Chickasaws became engaged in the European trade before making direct contact with Charles Town traders. In 1913 historian Almon Wheeler Lauber documented the long-distance movement of slaves through an intra-Indian slave trade network, and more recently Alan Gallay sees the intra-Indian slave trade as one of the mechanisms by which Europeans acquired slaves in the Southern slave trade (Gallay 2002, pp. 288–314; Lauber 2002, pp. 118–52). Ethridge (2006; 2009b, pp. 255–6), in characterizing the regionwide instability of the Indian slave trade as a shatter zone, also sees much movement of people over long and short distances, which would also facilitate intra-Indian movements of slaves and goods. And then there is the account of Lamhatty, a Towasa Indian from present-day north Florida, who was captured by Creek slavers in 1706. Through a series of intra-Indian exchanges, Lamhatty eventually found himself in Virginia. Lamhatty's story reveals that other Towasa Indians were already enslaved in Virginia and gives some indication that slaves, and presumably goods, circulated through a chain of transactions involving Indian groups from present-day Florida to Virginia, and perhaps beyond (Bushnell 1908; Swanton 1929; Waselkov 1988; 1989b, pp. 313–220).

English traders made their first forays into the lower South around 1674, when the slaver Henry Woodward, while on an expedition to the Westos, also surveyed the possibility of trade alliances with the Cowetas, Cussetas, and Apalachicolas who were living on the Chattahoochee River in present-day Georgia, groups who would later form the Lower Creeks (Crane 2004, p. 17). Under pressure from the Westos, however, Woodward and the Carolinians chose to abide by the Westo monopoly. They did not follow up on their contacts with the Lower Creeks until eleven years later, in 1685, after they had successfully broken Westo control of the slave trade. Woodward was then commissioned to go to Apalachicola at which time he also sent his agents further west to the Tallapoosas, Abihkas, and Alabamas in present-day central Alabama (groups that would later form the Upper Creeks) and to the Chickasaws in present-day northeastern Mississippi (Bowne 2005, pp. 82–5, 110–11; Galloway 1995, pp. 170–3; Nairne 1988, p. 50). The Creek groups soon afterward controlled the trade from approximately the Tombigbee River to the Atlantic coast, and it is reasonable to assume that the Chickasaw became directly involved with the Charles Town trade around this time although we have no documentary evidence for it.

The next documented traders into Chickasaw country occurred about a decade after Woodward's visit. Although the British superintendent, John Stewart, had sent an agent to the Chickasaws in 1692, it took six more years for the Carolinians to establish a firm Chickasaw trade alliance. This occurred in 1698, when two Carolina slavers, Thomas Welch and Anthony Dodsworth, journeyed to Chickasaw country (Atkinson 2004, p. 25; Crane 1919, p. 382; Gallay 2002, pp. 103, 155–64; Gibson 1971, p. 34). The Chickasaws responded positively to Welch's overtures. By 1700, the Chickasaws were relentlessly raiding the Caddos for horses and slaves up to 150 miles across the Mississippi River (Morgan 1997). In 1702, when Pierre Le Moyne d'Iberville settled Fort Mobile, the Chickasaws also were raiding as far south as the Gulf of Mexico and up the Mississippi River corridor perhaps as far as present-day St. Louis and maybe further, and throughout the Midwest perhaps as far as present-day Detroit. The Choctaws, however, took the brunt of Chickasaw raiding, creating an animosity that lasted into the eighteenth century (Atkinson 2004, pp. 28–9; Ethridge 2010, pp. 149–93; Galloway 2002, pp. 242–7; d'Iberville 1981, p. 172). Their eastern raiding was truncated, no doubt because of Creek control over the area. When they were involved in eastern raiding expeditions it appears to have been mostly as allies of other groups, most notably the Alabamas and Abihkas (Atkinson 2004, pp. 25–9; Du Pratz 1947, pp. 57, 291, 303–304; Galloway 1982, p. 157; McDowell 1992, pp. 123, 168, 215, 238, 249; Nairne 1988, pp. 37, 47, 75; Rowlands and Sanders 1929, pp. 39, 185; 1932, p. 22). By 1708, when Nairne visited the Chickasaws, the slave trade was a firmly established aspect of the their economy (Nairne 1988; see also Atkinson 2004, pp. 25–30; Ethridge 2010, pp. 149-231; Galloway 1995, pp. 308–10; Morgan 1997, pp. 94–99).[7]

In fact, two letters to d'Iberville from Tonti, written in 1702, establish the British-sponsored Chickasaw slaving beyond any doubt (Galloway 1983; Tonti 1702; 1983, pp. 166–73). Tonti wrote these letters as a report to d'Iberville when he journeyed to the Chickasaws to invite them to Mobile to speak with the governor. According to Tonti, the Indian guides took him on circuitous routes to the Chickasaw towns in order to avoid two raiding parties in the area; one party, apparently scouts, consisted of about ten warriors. The other party consisted of four hundred Chickasaw and Chakchiuma warriors. The Indian guides told Tonti that, on raids, this large group would break into smaller groups, attack a village, kill the men, and abduct the women and children. These victims were then bound and led to some sort of holding pen until enough had been accumulated to ship off to Carolina. Tonti, once in the Chickasaw towns, actually met the person in charge of purchasing the slaves and providing European-made goods. The man was a British slave trader, and Tonti at first did not recognize him as a European since he was dressed like his Chickasaw companions in a breech clout, blue long shirt, and "discs at his neck" (most likely some type of gorget; Tonti 1983, p. 168).[8]

The concept of a slave was not new to the Chickasaws or other North American Indians, as most Native groups had an indigenous form of slavery. Slaves were usually war captives who had been put into a version of slavery, although it was not chattel slavery. Therefore indigenous slavery was related to warfare, which was under the jurisdiction of the red moiety. In terms of commercial slaving, we have few descriptions of actual slave raids, but Nairne described a war event that clearly included commercial slaving. Nairne's description is quite detailed, indicating that he probably witnessed the event. Nairne (1988) described a surprise attack in which a small group of men fanned out into a half-moon and stealthily approached a village (p. 43). At a signal from the "Chief Officer" each warrior "gives the War Whoop, and then catch as catch can. After an exploit is done, good store of prissoners taken, and Danger a little over, they hang their bages about their prissoners necks and set them all advancing." This slaving was done with all the pomp and ritual of warfare, as detailed by Nairne.

Enslaving war captives, then, was nothing new to the Chickasaws and war captives could be easily linked to commercial slaving. Even so, some critical aspects changed dramatically. The war captives now consisted of hundreds of women and children, and they were now a commodity sold to European and Indian traders. And as commodities they were quite valuable. According to Nairne (1988), with a single slave, a Chickasaw man could purchase a gun, ammunition, a horse, a hatchet, and a suit of clothes. Nairne may have exaggerated the price in his report; still, slaving was a lucrative enterprise.[9] It should be no surprise, then, that Indian slaving expeditions were sometimes quite large with hundreds of men. Recall Tonti's 1702 trip to the Chickasaws and the 400-warrior raiding party. Tonti also related that when the raiders returned to their towns they locked the slaves in holding pens until the British traders were ready to export them (Galloway 1983, p. 159). Tonti's report, as well as others, clearly indicate that women and children comprised the largest number of captives and that there was usually an associated high toll of adult male deaths, both among those being raided and those doing the raiding (Boyd, Smith, and Griffin 1951, pp. 49, 93–4; Du Pratz 1947, p. 297; Galloway 1983, p. 159; d'Iberville 1981, pp. 171–5; Tonti 1983, p. 169).

Since slaving was part of warfare, the Chickasaws targeted enemy groups in their slaving and, conversely, slave raiding generated military enemies among those being raided. Because of their slaving, the Chickasaws were despised by other Indians throughout the range of their raiding, and they had many enemies. In other words, it was not just the brutality of slave raiding that created intra-Indian hostilities, but also the slave raids were acts of war and, according to the southeastern Indian code of warfare, these acts required retaliation (Hudson 1976, pp. 239–44; Perdue 1998, pp. 86–108; Reid 1970).[10]

As elsewhere throughout the South where commercial slaving was occurring, the impact of Chickasaw slaving was quite dramatic. The small, scattered Caddoan chiefdoms broke apart and the survivors began to coalesce into the Caddo confederacies. The Tunicas moved south to become a *petite nation*. Virtually all of the groups of the Yazoo Basin dispersed, with some moving south to become *petites nations*, some joining the Chickasaws, and many coalescing with refugees from Creek raiding to form the Choctaws, who then became the particular targets of Chickasaw raiding (Early 2000; Ethridge 2009b; 2010; Galloway 1995; Hickerson 1997; Johnson et al. 2008; Lorenz 2000, pp. 163–72; Perttula 2002; Ramenofsky 1987, pp. 42–71, 137–72, 173–6; Smith 2002, p. 17; Swanton 1911, pp. 296–7).

As slaving and disease spread, the entire geopolitical landscape in the Mississippian shatter zone was transformed. One of the most profound consequences was in Spanish Florida. The Spanish mission system, weak and flawed, could not withstand the early eighteenth-century onslaught of armed slave raiders. The results were calamitous and left Spanish Florida virtually devoid of Indians by 1710 (Worth 2009). Elsewhere in the South, remaining chiefdoms began to collapse in quick succession, the survivors joining the large, powerful coalescent societies. The coalescent societies themselves began to go through a series of changes as the new trade system undermined the inherited, hierarchal political order. Now young men and women with a new access to prestige, power, and influence through the trade system challenged chiefly and religious authorities and they began to craft a new form of governance based on the town council and achieved status (Ethridge 2010, pp. 82–4; Lapham 2005; Wesson 2008; 2002; Worth 2009).

Then, in 1715, the Yamasee War interrupted the European trade. But really, the slave trade was faltering in this new South. For one, as Paul Kelton (2007) has shown, in 1686, the entire region suffered from a devastating small pox epidemic carried far and wide by Indian slavers. Also, the most vulnerable populations such as the mission Indians of Spanish Florida had been slaved out. Slave catchers were simply running out of people to enslave. And those that remained had congregated into the large, formidable coalescent societies against whom raiding expeditions would have been difficult and quickly retaliated (Ethridge 2010, pp. 232–54).

After the Yamasee War a new South was indeed emerging. Gone were all the many polities that de Soto saw, replaced by large Indian nations such as the Creek Confederacy, the Cherokees, the Choctaws, the Chickasaws, the Catawbas, and the Caddo confederacies (see figure 2.1). The new South of the eighteenth century was born out of the sixteenth- and seventeenth-century Mississippian shatter zone. The Mississippian chiefdoms, structured to rise and fall, fell spectacularly with European contact, and they failed to rise again because of the turmoil and wide regional instability created by the introduction of Old World diseases and the increased violence and disruptions of the commercial trade in Indian slaves. Although thousands of Indians died and were enslaved, and virtually all Native polities were destroyed, there were survivors who regrouped and reformed new kinds of polities, and they reorganized and restructured their lives for living in the new geopolitical landscape of nations and a global capitalist economy that was in place by 1730.

Notes

1. The literature on the Mississippian period is quite extensive. Some good book-length treatments are Anderson (1994); Blitz and Lorenz (2006); Dye and Cox (1990); King (2003); Knight and Steponaitis (1998); and Pauketat (2004). On complex and paramount chiefdoms, see Anderson (1994, pp. 4–9); Hally, Smith, and Langford (1990, pp. 121–38); Steponaitis (1978).
2. In this scenario, the paramountcy of Coosa fell, and it did so along the timeline set by Smith (2000, pp. 96–121). The difference is that I propose the reasons for the fall were not primarily disease episodes and that this occurrence should not be projected across the Southeast as the total collapse of the Mississippian. This is in contrast to Paul Hoffman (1997), who, by examining the documentary evidence, challenged whether or not Coosa fell in the first place. Hoffman, however, did not reexamine the archaeological evidence for the decline of Coosa that Smith used in his reconstruction (pp. 25–9).
3. There is some discrepancy in the dating of the Chattahoochee River phases. The scenario here follows Jenkins (2009). In contrast, Worth (2000) repeats Knight's (1994). These are Stewart Phase, C.E. 1475–1550; Abercrombie Phase, C.E. 1550–1650; and Blackmon Phase, C.E. 1650–1715. Blitz and Lorenz (2006, pp. 71–2) date them as Stewart Phase, C.E. 1550–1600; and Abercrombie Phase, C.E. 1600–1650. Using these later dates, it is tempting to interpret the Big Eddy migration to the Chattahoochee as resulting from the fall of Tascalusa after the battle of Mabila.
4. Many scholars have proposed various scenarios for the origins and movements of the lower Mississippi valley and Yazoo River valley people. For an excellent summary of this work, see Jeter (2002, pp. 177–224).
5. Ferguson and Whitehead (1999) also understand militarization to be a result of the interface between expanding states and indigenous peoples.
6. The Tuscaroras, surrounded by Indian enemies because of their slaving, were defeated by a Yamasee/English army in 1713; the survivors migrated to Iroquoia where, in 1722, they joined the Great League as the Sixth Nation; see Merrell (1989, pp. 40, 54, 118) and Richter (1992, p. 238).

7. There is also some archaeological evidence for an early engagement with the European trade. For example, Johnson et al. (2008) present archaeological evidence for involvement in the European trade beginning as early as 1650. Sometime prior to the beginning of the Early period, the Chickasaw moved from hunting rabbits, squirrels, and other small mammals that would be used as food to a focus on beaver, otter, fox, and other fur-bearing animals whose skins they could sell on the market. The faunal evidence, then, complements the documentary evidence to indicate that the Chickasaw traded in small fur skins as well as slaves during the Early period. They also interpret the presence of bear on these Early sites to indicate that the Chickasaw owned guns by the late 1600s.
8. Tonti does not identify this man by name, but it may have been Thomas Welch, who probably spent much time with the Chickasaws as evidenced by his métis son, James Welch, who in 1727 applied for a license in South Carolina to trade among the Chickasaws. This document notes that James Welch was "related to the Chickasaws," which most likely meant that Welch's mother was Chickasaw; see the Report of the Joint Committee, 1727, Journal of the Council and Council in Assembly, Public Records Office, Document 18 transcribed in Maxcy (1999, p. 56).
9. The price of an Indian slave fluctuated over the years and also by country. In a careful examination of the documentary evidence, Gallay (2002) tracks the changing prices over time, and he also concludes that the English could pay the best price for Indian slaves (pp. 311–14).
10. Alan Gallay (personal communication) believes that this could help account for the endemic warfare between the Choctaws and Chickasaws and why the Choctaws continually spoiled French efforts to make peace between the two.

Chapter 3

Southeastern Indian Polities of the Seventeenth Century: Suggestions toward an Analytical Vocabulary

Eric E. Bowne

In the last two decades, scholars of Southeastern studies have considerably deepened our understanding of the complexities of Euro-American and Native American interactions in the seventeenth century (Bowne 2005; Braund 1993; Ethridge and Hudson 2002; Ethridge and Shuck-Hall 2009; Galloway 1995; Hahn 2004; Hall 2009a; Hudson and Tesser 1994; Kelton 2007; Smith 2000; McEwan 2000a; Merrell 1989; Milanich 1999; Oatis 2004; Rountree 1990; Usner 1992, 2003; Worth 1995, 1998). This turbulent century produced a number of important trends that by the second quarter of the eighteenth century had resulted in the development of an international theater of political intrigue, economic competition, and outright war. The colonizing strategies of the various European powers and their interplay have been described in some detail and though it is clear that Native polities reacted to these intrusions in a number of distinct ways, we have yet to describe their responses with any precision (Ethridge 2009c, pp. 422–4; Hudson 2002, pp. xxiv–xxxviii). It is my intent to make some preliminary suggestions toward the development of an analytical vocabulary that adequately describes these responses and the Native polities that subsequently emerged within the context of invasion and colonization.

Beginning in the 1980s, Charles Hudson and his associates undertook the Herculean task of tracing the routes of the Spanish conquistadors who explored the American South—particularly Hernando de Soto, Tristan de Luna, and Juan Pardo (Hudson 1987; 1990; 1993; 1994; Hudson, Smith, and DePratter 1984; 1990; Hudson, Worth, and DePratter 1990; Hudson et al. 1989). By combining archaeological information with the written accounts of Spanish exploration, Hudson developed a social geography of the Late Mississippian South that serves as a starting point for exploring both forward and backward in time (Hudson 1997). During the course of this research one thing became clear—the Southeastern Indian societies of the historic period were different in many ways from their prehistoric predecessors and had essentially developed during the early colonial period.

This led Hudson to propose, as my colleague Robbie Ethridge (2006) has noted, a "deceptively simple question": "What shaped the Indians of the eighteenth-century South? That is to say, what historical forces, trends, and events were attendant to the formation of the Indians of the colonial South?" (pp. 207; Hudson 2002, p. xii). Hudson advocates the social historical approach of Marc Bloch and Fernand Braudel as the research paradigm needed to answer it. Following that approach, Hudson has determined a number of factors involved with the transformation of Southeastern Indian societies: (1) military losses, (2) destabilization, (3) Old World diseases, and (4) political and economic incorporation into the modern world system. Hudson further subdivided the fourth factor into three distinct colonizing strategies: (i) Spanish missions (Florida and Texas), (ii) fur trade in the Northeast, and (iii) plantation system and Indian trade in the South (Hudson 2002, pp. xxii–xxxvi).

Not everyone reacted to these factors in the same way, however. In fact, members of the same culture and even the same societies often split into factions and pursued divergent paths toward survival. Because of this, Hudson has noted that the proper unit of analysis should be the polity, communities organized politically, as opposed to culture or society. Further, each polity followed its own historical trajectory and each trajectory must be understood within the context of the modern world system that superseded the Mississippian world (pp. xv–xvi). Hudson and Ethridge have called for the development of a vocabulary that adequately describes the several types of Indian polities that interacted with both Euro-Americans and African Americans in the seventeenth and eighteenth centuries (pp. xx; Ethridge 2009c, pp. 423–4). While it must be granted that it is somewhat reductionist to refer to four "types" of Native polities, I am not trying to reduce history to a set of models or make a statement about social evolution; rather I am using models to shape our research questions and help us understand the historical reality of the early colonial South. The four types are: (1) Neotraditional polities, (2) militaristic slaving polities, (3) Euro-dependent polities, and (4) confederated polities.

Before describing each type in more detail, it should be noted these polities developed within a context of macroregional coalescence, and all Native groups were affected by the phenomenon to some extent. In the past, many of us in Southeastern studies have used the term "coalescence" to refer to a type or class of society. Steve Kowalewski (2006), however, has made a strong argument that coalescence is in fact a macroregional phenomenon that gives new or greater emphasis to institutions that were already widely shared in the region. In the South as chiefdoms declined and new methods of political organization emerged, the importance of matrilineal clans increased because they "facilitated long-distance exchange...recruitment and community integration" (pp. 120). Societies throughout the region dealt with demographic upheaval in addition to the aforementioned political instability and though each came up with their own unique responses, broad similarities are recognizable (pp. 117). No matter which of the four polity types a particular group most resembled, they were composed of multiethnic and multilingual populations who joined in part to maintain viability and in part to provide themselves a measure of security.

Neotraditional Polities

Southeastern Indian societies were affected by the first three of Hudson's four factors within a context of macroregional coalescence for over a century before the intrusion of English commerce. During this time, many of the classic traits of Mississippian chiefdoms fell out of use (such as the building of platform mounds, hierarchical settlement patterns, and elite interments containing exotic goods) while others continued (King 2006; Smith 2000, pp. 97–98; Worth 2002, pp. 59–60). Between the time of the Spanish *entradas* and the intrusion of English commerce many polities shrank in size while migrating regularly over short distances, perhaps the most well-researched case being that of the chiefdom of Coosa (Smith 1987; 2000). Over the course of the seventeenth century the number of towns within the polity decreased dramatically, as did average town size, while the location of towns shifted regularly to the south and west (Knight 1994, 382; Smith 2000, pp. 100–17). Despite these disruptions there remained "clear signs of cultural, social, and political continuity from the sixteenth through the seventeenth centuries [and] long-term stability in certain towns as political centers" (Knight 1994, pp. 385). We might think of these societies as chiefdoms, but they were clearly not classic

Mississippian chiefdoms and therefore might be better thought of as "neotraditional" polities.

The Apalachee, whose territory was located in the panhandle of present-day Florida between the Ochlockonee and Aucilla Rivers, are one of the most well-documented examples of the neotraditional polity type (Hann 1988; 1994; McEwan 1993; 2000b; 2004; Scarry 1994; 1996). During the Middle Mississippian period the Lake Jackson site served as capital of a significant chiefdom with, at the very least, clear trade connections with Etowah to the north. As the multiregional exchange network broke down in the late fifteenth and early sixteenth centuries and other sweeping changes came to the Mississippian world, the Apalachee elite were forced to adjust in order to maintain their power (McEwan 2000b, pp. 60–1). The seat of government moved to Anhaica and authority seems to have been shared by both "peace" and "war" chiefs, but the hierarchical structure of a Mississippian chiefdom remained (pp. 62–3). The Apalachees were encountered by a number of Spanish exploring parties in the sixteenth century, including that of Hernando de Soto, all of whom found the group to be well organized and quite bellicose (Clayton, Knight, and Moore 1993; Hoffman 1994; Milanich and Hudson 1993).

Despite their relative success at driving off these early invaders by force of arms, the Apalachees were unable to muster a defense against European microbes or Spanish colonization efforts further east in St. Augustine. By the early seventeenth century the elite lineages of Apalachee were struggling to maintain the "old" social order, and they turned to an unlikely ally for help—the Spanish friars who established a mission in present-day Tallahassee in 1633. More correctly put, Apalachee leaders were trying to create a new social order based on old forms—with the primary goal of keeping themselves in a preeminent position (Worth 2002). Instead of living on mounds, they lived near the friars; instead of native copper and marine shell, they had European-manufactured goods; and in addition to traditional esoteric knowledge, they added literacy and Catholicism (McEwan 2000b, 65–7). Unfortunately for the Apalachees, the Spanish could not insulate or protect them from the expanding English trade in Indian slaves, deerskins, and beaver pelts, and in 1704 the Apalachee mission was abandoned after a series of English-led slave raids in the province (Crane 2004, pp. 75–80; Boyd, Smith, and Griffin 1951; Gallay 2002, pp. 135–47).

The Natchez Indians provide another good example of the neotraditional polity (Barnett 2007; Brown 1982; 1985; 1991; Lorenz 2000; Milne 2009; Neitzel 1983; 1997). The Natchez and their predecessors had inhabited the Yazoo Basin for over three centuries when they encountered members of the Hernando de Soto expedition in the early 1540s and drove the fleeing Spaniards down the Mississippi River with fleets of dugout canoes (Hudson 1997, pp. 387–97). In the ensuing 140 years it appears the Natchez maintained a relatively stable population in the basin and seem to have been less adversely affected by the changes taking place in the Mississippian world than groups closer to direct European contact (Lorenz 2000, pp. 147–50). There were still at least five mound centers occupied in the basin as late as 1680 and it is apparent the Natchez continued to practice a number of Mississippian traditions that disappeared from much of the South during the seventeenth century, including mound ceremonialism, retainer burial, and elaborate sumptuary rules related to chiefly lineages (Lorenz 2000, pp. 147; Swanton 1911, pp. 45–256). Though it is far from clear how they maintained these traditions so long, the distance from English markets may have been a factor until about 1685, when commercial slaving began to expand rapidly.

By the time the French arrived ca. 1700, the Natchez elite, much like their Apalachee counterparts, were in need of a buttress for their power. However, it is likely that the Natchez relationship with the French was predicated not only on the desire of Natchez elites to form a political partnership with the French, but also the general Natchez desire for French protection from the English-driven trade in Indian slaves. The irony, of course, is that the arrival of the French ratcheted up commercial competition in the region, which, besides the pressures it brought from the outside, led to internal factionalism between pro-French and pro-English groups (Neitzel 1997, pp. 55–7). Not surprisingly, the Great Sun sided with the French, who seemed to support his rule willingly but had trouble understanding why so many of the Natchez undermined their efforts. The pro-English faction among the Natchez wanted, among other things, the social mobility of the market and they sought the protection English firearms would provide them against Chickasaw slave raids (Ethridge 2006, pp. 213–16). The Natchez, who numbered between 4,000 and 6,000 in the early eighteenth century, could not long stand against the rising tide of the new market economy and were soon split asunder by internal factionalism and external competition (Lorenz 2000, pp. 172–3).

Remember these are the polities for which we have reliable data, but it is likely other interior groups were following similar strategies until forced down other paths by the development of the Indian slave trade. For example, when Hernando de Soto's expedition visited Cofitachequi in 1540, it was the seat of a large paramount chiefdom ruled by a woman known as the "Lady of Cofitachequi." In 1670, Henry Woodward of Carolina made a journey to the territory of Cofitachequi and met with the so-called Emperor (Cheves 1897, pp. 186–7). In the 130-year interim between de Soto's and Woodward's visits, Cofitachequi must have undergone some fundamental changes similar to those experienced by other Southern Native societies of the time. Yet, during his trip in 1670, Woodward "contracted a league with ye Emperor & all those Petty Caciques betwixt us & them, soe that some few weeks after my returne, our Provision failed us...[and] had not [we] releved ye General wants by what Provisions wee procured of the Natives [of Cofitachequi] it had gone very hard with us" (pp. 187). Thus, at the very least, there still existed a chiefly mechanism for the collection of (surplus?) food late in the seventeenth century.

A number of other interior societies seem to have also pursued the neotraditional strategy, though as with the case of Cofitachequi there is only indirect evidence. As discussed earlier, Marvin Smith (1987; 2000) has traced the movements of the remnant of the Coosa chiefdom during the late sixteenth and early seventeenth centuries, from northwest Georgia southwest into east-central Alabama where they where known as Abihkas. In the decades following the de Soto expedition, the Alabamas moved east from present Mississippi to the headwaters of the Alabama River (Waselkov and Smith 2000, pp. 248). Just to the east near Montgomery, the Tallapoosas appear to have been able to maintain their polity without relocating, though they would later survive only by accepting large numbers of refugees into their towns (p. 250). The Appalachicolas, though greatly reduced in numbers during the late sixteenth century, had established a chiefdom in the lower Chattahoochee Valley by the mid-seventeenth century after having migrated south along the river (Worth 2000, pp. 267–9). Meanwhile in the Piedmont of present Georgia, the remnants of several chiefdoms encountered by de Soto, including Ocute, Ichisi, and Altamaha, established a polity on the frontier of the Spanish mission system (Worth 2004, p. 251). Soon these groups would be forced to remake themselves again, however.

Militaristic Slaving Polities

Robbie Ethridge has argued that the intrusion of European commerce into the New World, which had the ability to transform Indian polities at great distances from Euro-American beachheads, resulted in the creation of "shatter zones," one of which she identifies as the whole of the eastern woodlands (Ethridge 2006, p. 208; 2009a). The introduction of commercial trade resulted in a dramatic shift in political economy within a single generation, and led to the rise of a "new social order" in the Deep South in which the primacy of hereditary chiefs was usurped by the effects of European technology and the intrusive world market (Worth 2006, p. 203). One of the driving forces behind the shift in political economy was the influence of a new livelihood that was adopted by a small number of groups, which Ethridge (2006) refers to as "militaristic slaving societies" (p. 208). These groups tended to be small in overall population and followed a predatory strategy—attacking other Native groups and selling the captives into slavery among the Europeans. This new commercial slaving livelihood developed because an unusual set of circumstances allowed a small number of polities to seize almost complete control of the market.

The first was Euro-American inexperience with Native languages and the geography of interior America. This inexperience kept Euro-Americans from maintaining direct access to interior Native groups—instead they had to rely on Indian allies as guides, interpreters, and providers of food for sustenance and wood for fuel (Bowne 2005, pp. 58–61). Indian allies were also required in order to truck trade goods into the interior, and sometimes those groups of Native "middlemen" were able to obtain arms and ammunition from their Euro-American trading partners. Once firearms were obtained, they could be used against "bow-and-arrow Indians" who had little experience with the loud and destructive weapons of the Europeans, which inflicted wounds beyond the ken of Native doctors. The particular circumstances that led to Native possession of firearms seems to have always been related to competing European powers—French, Dutch, and English in the Northeast; Virginia and Maryland in the mid-Atlantic; and Carolina, Virginia, and later Louisiana in the lower South (Fausz 1984; Gallay 2002; Hahn 1995; Richter 1992; Trigger 1978; Usner 1992). That is to say, when two or more European nations were competing for Indian trade in the same region, one nation often began selling arms to draw customers away from their competitors—a strategy that always resulted in the other nations being drawn into the arms trade as well.

Firearms were used to take captives for the burgeoning Southern trade in Indian slaves, which began in order to supply cheap labor for the tobacco fields of Virginia but quickly developed into an export business to the sugar islands of the Caribbean (Bowne, in press). The mission Indians under Spanish rule and the so-called pagan Indians of the Spanish frontier were among the first targets. At its height, the Spanish mission system in Florida amounted to no more than about forty towns of Christian Indians located throughout three provinces, including approximately 26,000 Indians, 300 Spanish soldiers, and a small number of priests (Bushnell 1989, p. 138). These missionaries and their Native flocks were thinly spread from coastal missions as far north as South Carolina and as far west as the Apalachicola River in the present panhandle of Florida, and this dispersion over such a wide area made them ideally suited for the depredations of Indian slavers (Bowne 2005, pp. 75–8). Further, because the Spanish friars made it illegal to trade arms and ammunition to either mission Indians or pagan Indians along the Spanish frontier, Native peoples of the region were at a military disadvantage to the northern invaders who had experience not only with European firearms but also with the commercial markets of the Atlantic (Waselkov 1989a, p. 120).

The Westo Indians in particular provide an illustrative example of the opportunities available as a result of the interplay of the three European colonizing strategies. The Westos first entered the historical record in the 1630s as the Eries, when they lived along the southern shore of the lake for which they are named (Thwaites 1896–1901:8, p. 115). In the 1640s, the Eries pursued a trading partnership with the Susquehannocks of northern Chesapeake Bay, exchanging beaver pelts for European-manufactured items the latter obtained from the Virginians, including firearms (Bowne 2005, pp. 44–9; Green 1998, pp. 10–11; Hoffman 1964, pp. 201–204; Weslager 1961, p. 117). By 1650, the insatiable European demand for beaver pelts led to plummeting beaver populations, which greatly increased competition between Native groups participating in the trade. The violent conflicts resulting from this competition became known collectively as the Beaver Wars (Richter 1992, pp. 50–66). The Eries, despite their access to European guns, fared poorly in the Beaver Wars and were forced to abandon their homeland and move south in 1656, beyond the easy reach of their enemies. Shortly after arriving on the southwestern frontier of Virginia, the Eries (known to Virginians as the Richahecrians) forged a trading partnership with the colony (Alvord and Bidgood 1912, p. 155; Bowne 2005, pp. 72–5; Burk 1805, pp. 106–107). The Virginians desired not only beaver pelts, but also Indian slaves to work their tobacco fields.

By 1659, the Richahecrians were staging raids against Indian groups in Spanish Florida, and in the mid-1660s they moved to the

Savannah River along the present boundary of Georgia and South Carolina, where they became known as the "Westos" (Cheves 1897, p. 166). They continued to raid the Spanish missions as well as surrounding groups in order to steal corn and capture Native peoples whom they sold into slavery in Virginia. Terrified local Indians were forced to seek the protection of the Spanish missions or the newly established Carolina colony (pp. 168, 194, 200–201). By 1674, however, the Lords Proprietors of the Carolina colony sought their own trade deal with the Westos, stipulating that slaves were only to be taken from interior groups unallied to Carolina (pp. 456–62). In exchange for "deare skins, furrs, & younge slaves," the Westos received the guns, powder, shot, and other English goods they needed (p. 462). Between 1674 and 1680 the Lords Proprietors exercised a legal monopoly on the Indian slave trade, and both they and the Westos benefited greatly from their business partnership.

Other, less well-documented, cases of Native groups pursuing a militaristic slaving strategy during the seventeenth century exist as well. For example, after the Westos migrated to the Savannah River valley ca. 1663, the Occaneechees replaced them as the preeminent Native brokers in the Virginia backcountry. From their island home in the Roanoke River, the Occaneechees served as middlemen for Indians trading from as far away as 500 miles and because of their access to European firearms, maintained a decided military advantage over their neighbors (Alvord and Bidgood 1912, pp. 209–26; DeMallie 2004, pp. 291–3; Everett 2009, pp. 83–92; Lederer 1958, pp. 24–6). The Chiscas were another militaristic slaving society associated with the Virginia backcountry, though they apparently migrated to the Spanish frontier before the Westos first negotiated their trade deal with the Virginians (Ethridge 2006, p. 212; 2009a, p. 33; Goddard et al. 2004, pp. 176–7). In addition, in 1673 the Tomahitans were encountered by English explorers in the Virginia backcountry as well, armed with sixty firearms and other European goods likely obtained at the port of San Marcos south of present Tallahassee (Alvord and Bidgood 1912, p. 214; DeMallie 2004, pp. 190–1; Waselkov 1989a, pp. 120–1). Most groups could not obtain the weapons necessary to follow the militaristic slaving strategy during the seventeenth century, however, and had to seek other means of security.

Euro-dependent Polities

Coastal Indian groups known to the English as "settlement Indians" and to the French as "*les petites nations*," were absolutely indispensable in helping maintain the European colonies during the first decades of colonization in any particular location. As noted earlier, early colonists and coastal Indian groups lived in a kind of symbiosis with each other, which, for a variety of reasons, quickly led to a dependence on the former by the latter. The Euro-dependent strategy pursued by a number of Indian polities, that is, relying on European material and military assistance in exchange for performing a number of tasks for which the colonists were initially unsuited, was obviously associated with the Atlantic and Gulf coasts because that's where the Euro-Americans were, but was there more to it than that? Remember that the coastal groups were not Mississippianized societies, so the neotraditional strategy wasn't open to them. It might also follow that non-Mississippianized coastal groups were less well-suited for joining the interior confederacies, which were composed almost exclusively of the remnants of Mississippian societies. In addition, official policy in Carolina kept settlement Indians from obtaining firearms, and thus from following the militaristic slaving strategy (Cheves 1897, p. 367; Salley 1928:I, p. 99). Meanwhile, the aggression of the Westos gave the settlement Indians little alternative but to seek Euro-American support.

Early reports from the Carolina colony often mention the willingness of Native peoples to trade food to the English in exchange for protection against the slave raids of the Westos: "They hoped by our Arrivall to be protected from ye Westoes, often making signes...wee should [engage them] with our guns" (Cheves 1897, p. 168). The ravaged coastal groups were "afraid of ye very footstep of a Westoe" (p. 334). These local groups, soon known as settlement Indians, became intimately associated with the Carolina colony, living among the settlers and performing menial tasks, including acting as guides and interpreters; cutting and transporting firewood; and piloting dugout canoes for a variety of purposes. Many of them learned European trades such as blacksmithing, and Indian-made pottery was widely used in colonial settlements (Lawson 1967, pp. 10, 175, 200; Usner 1992, pp. 149–90). As Carolina's Lords Proprietors noted in 1682, the settlement Indians were "of great use to ye Inhabitants of our province for the fetching in againe of such Negroe Slaves as shall Runn away from their masters and allsoe for fishing, fouleing, and hunting" (Salley 1928:I, p. 174). When the French established themselves in the lower Mississippi Valley at the beginning of the eighteenth century, they too relied extensively on the Native population, particularly the many small gulf coastal groups (Usner 1992, 2003).

What did settlement Indians and *les petites nations* gain by these alliances? First and foremost, they received access to European manufactured goods, with the exception of firearms. In fact, Euro-dependent Indians seem to have adopted these goods with less alteration than interior groups, who for at least the first half of the seventeenth century were apt to modify trade goods to suit aboriginal habits and tastes—for instance, using a brass kettle as the raw material for jewelry and arrowheads rather than for its intended use (Bamforth 1993, p. 53; Wilson and Rogers 1993, pp. 3–18). They also received a measure of protection from their proximity to Euro-American settlements; otherwise they didn't have the manpower or arms to survive the onslaught of the commercial slave trade. By living among the settlers on whom they depended, coastal groups were able to reduce their chances of being captured, since militaristic slaving polities, like predatory animals, sought to protect themselves from injury by attacking only weak and vulnerable prey beyond the easy reach of Euro-American assistance.

Confederated Polities

The groups that did manage to survive the initial wave of Old World disease and commercial slaving were those interior groups removed from direct contact with the colonies that formed confederated polities at least partially in response to the threat of Indian slavers bearing European firearms. That is to say, the various Indian confederacies likely began as nonaggression pacts between remnants of societies that coalesced based on such factors as language, geographic proximity, and shared cultural and historical experience. In particular, the threat of slavers strengthened the most integrative institution in the region—clans. At the same time, European commerce undermined the socioeconomic structure of chiefdoms, giving individuals access to wealth and prestige that the chief couldn't control. Taken together these factors led to the development of a new kind of political organization in the region—essentially autonomous towns joined together into groups that may be described as confederated polities. Productive research has recently been done on many of these late seventeenth- and early eighteenth-century polities, including the Upper and Lower Creeks, the Catawbas, and the Yamassees (Hahn 2004; Knight 1994; Merrell 1989; Smith 2000; Worth 1995).

It is difficult to pinpoint precisely when the political entity known in the eighteenth century as the Creek Confederacy formed, since it was likely a gradual process and is not directly reflected in the archaeological record (Jenkins 2009; Knight 1994; Shuck-Hall 2009). It has been argued that the Indian slave trade played a key role, however, serving as a potent mechanism that accelerated the development of the Creek Confederacy by forcing a number of neotraditional polities into nonaggression pacts for mutual self-defense (Bowne 2005, 2009). The core of what became the Upper Creeks between 1675 and 1715 consisted of the neotraditional societies discussed earlier: the Abihkas, Alabamas, and Tallapoosas (Waselkov and Smith 2000, pp. 242–55). Meanwhile the Lower Creeks coalesced around the remaining members of the neo-traditional polity known to the Spaniards as Apalachicola (Hall 2009b; Worth 2000, pp. 266–78). During the last quarter of the seventeenth century, Coweta and Cussita were the most prominent towns in the Chattahoochee Valley, in large part because they negotiated a trade deal with the Carolinians in 1685 (Hahn 2004, pp. 10–47).

Cofitachequi provides another example of the influence the slave trade had on Native politics if, as Woodward asserted, the "Emperor" of Cofitachequi exerted a certain influence over several villages at least as late as 1670. The "Emperor" of Cofitachequi and his petty caciques, however, disappeared from the written record during the middle years of the 1670s, and the old province of Cofitachequi soon became known as the country of the Catawbas (Beck 2009; Fitts and Heath 2009). No one has previously explained the disappearance of Cofitachequi, nor the timing or processes behind its demise. It is sometimes assumed that disease crippled the chiefdom of Cofitachequi before the English arrived on the Carolina coast. It is apparent from Woodward's account, however, that that was not entirely true. Instead I believe it likely that during the 1670s, the province of Cofitachequi became one of the principal targets of Indian slave raids. Archaeological evidence supports the idea that significant depopulation did not occur in the Carolina piedmont until after 1650 (Davis 2002, p. 143). Given this information, the idea that Indian slave raids were at least partially responsible for the downfall of the Cofitachequi polity must be entertained. If this was indeed the case, then these raids also provided some impetus for the formation of the Catawba Confederacy, which a Shawnee once described as consisting of "many nations under that name" (Merrell 1989, p. 92).

The Yamasee Confederacy also seems to have formed in large part because of the threat of Indian slave raids and, like the Upper and Lower Creeks, developed around the remnants of a neotraditional polity, in this case Altamaha (Bowne 2005; 2009; Worth 1995; 2004). The Yamasee formed between 1659 and 1663 in the territory adjacent to the Guale mission province along the coast of present-day Georgia and South Carolina (Worth 2004, p. 245). At first the Yamasees were forced to seek the protection of the Spanish missions, though most refused to convert to Catholicism, but the continuing pressure of slave raids forced many of them to flee from Florida in 1683 (p. 251). The following year with the help of a short-lived Scottish colony in present-day South Carolina, the Yamasee received the firearms necessary to become slave catchers themselves and began to raid the missions that had formerly offered them sanctuary (Crane 1929, pp. 25–31; Gallay 2002, pp. 70–98; Worth 2004, pp. 251–2). After the Scottish colony was destroyed by the Spanish, the Yamasee began trading with the Carolinians though eventually their relationship would sour (Worth 2004, p. 252).

European inexperience, which had been an advantage to coastal groups, militaristic slaving societies, and confederated polities alike did not last long however. Soon, experience and an increasing population of Europeans and African slaves helped spell the end for many Euro-dependent groups, since jobs that only Natives could perform in the seventeenth century could soon be done by colonists or black slaves. Coastal groups were also commonly subjected to Old World pathogens and for that reason perhaps more than any other, they did not last much into the eighteenth century. As their usefulness to colonists diminished, so did their overall numbers, and settlement Indians and *les petites nations* slowly faded out of the historic record and into extinction. At the same time, confederated groups began connecting directly to the developing Atlantic market, in part because Euro-Americans were able to make bolder and bolder forays into the interior. The expanding market spelled doom for neotraditional polities in part because its basic principles undermined the foundation of chiefly authority and in part because they were ravaged by slavers. It was also during this tumultuous last quarter of the seventeenth century, however, that Euro-Americans initiated a series of wars to wrest control of the trade from militaristic slaving polities, with the Westos again providing an illustrative example.

Between 1674 and 1680 the Lords Proprietors fought bitterly with a group of Carolina planters known as the "Goose Creek men" over control of the Indian trade (Cheves 1897, pp. 445–6; Salley 1928:I, pp. 100, 104–107). The proprietors' monopoly on trade with the Westos infuriated Carolinian planters, because exporting deerskins, beaver pelts, and Indian slaves was perhaps the most lucrative economic activity occurring in the colony at the time. The Westos' military advantage over other Native groups had to be overcome, however, before the planters could usurp control of the trade from the Lords Proprietors. Toward this end, in 1680 the Goose Creek men financed a secret war against the Westos, and by 1682 there were reported to be only fifty Westo warriors remaining in the South (Salley 1928:I, pp. 104–107, 115–16; 1911, pp. 182–3). Once this group was removed as an obstacle, adventurous Carolinian planters were able to quickly expand the market, entangling every Native polity as a result. In essence the Westo War and other conflicts of the same nature, such as Bacon's Rebellion and the Tuscarora War, marked the end of the militaristic slaving strategy described earlier (Ethridge 2009a, pp. 34–5; Everett 2009, pp. 83–95). In fact, only confederated polities survived long into the eighteenth century.

This is not to say, however, that Indian slavery came to an end along with militaristic slaving polities—quite the contrary. Between approximately 1685 and 1725, virtually every Native society in the region had access to European markets and was participating in commercial slaving to one degree or another, competing against each other to gain an upper hand in Euro-American commerce. As Robbie Ethridge (2006) has noted, "participation in the slave trade became one of the structural principles of life around which most everything else revolved" (p. 209). When the confederated polities that developed in response to the militaristic slaving strategy obtained significant numbers of firearms, they began their own slaving campaigns against neighboring groups. The dramatic lessening of social diversity in the South by the turn of the eighteenth century was a testament to the "success" of the second generation of Indian slavers. Confederated polities such as the Creeks and Catawbas survived the final turbulent quarter of the seventeenth century, but many of their neighbors, including the Guale, Mocama, Timucua, Calusa, and many others, ceased to exist as distinct ethnic groups. Meanwhile an untold number of groups such as the Hitchitis, Alabamas, Okmulgees, Esaws, Waterees, and Congarees saw their social identities partially subsumed within the developing confederations. Over the course of but a single generation a new social order had arisen in the South, and the struggle for control of the continent, a story with which we are all more familiar, had begun in earnest.

Chapter 4

From Captives to Kin: Indian Slavery and Changing Social Identities on the Louisiana Colonial Frontier

Dayna Bowker Lee

In the waning years of the seventeenth century, England and Spain were poised to extend their claims into the Mississippi River valley. With the consent of the government, but largely on his own initiative, René-Robert Cavelier de La Salle descended from Canada in 1682 to claim the river and all its drainages for France. Two years later, colonists in tow, La Salle failed to reach the mouth of the river through the Gulf of Mexico, and was murdered by his own men in Texas in 1687. Not until 1699 was Pierre Le Moyne d'Iberville permitted to spearhead occupation of lower Louisiana.

Fresh from victories in King Williams's War and long a proponent of reinforcing French claims to the river and gulf coast, Iberville was granted only a few troops and limited resources with which to represent French interests. This meager presence was to serve a dual purpose—to deny England and Spain control of the Mississippi River and the interior of the continent, and to advance opportunities for Indian trade. Many of the first soldiers/settlers to arrive on the gulf coast were seasoned French Canadians, accustomed to intimate dealings with American Indians and unfettered by bonds of matrimony.

By 1702, small French outposts were established near tribal villages at Biloxi and Mobile, and alliances with Indian nations to the east and west afforded the colonists a small measure of security. Missing were the settlers—the farmers, the tradesmen, the women, and the children—who would expand the colony and put it on an equal footing with the colonies of England and Spain. Iberville found little enthusiasm for his enterprise in Paris. Requesting a few French families and "some girls...for the Canadians," he received support only for the purchase of guns and other merchandise destined for Indian trade (Margry 1880, vol. 4, p. 484).[1] Louisiana, it seemed, had to survive with only minimal attention from France. Trade was the priority of French administrators who expected that alliances with Native nations would supply the livestock, provisions, and labor necessary to sustain the colony.

Embarking on a journey to France to garner support for the Louisiana enterprise, Iberville left his brother, Jean-Baptiste Le Moyne de Bienville, to command in his stead. Hoping to promote peace with the Indian nations, Iberville instructed his brother to allow no Indian slaves in the colony, to seize or purchase any that he discovered, and to return these captives to their homes. "By this practice," he declared, "we will gain the good will of the families and friends of those captured and of all the nations" (Higginbotham 1977, p. 83). Bienville would find these orders difficult to enforce. Just months after his departure, Iberville's affinal uncle, Louis Juchereau de St. Denis, initiated the practice of commodifying Amerindians that would persist in Louisiana throughout the eighteenth century.

Confined to Fort de la Boulaye on the lower reaches of the Mississippi River in 1702, St. Denis led his Canadian troops and Acolapissa warriors on an unauthorized exploration up the river to Bayou Lafourche. After allegedly coming under attack by a band of Chitimacha, St. Denis and his party pursued their assailants and captured several individuals to be taken back to Mobile and sold to the colonists (pp. 93–4; McWilliams 1981, p. 120). Bienville reprimanded St. Denis and ordered that the captives be returned, "but his orders were poorly carried out" (La Harpe 1971, pp. 41–2).

The Chitimacha were ever after suspicious of French intent, and resentment mounted toward their unwelcome neighbors. This general unease turned to open hostility when several Chitimacha warriors encountered and killed French priest Jean-François Buisson de Saint Cosmé and his party traveling from Natchez to Mobile in 1706. Bienville was acutely aware that France would lose face with her Indian allies should these murders go unavenged. Though it was a bitter decision, the governor was forced to call upon St. Denis, still nursing his rancor but always open to economic opportunities. Once again St. Denis led his Canadian troops and allied warriors against the Chitimacha, capturing several women and children whom he sold in Mobile for 200 *livres* each (Higginbotham 1977, pp. 289–92; Margry 1883, vol. 5, p. 433). With each skirmish against the now declared enemy nation, St. Denis increased his wealth through the sale of captives. The French war against the Chitimacha would last until 1718, making Chitimacha captives the "core" of the enslaved population in early colonial Louisiana (Usner 1992, p. 24).

The taking of captives was not uncommon among Indian nations prior to the arrival of Europeans. If kept alive, these captives could be gifted to allies, traded, or adopted by their captors to replace lost population (Lauber 1913, pp. 26–8). They also served as political currency in the exchange of captives, in peace negotiations, or to gain political advantage (Brooks 1996, pp. 280–90; 2002, pp. 1–10). That the French understood and employed this strategy is evinced in a 1723 decision by the Superior Council to liberate a Chickasaw woman and child captured by the Choctaw and enslaved in New Orleans. When four Chickasaw chiefs petitioned for the captives' freedom, the council granted the request "in order to retain them constantly in our friendship and in order that if we continue the war with them the unfortunates who may fall into their hands may find the same favor" (Rowland and Sanders 1927–1932, vol. 3, p. 358).

The French had some success with the use of Native labor in their upper Louisiana and Canadian holdings, but Indian slavery was neither as profitable nor as regulated as it was in the English system (Rushforth 2003, pp. 800–801). Governor La Mothe de Cadillac lamented the genius of the Englishman who could purchase an enslaved Indian for forty *livres*, while a Frenchman was forced to pay over one hundred *livres* for the same slave (Surrey 1916, p. 227). The governor acknowledged his failure to prevent Indian allies, as well as his own colonists, from trading with the English for slaves and other commodities (Lauber 1913, pp. 77–8).

Only a handful of African slaves entered the colony before 1719. Between 1702 and 1711, a mere 11 black slaves were present at Mobile, while 103 Amerindian males and 80 females made up the majority of the enslaved population at the post. This gender ratio reflects the needs of the nascent colony for male captives to serve as laborers, guides, interpreters, and hunters; but enslaved Indian women would soon outnumber men in the colony. Bienville owned 17 Indian slaves, more than any inhabitant of Mobile except for *Ordonnateur* Dartaguiette d'Iron with 19 (Higginbotham 1977, Appendix III).

In 1706, Bienville sought permission to exchange captive Indians for blacks from Saint-Domingue at a rate of two for one. The Ministry of the Colonies denied his request, stating that no French slave owner would agree to trade away valuable black slaves unless they were troublemakers. The inhabitants of Louisiana, the Ministry declared, must purchase slaves brought directly from Africa if they were to replace Indian slaves with blacks; however, few Louisiana colonials had the means to import African slaves. Commissary Nicolas La Salle petitioned the king in 1709 for two hundred Africans, complaining that Indian slaves "cause us trouble and...we receive very little service since they are not appropriate for hard labor like the blacks" (Hall 1992, p. 57).

The demand for captive Indian women, on the other hand, was increasing. Acquired ostensibly to serve as cooks, domestics, crafts people, and field hands, most captive women were in fact destined for lives of sexual servitude, or in some cases, marriage (Allain 1988, pp. 77–9; Gallay 2002, pp. 308–309). The dearth of French women in the colony left a void that Indian women, both free and enslaved, would come to fill. Young children who could be reared "in the French interest" were also highly valued (Hamilton 1897, p. 64).

The clergy mounted strong opposition to the enslavement of Indian women. Missionary François Le Maire denounced the Indian slave trade as having the singular purpose of furnishing concubines under the guise of domestic service. Although many enslaved women were Chitimacha, with whom the French were at war, others came from the Taensa, Chickasaw, Comanche, and the Missouri nations, and even the local allied Mobila. La Maire warned that the unabated raiding of allied nations in order to take captives would breed rebellion against the small French colony. The continued reluctance of the Crown to sanction marriages between French men and Native women or to regulate the commerce in Indian slaves, however, served to promote this practice (Giraud 1958, pp. 126–8; Hamilton 1897, pp. 63–4).

Captive-taking was largely ungoverned and very profitable. Colonial administrators held virtually no sway over Canadian *voyageurs* and *coureurs des bois*, many of them lured to lower Louisiana by the promise of high-paying wage work. Finding little in the small, struggling settlements to sustain them, these rugged individualists set about to create their own economic opportunities. The resultant "frenzy of enslaving" threatened to destroy the colony (Gallay 2002, p. 308). Bienville was ordered by the king in 1710 to put an end to the "shameless dissoluteness" of the traffic in Indian slaves, not out of regard for those being enslaved, but out of fear that these activities might impact trade or result in Native revolts that the government could ill afford to combat. Although he was charged with a near impossible task, Bienville informed Minister of Marine Pontchartrain the following year that he had confiscated a number of slaves that

Canadian *voyageurs* brought to sell in Mobile. Captives taken from allied nations were liberated and allowed to return to their homes. Before they departed, Bienville assured them that "the Court which permits the purchase of slaves is only on condition that these slaves shall be taken only from the nations that have killed Frenchmen." He issued orders forbidding *voyageurs* to trade in captive Indians "any more from any nation whatsoever," but the practice continued unabated (Rowland and Sanders 1927–1932, vol. 3, pp. 140–1).

French colonial entrepreneurs seized every opening to agitate tribal rivalries in order to acquire Indian slaves. Bienville's attempts to control the practice were futile, as was a 1720 edict issued by the Company of the Indies that declared these activities "not only contrary to the orders of the King, but...very prejudicial to the good of the trade" (Margry 1886, vol. 6, p. 316). French law—virtually ignored in the colony—dictated that no Christian could be held in bondage, implying that any slave would be freed upon conversion to Catholicism. Louis XV issued an edict—also ignored—banning the sale of female slaves and the children they produced with free, white colonists, declaring that the mothers and children should be freed after a certain period of time. The Code Noir, designed to address issues of slavery in the colony, had no separate provisions for enslaved Indians. Not profitable enough to warrant regulation separate from African slavery, the enslavement of Amerindians went practically unnoticed in France unless it interfered with commerce or threatened the precarious peace in the colony (Lauber 1913, pp. 65, 89–90).

Indian slave trade was an important component of French and Indian commerce in the colony. Allied nations traded the enemies they captured in punitive wars or gifted them to Frenchmen in symbol-laden exchanges, transforming these prisoners into commodities within the overall system of Indian trade. In Louisiana, this trade was controlled by a consortium of Canadian families connected through the bonds of kinship.[2] Shortly after he arrived at Mobile, St. Denis began to advance family and personal interests through the lucrative trade alliances he established with the Caddo on Red River and in Spanish Texas. Like the Canadian *voyageurs* and *couriers du bois*, St. Denis and his associates cultivated familial bonds with their Indian allies. Traders were entrenched in tribal villages, where they took the daughters of their allies as wives or companions and were often tattooed with symbols of tribal affiliation (De La Porte 1774, pp. 17–19; Higginbotham 1977, p. 126; Klier 2000, p. 249). Through St. Denis's personal alliance with the influential Caddo, the ill-equipped French colony was supplied with the necessities of survival—horses, cattle, buffalo and deerskins, bear oil, salt, and Indian slaves (Magnaghi 1981, p. 419).

Unlike women of African descent, who were subject to European laws banning miscegenation, Amerindian women were ultimately deemed to be legally marriageable. Many who entered colonial society enslaved eventually married their former captors. When the French established a post at the Natchitoches Caddo village on Red River in 1714, at least two men were accompanied by their formerly enslaved Chitimacha wives: Jeanne de la Grande Terre, wife of François Guyon des Prés Derbanne, keeper of the king's warehouse, and Marie Thérèse de la Grande Terre, wife of merchant Jacques Guedon (E. Mills 1981; Higginbotham 1977, pp. 444–5). Both women would outlive their husbands and remain at the post with their *métis* (offspring of French and Indigenous descent) children, founding lineages that would contribute to an increasingly complex frontier society. Enslaved Indian women would continue to supplement the female population at Natchitoches throughout the eighteenth century (Barr 2005, p. 30; D. Lee 1989, p. 91).

No doubt several Chitimacha captives were in the vanguard of settlers at the Natchitoches Post, established by inveterate slave trader Louis de St. Denis. No European women are known to have lived at the post prior to 1716, the same year that St. Denis married Manuela Sánchez Navarro y Gomes Mascorro in Spanish Texas, yet St. Denis already had a *métisse* daughter born between 1711 and 1716. Although posited that her mother may have been Natchitoches Caddo, it is more likely she was born to one of the enslaved Chitimacha brought to Natchitoches in 1714 by St. Denis. The girl was reared in the St. Denis household with his legitimate children and was identified in church records as Louise Marguerite Juchereau de St. Denis. Sometime before 1729, she married Pierre Coutoleau Duplessis, a St. Denis family ally who succeeded François Derbanne as keeper of the king's warehouse at Natchitoches. After his death in 1744, St. Denis's widow Manuela and her children apparently closed ranks and distanced themselves from Louise Marguerite, who received no mention in St. Denis's succession or in subsequent family records. Although she remained in Natchitoches until the mid-1750s, after the death of her father Louise Marguerite was never again identified as a child of St. Denis (Mills and Mills 1977, pp. 324–6; E. Mills 1985, p. 52).

St. Denis was appointed commandant over both the Natchitoches and Nasoni posts in 1721. The post at the Nasoni Caddo village upriver from Natchitoches was manned through the 1760s by a few soldiers/traders, most with Indian wives and *métis* children. Established by

Bénard de la Harpe and abandoned in 1720, this post was quickly reoccupied because of its strategic location. It soon became an important conduit for trade with the Wichita nations, called the *Mento* by the French (La Harpe 1971, p. 95; Rowland and Sanders 1927–1932, vol. 2, p. 265).

Hoping to extend French trade to those populous nations, La Harpe met with several *Mento* chiefs. Among the gifts La Harpe received during the negotiations was a young *Canneci* [Lipan Apache] slave of eight years old. The child's captors had eaten one finger from each of his hands to symbolize his slavery; and La Harpe noted that the *Mento* custom was to enslave *Canneci* women and children, while they ritually cannibalized the warriors (Margry 1886, vol. 6, p. 292). Although La Harpe would formalize trade relations with the Wichita, members of this confederacy were already trading in Natchitoches before his arrival. Claude-Charles Du Tisné, on a mission to the Illinois in 1718, sent a letter to Bienville by a *Mento* chief of whom he wrote: "I have seen him at the Osages and he sold me some slaves at Natchitoches" (p. 315).

When St. Denis assumed command of the entire Red River, his presence pulled the Caddo and the Wichita nations toward the French, shifting the source of Indian slaves from the southeast to the southwest. The Natchitoches post served as the seat of government for the region. Mostly subsistence agriculture was practiced at the post, the primary importance being its favorable position as an outlet from which French merchandise was distributed to the Indian nations and through which goods secured from the Indians were sent to other French posts. The Company of the Indies suggested to Governor Périer in 1727 that the true value of the Natchitoches post lay in its proximity to Los Adaes, the Spanish mission-presidio established some twenty miles to the west in 1721, but profitable trade with local Indian nations would provide "horses, pelts, bear oil or slaves, these things appearing to comprise all their wealth" (Margry 1886, vol. 6, pp. 226–36).

The placement of *Presidio Nuestra Señora del Pilar de Los Adaes* gave French traders at Natchitoches their long-awaited contact with Spanish Texas. Although strictly forbidden by Spanish law, trade between the outposts was constant and intense. The same French families who controlled trade in Louisiana shared close familial ties with equally influential families in Spanish Texas (Bridges and De Ville 1967, p. 239; Lemée 2003; E. Mills 1977, nos. 13, 168, 485, 490, 731, 879; Vogel 1976, pp. 110–11). St. Denis and his associates were able to carry on a profitable contraband trade "with the tacit consent, if not with the actual connivance, of [Spanish] officials" (Shelby 1923, p. 167). Although no records have been discovered that verify traffic in Indian slaves was a part of that trade, it likely did occur. Despite official policy, the Spanish engaged in constant warfare with the Lipan Apache, taking untold numbers of captives from that nation. The French—their neighbors and clandestine business partners—were inveterate Indian slave traders and provided a ready market for Spanish livestock and Indian slaves (Avery 1999, pp. 26–57; Dunn 1911, pp. 211, 251).

The Chitimacha negotiated their peace with France in 1718, and were no longer subject to capture and enslavement. Their relatives, the Natchez, would not fare as well. Relations between the French and the Natchez became increasingly strained with the growing sense of French entitlement and continued encroachment onto Natchez lands. After repeated insults, in 1729 the Natchez massacred almost the entire French population within their territory, initiating a three-year war. With the exception of those who escaped to join the Chickasaw, Creek, and Cherokee, most Natchez were either killed or enslaved. In the final year of the war, some 400 Natchez were captured and sold into the West Indian slave trade. That same year, a band led by the famed Flour Chief fled to Red River where they attacked the Natchitoches Caddo village and threatened the French post. With the assistance of Spanish troops from Los Adaes and a number of Indian allies, the French were able to rout the Natchez, killing over half of their force and enslaving twenty-eight women and children. St. Denis wrote in his account of the battle: "The nations have taken away the slaves they captured back to their own villages...I sent a few of the slaves of which the Indians made me a gift, to the Spanish to remove them from here and from the French colony" (St. Denis to Salmon, November 2, 1731, photocopy in the Deneise Palmer-Huggins Collection, Cammie Henry Research Center, Northwestern State University; hereafter CHRC). Officially the Spanish governor refused St. Denis's gift; however, ceramic sherds identified as Natchez-type Fatherland incised have been recovered at the Los Adaes archaeological site, suggesting that Natchez captives made their way to Los Adaes either by way of the mixed French and Spanish households or as a result of St. Denis's gift (Hiram F. Gregory, personal communication, March 17, 1989).

St. Denis retained at least one Natchez slave, the high status daughter of the Flour Chief. The young woman, christened Féliciane, lived most of her life in the St. Denis household where she married Julien, a black slave with whom she had at least two children (E. Mills 1977, nos. 31, 46, 378). French officer Dominique Monteche also kept at least one Natchez slave who he exchanged for a *Canneci* woman and her son in 1748 (Exchange of Indian slaves, May 23, 1748, and May 28, 1748, Docs. 78 and 79, loose copies, Colonial Archives, Natchitoches Parish Clerk of Court, Natchitoches, Louisiana; hereafter NPCC).

The population of enslaved Indians in French Louisiana was never significant when compared with black slaves. Blacks outnumbered Indians in all censuses taken at the Natchitoches post (table 4.1). Indian women outnumbered men in all French censuses in which gender was noted. Church registers document births, marriages, and deaths of baptized slaves, but some registers are missing and there are gaps in those remaining. The church registers denote a total of fifty-seven entries involving Indian slaves between the years 1729 and 1766, only four of which can be positively identified as individuals who appeared in other entries. These records note thirty-eight females, twelve males, and three with gender not given (E. Mills 1977).

Due to the nature of French trade and the distribution of traders at remote villages, an accurate demographic of enslaved Amerindians at Natchitoches is difficult to derive. It is unlikely that traders would take the trouble to baptize slaves they planned to sell or trade later, especially if they lived away from the post. It stands to reason, then, that a greater number of Indian slaves were owned by French citizens connected to Natchitoches than census information or church records might indicate.

The earliest existent record of an Indian slave baptized at Natchitoches was in 1729—Marie Louise, an Osage female belonging to François Viard (E. Mills 1977, no. 520). The Osage were bitter enemies of the Caddo, who probably captured this young woman and traded her to the French. Shortly after her baptism, Marie Louise appeared in the Superior Council records in a petition submitted for the deceased Viard, who provided for her emancipation and donated a hundred *pistoles* toward her Catholic education. Although approving her emancipation, the attorney general ensured that Marie Louise

Table 4.1 Slaves counts in Natchitoches post French censuses

Census years	1722	1726	1737	1766
Indian slaves	8	3	1m, 13f	11m, 19f
Negro slaves	20	32	64m, 43f	111m, 103f
Mulatto			9m, 6f	

Source: E. Mills (1981).

would remain a virtual prisoner when he ruled that the *Code Noir* forbade cash legacies to slaves. On his orders, Marie Louise was remanded to the Ursuline nuns for training and her inheritance donated to the hospital (Dart 1921, p. 355).

Both Indian and African slaves could be manumitted upon the deaths of their owners, as in the case of Marie Louise, and Féliciane, St. Denis's Natchez slave who was freed upon Madame St. Denis's death (Inventory and will of Dame Emanuel de Sanchez Juchereau de St. Denis, April 14, 1758, Volume I, Doc. 191, NPCC). More often, however, Indian slaves were inventoried as assets of the estate and were divided among the heirs. Three adult Indian women, one man, and five children inventoried in the estate of Commandant St. Denis were retained by members of his family (Inventory of Louis Juchereau de St. Denis, June 12, 1744, loose documents, NPCC).

Others were sold at the death of their masters, as was the case of a forty-year-old woman who was purchased along with an old cauldron for eighteen *livres* at the auction of the estate of Jean Riche (Sale of belongings of the late Jean Riche, May 21, 1758, vol. 1, Doc. 200, NPCC). Enslaved Indians were included in dowries or assets brought into marriages (Marriage contract of Dominique Monteche and Marie Bourdon, November 20, 1756, vol. 1, Docs. 171–172, NPCC), and were used to discharge debts (Release of debt of Sieur Marmillont by Juan Piseros, March 26, 1763, vol. 1, Doc. 542, NPCC).

Although some Indian slaves were eventually married by and/or emancipated by their masters, most who entered the Natchitoches post remained enslaved until death released them from captivity. As French women became more common and children were born and grew to adulthood in the colony, enslaved Indian women were less likely to be married by the men who owned them. The majority remained in domestic and sexual bondage until death or, if they were fortunate, manumission. Those who remained enslaved began to merge into the dominant slave population, producing children with both men of African and French descent. At least three *métis* infants born into slavery are noted in the church registers, and it is likely that these children of French fathers and Amerindian mothers remained enslaved if they survived. The designation *métis* was rarely used in notices of legitimate births of Indian/French children or in cases where the father claimed the child, but was used to indicate enslaved or freeborn Indian/French infants who were not awarded rights of paternity by their fathers, as in Simon the free *métis*, a well-known trader in the region (Depositions taken in the complaint of Jean Fromentin, July 12–13, 1757, Doc. 186, vol. 1, NPCC).

Throughout the eighteenth century, Natchitoches remained the primary point of entry for slaves traded from allied Indian nations to the north and west. This research has identified tribal origins for many enslaved Amerindians in Natchitoches during the French period: Chitimacha brought with the original inhabitants of the post, Osage traded through the Caddo, and Natchez acquired in war. By the end of the French colonial period in Louisiana, however, Lipan Apache acquired from the Comanche and Wichita and traded through the Caddo came to dominate the Indian slave population at Natchitoches. In fact, Governor Louis Billouart, Chevalier de Kerlerec, observed in 1763 that the majority of Indian slaves in all of Louisiana were Lipan Apache (Magnaghi 1981, p. 424). On the remote borderlands, captive women and children continued to enter the colony with trade goods obtained from tribal allies.

The lack of regulation on the part of the French government contributed to the persistence of this oppressive practice. After Spain took possession of Louisiana in 1765, the new government attempted to seize control of the Indian trade system. In 1769, Governor Alejandro O'Reilly set about to reorganize the colonial government and establish Spanish authority over trade in Louisiana (Kinnaird 1949, vol. 2, p. 61). Almost immediately, O'Reilly issued his "Ordinances and Instructions," an amalgamation of Spanish colonial laws, his own regulations, and the French Code Noir designed to place Indian trade under direct control of Spain. O'Reilly was particularly interested in the Natchitoches post, where he noted the presence of a number of traders who had "no other object in view than an illicit trade" (Gayarré 1903, vol. 1, p. 20). O'Reilly's intent was to eliminate the traffic in captive Indians altogether, declaring Indian slavery to be contrary to the laws of Spain. The new governor seemingly ignored the fact that, although outlawed in 1542, Indian slavery persisted throughout the Spanish provinces (Dunn 1911, pp. 207–11, 230, 251; 1914, pp. 407–10; John 1975, p. 416).

Under O'Reilly's instructions, citizens were forbidden to take or own Indian slaves and were ordered to manumit any they possessed. To compile a census of all enslaved Amerindians in the colony, owners were directed to submit a declaration stating the name, nation, age, time of ownership, and value of all Indian slaves in their possession. Commandants were instructed to enforce O'Reilly's directives, arrest any illegal traders, and confiscate their goods (Gayarré 1903, vol. 2, p. 24; Kinnaird 1949, vol. 2, p. 126). Although strongly worded and loaded with penalties for those who ignored his regulations, O'Reilly's decree did little to inhibit the trade or sale of Indian slaves, especially at the Natchitoches post. French traders based in Natchitoches continued to engage in the Indian slave trade throughout most of the Spanish colonial period.

O'Reilly appointed Athanase De Mézières to serve as lieutenant governor at the post of Natchitoches. Discharged from the French military when the colony was ceded to Spain, De Mézières had been in Natchitoches since at least 1743. He was a trader to the Caddo, wore marks of kinship in the form of tattoos, and married Marie Pétronille de St. Denis in 1746, bringing him into the St. Denis family cartel (Bolton 1914, vol. 1, pp. 79–84). De Mézières had the kind of rapport with the Red River tribes previously enjoyed by his father-in-law.

De Mézières set about to implement Spanish policy and to license traders residing at the important villages. These entrenched traders were themselves charged with controlling contraband trade and were ordered to arrest offenders and transport them to Natchitoches to stand trial. In accordance with O'Reilly's instructions, De Mézières called in all traders to register their Indian slaves (vol. 3, Docs. 618, 640, 642, 648, 654, 690; vol. 5, Doc. 836, 842; vol. 6, doc. 915, NPCC).[3] Among those who responded were partners Jacques Roulleau, Pierre Girard, and Nicolas Thibault. Roulleau declared three *Canneci* slaves—two girls aged ten and fifteen and a boy of thirteen, valued at 600 *livres* each. Girard claimed a *Canneci* girl, aged ten, as well as a woman and her male child acquired from the Caddo. Thibault declared no slaves at that time, but in the 1774 census he declared one adult female and one child (April 17, 1770, declaration of slaves, vol. 3, Doc. 618, NPCC; E. Mills 1981, p. 33).

Trader Jacque Ridde declared an eighteen-year-old *Canneci*, Angélique, who he received from another French trader at the Caddo. In the same document, Pierre Raimond claimed one *Canneci* woman, Françoise, and her son of about twelve, acquired through trade with an unnamed *voyageur*. Ridde manumitted Angélique in 1774 on the condition that she would remain in his service, while Raimond married his former slave four years later (June 27, 1770, declaration of slaves, vol. 3, Doc. 648; August 18, 1774, manumission of slave, vol. 4, Doc. 939, NPCC). The promise of freedom or marriage allowed traders to prolong the tenure of servitude for these women at a time when freedom for all Indian slaves was a real possibility (Barr 2005, pp. 39–40).

Infamous trader François Morvan, who lived in exile among the Caddo for seven years after murdering a French hunter, surrendered himself to De Mézières in 1770. He declared three Indian slaves—a fifteen-year-old Lipan Apache girl, a Tawakoni woman, and a *métis* who kept his horses at the Caddo village. Marie Anne, a twenty-five-year-old *Canneci,* and her son by Morvan were not enumerated as slaves and Morvan claimed to have manumitted them; however, Marie Anne was still noted as a slave in the 1774 Spanish census of Natchitoches. Presumably, Morvan did eventually wed Marie Anne, as they later appeared as man and wife in Spanish Texas (Documents relative to François Morvan, May 1770, vol. 3, Docs. 640, 642, 690, NPCC; 1784 and 1805 census of *Nuestra Señora del Pilar de Nacogdoches* for 1784 and 1805, Béxar Archives, CHRC).

All citizens registering Indian slaves in 1770 were instructed to educate them in the Catholic faith and to provide for their general welfare. Upon agreeing to follow these instructions, they were awarded provisional ownership pending a ruling on Indian slavery by King Carlos III. This ruling was still not issued in 1774, as evidenced in the will of François Clouseau in which disposition of a fifteen-year-old Indian girl named Geneviève was delayed "until His Majesty's decision on the subject of Indian slaves" (Bolton 1914, vol. 1, pp. 92–3).

Having dealt with the question of Indian slavery in Louisiana, albeit ineffectively, the Spanish colonial government faced another problem—how to structure interaction with the Wichita and Comanche, who had long been trade relatives of the Caddo and by extension, the French. These nations regularly raided Spanish settlements and outposts for goods, livestock, and citizens to barter with other Indians and the French, making relations with these tribes tenuous and unreliable for the Spanish. Conversely, the Spanish engaged in constant punitive expeditions against members of these nations and the Apache.

De Mézières worked to reconcile Spain with the enemy nations and thereby protect the lucrative Indian trade. Through careful negotiations in 1771, he was able to secure treaties between Spain and the allied Wichita nations. To the Spanish clerics who accompanied De Mézières, however, his accomplishments were tainted by his tolerance of practices that encouraged the perpetuation of the Indian slave trade. Fray Santo de Silva condemned the actions of a French carpenter who kept five captive Indian women at the Caddo village "for the illicit traffic of the flesh," and blamed De Mézières for the decadence of the traders who trafficked in Indian slaves (Bolton 1914, vol. 2, p. 74).

Despite these misgivings, relations were established with the Wichita and Comanche, adding impetus to the trade in Indian captives. There were only thirty Indian slaves counted in the 1766 French census of the post, while forty-one were enumerated in 1774—six men, twenty women, and fifteen children under twelve who were not classified by gender (E. Mills 1981, p. 33). De Mézières noted the presence of forty-four Indian slaves at the post two years later (Bolton 1914, vol. 2, p.120). This was the last enumeration of enslaved Amerindians separate from the total enslaved population in Natchitoches.

An unusual situation involving an enslaved woman, Marianne, arose in 1773. The slave, owned by Silvie Hubardeaux, escaped from her mistress and took refuge with Madame Alexis Grappe. Madame Grappe sent the slave Marianne, identified as either Apache or Comanche, to the Caddo village and induced the Caddo to claim Marianne as one of their people. Hubardeaux filed a complaint in which she demanded that Madame Grappe be brought before authorities to answer charges. Commandant François De Villiers, acting in De Mézières's absence, noted in his response that judgment would be suspended pending the receipt of responses to inquiries he sent to the Caddo villages (July 17, 1773, Hubardeaux complaint against Dame Grappe, vol. 5, Doc. 842, NPCC). No further action on this complaint was found in the colonial records.

In 1773, Louise Marguerite and Alexis Grappe were two of the wealthiest members of the Natchitoches community. Grappe was closely associated with the St. Denis family and De Mézières, and served as the licensed trader to the Nasoni Caddo village. Alexis Grappe declared two Indian slaves in 1774, but none were enumerated in the 1796 final accounting of Madame Grappe's succession (Mills 1981 p. 31).

Louise Marguerite Guedon Grappe was the daughter of Marie Thérèse de la Grande Terre, one of the two formerly enslaved Chitimacha women who were among the first to settle in Natchitoches with their French husbands. Alexis and Louise Guedon Grappe reared their family at Ft. St. Louis at the Nasoni Caddo village and as such, she was familiar with the captives traded through their villages. Madam Grappe often served as godparent to Indian slaves belonging to other inhabitants (E. Mills, 1977), and likely had great empathy for the enslaved women and children with whom she had contact. Madam Grappe's involvement in this situation is unclear, as is the fate of Marianne, but this complaint demonstrates the complex nature of Indian slavery in colonial Louisiana.

Captive Indians continued to be sold and traded in Natchitoches, regardless of legal restrictions. In 1787, trader Pierre Rousseau sold an Indian (no age, ethnicity, or gender noted) to Pierre Dolet (1787 sale of Indian slave from Rousseau to Dolet, NPCC). The following year, Dolet sold an Indian slave for a term of years to Pierre Sorel *dit* Marly (1788 sale of an Indian slave for a term of years, Dolet to Marly, NPCC).[4] Like other chattel property, slaves were used to satisfy debts or were leased out to perform services. De Mézières himself contracted in 1774 to lease two *Canneci* slaves, Hector and Felix, to trader Augustin Duchene at the Caddo. In return, Duchene was to deliver twelve gelded horses, "each having a good halter,...well trained...and without Spanish brands" (December 22, 1774, promise to deliver slaves, vol. 6, Doc. 915, NPCC). François Baudouin's *Canneci* slave was seized by arbiters and awarded to his creditor to satisfy a 900-*livre* debt (February 9, 1775, arbitration of suit brought by Pierre Gagnard, vol. 7, Doc. 1048, NPCC), while François Frederic donated a sixteen-year-old Apache girl, Julie, to his doctor to pay for medical services. Frederic declared that he was no longer able to "maintain and bring [her] up in the Apostolic Catholic religion" (July 21, 1773, donation of slave from Frederic to Mercier, vol. 5, Doc. 836, NPCC). Men also left property or funds to support Indian slaves who had served as their companions or borne children for them (Agreement to administer cash legacies, November 3, 1764, and September 18, 1768, vol. 2, Docs 480, 481, NPCC). In 1791, Jean Baptiste Dupre manumitted Balthazar and Cecile, aged around seven and nine years old, respectively, "in consideration of the good service of their Indian mother" (Succession of Jean Baptiste Dupre, May 1791, Folder 582, Melrose Collection, CHRC).

Of the enslaved Indians just mentioned—De Mézières's Hector and Felix, Madam Huberdeaux's Marianne, the slaves sold by Dolet and Marly, the slave who satisfied Baudouin's debt, the mother of Balthazar and Cecile, even Frederic's Julie, whose Catholic education he could no longer maintain—none appear in the Natchitoches church registers, although at least some of them were probably baptized. As in the French period, it is difficult to ascertain the true number of enslaved Amerindians at Natchitoches, still a frontier post far removed from the Spanish capital at New Orleans.

Although it did little to deter the practice in Louisiana, O'Reilly's 1769 ban on Indian slavery was reissued in 1787 by Governor Esteban Miro in response to several lawsuits brought before him by slaves of Amerindian descent. Miro ruled in favor of these petitioners, who claimed freedom based on their Indian ancestry and on the fact that Indian slavery was outlawed in the colony in 1769. Slaves of Amerindian descent continued to sue for their freedom until 1791, when several planters petitioned Governor Francisco Luis Carondelet to suspend all lawsuits filed by slaves claiming Indian ancestry. The planters maintained that the suits set a dangerous precedent and challenged the entire system of slavery, thereby threatening the overall economy of the colony. Persuaded by their arguments and discovering that O'Reilly's orders had never been formally filed, Carondelet put an end to the litigation (Webre 1984, pp. 130–4). No records of proceedings initiated by slaves claiming Indian heritage have been identified in the colonial records of Natchitoches.

The status of Indian slaves in Louisiana grew more uncertain, as they were legally afforded rights of freedom but increasingly identified as black or mulatto by the masters determined to retain their services. The case of Dorothée Monet, born enslaved in 1778, demonstrates this ambiguity. The priest who registered Dorothée's baptism failed to include her ethnicity in the record of her birth, but in subsequent church records she was noted as a *mulatresse*. Her owner and probable father, Louis Monet, who gave her a valuable piece of property along with his surname, eventually manumitted Dorothée. Upon assuming her freedom and her property, Dorothée became involved with a white planter with whom she had a number of children. When these children were baptized, Dorothée's ethnicity was entered in the church register as *Canneci*, and on the 1796 survey map of her property, she was listed as a free *métisse* (G. Mills 1977, pp. 86–7; Survey of the property of Dorothée Monet, 1794, Pierre Maes, surveyor, photocopy in CHRC).

Was Dorothée the daughter of an Apache slave who was misclassified as a *mulatresse* so her father could keep her enslaved? Was she a Creole of color whose relationship with a wealthy white planter allowed her racial designation to be adjusted in order to afford their children the rights and privileges of their father? Whatever the situation, Dorothée Monet was able to use legal means and social connections to ensure that at least some of her children could assume the status of their white father. Those without family connections or assets were rarely as successful at negotiating legal identity as Dorothée Monet, who founded two divergent lineages—one white and one Creole of color—that continue today.

Children of enslaved Indian mothers might be liberated by their fathers or purchased so that they could marry prominent free Creoles of color (G. Mills 1977), themselves the children of white fathers. Such was the case of Thérèse Le Comte, daughter of an enslaved Lipan Apache and a French Creole planter. Thérèse married Louis Metoyer, the wealthy and acknowledged son of a former black slave and a French father. Their union produced one of the core lineages of the contemporary Creole of color community in Natchitoches Parish (E. Mills 1977, no. 3049; G. Mills 1977, pp. 85–6).

From 1766 to at least 1792, Indian slaves continued to appear in civil and church records in Natchitoches. The influx of Indian slaves, primarily Lipan Apache, peaked in about 1784. A spate of baptisms between 1778 and 1784 were probably of captives acquired to fill voids in the population left after an epidemic swept the post in 1777. Twelve out of thirteen Indian slaves baptized between 1776 and 1792 belonged to known traders, indicating that trade in captive Indians continued through the late eighteenth century (Bolton 1914, vol. 1, p. 84; E. Mills 1977).

The last baptism of an Indian slave in Natchitoches was recorded in 1792 (E. Mills 1977, no. 2689). As the Spanish era in Louisiana drew to a close, trade in Indian slaves through and in Natchitoches also came to an end. A survey of colonial records indicates that active trade in Indian slaves died out after 1790. The Amerindian slave population, not replenished after the 1790s, slowly blended—creolized—into the multiethnic population in Natchitoches.

A more balanced population of European men and women, the decreasing importance of Indian trade, and tribal consolidations and relocations all contributed to the decline of Indian slavery, which waned along with the influence of the French Creole families who controlled it. Anglo-Americans who poured into Louisiana after the purchase in 1803 brought with them thousands of black slaves, Protestantism, and a binary approach to race and ethnicity.

The century of colonialism in Louisiana saw the beginning and the end of the brutal practice of commodifying captive American Indians. Reporting on the local nations in 1805, U.S. Indian agent John Sibley noted a number of Lipan Apache in the vicinity. He attributed their former enslavement to the Spanish at Los Adaes, declaring that "a considerable number of them were brought to Natchitoches and sold amongst the French inhabitants, at forty or fifty dollars a head." Sibley's notion of Spaniards as the source for these slaves in Natchitoches is not borne out by the records, nor is his belief that a formal emancipation of Indian slaves had taken place. While the proclamation was issued it was certainly not enforced, at least not in outposts such as Natchitoches where the French Creole family consortiums still dominated politics and practice (Sibley 1832, pp. 722–3).

While descendants of Louisiana's colonial families today often take pride in their Indian ancestors, few are aware that these progenitors may have entered their lineages unwillingly. Descendant communities with the greatest understanding are those whose cultural identity is defined by their multiethnic ancestry—the Creoles of color (G. Mills 1977)—whose careful genealogical documentation may best illuminate the lives of their enslaved relatives, both African and Amerindian; and members of the Choctaw-Apache[5] tribal community, who have crafted a tribal identity from their Indo-Hispanic heritage and reestablished connections with their distant Apache relatives in the American southwest and in Mexico.

Louisiana history is filtered through the lens of European experience. Left out of the telling are the stories of those whose lives were unwillingly transformed by the colonial process. Enslaved American Indians, primarily women and children, were caught in a system of social, economic, and political exchange that cast them as involuntary partners in Indian/European interrelations. Taken from their homes and families, their identities stolen and forgotten, enslaved Indians helped reinforce population and forge new social identities in colonial Louisiana.

Notes

This essay evolved out of research undertaken for my master's thesis, Indian Slavery in Lower Louisiana, during the colonial period, 1699–1803 (Northwestern State University, Natchitoches, 1989).

1. All translations from the French are by the author unless otherwise noted.
2. For a more complete picture of the trading families in colonial Louisiana, see A. Lee (1989).
3. Documents cover the years 1770–1774 and deal with the sale, possession, trade, or relinquishment of Indian slaves.
4. These documents are missing from the archives and are referenced from the index of colonial documents compiled ca. 1900 and kept at the Natchitoches Parish Clerk of Court's Office, Natchitoches, Louisiana.
5. The Choctaw-Apache Tribe of Ebarb, Louisiana, is the second largest of eight state-recognized American Indian communities in Louisiana. Located primarily in Sabine Parish in northwestern Louisiana, the tribe traces its origins to enslaved Apache brought into the region by French and Spanish colonials. After Indian slavery was outlawed under the Americans, these formerly enslaved Apache and their descendants merged with a small band of Choctaw. The Choctaw-Apache Tribe is currently seeking federal recognition (CATE n.d.).

Chapter 5

Capturing Captivity: Visual Imaginings of the English and Powhatan Encounter Accompanying the Virginia Narratives of John Smith and Ralph Hamor, 1612–1634

Stephanie Pratt

This chapter concerns what might be called the "early contact" history of coastal Virginia and its visual representation,[1] and consists of an examination of a small group of graphic images created in Britain and Europe between 1612 and 1627. These engravings sought in their separate ways to imagine and visualize what had occurred in the early years of first contact between the Powhatan peoples of coastal Virginia and the English newcomers to their shores. Given the historical accounts they were illustrating, some of them inevitably focused on situations where exchanges, misunderstandings, and even conflicts were in evidence. As surveyed in the editors' introduction, only a small number of illustrations were made during this period in colonial history and of these only a handful engage with the central topics in this book, the themes of captivity, adoption, and slavery. It has also been observed here that the scope for the study of images of American Indian captivity, adoption, and slavery is still to be fully developed. Over thirty years ago the anthropologist and historian Christian Feest (1967) presented his analysis of these same few illustrations of coastal Algonquian peoples in two essays titled "The Virginia Indian in Pictures, 1612–1624, Parts I and II" (I, pp. 1–30). His account made seminal points about the nature of illustrations of indigenous Americans in this period and he noted that the earlier images created by Theodor de Bry and family from 1590 until 1634, especially those elaborated from the Sir Walter Raleigh funded Roanoke Voyages to the lands the English named "Virginia," were the major source for the corpus of imagery about "Virginia Indians." Feest also located in the illustrations elements of knowledge gained from direct contact with indigenous peoples. It is instructive that he wrote of these images as a group and that he was able to see both their stereotypical and their anthropological relevance. I want to take the analysis of some of these early images deeper to consider the ways that the notion of captivity with American Indians, and to a lesser extent, the captivity of Indians by Europeans, was a main structuring device for many of the American Indian images created at this time.

Although it would be dangerous to attempt to encompass the English and Powhatan encounter only through the lens of the contemporary graphic illustrators who were called upon to create such imagery, they provide useful data when analyzed. What the images offer is further explanation as to why the North American "captivity" in particular made such a convenient trope for summing up the newcomers' experiences and, later in the period, how such images could help the colonizers to portray a common threat to all the colonies from their frontier areas, thus creating a sense of unity where one did not yet exist. Capture by indigenous North American peoples during the colonial period was certainly a reality, even if only directly experienced by a minority of the newcomers. Indeed, some scholars have viewed captivity with the Indians as the quintessential North American colonial experience in terms of the historical record (Colley 2003, pp. 140–1). This important element in the encounter between indigenous North Americans' and newcomers' cultures is underwritten by a vast primary literature that runs to about two thousand volumes (taking in numbers of separate editions) and relates to more than five hundred "canonical" instances of newcomer captivity among the Indians [a summary of this extensive literature is provided by Levernier and Cohen (1977, p. xiv)]. Captain John Smith was captured by the Powhatan Indians in Virginia in 1607 during the founding of the colony at Jamestown. His recitations of his captivity, the central focus of this chapter, were published in different versions throughout his lifetime. Smith's narrative is, arguably, the first widely disseminated account of captivity by American Indians that was offered to English readers, thus starting off a long tradition that would last well into the nineteenth century (Barbour 1986; Rennie 2007).[2] It is through such accounts of captivity, with their often graphically precise descriptions (and including the earliest English illustrations of Indian culture), that an image of a threatening and terrifying indigenous opponent is first formulated. It would become a central theme in the ways American Indians have been and continue to be imaged in the Anglo-European consciousness from the 1600s up to the present day (Honour 1975; Pratt 2005; Stedman 1982; and in films such as Michael Mann's *The Last of the Mohicans*, 1992).

Archaeological and anthropological studies in this volume and elsewhere have examined the actual levels of violence in the North American pre-Columbian world, recounting the means by which acts of cruelty and torture were elements of the preexisting intertribal warfare and aggression that had specific functions within the societies in which such practices existed, both before and after the initial contact period (chapter one in this volume; Gallay 2002; Richter 1992; White 1991). These studies have elucidated more fully the ways that this complex of captivity, adoption, or slavery practices, often with violent outcomes, functioned historically and how in some instances it became deeply affected as the shock waves of the newcomer invasion created the "shatter zone" effect discussed here and elsewhere (Ethridge and Shuck-Hall 2009; Richter 1992; 2001, p. 63; White 1991). A rather less-studied phenomenon is the case of captive American Indians, taken against their will or coerced into captivity, whose experiences have been underplayed in light of the supposedly more sensational aspects of white captivity among the Indians (chapter four in this volume, Foreman 1943; Vaughan 2006).

This account will take as a main framing device the ways that the experience of captivity and its illustration were viewed habitually as phenomena of Anglo-European contact with American Indians but whose practice in reality relates to a wider complex of social incorporation techniques and specific societal functions that had developed historically after the newcomer invasion. Captivity was to become a key thematic in the representation of English colonial experience long before the 1682 publication of Mary Rowlandson's account of her captivity, which had occurred in 1675 during King Philip's War. It is perhaps due to John Smith's accounts in 1612 and 1624, which were published with engravings revealing his captivity experience, that this theme took hold the way that it did. Crucially, as Linda Colley and others have shown, the experience of captivity was not a new phenomenon when the English first arrived in North America in the late sixteenth century, but had a history going back to earlier contacts between Europeans and the Eastern or Middle Eastern empires, with the captivity experience being linked significantly in many cases to a trade in captured "white" slaves (Banerjee 2005; Colley 2003). Captivity may be the keynote to the discussion here but as we have argued elsewhere in this volume, it is almost meaningless to discuss this activity in isolation from the other related practices of social incorporation, such as slavery, bondage, forced labor, ritual execution, or adoption as well as forced marriage or concubinage (Turner Strong 2002, pp. 339–56).

The first set of images to be discussed are the illustrations that accompanied Captain John Smith's accounts of his captivity among the local indigenous people of Virginia living near the English settlement at Jamestown. Historically, via his accounts, Smith has come to be almost exclusively associated with this first permanent English settlement (whether or not one can actually prove that the series of events at Werowocomoco that he describes in his writings on Virginia did in fact take place) (Rennie 2007, p. 11). But of even more significance to the analysis here is the capture and forced acculturation of the Powhatan woman, Pocahontas, or Matoaka, as she is known more correctly, who would live with the English for the rest of her life. This took place in 1613, four years after Smith had left the colony permanently. Pocahontas/Matoaka has been described very aptly as an important American Indian woman "mediator" whose role in securing for the colony a peaceful coexistence with the Powhatan Indians cannot be underestimated (Kidwell 1992, p. 97). Her status as an American-origin myth has been extensively covered in the secondary literature to date (Mossiker 1976; 1996; Tilton 1994). However, it is her blatant capture and "incorporation" into English society that is often underplayed in recounting her importance for American history, with her loyalty or devotion to the English being made much more prominent in the narrative. Her capture by the English is only infrequently illustrated and in contemporary accounts is shown only in two images created by Georg Keller in 1617 to illustrate Ralph Hamor's *Present State of Virginia* (originally published without plates in 1615).

John Smith's captivity with the Powhatan Indians, according to the English sources, took place sometime in late November–early December 1607 while he was conducting a trading and upriver exploration in Chickahominy territory (Rennie 2007, p. 5). The veracity of his account has frequently been challenged but it is important here to recount the story of his captivity as it was first iterated.[3] Originally, John Smith was captured by a hunting party of Pamunkey men and taken to the Pamunkey werowance or leader, Opechancanough, a half-brother of Powhatan, the headman of all the allied peoples of this region. This primary leader is often simply referred to by his title "Powhatan" in the histories. He is now more correctly referred to as Wahunsenacock/Wahunsenacawh, his personal tribal name. After some deliberation among the council at Opechancanough's home village, including a ceremony of divination requiring the medicine leaders to paint themselves in red, black, and white pigment and the identification of Smith as not being one of the murderous Englishmen who had visited a few years previously, the Pamunkeys decided to take Smith to see the headman, Wahunsenacock, at his home village of Werowocomoco (Smith 1624, II, pp. 47–8). It is here that the most familiar part of the John Smith captivity narrative was enacted. Simply put, Smith was brought before the headman Wahunsenacock, or in Smith's narrative, more frequently referred to as "Powhatan." Smith's hands were cleansed and he was given some food to eat. At some point two large stones were brought into the meeting house, put before Powhatan, and Smith was forced to place himself across them with his supposed executioners standing close by holding clubs with which to kill Smith or knock him senseless (p. 48). [This style of execution was referred to one other time by Smith apart from this main description of his "rescue" by Pocahontas. See Leo Lemay (1992, pp. 2–3, 17).] Before the next step was taken, a young daughter of the headman (of about eleven years) ran forward to place her head on top of the Englishman's, thus offering herself up for execution instead. Smith was then released and, after further ceremony in which Wahusenacock appeared to him painted in black, the Englishman was given his own house and lands in a local village located within the territories of the headman's remit and was thereafter to be considered as one of Powhatan's own sons.

Modern scholarship has interpreted this series of events to mean a ritualized social incorporation giving Smith some status in Powhatan society (Gleach 1997, pp. 118–21; Kupperman 2000, pp. 114, 174; Smith 1624, II, p. 49). Although it is never fully stated as such, the preceding narrative could be likened to an indigenous form of ceremony creating an identity for Smith within the tribe—as it was iterated in Smith's own writings—although for the English authorities Smith's status in a Virginian indigenous society was not of real importance in itself, their main concern being the legitimacy of their claim to Virginian lands. Smith's description of the use of feathers and colored pigments, especially black and red, and the need for cleansing and some sequestering from the group during such rituals all point to some element of truth in his descriptions at least, even if the events themselves bear no professional anthropological scrutiny. Helen Rountree (1990) has firmly asserted her doubt that this account recalls an actual ceremony in the Powhatan society but the details seem too precise to be entirely imagined out of nothing (p. 39). Many historians have simply moved on from ascribing truth or falsity in Smith's narratives and instead look for archetypal structures or truths to certain forms of expression, such as romanticism and frontier mythification (Rennie 2007).

Pocahontas's captivity occurred a few years later, after Captain Smith had been forced to leave the colony in 1609 (due to injury and dissention) but prior to his final return to England. In brief, in the early spring of 1613 both the English captain Samuel Argall of the Jamestown colony and the Powhatan girl "Pocahontas" (the same individual who had "saved" Smith in his ritual mock-execution and tribal "adoption") were visiting the Potomac area. Captain Argall discovered that Pocahontas was staying at the Potomac chieftain's house, whose lands were at the furthest northern extent of Powhatan's external alliances (Rountree 1993, pp. 131–2). A brother of the Potomac leader, called either Iapassus/Iopassus or Japasaws depending on which English account one consults, was blackmailed by Argall into bringing the then seventeen-year-old Pocahontas to Captain Argall's waiting ship and somehow enticing her to be brought on board. The entrapment of Pocahontas was successfully carried out by deploying Iapassus's wife whose supposed desire to go on board the English ship could only be fulfilled if she was accompanied by Pocahontas. Once on board, Captain Argall let Pocahontas know that she could not return to her people and that she would be held ransom until her father, Wahunsenacock, returned the Englishmen and guns he had recently captured (Hamor 1615, pp. 19–21). In the end, Wahunsenacock refused to go along with the English demands and thus Pocahontas was kept with the English against her will and the process of her acculturation began within the colony of Jamestown. She eventually became the wife of an English tobacco entrepreneur, John Rolfe, and traveled with him and their son Thomas to London in 1616. She succumbed to a smallpox infection and died before the return voyage, being buried in Gravesend in Kent (Barbour 1970; Mossiker 1976; 1996; and Rennie 2007).

The first printed account to describe either of these two captivities is John Smith's report of the colony, *A True Relation* (1608). It was not intended to be published by Smith and did not contain illustrations but its popularity and impact must have encouraged him to continue to relate in print his experiences in the American colonies and to elaborate on his views about the Native peoples he encountered there. In *A True Relation* Smith's captivity is reported, but no mention is made of his being saved by Powhatan's supposed favorite daughter, Pocahontas. The next account to be published is John Smith's book entitled *A Map of Virginia* (1612). This small book was printed in

Oxford and missed being registered at the Stationery's Office and so has virtually dropped out of official book history as a result. It contains both a written description and a cartographic representation including within its borders some vignette illustrations. This engraved image was extremely successful and went through twenty-seven various reprintings and adaptations in the seventeenth century (Rennie 2007). Although Smith himself is not depicted, his captivity is alluded to in the inscription under the image of Powhatan's meeting house: "POWHATAN held this state and fashion when Captain Smith was delivered to him prisoner. 1607." Again, Pocahontas's intervention is neither described nor illustrated.

The next publication to appear chronologically concerns the experiences of the Virginia colony at Jamestown after Smith's departure. This account was written by the secretary to the colony Ralph Hamor and appeared first in 1615 under the title *A True Discourse of the Present Estate of Virginia*. Hamor's narrative is the first to mention the abduction of Pocahontas and in its 1617 edition was illustrated with two engravings, as already mentioned. This account was printed again in 1618 (in German) and 1619 (in Latin), together with John Smith's report from his *Map of Virginia*, as one section of part 10 of the series of illustrated travel accounts to the New World published by the de Bry family of engravers often referred to as *The Grand Voyages*. Six of the illustrations in de Bry's volume deal with Virginian topics and three of these concern Pocahontas: (1) *Pocahontas deceitfully handed over to the English* (plate 7 in vol. X); (2) *Pocahontas's brothers coming to reclaim their sister* (plate 8 in vol. X); and (3) *Ralph Hamor is sent to Powhatan to ask for the hand of his daughter Pocahontas on behalf of John Rolfe* (plate 10 in vol. X). In de Bry's volume the images have been flipped from right to left when the engraver copied them directly from the earlier published account.

John Smith published yet another version of his experiences, this time under the title *The Generall Historie of Virginia, New-England and the Summer Isles* (London, 1624). In the *Generall Historie* a single engraved plate is added to the text to give an indication of the dangerous and aggressive conflicts that were taking place during the foundation of England's first permanent North American colony. It is also here that the trope of Pocahontas acting as Smith's personal savior is first mentioned and elaborated upon, verbally and visually. It remains a matter of conjecture why it had taken Smith sixteen years to mention this incident in print, but I think it likely that he wished to establish his primacy in a story whose later episodes featured Hamor and Rolfe so prominently. However, prior to the *Generall Historie*'s appearance, Smith penned an introductory letter to Queen Anne on the occasion of her reception of Pocahontas during the latter's stay in England in 1616, which does mention Pocahontas's role in his salvation. Although perhaps without a wide distribution, the letter contained a description of Pocahontas's rescue of Smith thus bringing her role in the affair to the attention of King James and this account was never contradicted by those survivors of the colony who were in London after Pocahontas's death (Lemay 1992, p. 17).

Finally, in the last publication to be discussed, both John Smith's *The Generall Historie of Virginia* and also his *Description of New England* (1616) are contained within the thirteenth and final part of De Bry's *Grand Voyages* series published first in 1627 (in German) and then in 1634 (Latin edition), encompassing the English colonization efforts in North America and the voyages made to Tierra del Fuego. Topics from the Virginia colony's history take up six of the engraved illustrations, all of them new and one of them, to which I will turn shortly, illustrating Smith's captivity and Pocahontas's intervention.

Let us look, then, at the various illustrations in these publications. Given that John Smith's initial account, the *True Relation* of 1608, was not illustrated, one might argue that the inclusion of engraved images in later versions and editions came somewhat as an afterthought. Nevertheless, the first collaboration between Smith as author and William Hole as engraver, in Smith's *A Map of Virginia* (1612), produced an image that proved influential in its twenty-seven reprintings. My contention with much of the illustrated travel literature of this period is that its format of text and image make for a particular visual and informational package, which in Mark Wagner's (1995) formulation we might describe as an *iconotext*. Because the image and text are required to make their impact on one viewing (as opposed to the progressive development during the course of a narrative) the resultant "iconotext" condenses time and place to offer a simultaneous present of the protagonists and events in Smith's account of his captivity. Thus, for a contemporary who must "read" the iconotext, the incorporation of many disparate events into one plate is neither confusing nor without sense. Its condensed language is understood and was created for an audience who would be conditioned to understand how such images were structured and held meaning.

The illustration in Smith's *A Map of Virginia*, the first plate under discussion, amounts to a visual/informational system that produces narrative structure in its use of map-like constructions and devices. Here, vignette scenes placed at the corners or on the edges of the map's boundaries help to formulate a set of discrete and varied information "bundles." In the one reference this image makes of Smith's being held captive, the view showing the interior of the Powhatan's lodge or meeting house is combined with the following inscription: "POWHATAN Held this state and fashion when Capt Smith was delivered to him prisoner." This textual element helps the viewer to understand Smith's position as prisoner by showing us looking into the dark depths of the lodge, crowded with the women and men of Powhatan's intimate circle. The use of vanishing point perspective in the way the lodge is delineated virtually places the viewer in Smith's position (detail, top left corner, figure 5.1).

Yet, despite the image's success in visualizing a Powhatan meeting house, it is not an original but borrowed from an earlier set of imagery published by the de Bry family in 1590 and 1591, in reproductions of visual materials garnered from the earlier Roanoke colonizing venture of the 1580s. The watercolor images created by John White at Roanoke, in present-day North Carolina, were drawn from his direct colonial experiences with the local Algonquians. White's "Tombe of the Weroans, a priest guards the mummies" (printed with additions

Figure 5.1 Detail, "Map of Virginia" engraved map (frontispiece) in John Smith's *Generall Historie of Virginia* (London, 1624; shelfmark G.7037). © The British Library.

and alterations by de Bry in 1590) is recycled here to stand for the Powhatan meeting house (figure 5.2). In William Hole's reimagining of the Smith captivity, the figure and pose of the headman Powhatan or Wahunsenacock seated on a raised platform toward the back of the structure is also derived from a de Bry engraving from 1590 showing

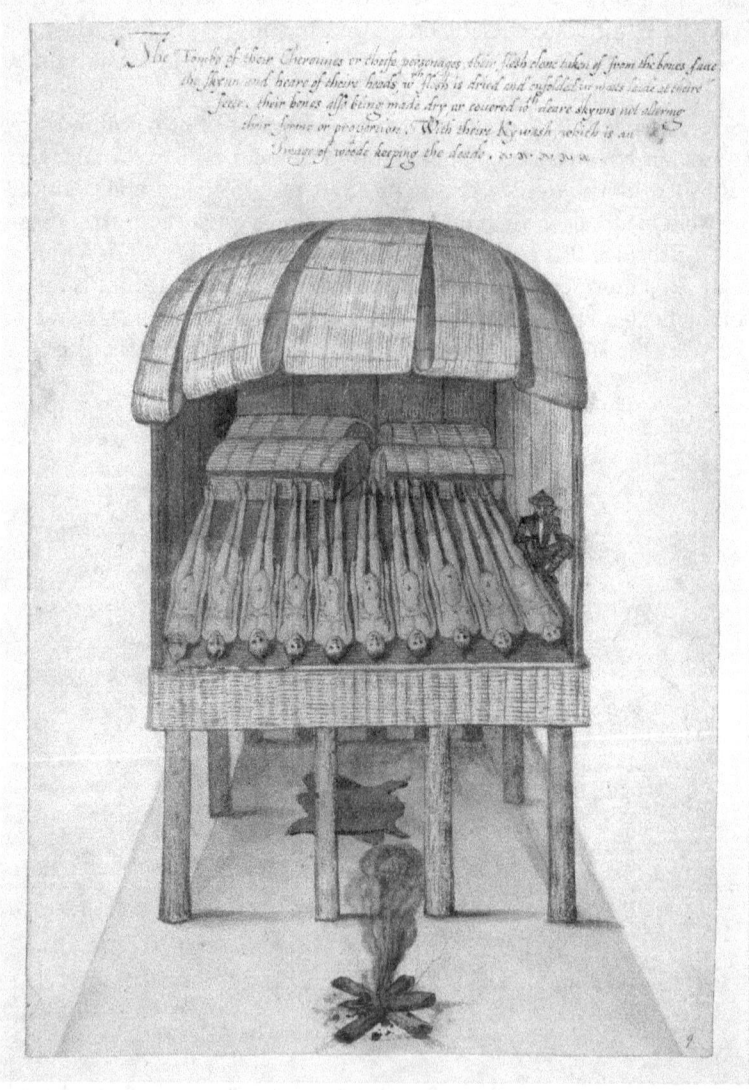

Figure 5.2 *Tombe of the Weroans* watercolor drawing by John White, *ca.* 1590. © The Trustees of the British Museum, London.

the Roanoke Algonquian's "idol Kiwasa" (figure 5.3). The text for the 1590 volume was written by the Roanoke expedition's scientific officer Thomas Hariot who states that

> The people of this country have an idol, which they call Kiwasa: it is carved of wood in length of four foot; its head is like the heads of the people of Florida...This idol is placed in the temple of the town of Secota, as the keeper of the kings' dead corpses. Sometime they have

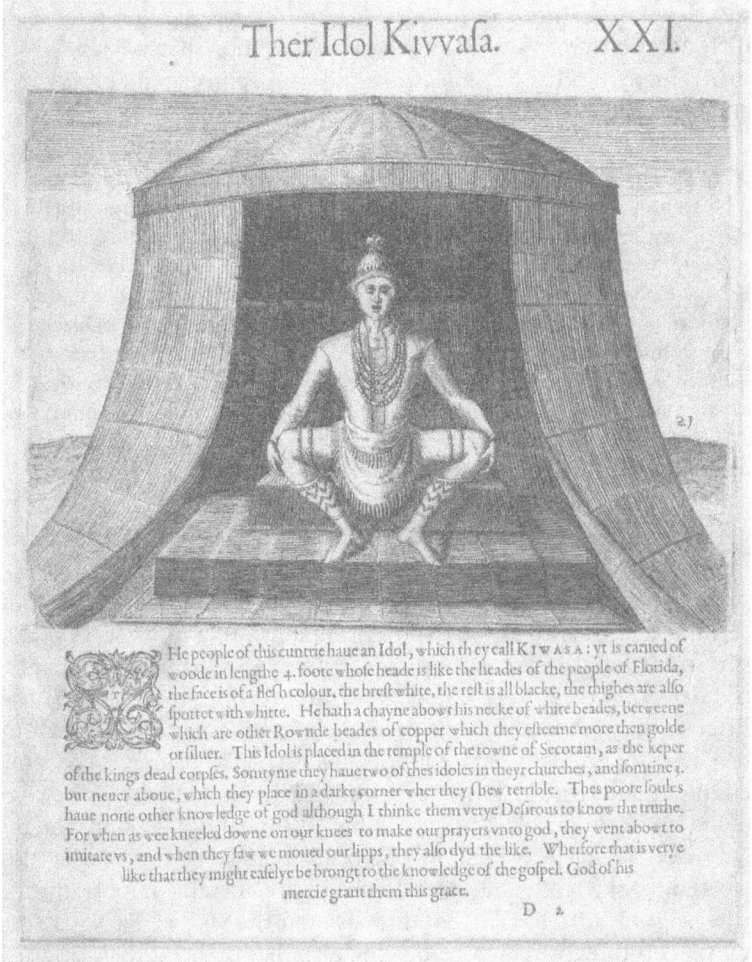

Figure 5.3 *Their Idol called Kiwasa* engraving by Theodore de Bry, after John White, published in Theodore de Bry, *Grand Voyages*, Part I, London, 1590. © The British Library.

two of these idols in their churches, and sometime three, but never above, which they place in a dark corner where they show terrible. (Hariot 1588, 2007, p. 71)

Hole's decision to take an idol from the 1590 volume and reuse it as the living Powhatan is intriguing. Clearly, the gloomy interior confronting Smith is made more forbidding if the viewer is aware of the original context of this iconography, although any purchaser of the *Map* of 1612 may simply have read this pose as regal and authoritative. Ironically, in one of his retrospective narratives, first published in 1624, Smith refers to Wahunsenacock as "more like a devil than a man," implying that he, at least, would have appreciated Hole's recycling of a pagan idol to stand for his captor.

> Two dayes after, Powhatan having disguised himselfe in the most fearefullest manner he could, caused Capt: Smith to be brought forth to a great house in the woods, and there vpon a mat by the fire to be left alone. Not long after from behinde a mat that divided the house, was made the most dolefullest noyse he ever heard; then Powhatan more like a devill then a man with some two hundred more as blacke as himselfe, came vnto him and told him now they were friends, and presently he should goe to Iames towne, to send him two great gunnes, and a gryndstone, for which he would giue him the Country of Capahowosick, and for ever esteeme him as his sonne Nantaquoud. (Smith 1624, II, pp. 48–49; 1907, p. 102)

The next imagery in chronological order of its appearance is the set of plates published in 1618 and 1619 in Volume 10 of de Bry's *Grand Voyages*, especially those illustrating Ralph Hamor's account concerning the Virginia colony and Pocahontas's role in its success and survival through these early years (figure 5.4). Of the three images, the depiction of how Pocahontas was duped into going aboard the English ship and thus made a permanent captive and English "adoptee" is my main focus of attention. This particular plate was probably engraved, after the originals by Georg Keller, by one of the descendants of Theodore de Bry, either his son Johann Theodore, or his grandson Mattaeus Merian or one of his grandsons-in-law who also worked for the family business. In the plate's overall composition the three figures of Iapassus, Pocahontas, and the wife of Iapassus take up the left foreground space but the plate has reversed their original positions in Keller's engraving and given the scene more dynamism by moving the narrative sequence from left to right (as opposed to from right to left). This makes the viewer look across the image as one

Figure 5.4 "Pocahontas deceitfully handed over to the English" engraving (plate 7) by Abelius after Georg Keller in Theodore de Bry and family, *Grand Voyages*, Part X (London, 1619). © The British Library.

would read a page of text. Pocahontas is thus figuratively and historically surrounded by the narratives of her entrapment, captivity, and eventual incorporation within the Jamestown hierarchy. Depicted more distantly in the middle ground of the image is the actual enticement and captivity of the Powhatan's daughter where she is shown sitting for the meal prepared for the group as part of the ploy to get her to go on board and to stay some time with the English adventurers. In a stylized Judas-type payment for his duplicity, the figure of Iapassus is shown in the mid-ground receiving a chest from the mariners who will take Pocahontas on board. As the viewer's eye circles back to the main group of the three central actors in the drama, one notices in Iapassus's left hand the copper kettle that served as his payment for the "betrayal" of a "saviour" of the English and their colony. The underlying symbolism seems more than incidental. In fact, the group of the three figures in the left foreground recalls the scene of "virtue and vice" depicted widely in the emblem books being printed in the late sixteenth and early seventeenth centuries (a good example can be found in the *Emblemata* of Junius of 1565).

The figure of Iapassus is drawn in profile and has what looks like a small goatee beard on his chin, a physical feature that is highly unlikely ethnographically and contradicts Smith's report that the Indians were essentially beardless. Iapassus's feather adornments and animal skin clothing reveal that the engraver has looked back to an original de Bry figure, the "Weroan or Chief Lorde of Virginia" first engraved in 1590 and based on an existing John White watercolor (see White's images as reproduced in Hulton 1984, plate 48, p. 78). However, in the new formulation, de Bry's elegantly depicted warrior who dresses up for war and for feasts in the same attire is now shown in the guise of duplicitous Iapassus wearing the skin of a panther or mountain lion with its tail trailing behind. In John White's original drawing the same lion's tail hangs between his legs and, as it is a frontal figure, is not immediately visible. In this 1618/19 reimagined Indian man, the tail is more obtrusive; the curving feathers in de Bry's engraved image are altered in Iapassus's headdress to become stiff and pointed knife-like projections coming out of the back of his head, which, at first glance, have more the appearance of hard horns than soft feathers. It is possible, in short, that connotations of the devil have been mobilized by this manipulation of imagery.

So far, then, I have offered conjectures concerning two images—one of the Powhatan's meeting house, the other the figure of Iapassus—that propose the insinuation of pejorative connotations, specifically references to the diabolical, in the visualization of these Powhatan peoples. And in both instances this has been achieved by taking positive or peaceful visualizations of the Algonquians of Roanoke, first produced in the 1590s, and adjusting that iconography to fit these later accounts of other Native peoples. Nowhere is this process clearer than in my next example.

The plate engraved by Robert Vaughan in 1624 was printed as one scene in a foldout plate to John Smith's *Generall Historie of Virginia* (figure 5.5). It shows the Native American medicine peoples' "conjurations" about Smith and, at bottom right, his eventual rescue by Pocahontas. Here we find again that the imagery in de Bry's first volume of the *Grand Voyages* published 1590 is the main source for much of the iconography (Feest 1967, I, pp. 1–30). I'd like to take just one part of Robert Vaughan's six-part plate to reveal how an original John White image, via a de Bry reproduction of it, is translated from a North Carolinian context to one relevant to Native peoples living near the Jamestown colony in Virginia and how the reimagining of a new scene using older and outdated information is made plausible

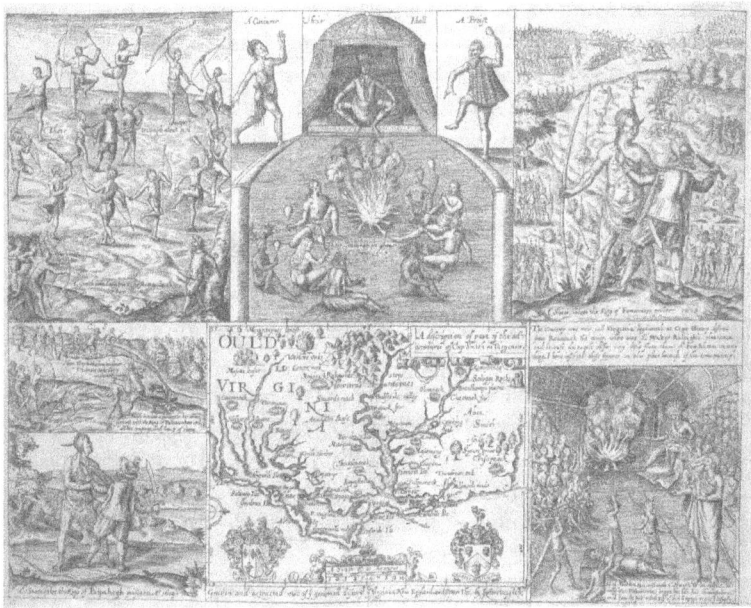

Figure 5.5 "Various scenes in Virginia", engraved illustration (between p. 40 and 41) in John Smith's *Generall Historie of Virginia* (London, 1624; shelfmark G.7037). © The British Library.[4]

within the context of the "iconotext" configuration. Vaughan reused White's scene of the circular dances of the Carolina Natives around carved poles, "which they use at their hyghe feastes," an image of peaceful celebration, to articulate the position John Smith must have felt on being captured and surrounded by Virginian Natives carrying weapons and dancing in "their triumph about him" (figure 5.5). Vaughan, or more likely Smith, provided a rationalization of this reconfiguration (figure 5.5) by stating in the legend to the plate that

> the Countrey wee now call Virginia beginneth at Cape Henry distant from Roanoack 60 miles. Where was Sr. Walter Raleigh's plantation: and because the people differ very little from them of Powhatan in any thing, I have inserted those figures in this place because of the conveniency.

Smith's candor in confessing his reliance on Roanoke imagery offers a welcome insight into the world of seventeenth-century engraving and the dangers involved in relying on this visual material for accurate historical information.

The last image to be considered in detail is also the final one to appear chronologically in publishing terms. It is the plate in de Bry's volume 13 published in 1627 that shows the combined scenes of Smith's first captivity with Opechancanough and the final and cathartic release and transformation of Smith into an adoptee or "son" and thus a leader in his own right within the Powhatan confederacy with his "rescue" by Pocahontas. In the narrative Smith retells the story of his captivity, and in this version repeats Pocahontas's role in his salvation, as first published in his *Generall Historie of Virginia* of 1624. Interestingly for the depiction and its position in this brief art history I have related, the action of Pocahontas's intervention is less obvious than it was in Vaughan's engraving of 1624. In the 1627 version it is pushed away into the mid-ground of the composition and the role of Opechancanough and his "conjurors" takes up the center stage. Repeated here again is the architectural feature of the meeting house or lodge that was first shown in de Bry's original plate, repeated on the *Map* of 1612 and now housing some other form of ceremonial or divination (figures 5.2 and 5.6).

A final observation concerns another of those same images that were first discussed by Feest in his original study mentioned at the beginning of this chapter. Feest offers a thorough analysis of two "Virginian" Indian figures found on the Virginia Company Standing Lottery broadside of 1615, now housed in the collections of the Society of Antiquaries of London (see figure 6 in Feest 1967, preceding pp. 10–11). His analysis is instructive for how we can view these figures as being both individual and yet offering another variant on the typical de Bry-inspired figure (Feest 1967, I, pp. 10–13). The fact that both figures in the broadside are given American Indian names is puzzling. Neither name appears in other documentation of the time, making it very difficult to determine who these figures represent and why they have found illustration in the visual record. "Eiakintomino" and "Matahan" could be completely invented, but a better supposition is that these must be actual Algonquian names and refer to real individuals known to the colony officials or promoters of Virginian settlement (Pratt 2009, pp. 36–37). Irrespective of the de Bry formula used for their representation, with its typical poses and disposition of costume, weapons, and ornament, if the representation points to actual Indian people then who were they? Might they too, like Pocahontas, be in fact captive peoples, taken from nearby the colony and brought to London to promote its new ventures into capitalism? This was certainly one of Pocahontas's main roles and a reason why she was brought to London by her husband John Rolfe

Figure 5.6 "Smith saved from death by Pocahontas and religious ceremonies", copperplate engraving from Johann Ludwig Gottfriedt's *Newe Welt vnd americanische Historien* (Frankfurt: Bey denen Merianischen Erben, 1655). This is an abridged version of Theodore de Bry and Sons, Grand Voyages, Part XIII (London, 1634). © The Wisconsin Historical Society. WHi-23856.

in 1616. Pocahontas's captivity was further removed from the main narratives once she became Christianized as Rebecca and once her original captivity became codified in image and text as an action of her duplicitous and "evil" Indian compatriots, Iapassus and his wife as related in the account by Hamor. Coincidently, both of these Virginian Indian figures who appear in the 1615 Broadside adopt the pose of classical support figures, traditionally placed on either side of a main escutcheon or military coat of arms, and thus refer back to an original derivation in Roman and other antique triumphal architecture where captive "barbarians" were used to symbolize the conquests of the Imperium (Pratt-Smiles 1992, pp. 14–24). In 1615, the Standing Lottery notice with its American Indian supports attributing the figures to a new Virginian "heraldry" was a clever way to promote the colony and offset the effects of its unpopularity.

By way of a conclusion, I would like to reflect on the images I have discussed and to tease out from them some general issues bearing on the themes of this volume. The key point they raise is one of narratives and their coding—visual and verbal narratives of captivity and adoption. The verbal accounts of what happened to John Smith and Pocahontas are the earliest to receive illustrative treatment in the English colonial context and these often unassuming prints thus provide a witness of the mediation processes that turn American experience into European commodity. For the reader/viewer to experience vicariously what took place in early 1600s Virginia it was necessary that author, engraver, and publisher fabricate a system of verbal and visual cues to guide the reader's response. The novelty of the enterprise was such that its mechanisms are more visible than is true of later verbal and visual narratives—the process of signification is laid out for us.

My chronological account of the various telling and retellings of Smith's and Pocahontas's stories indicated how several elements coalesced into the narrative we are familiar with today, albeit the fact that in the more popular accounts that appeared over the next two centuries the story of Pocahontas's dramatic intervention in Smith's fate becomes the image of choice, eclipsing her own abduction by the English six years later. And in the presentation of Smith's captivity we also see, perhaps, the origin of all those later accounts of hapless white victims surrounded by violent savages undertaking alien rituals.

From a visual point of view what is most telling is how difficult it seems to have been to represent these incidents in the early 1600s, and this difficulty perhaps derived from the fact that the boundaries between abduction and adoption, captivity and co-option were so fluid. In these circumstances it is understandable that the seemingly less ambiguous experiences of Smith's physical restraint and preparation for execution would be the ones that subsequent treatments of the narrative tended to concentrate on. It may also explain why the story of Pocahontas's captivity was replaced by her intervention in Smith's "execution." Simply put, in narrative the demands of graphic illustration are better satisfied with memorable actions.

Notes

1. English colonizing efforts in this area of North America only began seriously in the 1580s and so it is reasonable to consider the first half of the seventeenth century as a time of early contact between

indigenous peoples and the English "newcomers." See Kicza (2002, pp. 35–8).
2. John Smith's published writings are as follows: *A True Relation of Such Occurrences and Accidents of Note as Happened in Virginia* (1608); *A Map of Virginia* (1612); *The Proceedings of the English Colony in Virginia* (1612); *A Description of New England* (1616); *New England's Trials* (1620, 1622); *The Generall Historie of Virginia, New-England, and the Summer Isles* (1624); *An Accidence, or the Pathway to Experience Necessary for all Young Seamen* (1626); *A Sea Grammar—the first sailors' Word Book in English* (1627); *The True Travels, Adventures and Observations of Captain John Smith* (1630); and *Advertisements for the Unexperienced Planters of New England, or Anywhere* (1631). Smith's *Generall Historie* is perhaps the text most frequently reprinted and cited regarding his time in Virginia.
3. There will be some repetition of the captivity stories of figures such as John Smith and John Marrant whose experiences feature in several of the chapters in this part of the present volume. It is important that each of the several contributors recount their understandings of these historical events as different aspects have been emphasized in each.
4. For a more detailed image of this engraving, please see it reproduced in my article, Stephanie Pratt, 2009 "Truth and Artifice in the Visualisation of Native Peoples, from the time of John White to the beginning of the eighteenth-century," *European Visions: American Voices*, British Museum Publications 172, London: British Museum Press, 33–40, online access at http://www.britishmuseum.org/pdf/1-Pratt-Truth20%and20%Artifice.pdf.

Chapter 6

Strategies of (Un)belonging: The Captivities of John Smith, Olaudah Equiano, and John Marrant

Susan Castillo Street

One of the most exciting areas of Early American scholarship in recent years has been that of narratives that relate an individual's experience of captivity or enslavement. Often, however, these texts have been interpreted through a Eurocentric lens. Pauline Turner Strong (2002) comments: "the assumptions embedded in conceptualizing indigenous practices such as 'captivity,' 'adoption,' and 'slavery'...have led to blind spots, misconceptions, and poorly framed controversies." She suggests that incorporation and subordination are more satisfactory terms to designate the processes of transformation following "captivity," which is in turn defined as "the assertion of power over a person or group resulting in dislocation, physical confinement, and social transformation" (p. 339).

In this chapter, I look at three individuals who underwent such a transformation as a result of being incorporated into or subordinated by a more powerful group: John Smith, one of the founders of Jamestown, taken captive by Powhatan in early Virginia; Olaudah Equiano, captured by slavers on the African coast; and John Marrant, an African American missionary captured by the Cherokees. In what follows, the focus will be of necessity anecdotal. Stephen Greenblatt (1992), in *Marvelous Possessions: The Wonder of the New World*, states that the anecdote "is the principal register of the unexpected and hence of the encounter with difference" (pp. 2–3). He adds:

> Anecdotes then are among the principal products of a culture's representational technology, mediators between the undifferentiated succession of local moments and a larger strategy toward which they canonly

gesture. They are seized in passing from the swirl of experiences and given some shape, a shape whose provisionality still marks them as contingent—otherwise we would give them the larger, grander name of history—but also makes them available for telling and retelling. (P. 3)

Obviously, this anecdotal telling and retelling is mediated by language. Language here is seen, however, not as a transparent window on univocal historical Truth, but rather as the medium through which Smith, Equiano, and Marrant articulated not only their personal experience of captivity and of contact with a culture very different to their own, but also their struggles to understand or be understood by their captors. John Smith had a limited knowledge of Algonquin; Olaudah Equiano initially had no understanding at all of the language of the slavers who took him captive; and John Marrant literally owed his life to an encounter with a Cherokee hunter who taught him the rudiments of the Cherokee language. Another important feature of these three narratives is they tend to blur cultural boundaries and subvert traditional binaries that view captives or enslaved people as victims without agency. All three men were well aware that to escape from situations of powerlessness, it is vital to command and manipulate not only one's own linguistic resources, but also to command and if necessary manipulate the language of the powerful.

John Smith's life was nothing if not eventful. Born in 1580 to a farming family in Lincolnshire, he was apprenticed at the age of fifteen to a shopkeeper, but hankered after adventure. After his father's death, Smith managed to waive his indenture and volunteered to fight on behalf of the Dutch in their struggle against the Spanish crown. After a time as a privateer in the Mediterranean, he joined the Austrian army and fought against the Turks, allegedly beheading three Turks in a single battle in Romania, a deed commemorated on his coat of arms. Later, however, he was taken prisoner and sold to a Turk, who passed him on to his betrothed as a slave. According to Smith, this woman fell in love with him, but he then repaid her affections and escaped by murdering his master, returning to England in the winter of 1604.

Smith did so at a time that was propitious for adventurers. In London, he became involved in the projects of the Virginia Company, which had received its charter from King James I as a profit-making venture to colonize Virginia. The expedition embarked for the New World in 1606, and Smith immediately gained a reputation as a troublemaker, to the extent that the leader of the expedition threatened him with execution. When, however, the list of council members was opened on shipboard, Smith's name was on it, and he was spared by Captain Newport and sworn in to the council of the colony. The beginnings of the Jamestown colony were not auspicious, however. The harsh winter and epidemics of fever carried off many of the colonists, and many were not remotely fit for the rigors of colonial life. Smith was put in charge of procuring foodstuffs and supplies for the colony, and it was in the course of carrying out his duties and seeking food along the Chickahominy River that he was taken captive for a period of six or seven weeks by a group of Native Virginians. The only version that we have of events is Smith's own, first in his 1608 *A True Relation of Such Occurences and Accidents of Note, as Hath Hapned in Virginia* and his 1624 *The Generall Historie of Virginia, New England, and the Summer Isles*. By any standard, and even taking into account Smith's tendency toward exaggeration and self-aggrandizement, it is quite a tale. It is told in the third person, which enables Smith to foreground his own bravery and resourcefulness.

While foraging for food with two other colonists, Jehu Robinson and Thomas Emry, and two Powhatan Indian guides, Smith ordered the guides to go ashore so that he could explore the woods, leaving behind the two other Englishmen and one of the Indian guides, and taking another Indian guide with him. In the forest, Smith was ambushed by a group of Indians, and used his Indian guide as a shield to ward off their arrows. (What happened to his unfortunate guide is not recorded). Smith sustained a minor wound in the thigh, and was taken prisoner; the other two Englishmen were killed. At this point, he demanded to be taken to the Indians' leader, and when he was brought before Opechancanough, Smith showed the indigenous leader the marvels of Early Modern technology:

> He demanding for their captain, they showed him Opechancanough, King of Pamunkey, to whom he gave a round ivory compass dial. Much they marvelled at the playing of the fly and needle, which they could see so plainly and yet not touch it because of the glass that covered them. But when he demonstrated by that globe-like jewel the roundness of the earth and skies, the sphere of the sun, moon and stars, and how the sun did chase the night round about the world continually, the greatness of the land and sea, the diversity of nations, variety of complexions, and how we were to them antipodes and many other such like matters, they all stood as amazed with admiration. (Smith 1624)

Here Smith portrays some of the qualities that made him such a natural survivor: ruthlessness, courage, sheer nerve (in demanding to see the leader of the Indians), and quick thinking, as demonstrated in his attempt to establish ascendancy over his captors with a demonstration of advanced technology, since glass and indeed the compass were unfamiliar to the Indians. This manifestation of technological superiority is a trope we frequently encounter in texts describing colonial encounters between Europeans and indigenous groups. There are obvious reasons for its appeal to European writers as a strategy of empowerment in situations when the balance of power is apparently not in their favor, in that it reinforces the authority not only of the narrator but also of his allegedly more advanced culture. How well Smith was actually able to convey his ideas is unclear. He did have a rudimentary grasp of Algonquin (as the list of words in the Vocabulary, which accompanies his *Historie of Virginia and the Summer Isles*, attests) but was hardly a fluent speaker. But all this notwithstanding, his captors tied him to a tree and presumably were preparing to shoot him when Opechancanough held up the compass and they laid down their bows and arrows. After this, he was taken to the settlement of Oropaks, guarded by "three great savages holding him fast by each arm," with six more on each side, and was given food and drink. After this, Smith describes their dancing in a ring, "with hellish notes and screeches":

> Every one (had) his quiver of arrows and at his back a club, on his arm a fox or an otter's skin or some such matter for his vambrace, their heads and shoulders painted red with oil...which scarlet-like colour made an exceeding handsome show, his bow in his hand and the skin of a bird with her wings abroad, dried, tied on his head, and a piece of their snakes tied to it, or some such like toy. (Smith 1624, p. 47)

Clearly, Smith was in fear for his life, and his text is a curious mixture of remarkably close observation of his surroundings and figurative language, particularly depth tropes such as metaphor, which literally demonizes the Indians and reflects his own terror, with the Indians characterized as "devils" and "hellish." Smith was then taken to a long house and given even more venison and bread. Unsurprisingly, he tells us that he had little appetite, and was convinced "that they would fat him to eat him." This is a trope that occurs over and over again in early texts, and perhaps reflects not only the captive's literal fear of being eaten, but also his or her horror on a symbolic level at being ingested and engulfed by the culture of the Other, with the concomitant loss of individual identity. Nonetheless, Smith does mention individual acts of kindness, such as that of one elderly Indian he had met on arriving in Virginia to whom he had given beads.

In the following days, Smith was taken to several other settlements. Finally, he was brought to Powhatan's camp in Pamunkey. He describes the ritual that took place, framing it at both beginning and end with couplets highlighting the Indians' diabolical attributes:

(where they entertained him with most strange and fearefull Coniurations;
As if near led to hell, Amongst the Devils to dwell.
Not long after, early in a morning a great fire was made in a long house, and a mat spread on the one side, as on the other, on the one they caused him to sit, and all the guard went out of the house, and presently came skipping in a great grim fellow, all painted over with coale, mingled with oyle; and many Snakes and Wesels skins stuffed with mosse, and all their tayles tyed together, so as they met on the crowne of his head in a tassell; and round about the tassell was as a Coronet of feathers, the skins hanging round about his head, backe, and shoulders, and in a manner covered his face; with a hellish voyce and a rattle in his hand. With most strange gestures and passions he began his invocation, and environed the fire with a circle of meale; which done, three more such like devils came rushing in with the like antique tricks, painted halfe blacke, halfe red: but all their eyes were painted white, and some red stroakes like Mutchato's, along their cheekes: round about him those fiends daunced a pretty while, and then came in three more as vgly as the rest; with red eyes, and white stroakes over their blacke faces, at last they all sat downe right against him; three of them on the one hand of the chiefe Priest, and three on the other. Then all with their rattles began a song, which ended, the chiefe Priest layd downe fiue wheat cornes: then strayning his armes and hands with such violence that he sweat, and his veynes swelled, he began a short Oration: at the conclusion they all gaue a short groane; and then layd down three graines more. After that, began their song againe, and then another Oration, ever laying downe so many cornes as before, till they had twice incirculed the fire; that done, they tooke a bunch of little stickes prepared for that purpose, continuing still their devotion, and at the end of every song and Oration, they layd downe a sticke betwixt the divisions of Corne. Till night, neither he nor they did either eate or drinke, and then they feasted merrily, with the best provisions they could make. Three dayes they vsed this Ceremony; the meaning whereof they told him, was to know if he intended them well or no. The circle of meale signified their Country, the circles of corne the bounds of the Sea, and the stickes his Country. They imagined the world to be flat and round, like a trencher, and they in the middest. After this they brought him a bagge of gunpowder,

which they carefully preferred till the next spring, to plant as they did their corne; because they would be acquainted with the nature of that seede. *Opitchapam* the Kings brother invited him to his house, where, with as many platters of bread, soule, and wild beasts, as did environ him, he bid him wellcome; but not any of them would eate a bit with him, but put vp all the remainder in Baskets. At his returne to *Opechancanoughs*, all the Kings women, and their children, flocked about him for their parts, as a due by Custome, to be merry with such fragments.

But his waking mind in hydeous dreames did oft see wondrous shapes, Of bodies strange, and huge in growth, and of stupendious makes. (Smith 1624, p. 48)

This passage is notable for many reasons. For Smith and his captors, interpreting each other's meanings was literally a matter of life and death. Clearly, Smith was in a state of extreme apprehension, and it is possible that by representing his captors as diabolical alien creatures he is highlighting his own bravery and also rendering his narrative more marketable. He had notable powers of observation, and this description is one of the few extant accounts of the ritual practices of the indigenous inhabitants of early seventeenth-century Virginia, characterized by remarkable richness of detail. According to Smith, the Indians explained to him their worldview and the meaning of different facets of the ceremony performed. Smith also conveyed the fact that the apprehension was not only on his side; clearly it was to the Indians' advantage to ascertain the intentions of Smith and his fellow colonists and the meaning of their gifts. The image of the Indians planting gunpowder as though it were seeds is a fascinating one. In the couplets taken from a translation of Lucretius by Fotherby, which frame the narrative, however, we gain an insight into the sense of alienation and estrangement that Smith was experiencing. The text as a whole is characterized by this curious oscillation between factual information gained from close observation of Smith's captors, conveyed in a dispassionate tone, and lurid imagery. This may be in part due to the fact that Smith's *Generall Historie* was intended to promote settlement in Virginia (and thus convey information about conditions in the colony), but at the same time to replenish Smith's own coffers by selling well, which would account for the tone of derring-do and adventure. It has been suggested as well that this ceremony bears no resemblance to rites of divination practiced by Native Americans in this period, and may in fact have been a version of the Delaware Big House ceremony or *Gamwing*, a ritual renewal of the world. (Gleach 1997)

The narrative goes on to describe one of the most famous—and enigmatic—episodes in American literary and cultural history. Smith is brought before Powhatan and two hundred of his courtiers:

> At his entrance before the King, all the people gaue a great shout. The Queene of *Appamatuck* was appointed to bring him water to wash his hands, and another brought him a bunch of feathers, in stead of a Towell to dry them: having feasted him after their best barbarous manner they could, a long consultation was held, but the conclusion was, two great stones were brought before *Powhatan*: then as many as could layd hands on him, dragged him to them, and thereon laid his head, and being ready with their clubs, to beate out his braines, *Pocahontas* the Kings dearest daughter, when no intreaty could preuaile, got his head in her armes, and laid her owne vpon his to saue him from death: whereat the Emperour was contented he should liue to make him hatchets, and her bells, beads, and copper; for they thought him as well of all occupations as themselues. For the King himselfe will make his owne robes, shooes, bowes, arrowes, pots; plant, hunt, or doe any thing so well as the rest. (Smith p. 49)

Clearly, Smith was convinced that he was about to breathe his last, and that he had been saved only through the intervention of Pocahontas. Scholars such as Karen Kupperman (2007) and Frederic Gleach (1997, p. 113) have suggested that she was actually acting as cultural mediator by taking part in an adoption ceremony in which Smith underwent a symbolic death and was then adopted into Powhatan's family. In this perspective, Clara Sue Kidwell (1992) suggests that Smith would be undergoing a ritual death so that he could be reborn into a new world of cultural relationships (pp. 97–107; see also Kidwell and Velie 2005). Smith himself mentions that two days after the ceremony Powhatan had said that if Smith brought him two cannons and a grindstone from Jamestown he would give him a territory of his own and "for ever esteeme him as his sonne Nantaquoud." Indeed, Frederic Gleach comments, "Powhatan's intention at the end is clearly to have the English settle within his territory, as his subordinates." This clearly was not what Smith understood, as subsequent events would demonstrate. In the *Interesting Narrative of the Life of Olaudah Equiano, or Gustavus Vassa, the African, Written by Himself*, written and published nearly 200 years after Smith's account (in 1789), we gain an alternative perspective of captivity. Olaudah Equiano, like John Smith, was taken captive by a group of individuals very different to himself, and his *Narrative* shows many rhetorical parallels to that of Smith. At the same time, however, the two men were unalike in many ways.

The *Narrative* tells the story of Equiano's life from his birth in Africa around 1745 until the year of its publication (1789). It is an extraordinary tale by any standard. Much of Equiano's life was spent at sea, first on the slave ship that took him to the Caribbean, later on a second slave ship that carried him to Virginia, then serving on ships that sailed back and forth across the Atlantic between England, the Caribbean, and the United States, including as well trips to various ports in the Mediterranean, a failed venture intended to establish a colony in what is now Nicaragua, and a voyage of exploration to the North Pole. Eventually, as a personal servant to several sea captains, Equiano was able to save up enough money to purchase his freedom. But freedom in the early Atlantic was a precarious thing, and Equiano was several times on the verge of being sold back into slavery. He finally settled in London, where he converted to Christianity and became very active in the abolitionist movement. His *Narrative* went through eight editions in only six years, and was frequently cited in the Parliamentary debates on the slave trade. Its importance in bringing an end to the slave trade was incalculable.

In the course of his eventful life, Equiano was constantly thrust into direct contact with other cultures. After his kidnapping in Africa, his experience on the slave ship was harrowing. When he sees his captors, he reverses the usual Eurocentric racial stereotypes of whites as civilized and Africans as primitives, describing the former as "white men with horrible looks, red faces and loose hair"; initially he believes they are spirits, later adding that this belief was confirmed by "their complexions too differing so much from ours, their long hair, and the language they spoke, which was different than any I ever heard" (Equiano/Vassa 2001, p. 39). When he sees a boiling furnace, like John Smith, he is convinced that he is about to be eaten by his captors. He recounts the horrors of the Middle Passage, with slaves jumping overboard in despair or confined below decks in insalubrious conditions, and cites instances of the brutality of the whites, flogging one of their own number to death, and tossing fish overboard rather than give them to the slaves to eat. Later, on reaching Barbados, Equiano and his fellow Africans are made to jump ashore, and again he thinks that he is about to be devoured by his captors ("these ugly men"). He is amazed, first at the stone houses built with many stories and then at the horses, which he had never encountered, concluding again that the white people who surround him are spirits. Later Equiano is taken to Virginia, still grieving for his family, and encounters still more disconcerting novelties: the iron muzzle worn by a slave cook;

the ticking noise of a clock on the mantelpiece; the eyes of a man in a portrait, which seem to follow him around the room. He reacts to these phenomena with terror and deep sadness, particularly because of his incapacity to speak the language of his captors and decode their culture. Equiano tells us,

> I now totally lost the small remains of comfort I had enjoyed in conversing with my countrymen...We were landed up the river a good way from the sea, about Virginia County, where we saw few of our native Africans, and not one soul who could talk to me...I was exceedingly miserable, and thought myself worse off than any of the rest of my companions; for they could talk to each other, but I had no person to speak to that I could understand. (Equiano 2001, p. 44)

As Susan Marren (1993) has pointed out, however, the insight of the young enslaved man into these asymmetries of colonial power is in inverse proportion to his command of English. She comments, "When he begins to comprehend, he apparently loses the ability to defamiliarize and thereby to problematize the value system of the English culture" (p. 99). Later, Equiano is sold to another master, who sends him to England as a gift to a friend. On board, he is well-treated, and concludes that perhaps not all the white people "are of the same disposition." Here, he meets a young American boy called Dick, who becomes a close friend and instructs him in English and in the tenets of Christianity. When they reach Falmouth, he is fascinated by snow (which he had never seen) and by books. He describes them thus:

> I had often seen my master and Dick employed in reading; and I had a great curiosity to talk to the books, as I thought they did; and so to learn how all things had a beginning: for that purpose I have often taken up a book, and have talked to it, and then put my ears to it, when alone, in hopes it would answer me; and I have been very much concerned when I found it remained silent. (Equiano 2001, p. 48)

This trope of the talking book is one that often appears in texts describing colonial encounters, and European writers often employ it to invoke the superiority of European scribal culture. What is notable here is that it describes the perspective of a preliterate person on encountering print culture and experiencing its power to disseminate ideas. As Equiano's command of English increases, so does his assimilation into English culture, and indeed a growing awareness of his capacity to advocate his own ideas in print. He describes the process vividly:

> I have often reflected with surprise that I never felt half the alarm at any of the numerous dangers I have been in, that I was filled with at the first sight of the Europeans, and at every act of theirs, even the most trifling, when I first came among them, and for some time afterwards. That fear, however, which was the effect of my ignorance, wore away as I began to know them. I could now speak English tolerably well, and I perfectly understood everything that was said. I now not only felt myself quite easy with these new countrymen, but relished their society and manners. I no longer looked upon them as spirits, but as men superior to us; and therefore I had the stronger desire to resemble them; to imbibe their spirit, and imitate their manners. (p. 58)

It is clear throughout Equiano's narrative that he is torn between two loyalties: as an African (as explicitly stated in his title), and as a free British subject campaigning for abolition of the slave trade. This shapes his authorial strategies: he presents his own Igbo culture as a group not unlike the English: monotheistic, hard-working, valuing chastity in women, and cleanliness. This he does very subtly in order to force his audience to accept not only the injustice of the slave trade but also Equiano's own status as a civilized interlocutor (and consequently that of his people as well) and not as an exception to what Europeans viewed as the rule of black primitivism. As well, he clearly realizes that in order to be an effective advocate for the end of the slave trade, he must plead his cause in terms that his readers (who belonged to the dominant culture) could understand; it is clearly in his interest to describe English culture in favorable terms. At the same time, however, what emerges clearly in the text is the extent to which Equiano underwent over the years a process of genuine acculturation, transforming himself from an African to, in his own phrase, "almost an Englishman," positioning himself as a cultural insider. This is apparent in the slippery pronouns we encounter in his text. After he purchases his own freedom, we see in the text that he refers to slaves as "these unfortunate wretches," "the poor creatures." When he agrees to serve as overseer on a Jamaica plantation, we find textual evidence of this double consciousness: "Our vessel being ready to sail to the Musquito shore, I went with the Doctor on board a Guineaman, to purchase some slaves to carry with us, and cultivate a plantation: and I chose them all of my own countrymen" (p. 155). Here, we see that Equiano identifies with the English (*our* vessel) to buy slaves to carry with *us* (English), but then foregrounds his African identity with a reference to his own countrymen.

Another figure of the Black Atlantic who was forced to negotiate between cultures was John Marrant. Marrant (1995) was born into a free black family in New York, and lived in Florida and Georgia before going to live with his older sister and her husband in Charleston, South Carolina. From the age of eleven–thirteen he was apprenticed to a music master, who taught him to play violin and French horn; this enabled him to earn money playing for the white elites of Charleston in the evening. He describes himself as "devoted to pleasure and drinking in iniquity like water; a slave to every vice suited to my nature and to my years" (p. 77). One day, on passing a meeting house, he is urged to disrupt the services by blowing his French horn as a prank. As he prepares to do so, the minister points at him and tells him to prepare to meet his Maker. This causes the child to faint in terror. When he is revived, he feels the minister's words "like a parcel of swords thrust in me" (a metaphor reflecting his fear of violence and bodily harm or penetration) and says that he sees the devil everywhere (p. 78). After being sent home, Marrant is low and restless, but a minister comes to speak to him and finally sets his mind at rest and confirms his conversion. The young man embraces his new faith with what can only be described as terrifying alacrity, and his family try to dissuade him from devotional excesses, but Marrant, with adolescent stubbornness, clings to his new beliefs: "The more they persecuted me, the stronger I grew in grace" (p. 80). When his family tells him he is crazy, he decides to embark upon a pilgrimage into the "desart" (i.e., the wilderness) with his Bible.

In the forest, Marrant meets an Indian hunter, and spends some weeks with him hunting deer and learning the Cherokee language, a skill that was to save his life. He and the hunter go into a Cherokee village, but there he is apprehended. When he is told that he will be put to death, he bursts into tears and begins to call upon the Lord Jesus. He is taken away to a place of confinement, and spends the night praying and singing aloud to Christ. When the time of his execution rolls around, he is taken out and shown a basket of small skewers, which are to pierce his flesh (reflecting his early vision of being pierced by swords) and then be set on fire, and when they are burned out he is to be tossed into the flame by four men. He begs the executioner to be allowed to pray, and sinks to his knees, praying first in English and then in Cherokee, saying, "The Lord impressed a strong desire upon my mind to turn into their language, and pray in their tongue" (p. 85). Whether or not the inspiration was divine or earthly, it almost certainly saved Marrant's life: the executioner embraces him and refuses to carry out the sentence. Later, in an audience with the Cherokee leader, Marrant's fervor prompts the chief's daughter to kiss his Bible; as is the case of Pocahontas and John Smith, a young woman is described as cultural mediator. When she is converted, Marrant is released and adopted by the Cherokees. He describes it thus:

> A great change took place among the people; the king's house became God's house; the soldiers were ordered away, and the poor condemned prisoner had perfect liberty, and was treated like a prince...I had assumed the habit of the country, and was dressed much like the king, and nothing was too good for me. The king would take off his golden ornaments, his chain and bracelets, like a child, if I objected to them, and lay them aside. Here I learnt to speak their tongue in the highest stile. (p. 87)

After a sojourn of around nine weeks with the Cherokees, Marrant eventually travels to the Choctaw and Chickasaw nations. He later decides to return home, but his family does not recognize him because he is wearing animal skins and carries a tomahawk. Rafia Zafar (1991) has suggested that Marrant has cast his story in biblical terms so that Christian readers could establish typological parallels with the Scriptures, particularly the story of John the Baptist's sojourn in the desert (p. 30). Although there is little reference in the text to Marrant's African origins, it is unclear whether such references were removed by the editor of his *Narrative*, A. Waldridge. Marrant (1995) does comment, however, that the Choctaw and Chickasaw people he encounters mention their anger at colonization: "When they recollect, that the white people drove them from the American shores, they are full of resentment" (p. 88). It is conceivable that the Choctaw and Chickasaw were able to express their opinions of Europeans so freely precisely because Marrant was not white himself. Marrant became a protégé of the Countess of Huntingdon, and his *Narrative* was published in 1785 with a preface by W. A. Aldridge, a Methodist minister and friend of the Countess.

In these three narratives, we have seen how Europeans, Africans, and indigenous peoples of the Americas attempted to make sense of one another. John Smith, the Early Modern European, was an acute observer of Indian culture in order to survive and to ensure the survival of his group, but there is no suggestion that he values Indians or Indian language and society except in an instrumental sense. Particularly when he himself fears death, he paints his Indian captors as cannibalistic "devils" and "great grim fellows," and if he was adopted by them, he is incapable of perceiving their intentions. Equiano similarly views his captors as "ugly," "red-faced," with "horrible looks," who (he thinks) are about to eat him. In both these texts, however, as Smith and Equiano spend time among their captors, they begin increasingly to perceive them as individuals, and Equiano at least is able to perceive some positive facets of their culture. Marrant and his text are imbued with missionary zeal and biblical typology, and (perhaps reflecting the fact that he was an adolescent at the time of his capture) his *Narrative* is remarkably self-centered, focusing on his own reactions, emotions, and strongly held opinions rather than on those of the Cherokees he encounters. For both Marrant and Equiano, Christian ideology is a strong factor leading to their acculturation. What is the case, however, is that all three encounters were mediated by language, and that for all three men a capacity to understand the language of their captors in order to interact with their culture was ultimately a matter of life and death. Finally, all three use English, the language of their captors, in order to present their own personal agendas and visions of events to a wider Atlantic audience.

Chapter 7

Captive or Captivated: Rethinking Encounters in Early Colonial America

Patrick Minges

One of the most popular forms of literature in both America and Europe from the seventeenth century until the latter half of the nineteenth century was the genre that came to be known as the "captivity narrative." From the amazing third-person narrative of John Smith that detailed his narrow escape from death at the hands of the Powhatan to the classic best-seller of the colonial period *A true history of the captivity & restoration of Mrs. Mary Rowlandson, a minister's wife in New-England.: Wherein is set forth the cruel and inhumane usage she underwent amongst the heathens, for eleven weeks' time: and her deliverance from them* (Rowlandson 1682), the genre was America's first flirtation with mythoprosaic representation. According to scholar Denise MacNeil (2005), the narrative "illustrates Rowlandson's place as a cultural hero, capable of furnishing the raw materials necessary for the formation and emergence of the American frontier hero from within the *Narrative*. As such, Rowlandson's text provides the primary American literary roots of this American frontier hero" (p. 626). Rowlandson's work established the pattern for the early texts in this tradition: a confirmation of the election of God's people, the piety of the captives, and the justification for Indian removal; the narrative went through four editions in its first year and to date, at least forty editions have appeared (Elliott and Davidson 1991, p. 32).

One of the more interesting narratives of this genre was that of the free black John Marrant whose story was lifted up by Henry Louis Gates in his work *The Signifying Monkey: A Theory of African-American Literary Criticism* (1989). Gates describes Marrant's *A Narrative of the Life of John Marrant, of New York, in North America With [an] Account of the Conversion of the King of the Cherokees and*

His Daughter as an "Indian captivity tale" and "one of the three most popular stories of Indian captivity, surpassed in number of editions only by those of Peter Williamson (1757) and Mary Jemison (1784)" (p. 142). In writing of Marrant's capture, Gates describes it thus: "Marrant, like Gronniosaw, was fifteen when captured. Wandering through the wilderness, Marrant encountered an Indian 'fortification' protected by strategically placed 'guards.' The Cherokee guard politely informed him that he must be put to death for venturing onto Cherokee land" (pp. 142–3). When brought before the executioner, Marrant began to engage in what Gates describes as a "divinely inspired fluency in Cherokee" and again later Marrant engaged in his "gift of tongues" before the Cherokee; time and again, Gates describes Marrant's fluency in Cherokee as "inspired by God."

As often occurs in the tropes of American history, there is a little bit more to this story than Marrant's "captivity" and his fluency in Cherokee being "inspired by God." Though his interpretation is literary and inspirational, Gates chooses to ignore a very simple fact expressed by Marrant early on in this narrative:

> As I was going on, and musing upon the goodness of the Lord, an Indian hunter, who stood at some distance, saw me; he hid himself behind a tree, but as I passed along he bolted out, and put his hands on my breast, which surprised me a few a moments. He then asked me where I was going? I answered I did not know, but where the Lord was pleased to guide me... To this he made me no answer, only said, I know you, and your mother and sister, and upon a little further conversation I found he did know them, having been used in winter to sell skins in our town. This alarmed me, and I wept for fear he would take me home by force; but when he saw me so affected, he said he would not take me home if I would go with him... Our employment for ten weeks and three days, was killing deer, and taking off their skins by day, which we afterwards hung on the trees to dry till they were sent for; the means of defense and security against our nocturnal enemies, always took up the evenings... A fire was kindled in the front of our temporary lodging room, and fed with fresh fuel all night, as we slept and watched by turns; and this was our defense from the dreadful animals, whose shining eyes and tremendous roar we often saw and discard during the by constant conversation with the hunter, I acquired a fuller knowledge of the Indian tongue: This, together with a sweet communion I enjoyed with God, I have considered as a preparation for the great trial I was soon after to pass through. The hunting season being now at an end, we left the woods, and directed our course towards a large Indian town, belonging to the Cherokee nation; and having reached it, I said to the hunter, they will not suffer

me to enter in. He replied, as I was with him, nobody would interrupt me. (Marrant 1785, p. 13)

So Marrant did not just wander in the Cherokee Nation nor was his fluency in Cherokee "inspired by God," but he was invited by his friend to enter the town and his fluency was acquired by nearly three months of being daily in the presence of the Cherokee. Though it is certain that neither Marrant nor the "Indian hunter" he had befriended expected that he would be seized and charged with a capital crime, it is not exactly correct to view Marrant's story as an "Indian captivity tale." That John Marrant lived among the Cherokee for another six months and served as an emissary to other Indian nations in their immediate territory only further complicates the notion of his mission as a captivity narrative.

The idea that Marrant's story does not fit the paradigm of an "Indian captivity tale" is not a unique one. In her work "Recapturing John Marrant," Benilde Montgomery (1993) argues that "Marrant does not understand himself as the victim of frivolous circumstance, but as an active participant in the evolution of a providential design" (pp. 106–107). Furthermore, she believes that Marrant sees himself as a missionary such as Jonathan Edwards or his hero George Whitefield. Rosalie Murphy Baum agrees and sees Marrant's narrative as resembling the religious essays and conversion narratives of Jonathan Edwards, John Woolman, and Roger Williams as opposed to the captivity narrative (Baum 1994, p. 537). Cedrick May (2004) sees Marrant's narrative as an ordination sermon and believes that "to study [Marrant's Narrative] primarily as a captivity narrative is to discount its emphasis on...proper Christian knowledge" (p. 556). Philip Gould (2000) asserts that Marrant's narrative turns the idea of a captivity narrative on its head: "Traditionally seen as an Indian captivity narrative (and included in modern anthologies of the genre), Marrant's work actually inverts the moral geography of Indian captivity" (p. 669).

Marrant's narrative epitomizes the complexity of dealing with early colonial encounters and the fluidity of definitions such as adoption, captivity, and slavery. What the very persons themselves may describe as "captivity" for their kin, community, and avid audiences may not have been captivity at all but something more akin to adoption or, as in Marrant's case, absorption or a communal embrace. As all of us know, families and friends are less than excited when we abandon them for even the most mundane things such as going off to college, getting married, or moving to a distant city. Therefore, the prospects of being taken from one's immediate home and being delivered into the hands of the enemy, especially when that "enemy" was considered hostile and even lacking humanity, encourages one to bend and shape the conditions of capture to better accommodate the social conditions of the time. In her work "Going Native, Telling Tales: Captivity, Collaborations, and Empire," historian Linda Colley (2000) correctly notes,

> Almost by definition, captivities of this sort, especially when protracted, involved all kinds of circulations, mixings and inversions of customary power-relations. To assume in this context a stable, binary divide between European and non-European would be to exaggerate the unvarying power of this kind of group identity and the degree to which cultures are closed. (pp. 175–6)

If this "stable, binary divide" was not true for Europeans and Indians, then the "circulations, mixings and inversions" were even much more a fluid phenomena when talking about the interactions among non-Europeans during the colonial period. Though the story of John Marrant's "captivity" among the Cherokee is most familiar, it is not the sole narrative of non-Europeans taken from the colonial establishment into a different communal environment. As early as the sixteenth century, we have the story of Estavanico, "an Arabian black, native of Acamor," who accompanied Pamphilo de Narvaez into the colonial wilderness, was captured, and spent some six years as slaves of Indians in what is now western Louisiana or eastern Texas. Estavanico became extremely fluent in indigenous languages and after he escaped his "enslavement," he served as a liaison between the Spanish and the indigenous people of the American Southwest; he was renowned as a skilled "healer" and used this ability as an *entrada* into Native communities. Ultimately, Estavanico overextended his boundaries and was killed by the Lord of Cibola:

> For three days they made inquiries about him and held a council. The account which the negro gave them of two white men who were following him, sent by a great lord, who knew about the things in the sky, and how these were coming to instruct them in divine matters, made them think that he might be a spy or guide from some nations who wished to come and conquer them, because it seemed to them unreasonable to say that the people were white in the country from which he came and that he was sent by them, he being black. Besides these other reasons, they thought it was hard of him to ask them for

turquoises and women and so they decided to kill him...(Castenada, quoted in Logan 1940, p. 49)

In his 2006 article "Following Estevanico: The Influential Presence of an African Slave in Sixteenth-century New World Historiography," Richard Gordon (2006) notes not only the complexities of representation of a "more complicated and nuanced captive state," but also the problematic historiographical representations of Estavanico (p. 187). Historians' attempts to portray Estavanico are themselves heuristic devices used to propel particularities and situational variables that suit the author's intent and not necessarily an accuracy of representation. Gordon states:

> Written from the mid-sixteenth to early-seventeenth centuries, these texts variously exploit the air of ambiguity, hybridity, and mutability that surrounds Esteban, some of which the enslaved explorer himself had cultivated. On the one hand, the writers exploit Esteban's changing states of freedom and captivity and the unclear nature of his final imprisonment and execution. On the other hand, they attempt to harness his ethnic complexity. (P. 189)

In 1526, Lucas Vasquez de Ayllon, a royal judge residing in Santo Domingo, led a voyage of 500 men and women, including African slaves and Dominican friars, to establish a Spanish colony called San Miguel de Gualdape on an island just off the coast of Savannah Georgia (Bourne 1904, p. 67). It is also reported that Lucas Vasquez de Ayllon led a group of Spanish sailors and established a temporary colony in North Carolina, probably located at the mouth of the Cape Fear River (State of North Carolina). Some historians even report that Vasquez de Ayllon attempted to settle on the Chesapeake River near what would become Jamestown Island about this same time; he is said to have brought 600 men and women, including many Negro slaves, 100 horses, and a Jesuit priest named Antonio Montesino (Fiske 1892, p. 83).

In October of that year, there was a slave revolt among the Africans under de Ayllon's command at San Miguel de Gualdape and the colony was overthrown and the Spanish departed; in a footnote in Peter Wood's *Black Majority*, he states that it is speculated that "Indians instigated the revolt" (Wood 1974, p. 3). What remained of the colony—largely African slaves—fled the aborted colony and became members of a community of the Cofitachequi Indians at the head of the Santee River in what Herbert Aptheker (1963) refers to as "the first permanent inhabitants, other than the Indians, in what was to be the United States" (p. 163). Further evidence of the permanence of this settlement of Africans among the Indians is provided for us by a later visitor by the name of Hernando de Soto who, when he plundered a temple mound at the holy city of Talomeco, found "Biscayan axes of iron and rosaries with their crosses" and other items of European descent that had been left there by the refugee African slaves (Bourne 1904, p. 69). Now, if the slave revolt were indeed inspired by the local Indians and the African slaves fled to live among the Cofitachequi, then we, again, encounter a complex scenario in which the traditional understandings and language of colonial encounter becomes exceedingly problematic.

When Hernando de Soto arrived among the very same Cofitachequi Indians of the coastal Carolinas in 1540, he also brought with him African slaves bearing Spanish surnames including the slave of one Andre de Vasconcelos. When Hernando de Soto and his party first met with the "Queen of the Cofitachequi," she noticed this slave of Andre de Vasconcelos and in a matter of seconds, the borders that separated the "old world" and the "new world" were crossed and matters of state became superseded by matters of the heart. A few days later, de Soto seized the Beloved Woman and forced her to lead his expedition into the interior coastlands in search of gold. As she was leading them on their way, she "left the road, with the excuse of going in the thicket, where, deceiving them, she so concealed herself that for all their search she could not be found" (Jameson 1907, p. 177).

De Soto, all the more frustrated because the Beloved Woman had fled with a box of "unbored pearls" of great value, decided to move on to Guaxule (ibid.). However, it seems that the lady had made other plans and had arranged for a rendezvous with other members from de Soto's party. These included an "Indian slave boy from Cuba," a "slave belonging to Don Carlos, a Berber, well versed in Spanish," and "Gomez, a negro belonging to Vasco Goncalvez who spoke good Spanish" (Bourne 1904, p. 104). Alimamos, a horseman sent by de Soto to find the fugitives, "got lost" and happened upon the refugee slaves. He "labored with the slaves to make leave of their evil designs." Two of the slaves did just that and returned to de Soto but "when they arrived, the Governor wished to hang them" (Jameson 1907, p. 178).

However, the horseman Alimamos reported yet another story that was something altogether shocking. He stated that "the *Cacica* remained in Xuala, with a slave of Andre de Vasconcelas, who would not come with him (Alimamos), and that it was very very sure that they lived together as man and wife, and were to go together to Cutafichiqui" (p. 172). In an effort that would be repeated countless times over the next 300 years, refugee slaves fled from their masters to the sanctuary villages of the neighboring Indians and were thus welcomed and protected. Equally important to our collective history, the "Queen of Cofitachequi" and the "slave of Andre de Vasconcelas" returned to their "village of the dogwoods" on the banks of the Savannah River near Silver Bluff, S.C. where they would begin a life together in what would become a prominent Aframerindian community.

Some years later in 1619, Sir Edwin Sandys—the newly appointed treasurer of the Virginia Company headed by Captain John Smith—put forward the idea of a college where "Indian youth would be acquainted with the more sophisticated aspects of Christianity and civility" (Morgan 1975, p. 98). In order to finance this enterprise, the Virginia Company acquired a particular commodity described in a letter from John Rolfe, widowed husband of Pocahontas, to Sir Edwin Sandys:

> About the latter end of August, a Dutch man of Warr of the burden of 160 tons arrived at Point Comfort, the Comandor's name was Capt. Jope, his Pilot for the West Indies one Mr. Marmaduke an Englishman. They mett with the "Treasurer" in the West Indies and determined to hold consort shipp hetherward, but in their passage lost one the other. He brought not anything but 20 and odd Negroes, which the Governor and Cape Merchant bought for victualle [whereof he was in greate need as he pretended] at the best and easyest rate they could. He hadd a lardge and ample Comyssion from his Excellency to range and to take purchase in the West Indies. (Kingsbury n.d.)

These Africans were not "slaves" as many people think because there were no slave laws in place at this time; these "20 and odd Negroes" were initially treated as indentured servants and given the same opportunities for freedom dues as whites. These Africans were settled on "the governor's land," Governor Yeardley's 2,200-acre tobacco plantation. That land was home to the Weyanoke people, in what is now Charles City County, Virginia (Weyanoke Association).

When these Africans had worked off their period of indentured servitude, they joined the immediate community and sought out those persons most like themselves with whom they could settle. They found the Native peoples of southeastern Virginia who shared with them a culture similar to their own—one rooted in a sacred relationship to the subtropical coastlands of the middle Atlantic. They forged ties and kinship and bonds of love into a culture that would forever change the landscape of southeastern Virginia. It has been estimated that as many as 80 percent of those persons in southeastern Virginia who are known today as African Americans have significant Native ancestry (Weyanoke Association).

However, Sandys's school would carry forward as he had envisioned it; yet it encountered a certain problematic nature: it seems that the Native peoples of southeastern Virginia had little or no inclination to becoming "acquainted with the more sophisticated aspects of Christianity and civility." Governor George Yeardley of Virginia supported Sandys's plan for a school and devised a plan to find students to fill the school. As the Powhatan chief and his people were reluctant to give up their children to be educated, Yeardley proposed that a group of English and Indian soldiers could engage in a raid upon a Siouan group beyond the falls of the James River. The raiding party would split the captured corn, land, and "booty of male and female children." Yeardley believed that the male children taken might serve to "furnish the intended college at Henrico" (Axtell 1985, p. 190).

A primary goal of the Virginia Company was "[the] propagating of Christian religion to such People, as yet live in Darkness and Miserable ignorance of the True Knowledge and Worship of God, and may in time bring the Infidels and Savages, living in those Parts, to Human civility, and to a settled and quiet government" (McDonald 1914, p. 24). The building of the missionary "university" was supposedly a major vehicle through which this goal was to be accomplished. In January 1691 the Reverend James Blair was in London seeking a royal charter for the College of William and Mary in order to keep Indian children "in Sicknesse and health, in Meat, drink, Washing, Lodgeing, Medicine, Cloathes, books, and Education from the first beginning of Letters til they are ready to receive Orders and be thought Sufficient to be sent abroad to preach and Convert Indians." As, again, the people of the Powhatan Confederation were less than willing to have their children adopted in colonial society, a cost was included in the budget of the new college for "buying or Procureing such Children" (Axtell 1985, p. 190).

Still having problems filling their new "university," the Virginians turned to their neighbor in the south to provide Indian children. When the Tuscarora Indians of North Carolina arose against colonial depredations, Lieutenant Governor Alexander Spotswood marched a large troop of Virginia militia to the border and demanded that the Tuscarora sign a treaty with the Virginians. Terms of that treaty included sending two sons of Tuscarora headmen as "hostages" to be "brought up at the college" there to serve as "security" for the Tuscarora's fidelity and to take the first step toward the conversion of the "whole Nations...to the Christian faith" (Axtell 1985, p. 191). The Tuscarora sent twenty sons to the Virginians to prevent military retribution; not happy, the college governors continued the practice of "buying Indians of remote nations taken in war to be educated" (ibid.). The Indians continued in their reluctance to send their children to be educated because they remembered the time they had tried to do so earlier—they had been shipped off to other countries and sold as slaves.

We have many captivity narratives within the canon of American literature, but we have very few, if any, that reflect the story of these young persons taken captive and brought up within an alien environment in which the line between evangelism and enslavement grew very thin. The story of missionary schools throughout colonial America is that of students brought forcibly into institutions where they were taught the civilized values of European society such as farming and husbandry for the men and housework for the women. "Hostages" all, their conversion came at a very high price. The poignant stories of these individuals serve to remind us that the lines between "adoption, captivity, and slavery" must be framed within a discussion of the function of the power to define more so than the ability to describe. We adopt. We educate. We civilize. They capture. They enslave. They destroy.

The focus of this book has been on the complexity of the interactions among the various people of the early colonial period and how the language that we have used throughout history to describe these relations has failed to capture the true nature of these relationships. Nowhere is this more valid than in the descriptions of the interactions among the people of the American Southeast. As discussed in chapter five, the very words and images that form the core of our collective understanding of this period are themselves distorted by the cultural and ideological inclinations of these so-called first-person accounts as well as those who promoted them. Slavery is a critical part of our southern history but that history itself, as we learned from chapters one–three, is myopic because it ignores the role that slavery played in transforming American society long before slavery became that "peculiar institution."

In reality, our understandings, today, of the meanings of "adoption, captivity, and slavery" are as fluid as were the actual practices themselves during the colonial period. In the stories given in this chapter, it is difficult to identify the captive and the capturer or even the enslaved and the enslaver. Often, as in the case of enslaved runaway Africans among the Seminole of Florida, the line between adoption, captivity, and enslaved becomes so fuzzy as to challenge even the greatest of our scholars much less the poor slave-owners of the Old South. Perhaps it was this very liminality that led the federal government to remove the Seminole to the Indian Territory in what was the bloodiest war in American history up to the civil war. Perhaps it is this very liminality that speaks to the heart of the struggle of who is and who isn't a Seminole, Mvskoke, or Tsalagi even unto this day; the whole term "Freedmen" is itself a paradox because the African American presence among the Five Nations cannot be collectivized into a singular term such as "Freedmen." Our collective histories are so interwoven and the lines of relationship so complex that to begin to define is an arbitrary exercise in power if not in futility. We can, at best, only describe these relationships.

Emblematic of the challenges we face as historians describing the relationships among various cultures in collision and collusion during the colonial period is that of Nancy Ward, or Nan'yehi, of the Tsalagi. Some consider Nan'yehi to be the first slave-owner within the Tsalagi Nation of the Old South, but, again, things are a little more complicated than this. Nan'yehi was born in 1738 in the Cherokee town of Chota, a "Peace Town" or "Mother Town" in the Overhill region of the Cherokee Nation. She was a member of the Wolf Clan. Her mother, whose actual name is not known, is often called Tame Deer, and was a daughter of Chief Moytoy I and a sister of Attakullakulla. Her father, Fivekiller, was probably part Leni Lenape (Cengage Learning 2008).

Nan'yehi's first husband was the Cherokee man by the name of Kingfisher. Nan'yehi and Kingfisher fought side by side at the Battle of Taliwa against the Mvskoke in 1755; she was about eighteen years old at this time. When Kingfisher was killed, she took up her slain husband's gun and, singing a war song, led the Cherokees in a rout of the enemy. Out of her loss was born a decisive victory for her people and a title of honor for her: the title of "Ghighua" or "Beloved Woman." For her valor in the Battle of Taliwa, Nan'yehi was given the life of a captured African American who had fought on the side of the Mvskoke (Access Genealogy 2008). Although she did take him home with her, whether or not he was "adopted" or "enslaved" is a story much to the preference of the storyteller. Whatever the case, he returned with her to the Cherokee Nation and became part of her entourage (Hoig 1998, p. 33). Some people refer to him as a slave; I like to think of him as a person who was able to snatch victory from the jaws of defeat.

It was up to the "beloved women" of the nation such as Nan'yehi to decide the fate of these individuals; they could "by the wave of a swan's wing, deliver a wretch condemned by the council, and already tied to the stake" (Timberlake in Williams 1948, p. 37). The Cherokee *atsi nahtsa'i,* or "captives without clans" (Perdue 1979, p. 12), were individuals captured through warfare and often given to clans who had lost members in the conflict (Reed 1970, p. 192). Women were in control of the system of indigenous slavery prior to contact with European society (De Vorsey 1971, p. 73). Once rescued, these persons owed their life to the Cherokee Nation. If accepted into the clan to replace lost members, they gained identity and protection through the clan and citizenship in the nation. If not, these individuals existed outside of the clan structure and on the periphery of Cherokee society. Though not members of the Cherokee Nation, neither were they considered to be a commodity (Perdue 1979, p. 13).

In 1780, following a Cherokee attack on the Fort Watauga settlement on the Watauga River (in present-day Elizabethton, Tennessee), Nan'yehi used her power as *Ghigau.* She came upon Mrs. Lydia Russell Bean, who was tied to a post and was about to be executed by two Tsalagi soldiers (Kidwell 1992, p. 103). Nan'yehi rescued Mrs. Bean and then she took her into her home and nursed her back to health from injuries she suffered in the battle (Mooney, 1900, p. 490). Mrs. Bean taught Nan'yehi how to weave, revolutionizing the Cherokee garments, which at the time were a combination of hides and cloth bought from traders. Mrs. Bean also rescued two of her dairy cows from the settlement, and brought them to Nan'yehi. From her "slave," Nan'yehi learned to raise cattle and to eat dairy products, which would sustain the Cherokee when hunting was bad (Perdue 1998, p. 116). Thus, in saving the life of her captive, she was able to prolong the life of her people. Throughout her long life, Nan'yehi used her remarkable power and presence to save the lives of captives time and again and worked pervasively to promote the best interests of her people. When she died in 1822, a different sort of captive was released, "a light rose from her body, fluttered like a bird around the room, and finally flew out the open door"; the light was last seen moving in the direction of Chota—mother town of the Cherokee (Carney 2001, p. 137).

Before we conclude, let us return again to the story of John Marrant and address a part of his life that is often not something that finds common discussion. Having become an Indian and returned to his family who did not recognize him as such, Marrant stripped away his Cherokee identity and escaped the bondage of a person that he was not. "I was then made known to all the family, to my friends, and acquaintances, who received me, and were glad, and rejoiced: Thus the dead was brought to life again; thus the lost was found" (Marrant 1785, p. 4). In a remarkably perceptive analysis, John Saillant (1999) notes that Marrant was no longer the black boy entertainer, nor the Indian, but had emerged as a black man, "who came to identify himself as African" and had become "a black visionary laboring among the dispossessed and forging an Africanist theology for them." As Saillant describes it, Marrant located his blackness "not only in his skin but also in his immersion in a black community" (p. 303). If we are to understand Saillant correctly, perhaps Marrant was indeed "captured" by the Cherokee; we might even say he was captivated. However, eventually he returned to who he was or perhaps emerged as someone he had never been.

John Marrant took a position as a "free carpenter" on the Jenkins plantation just outside of Charleston where he encountered enslaved "negro children" and his heart went out to them and he endeavored to teach them the rudiments of his Christian faith. What started out small soon blossomed into a full-blown mission; Marrant set up an evening school for about thirty slaves on the Jenkins plantation (Brooks 2003, p. 91). As with the Cherokee, Marrant sought to bring to the slaves on the plantation the word of the holy gospel. However, the mistress of the plantations was less than pleased at Marrant's efforts. Being shocked to find her slaves at prayer, she had her husband round up a posse and raid the prayer-meeting. "As the poor creatures came out they caught them, and tied them together with cords," Marrant reported, "till the next morning, when all they caught, men, women, and children, were strip'd naked and tied, their feet to a stake, their hands to the arm of a tree, and so severely flogged that the blood ran from their backs and sides to the floor, to make them promise they would leave off praying." Marrant warned the slave-owners "that the blood of these poor negroes that he had spilt that morning would be required by God at his hands" (Saillant 2008). In spite of their beating and the threats to Marrant, he continued to "steal away" with his congregation for nightly meetings in different corners of the plantation. When the slave-owner's wife passed away from illness, he joined with Marrant and the slaves in worship though he was never to free his slaves (Saillant 1999, p. 304). Though we may engage in semantic differentials among the definitions of adoption, captivity, and slavery, John Marrant had come to know first hand the very profound differences among these various words not by description but by experience. These experiences would shape his future life and work.

Not long after taking up his mission, Marrant was again captured. He describes it in his narrative, "In those troublesome times [the American revolution], I was pressed onboard the Scorpion sloop of war as their musician as they were told I could play on music." Unlike his "captivity" with the Cherokee that lasted a mere six months, Marrant was held by the British for more than six years and even began to lose faith; with great shame, he confessed, "that a lamentable stupor crept over my spiritual vivacity, life, and vigour; I got cold and dead" (Ennis 2002, p. 132). Even in the face of hardship, Marrant found biblical metaphors for his nearly daily challenges; in the battle of Charleston, he was swept overboard and nearly drowned but escaped death by praying as had Jonah when he faced a similar ordeal. In 1781, Marrant was discharged from the Royal Navy after his wounds made him incapable of "serving the King again"; it seems, as though with the Cherokee, his "captivity" had led him to an identification with his captors that again caused him to redefine himself. Some argue that Marrant joined the British Navy to escape slavery; however, he was never a slave but a free black who certainly knew first hand what slavery was and what freedom meant. Marrant is now considered a "Black Loyalist" and moved to Nova Scotia following his release from the British Navy. Again, we must wrestle with the problem of definition; was Marrant captured by the British or captivated with life as a Briton?

Many years later, John Marrant again appeared on the American scene, this time in Boston at African Lodge #459 chartered to Prince Hall and fourteen men of color by The Grand Lodge of England on September 29, 1784, as the first lodge of Black Freemasons in the United States of America. Prince Hall, himself, believed that all persons possessed "a natural and unalienable right to that freedom that the great Parent of the Universe hath bestowed equally on all mankind" (Hall, Bess, and others 1947, p. 5). On June 24, 1789, African Lodge #459 held its annual St. John's Day celebration. The Chaplain of African Lodge #459, the former "savage" John Marrant, delivered the St. John's Day sermon to assembled brothers. He beseeched them to "present your bodies a living sacrifice, holy, acceptable to God...let love be without dissimulation, abhor that which is evil, cleave to that which is good. These and many other duties are required of us as Christians, every one of which are like so many links of a chain" (Marrant, A Sermon Preached on the 24th Day of June 1789, Being the Festival of St. John the Baptist, At the

Request of the Right Worshipful the Grand Master Prince Hall, and the Rest of the Brethren of the African Lodge of the Honourable Society of Free & Accepted, 1789, p. 7).

Marrant told his audience that a black exodus to Africa, the restoration of a pure and covenanted black community to their Zion, was an element of God's providential design. Marrant preached that this restoration would be as a benevolent overruling of the sins of the slave traders and slaveholders (Saillant 2008). Marrant spoke strongest against those that would despise their fellow men, as "tho' they were not of the same species with themselves, and would in their power deprive them of the blessings and comforts of life which God in his bountiful goodness hath freely given to all his creatures to improve and enjoy. Surely such monsters never came out of the hand of God in such a forlorn condition" (Marrant, Sermon, 1789, p. 7).

In conclusion the lines between adoption, captivity, and slavery are quite nebulous and the challenge for us today in identifying among adoptee, captive, and slave as well as adopter, captor, and enslaver is as complex and complicated as it was during the actual colonial period itself. This is nowhere more true than among persons of indigenous or African descent as we have explored in this chapter: John Marrant's experiences ran the panoply of concepts envisioned by the editors of this volume; the "Queen of the Cofitachequi" was both the captive and captor; the slaves of Ayllon rebelled against their enslavement and would ultimately become adopted into neighboring indigenous peoples; the "endentured servants" of Sandys's experiment in a "missionary university" fared far better than those who ultimately became the "students" of what would become William and Mary [or many of the other elite institutions of the colonial period]; Nan'yehi's role as *Ghigau* gave her the power of definition over Cherokee captives and her decisions regarding life or death were as much utilitarian as merciful.

As mentioned earlier, we must be comfortable with our role as describing the particular events in the encounters between colonial forces and be reticent to easily define these as "adoption," "captivity," or "slavery." Even with our descriptions, we must recognize the tentative nature of these expeditions and appreciate the subtle contexts from which these descriptions arise, the profound nature of power relationships entailed in any cultural encounter, and the challenge of distance both temporal and intellectual that seems a prerequisite of scholarly engagement. If Henry Louis Gates misses the boat by referring to John Marrant's story as a "captivity narrative," then we must appreciate his "original intent" (borrowing a term from politics). Today interpretists on the web and elsewhere refer to Nan'yehi as "the first Cherokee slaveowner" (Cengage Learning, 2008), then we have to understand that this term is not so much a function of ignorance but one of the comfortable power of hermeneutical distance or (to borrow a phrase once again) an heuristic algorithm. When scholars meet to try to come to terms with the very nature of the colonial encounter, we must emerge with the recognition that we can, at best, grasp cautiously at the very fluid and permanently itinerant nature of these concepts yet only in expression and not in actuality.

This fact, however, must not inhibit our endeavors. There are those who seek to understand these early encounters in discrete, almost finite, terms; they are uncomfortable around uncertainty. In this world, description without definition is somehow inadequate. This is the very nature of the academy; this is the raison d'etre of the scholarly endeavor. However, we have a higher responsibility; we have to understand and appreciate the majesty of the mystery of these colonial encounters.

In the stories of both the Tsalagi and the Mvskoke of the American Southeast, there is the lesson of the corn mother; in both of these stories, the curiosity of the sons to understand the workings of magic leads to the unbecoming of the corn mother. In her telling of the Mvskoke version of this story, Jean Chaudhuri states that the corn mother admonishes her progeny for the implications of his inquiry, "Now, you have to take care of everything and work to deal with the responsibilities of your curiosity" (Jean Chaudhuri; Joyotpaul Chaudhuri 2001, p. 63). The responsibility of our curiosity is the recognition of the probability that our every attempt to articulate, define, and refine the parameters of these colonial encounters is simply an exercise of sisyphean proportion.

That this exercise remains ever elusive and our understandings remarkably muddled even to this day needs no further evidence than that struggle among the Five Nations of the American Southeast over the definition of its own citizens of mixed heritage. In her pivotal work *Blood Politics: Race, Culture, and Identity in the Cherokee Nation of Oklahoma,* Circe Sturm attempts to deconstruct the clever narratives that reconstruct the identity of persons of mixed Native/African descent within the Cherokee Nation as persons who belonged to the nation yet were not of the nation. As the work of scholars such as James Brooks, Claudio Saunt, Tiya Miles, and Celia Naylor have brilliantly shown, the identity of persons of mixed race within the Five Nations is as much a matter of social and political construction today as it was a literary one within the earlier period. The history of the legal cases of persons of mixed heritage within has been so lengthy and complex that the Cherokee Nation, only a few years ago, set aside the legal wranglings and voted to disenfranchise persons in the Cherokee Nation of African descent.

The U.S. Congress, in H.R. 2824, seeking to punish the Cherokee Nation of Oklahoma for that vote aims to "sever United States' government relations with the Cherokee Nation of Oklahoma until such time as the Cherokee Nation of Oklahoma restores full tribal citizenship to the Cherokee Freedmen disenfranchised in the March 3, 2007, Cherokee Nation vote and fulfills all its treaty obligations with the Government of the United States, and for other purposes" (CONGRESS 2008). The Cherokee Nation, as late as January of 2011, filed an appeal in its tribal Supreme Court to defend the constitutional amendment that effectively barred freedmen who don't have tribal blood from Cherokee citizenship. If the Cherokee Nation of Oklahoma can't even to this day define its own citizens without regard to race, how are we to distinguish among who was held captive by one culture or another or who was simply captivated with one culture or another.

Perhaps that is a good thing. It seems that far too many Americans have little tolerance for ambiguity and go about the world exercising their predilection for defining words such as "freedom" and "democracy" not just for ourselves but for "other" folks, too. Perhaps we should just learn an appreciation for the complexity that renders our past all the more intriguing and the future all the more challenging. Maybe I just have a little bit too much affection for the foggy valleys that make up the mountains of our historical research. Maybe that doesn't make me a good scholar. Maybe, it doesn't even make me a good American. However, I firmly believe it makes me a better person.

Chapter 8

A Christian Disposition: Religious Identity in the Meeker Captivity Narrative

Brandi Denison

On September 29, 1879, at the White River Ute Agency near present-day Meeker, Colorado, Ute Native Americans captured Arvilla Meeker, Josephine Meeker, Flora Price, and Flora's two children.[1] Nestled in a lush valley with craggy mountains on every side, the White River Ute Agency was an outpost for the U.S. government's plan to lead Native Americans to civilization. On this particular afternoon though, the agency's "civilizing" activity ceased as Ute men fired shots at Euro-American employees. To protect themselves, the women seized the children and hid in the milk house, which protected them until they smelled smoke. Fearing the Utes would set fire to the building, they sneaked into the juniper trees surrounding the agency. At first, they did not see the extent of the bloodshed; all nine of the agency's men, including Nathan Meeker, the U.S. Indian Agent to the Utes and the patriarch of the Meeker family, were dead. Twenty miles away in a separate but related confrontation several Cavalry soldiers and over thirty Utes had died. Out in the open, the escapees attracted the attention of the Ute men. Sixty-three-year-old Arvilla had broken her leg two years earlier and suffered a gunshot wound that day—the bullet grazed the skin of her thigh, "plowing a three-inch deep path" (J Meeker 1976, p. 13). Arvilla's injuries and the two children limited the women's escape; they had no choice but to surrender to the Utes. Abandoning the corpses of agency men, the women rode over ninety miles through mountainous terrain as the Utes attempted to escape the U.S. Cavalry (Congressional Record 1880; J Meeker 1976).

Although western Colorado was the Ute's ancestral home, their familiarity with the rocky canyons, winding streams, and towering mesas did not prevent the Cavalry from locating the group. Twenty-three days after the outbreak, on October 21, 1879, Charles Adams, former Indian Agent to the Utes and special agent of the Post Office, successfully led the Cavalry to the Ute encampment. Adams's presence precipitated the men to debate the captive's release. In a newspaper article and captivity narrative, Arvilla provided insight into the Ute arguments. It was a lengthy and stormy tribal council meeting, with the "war party" advocating using the captives to negotiate clemency for the Utes that had killed the agency employees. The "peace party" stood in opposition, advocating the immediate release of the captives. Resolution seemed impossible. However, all debate ceased when Susan, a Ute woman and sister to the prominent chief Ouray, "burst into the lodge in a magnificent wrap and demanded that the captives be set free, war or no war." At Susan's insistence, the Ute men decided to release the captives. The captivity narrative explained Susan's actions were because of her "kind, noble, Christian disposition" (J Meeker 1976, p. 13; *Greeley Tribune*, November 12, 1879).

This chapter will contextualize the captive narrative's description of Susan's "Christian disposition." Rather than documenting the historical Susan's religious beliefs, this chapter will examine the role her representation played in the late nineteenth century. Native Americans throughout the history of contact with Euro-Americans did convert to Christianity, and as James Axtell (1990) has noted, scholars cannot dismiss these conversions (pp. 100–21). Rather than accounting for Susan's religious beliefs or practices, this essay augments Axtell's (1992) argument that Euro-Americans remade Native Americans through a set of normative stereotypes of the "Other." In the late nineteenth century, Euro-Americans drawing on representations of religiosity in order to convey representations of Native American religiosity was one way Euro-Americans attempted to remake America's inhabitants through a set of normative stereotypes.

Scholars often ignore the religious language in nineteenth-century captivity narratives, suggesting that after the Puritan era, captivity narrative authors aimed to spread anti-Native American propaganda rather than express religious experiences (Derounian-Stodola, Zabelle, and Levernier 1993; Fitzpatrick 1991, pp. 1–26; Namias 1993; Pearce 1947; VanDerBeets 1984). However, religious language infused the nineteenth-century propaganda narratives. While few nineteenth-century captives framed their experience as religious awakening, many used religious language to understand their experience of colonial contact, fueling the fire of propaganda. The common use of religious language in nineteenth-century captivity narratives reflects the religious fervor of that era as well as Euro-American interest in converting Native Americans to Christianity. Scholar of U.S. religious history Jon Butler (1990) has argued that the nineteenth century in America was a "spiritual hothouse," indicating ascension of religious beliefs and practice rather than a declension after the Puritan era. Religious groups also had a historic interest in Native American missions, as demonstrated by the Massachusetts Bay Colony Seal, with an image of a Native American begging Englanders to "Come and Help Save us" to the American Board of Foreign Mission's funding of missions to Native American reservations (Bowden 1981). Given the religious electricity of nineteenth-century United States and long-standing efforts on behalf of religious groups to convert Native Americans, religious themes in the era's captivity narratives are to be expected.

The Meeker captivity narrative is a propaganda piece; however, it reflects the uncertainty of a nation struggling with reconciling the principles of "manifest destiny" with Christian reform movements (Stephanson 1995; Weinberg 1963). On the one hand, *vacuum domicilium* granted "unfarmed" land to Euro-Americans, but on the other, a Christian nation had a responsibility to lead undeveloped peoples toward civilization. The Meeker outbreak occurred during national debate about governmental policy toward Native Americans, with Christian reformers advocating assimilation on the one hand and Western settlers advocating removal or extermination. This chapter will examine (1) the religious idealism that framed the national policy toward Native Americans; (2) the religious idealism that carried Nathan Meeker and his family to the agency; and finally (3) the representation of Susan's Christian disposition and the role it played in simplifying the complex issue of Euro-American settlement in Native American lands.

These questions have been informed by postcolonial studies that suggest Euro-American representations of the Other reveal more about Euro-American culture than about the cultural practices of the Other (Pratt 1992; Said 1978; Takaki 2000). Susan's religious representation in the captivity narrative occurred within the highly charged political arena of the American West contact zone, "social spaces where disparate cultures meet, clash, and grapple with each other...in highly asymmetrical relations of domination and subordination" (Pratt 1992, p. 4). While Susan's actions were extolled, the captivity narrative filtered the explanation of her courage and protection through a Euro-American, Christian worldview.

In order to understand the captivity narrative, a brief overview of Ute involvement in the southwest captivity economy is necessary. Before the pressures of U.S. colonial expansion, Ute nomadic life followed the cycle of the seasons. They summered in the mountains, collecting fruits, berries, and hunting large animals. In the fall, they would camp at lower altitudes, continuing to hunt. When the cold mountain winters arrived, they migrated to lower valleys for the mild winters. The arrival of spring signaled a return to higher grounds, the harvesting of fruits and greens, as well as fishing in cool mountain streams. While the Utes controlled a large territory, family groups returned to the same places year after year. Like many other Native American groups, gender determined labor activities. The men were the primary hunters and defenders of the tribe. Women gathered fruits, vegetables, and nuts. They also processed the results of the men's hunt, tanning hides and drying meat (Jefferson et al. 1972; Lewis 1984, pp. 22–3).

The arrival of the Spanish in the seventeenth century altered the cultural landscape of the Southwest and the mountainous west through the introduction of the horse and the exploitation of the region's captivity economy. Smaller in number than surrounding nations, the Utes were frequent victims of the slave trade. Eager to protect themselves, the Utes aspired to acquire numerous horses through trading pelts and furs with the Spanish. Like other Plains Indians, the horse transformed Ute culture by opening up a wider range of hunting territory, intensifying the male warrior culture. In 1879, Utes acted out of a long history a captivity economy, in which human captives were a key component of political negotiations (Brooks 2002, pp. 148–59, 301–303; Jefferson et al. 1972). The incident at the White River Ute Agency and the subsequent captivity was the result of several years of tension between the White River Utes and the U.S. government (Coneah 1982, p. 18; Quintana 2004, p. 6).

The expanding Euro-American interest in the Colorado territory led to a series of treaties with the Utes. In 1863, the Tabeguache band of Utes agreed to a treaty that restricted Utes to the western portion of the Colorado Territory. In exchange for the land and mineral rights, the U.S. government agreed to pay the Utes $10,000 annually in livestock, goods, and provisions that would transition them into a farm-based life. In 1868, the Utes signed the Kit Carson treaty, which expanded the acreage of Ute land but restricted Ute movements outside the reservation. The treaty established the White River Ute Agency to aid the "civilization" of the Utes as well as to distribute the annuity goods granted under the 1863 treaty (Osburn 1998, pp. 9–20; Quintana 2004, pp. 1–9).

At the same time, the U.S. government policy toward Native Americans had been under scrutiny by Eastern religious reformers. In response, President Ulysses S. Grant formalized the "Peace Policy" in 1873. The policy reflected strategies that had already been in place, such as placing Native Americans on reservations and distributing rations, with a focus toward transforming Native Americans from their hunting/gathering culture into an agriculturalist and husbandry culture. However, the distinctive aspect of the policy was that the government turned over the reservation administration and ration distribution to American churches. The religious organizations were in charge of appointing Indian agents who were "competent, upright, faithful, moral, and religious." In addition to distributing high-quality government rations, the Indian agents were to manage the construction of schools and churches on the reservations that would teach Indians to appreciate "the comforts and benefits of a Christian civilization and thus be prepared ultimately to assume the duties and privileges of citizenship" (Prucha 1984, p. 153). The government divided the agencies among the Methodists, Quakers, Presbyterians, Episcopalians, Catholics, Baptists, Lutherans, Congregationalists, and Unitarians (p. 161).

At the White River Ute Agency, most of the Native Americans retained their nomadic lifestyle, viewing the agency as a new stop on their itinerant lifestyle. They were not interested in remaining at the agency year-round because of its location and climate. At nearly 8,000 feet above sea level, the growing season was between three and four months, with temperatures regularly well below freezing in the winter. Most preferred to return to lower altitudes and warmer climates during the cold months. The agency could not be a center for agricultural and religious instruction without "students." The Unitarian church that was responsible for appointing agents to the White River Agency was in Boston, far removed from the pragmatic concerns of living in the isolated mountains of Colorado. While the agents posted were spiritually qualified, they did not have the practical tools necessary to cope with the cold winters, the language skills to communicate with the Utes, or the administrative skills to deliver the government rations (Decker 2004, p. 64).

During the 1870s, the Utes were dissatisfied with the government's recognition of the treaties. They were unhappy about the distribution and the quality of rations and the continued encroachment of miners and ranchers onto their reservation. Disputes over the government-issued rations began in 1877 with the Unitarian-appointed Indian agent before Nathan Meeker, Reverend E. H. Danforth. Due to miscommunication and confusion about shipping cost responsibility, the 1877 ration shipment sat in a warehouse in Rawlins, Wyoming. The rations that the Utes did receive while Danforth was the agent were subpar. Danforth filed his monthly reports to the Indian Commissioner with complaints on the Utes' behalf. He reported the coffee was "not enough and not so good as the previous years," the tobacco was not strong enough, and the sugar was "damp and heavy" (Letter from Danforth to CIA, February 22, 1879). The quality of the goods along with the lack of flour at the agency meant that few Utes camped around the agency. Without flour rations, the Utes needed to rely more heavily on game in order to fulfill their nutritional needs. Rather than using bow and arrows to hunt, the Utes used the more efficient rifle. However, the Office of Indian Affairs issued a circular prohibiting the sale of ammunition to the Utes on reservation land and required a military escort for the Utes every time they left the reservation. As a result, Utes frequently sneaked off the reservation in order to travel about ninety miles to trade for ammunition, alarming the surrounding Euro-American settlers. In 1878, residents near the reservation sent a letter to the Boston Unitarian church, to complain about their administration of the agency. They argued Danforth's "course of administration is revolutionary and if pursued it will cause a collision between the Indians and the settlers in the Snake and Bear River Valleys" and that the geographic isolation of the settlers would result in extraordinary casualties if a "collision" were to occur (Letter from settlers of Snake and Bear River Valleys). Danforth's unpopularity with the Utes, the settlers' complaints, and the rotting supplies in Rawlins contributed to his loss of appointment (Decker 2004, pp. 64–5).

The change in administration at the White River Ute Agency reflected a change in policy at the national level. President Hayes, elected in 1876, appointed Carl Schurz as the secretary of the interior. Schurz was a vocal opponent of the Peace Policy and by 1882 the government had regained all administrative control of Native American agencies. However, Schurz maintained the same goal for Native Americans, assimilation into the United States. He even retained the same means—education of Native American men in agriculture and women in housekeeping. Yet, he disagreed that churches were best equipped to solve these problems and instead hired agents that were agricultural experts (Prucha 1984, pp. 194–5). In short, the governmental policy shifted from cultivating souls to cultivating soil.

In 1878, the commissioner of Indian affairs selected Nathan Meeker as the representative to the White River Ute Agency because of his agricultural experience and his political connections. Meeker provided a bridge between the reformers who advocated that Indians must become Christians before they could be farmers and those who argued that mechanical and agricultural skills were the path to assimilation. Meeker was born in Euclid, Ohio, in 1817. He attended Oberlin College, an intellectual center for the abolition movement. While attending school, he was part of the Campbell/Stone Movement, a Bible-centered restoration movement that later developed into the Disciples of Christ. After his marriage to Arvilla Delight Smith, he moved to the Trumball Phalanx, an agrarian socialist experiment based on the ideas of Charles Fourier and the Brook Farm experiment. Four years of failed crops and mounting debt forced Meeker to leave the commune. Despite being a lifelong temperance man, he opened a pharmacy that also sold liquor. When they applied to a Disciples of Christ church, the membership board rejected their application based on Meeker's store. Disenchanted with the board's decision, he left organized religion forever, though he continued to consider himself a highly religious person (Decker 2004, pp. 69–90; Werner 1985, pp. 2–14).

During his youth, Meeker wrote for several newspapers, as a Civil War correspondent and as an agricultural commentator. His work attracted the attention of Horace Greeley, who offered him a job as the agricultural editor for the *New York Herald Tribune*. On his way to Utah to report on the irrigation practices of the Latter-day Saints (LDS), a snowstorm forced Meeker to stop in Denver. Upon the recommendation of a fellow traveler, he journeyed about sixty miles north of Denver, along the Cache de Poudre River. Always a visionary, he looked at the vast, flat plains with a river nearby and saw opportunity. He abandoned his project to report on the LDS and returned to New York with ideas of a cooperative township floating in his head. In 1869, Horace Greeley and Meeker drafted the charter for the Union Colony—with Meeker as the president and Greeley the treasurer. They published an advertisement in *Tribune*, calling for temperance men, a strong work ethic, and with at least $3,000 in liquid capital to form an upstanding, moral society on the plains of Colorado. The response was overwhelming, with over six hundred letters of interest received. Meeker selected people who would be able to sustain themselves financially, who had a sense of the hardships of agricultural life, and those that upheld the spirit of temperance ideals. The project attracted the attention of P. T. Barnum, who brought his celebrity to the project as well as his funds. In 1870, hundreds of settlers arrived in the northern plains of Colorado from the East Coast in order to realize Meeker's visions of an agrarian utopian community (N. Meeker Papers, Denver Public Library WH1680; Colorado Historical Society).

Like most experiments in utopian communities, Meeker's attempt was marred by more failures than successes. Although his irrigation system became the basis for western water management, it was expensive and flooded basements (Ganoe 1938, pp. 59–78; Hess 1912, pp. 807–33). The land was rocky and dry. Without a working irrigation system, 1,400 newly planted trees withered and vegetable gardens blew away. Many settlers left angry with the management of the project and overwhelmed by the labor of turning an arid land into a lush garden. Just a few years after the settlers arrived, Greeley died with Nathan Meeker in debt to his estate. Greeley's daughters urged Meeker to repay the debt. While Meeker was able to maintain a subsistence level of pay, he could not repay the debt while continuing as editor to the Greeley *Tribune* and as the colony founder.

Meeker began sending out letters of interest, applying for government posts in the agricultural department, and asking for favors from his well-connected friends. When the governor of Colorado, Frederick Pitkin, started to receive numerous complaints about the ineffective management of the Ute Indians by Danforth, Meeker stood out as an adequate replacement. Not only was he an expert in agriculture, he had also brought together a variety of people to create an agricultural community. With letters of support from governmental officials, Meeker sought and obtained the White River Ute Agency job. In order to assist him, he hired his twenty-one-year-old daughter, Josephine Meeker, as the agency teacher and physician. In preparation for her new position, he encouraged her to attend a business college in Denver, to be able to assist with the bookkeeping. Arvilla also followed Meeker to his new post, in order to maintain the house, to assist Josephine with the physician position, and to teach domestic skills to the Native American women (N. Meeker, "Letter to Arvilla," July 1, 1878). While money troubles led Meeker to seek the Indian agent position, he brought to his position of Indian agent the same fervor with which he approached all his projects. He took seriously the U.S. government's call to Christianize and civilize the Ute Indians, which he aimed to achieve through a strict application of governmental laws. Through teaching "the cultivation of the soil, the value of hard work, and the importance of a fixed and comfortable home," Meeker believed that Indians' souls could be transformed into "civilized" people (N. Meeker April 1879, pp. 224–6).

Meeker's approach to managing the agency was aggressive, aiming to rectify the deficiencies of past administrations. When he first arrived, Meeker reported, "The whole agency is in a state of disorganization." Aside from the lack of flour and seed, "there [have] not been enough crops raised here in 8 years to sustain a small family all year" (N. Meeker, May 27, 1878). He labored to bring order to the agency, first by retrieving the unclaimed 1877 rations from Rawlins. He also moved the agency from the high altitude to a lower valley more suited to agricultural endeavors and closer to where the Utes wintered. Hiring men from the Union Colony, he dug an irrigation ditch and planted new crops. In the spring of 1879, he was able to convince several Ute men to work on the irrigation ditch for pay, though he claimed "they need close following up and constant oversight" (N. Meeker, May 19, 1879).

Despite all the progress at the agency, Meeker was frustrated and impatient. Few Utes stayed at the agency. Josephine only had one student, whose father eventually removed from her school. Not even the white laborers could live up to Meeker's expectations of work ethic. In a letter to his coeditor of the *Greeley Tribune*, Meeker admitted to firing two of the Greeley boys when he had discovered they had forgone work in favor of swimming in the river. When they begged to be rehired, he did, though he said that he saw "how they [were] going, and they must be watched like anybody else" (N. Meeker, July 10, 1879). In addition to problems with the agency employees, Meeker was frustrated with the Ute attitude toward work. In a satirical article to the *Greeley Tribune*, Meeker suggested that the Utes were already civilized because they enjoyed the same luxuries as the aristocratic class, "for they both think labor a disgrace, both pass their days in frivolous amusements, both dearly love horse racing, dancing, and discordant music, and both live on the labor of other people" (N. Meeker, April 2, 1879).

From the Ute perspective, the Great Spirit intended the whites to work for the Utes. In an 1867 Southern Ute explanation, the Great Spirit created the first man an Indian. When the population increased, they created a ladder to reach the Great Spirit, but the Great Spirit scattered them and "made them speak several languages." The whites resulted from fear, "and the Great Spirit then said that is was now the wish of the Great Spirit to have the white man work and plant for the Indian" (Lewis 1984, p. 41). The pattern at the White River Ute Agency fit with Ute expectations that the whites should work for them. Meeker and his white employees built the store house, took care of agency cattle, built the irrigation ditch, plowed fields, tended to the crops, and distributed rations. Meeker's perception was that Utes did not care to work their own ground and preferred that the U.S. Indian agents do it. In the spring of 1879, he changed the ration distribution system that he thought would address this problem, but may have set the stage for the fall outbreak.

In order to curtail the Ute perception regarding work, Meeker enacted his interpretation of the governmental policy on rations. When Meeker first arrived at the agency, he had a perceptive approach to ration distribution. In a letter to Senator Teller, he wrote: "I have two or three circulars from the Department of Interior to the effect that no rations are to be issued to any Indian unless he works...I presume there could be an outbreak if I should obey. On the whole I think the Utes have been treated badly and they know it as well as you and I" (N. Meeker, May 27, 1878). However, Meeker began to see that the Utes, like many other humans, would not work just for the sake of working, they needed incentives. Meeker continued to distribute basic rations to everyone, but he increased the rations of "luxury items" to those who worked. Withholding rations was "equivalent to 'compulsory education,' and it is the only power that can be made to operate." Meeker suggested that "with plenty of coffee, sugar, and dried peaches I can lead them forward to civilization" (Emmitt 2000, p. 86). Many Utes perceived this action as blatant favoritism at best, or governmental stinginess with rations at worst. For a population that was struggling to adjust to a new means of subsistence as well as recent memories of inconsistent deliveries of rations, the Utes may have perceived this policy as being a direct threat to their well-being and an unapproved revision of the treaties.

In addition to trouble with rations, Meeker and the Utes disagreed about the horses. Danforth's 1877 estimation was that there were over 4,000 horses for 600 Utes on the reservation (Annual Report to the Commissioner of Indian Affairs, 1877). Many horses roamed free, pasturing themselves. However, there was prime pasturing land near the new location of the agency. The best pasture for Utes' prized racing horses was also a prime agricultural location for Meeker. In the spring of 1879, Meeker reached a compromise with the Utes on which ground he would cultivate. At the same time, Johnson, a medicine man and Susan's husband, asked Meeker to break two horses for plowing. Meeker took this as an encouraging sign that his efforts to transform the Utes into farmers was taking hold. However, Meeker soon learned that Johnson merely wanted Meeker to get the horses into shape, so they would be better racers. Meeker asked that Johnson kill his horses. In response, Johnson pushed him to the ground, injuring Meeker's shoulder. A few weeks later, in early September, Meeker had agency employees plow the pony pasture near the agency. The agency employees reported that as soon as they began plowing, one of the Ute men shot at them. Meeker grew increasingly concerned when the Ute women and children who lived nearby the agency moved further back. Fearing an outbreak, he wrote a telegram to Governor Pitkin, asking for assistance from the Cavalry. When the Cavalry entered reservation land, the Utes at the agency attacked the agency men and captured the women and children (N. Meeker, September 8, 1879; N. Meeker, September 10, 1879; Coneah 1982, pp. 97–100; and Lewis 1984, p. 46).

The outbreak occurred at a time when national debate about "the Indian question" was shifting from assimilation to removal. As the North American plains became more populated with Euro-Americans, settlers pushed the government to use more "pragmatic" techniques, namely, to transfer the Indians Affairs Department from the Department of the Interior back to the War Department, so that the Army, not reform-minded individuals, would have responsibility for interactions with Native Americans. While Meeker's appointment represented a transition away from the Christian-based Peace Policy, increasing numbers of settlers in the western United States were calling for more extreme actions as patience for the slow-moving reform policy was wearing thin. In addition to the day-to-day fear that settlers in the American west had of Native Americans, there was a shifting opinion of the ability of races to progress toward civilization, challenging the government's policy that Native Americans could assimilate into Euro-American society (Hoxie 2001).

In the middle of national debates about race, progress, and Indian policy, the Ute outbreak provided a fulcrum for conversation about the direction of Indian policy. In the haze of their grief, Flora Price, Josephine, and Arvilla Meeker allowed Ralph Meeker, the oldest child of Arvilla and Nathan, to publish their stories in the *New York Herald Tribune*. Ralph was a successful journalist, working for *Frank's Illustrated Newspaper* and the *New York Herald Tribune* and had contacts with newspaper publishers around the country. The incident captured the attention of the nation, appearing on the front page of *Chicago Tribune* and the *New York Times*, the *Philadelphia Inquirer*, as well as western newspapers such as the *Denver Tribune*, the *Colorado Republican*, the *Omaha Herald*, the *Greeley Tribune*, and the *Deseret News*. *Frank's Illustrated Newspaper* carried an article about the outbreak, as well as pencil drawings of the incident. Several months after the confrontation at the White River Ute Agency, the Denver Tribune Publishing House complied the women's stories, edited from the longer versions that appeared in the *New York Herald Tribune* and the *Greeley Tribune* of their captivity in a narrative titled *The Ute Massacre: Brave Miss Meeker's Captivity, Her Own Account of it: also the Narratives of Her Mother and Mrs. Price, to which is Added further Thrilling and Intensely Interesting Details, Not Hitherto Published, of the Bravery and the Frightful Sufferings Endured by Mrs. Meeker, Mrs. Price, and Her Two Children, and by Miss Josephine Meeker* (J Meeker 1976 rpt).

Susan's dramatic rescue of the captives appeared in headlines in the *Denver Tribune* and the *Chicago Tribune*, several smaller newspapers, and in the captivity narrative. The story has inspired poetic interest in the past century, with numerous odes written lauding Susan's eloquent, liberating speech, though one poem misnamed her as Ouray's wife, Chipeta (Field pp. 22–3, in Caldwell 1911; Haskell 1889; Howard 1902; Stephens 1976). Not all the accounts of the incident recount Susan's role in the release of the captives. In her Congressional Testimony, Josephine focused on the circumstances at the agency that led to the outbreak instead of the details of her release. Charles Adams provided Congress this information, suggesting that the women were not present at the negotiations but at a camp several miles away. Susan did not even warrant a mention in the Congressional testimony (Congressional Record 1880).

While Susan did not enter into official record, her wisdom and bravery captivated newspapers across the country. Susan's intervention in the tribal council meeting developed as the stories of the women's captivity traveled along telegraph wires to newspapers offices. At first, Susan's role in the women's release was limited to brief praises of her character by the women. Drawing on June Namias's (1993) categories, these news reports characterized Susan as a Native American "Amazon" protecting the "frail flowers" of Arvilla, Josephine, and Flora (pp. 29–48). Initial reports published in the Denver newspapers gave brief statements from Arvilla Meeker that Susan was a shining sun in the bleak cloud of captivity, and because of her motherly tenderness toward the captives, they were spared from the discomfort of being hostages. Arvilla said that Susan "did more than all others to save their lives. She was as kind to them as a mother" (*Denver Daily News*, October 29, 1879). Several days after these nonspecific references to Susan's kindness, longer articles appeared in the *Denver Tribune*, rippling out to the *Chicago Tribune* and the *Philadelphia Inquirer*. These articles expanded the role of Susan from a caring, motherly figure to a woman who traversed the barriers of her position in Ute society to demand the release of the women. Appearing on the front pages of the *Chicago Tribune*, Susan was declared a "strategic squaw," a "faithful friend," a protector, "shielding [the captives] from indignities which the Bucks offered," all things that were "never before heard of in Indian history." The respect that the men gave Susan's words of peace was rare, because "the Utes make slaves of their women" and force them into silence in political meetings, similar to "the way St. Paul did." The article attributed the respect to Susan's relationship to Chief Ouray—a Ute Indian that had attained respect from the U.S. government for his role in negotiating treaties—not to her natural religious inclination (*Chicago Tribune*, October 29, 1879).

A few days following this report, the *Chicago Tribune* reported that Susan's motivation for intervening in the council was not because of her relationship with Chief Ouray but because of her past. Susan had been a captive of Cheyenne Indians when she was young. According to an interview with past Ute Indian agent Simeon Whitely, Susan was hunting with her family on the eastern plains of Colorado in 1863 when the group was attacked by Cheyenne Indians. In the chaos of defending themselves and their livestock, Susan was taken captive. Johnson, Susan's new husband, alerted the Calvary. The Calvary successfully located the raiding party along the Cache de la Poudre, and not a moment too soon, because as they were riding up Susan was bound to an unlit pyre. The soldiers transported her to Simeon Whitely, where she lived for several months, learning English, and enjoying the luxuries of civilized life. When Whitely was able to locate her family, she returned. Whitely reported he had not heard of her again until he read the *Chicago Tribune*'s article. He was certain that Susan's empathy and defense of the captives emerged from her own harrowing experience in captivity (*Chicago Tribune*, October 30, 1879). The story of Susan's own experience with captivity attracted the attention of numerous newspapers across the country, including the New Hampshire *Farmer's Cabinet* and the *Macon Weekly Telegraph* (*Farmer's Cabinet*, November 25, 1879; *Macon Weekly Telegraph*, November 11, 1879). However, it did not appear in the captivity narrative. Instead of arguing that Susan intervened on behalf of the captives because of her own brush with captivity, she acted because of her inclination toward Christian kindness.

The Meeker captivity narrative is primarily a propaganda piece, similar to other captivity narratives produced in this era. However, Susan's religious identity plays a large role in mitigating the propaganda, serving as social currency in the volatile market of Indian policy. The preface of the narrative states that white men will continue to be murdered and women and children will continue to be captured "until the whole Indian question is placed in the control of the War Department... If the Government were to appoint General Grant or Sherman or Sheridan, as Indian Commissioner, with free power to control the whole question, we do not believe there would ever be an other [sic] Indian outbreak of any description" (J. Meeker 1976, p. 4). As mentioned earlier, Grant's Peace Policy had lost support. The 1876 Battle of the Little Bighorn and the 1872 Modoc War had swayed public opinion away from the reform movements of the peace policy back to war. In the minds of many Anglo-Americans, war could accomplish what reforms and policies could not (Hoxie 2001; Keller 1983; Prucha 1984).

The White River Ute Agency outbreak occurred amid this national debate about the best governmental policy toward Native Americans. In the weeks after Nathan Meeker's death, the *Weekly Denver Post*, the *Rocky Mountain News*, and Colorado's governor, Frederick Pitkin, echoed the sentiments of the war party. The *Post*, reporting on the confrontation at the White River Ute Agency, declared in bold, large headlines that the "Utes must go!" (Sprague 1954, p. 164). Governor Pitkin's solution to the ongoing friction between the Utes and Coloradoans was to raise a militia of 20,000 men. Pitkin had promised to lead the militia in a full-scale genocide (Decker 2004, p. 152). The prologue to Josephine Meeker's captivity narrative reflects the sentiments of Governor Pitkin and the many ranchers and miners who wanted the Utes gone. Economics and infrastructural developments drove this approach; the Utes' reservation was expansive and full of resources. Land that had once been inaccessible to Euro-Americans became a tangible possibility. Railroads and mining roads had slowly carved a path through the mountains. Having nearly moved mountains to reach the Rocky Mountains' resources, 3,000 Ute Indians no longer seemed immovable. Meeker's death had given the governor a rational reason to mobilize against the Utes. Only the reform policies of the Department of the Interior stood in the way of the immediate settlement of western Colorado.

Susan's heroic role and her ascribed religious identity stand in contrast to the prologue and Governor Pitkin's militaristic stance. The captivity narrative concludes with an appeal to the readers, urging them to look beyond their sympathy for the captive women, and to not

> like the Indians themselves visit anger and punishment indiscriminately on the latter as a people. For where among all our civilized selves can we find a woman who, under the same circumstances, would have shown such a noble, tender, Christian disposition and heart as Susan, the good squaw, the sister of Ouray. (J. Meeker 1976, p. 46)

Perhaps this statement merely was arguing against Pitkin's blanket condemnation of Utes, or it could have been an appeal to reformists on the East Coast to continue their efforts at civilizing Native Americans, because Susan's actions demonstrated either that some Indians are inherently good or that the civilization programs were working.

Historical record also has erased the chance to determine who compiled the captivity narrative, though most likely it was Ralph Meeker. However, questions of authorship obscure more compelling questions, namely, what purpose did the representation of Susan's intervention serve? The narrative reveals power structures that scholars have come to expect in colonial relationships; the Anglo-Americans portray the Native Americans as brutal, uncivilized savages while the Anglo-Americans are gentle, religious survivors. However, Josephine Meeker's captivity narrative reveals fissures in this narrative structure. The most powerful figure is a Ute woman. Susan does not have a voice in this narrative, but the significance of her role for the captives is powerful. Religious identity becomes a social currency for negotiating stereotypical identities assigned within a colonial context. In other words, the captivity narrative ascribes a Christian identity to assist readers in sorting out the "good" Indians from the "bad."

Why use a Christian disposition as the explanation? Why not explain it as a Native American custom for powerful women to decide the fate of the captives, as was common among the Iroquois? Second, what might Josephine and her family understand a Christian disposition to be, and how did Susan fulfill this? Finally, what cultural work did this episode in the captivity narrative do and what benefits would scholars of colonial contact have in adding religion as an analytical category?

There is a long tradition in European history of trying to determine the origin of the Native Americans through religious categories. Thomas Thorowgood's 1650 volume *Jews in America, or, Probabilities that the Americans are of that Race* was one of the first books in English to argue that the Native Americans were from the lost tribes of Israel. In 1775, James Adair's *History of the American Indians* argued that the Native Americans were descendents of Jewish tribes. In 1830, Joseph Smith published the *Book of Mormon* that also argued that Native Americans were the remnants of a once glorious empire of the lost tribes of Israel. The early colonial theologians and scholars in England, France, and Spain worked to integrate the existence of Native Americans into their cosmology, using familiar religious categories. Colonizers used the constructed religious identity of Native Americans to model appropriate types of action toward indigenous populations. In the case of the Latter-day Saints, the idea that Native Americans were descendents of one of the lost Tribes of Israel compelled the LDS church to send missionaries in order to bring the Native Americans back into the fold (Vogel 1986).

The Meeker captivity narrative does not make similar attempts to locate the origin of Native Americans, though the description of Susan's motive for intervening in the tribal council meeting is within the same discursive framework. For earlier European settlers, the question of origin was one of the factors that framed the colonial response to indigenous populations. In the case of the narrative, the question of motive for Susan's intervention in the council meeting led to recommendations for appropriate reactions to the Ute uprising. Using a religious identity familiar to the readers, the captivity narrative links Susan and other "good" Indians to the political tropes of "Christianize and civilize." The captivity narrative's description of Susan, with her natural tendencies toward doing Christian things, urges readers to take action, specifically to remember the "good" Indians and, presumably, work toward their preservation.

What might the Meeker family understand a Christian disposition to be? It is difficult to determine precisely the family's religious beliefs, though through their diaries, letters, and involvement in Christian-based agrarian utopia projects, one can surmise their understanding of Christianity. The Meeker family history is best understood in the context of nineteenth-century religious fervor and American expansion. Institutionally, the Meekers' religious membership looks like a roster of the prominent Protestant churches of the day. Nathan Meeker, as mentioned earlier, associated with the Disciples of Christ before leaving organized religion. In her brief autobiography, Arvilla Meeker tells her children she became a Presbyterian when she was twelve. Later in life, she was a Congregationalist, and then a Methodist (A. Meeker, March 5, 1897). Arvilla based her religious life on the notion of hard work and the cultivation of her mind (A. Meeker

1846). For both Nathan and Arvilla, marriage provided the greatest source of spiritual development. In an unpublished manuscript titled "A New Spiritual World," Nathan Meeker revealed the importance of marriage to his spirituality, arguing "no apology can be made for those who disregard marriage," and in punishment, "there will be long stages of painful probation extending perhaps through many millions of years or until the individual shall be thoroughly purged from his sin, when he will understand what this kind of purity signifies" (N. Meeker Papers, unpublished manuscript, Denver Public Library WH1680, Colorado Historical Society, unpaginated n.d.).

The Union Colony, the Colorado community Meeker founded with Horace Greeley, reveals Nathan Meeker's ideal of a religious community. People ought to exist in a harmonious community with a mixture of privately and publicly held lands, citizens should gain their living through farming, only one church should exist in the community that people could choose to attend, and their lives should be pious, avoiding alcohol, gambling, and other vices. The family should be the central social structure and everyone should labor hard and spend their spare time educating himself or herself. In 1879, the community of Greeley continued to live up to these ideals by formalizing a ban on alcohol and forming the "Union Society," which met on Sundays in order to discuss topics of religious significance, including topics as diverse as the merits of Islam, the necessity to educate children, and the efficacy of mesmerism. For the Meekers, religious ideals provided a template for a moral and intellectual life. In an article in the *Greeley Tribune*, Nathan Meeker's understanding of proper gender roles for Christian women emerges. "Susan, Johnson's wife, is a good genius," he wrote, "she has dignity and good sense, and she makes her husband do as she bids" (N. Meeker, December 11, 1878). Like many of his Victorian contemporaries, Meeker believed that women civilized and controlled men, regardless of their race.

Meeker's worldview is difficult to pinpoint. He was a freethinker that resisted institutions telling him how to live, even if he upheld those beliefs that structured the institution's rules, as in the case of his Ohio liquor store and confrontation with the Disciples of Christ. The plans for the Union Colony suggest that above all, Meeker stood for freedom of choice tempered by community responsibilities, as well as a constant drive toward self-improvement. One can assume that a Christian disposition for Meeker would mean independence, temperance, and a commitment to hard work through farming. A true Christian man would seek marriage with a Christian woman, who would provide a moral compass for her husband, "biding him to do as she bids," never afraid to stand up for what she believed to be right and true.

While the narrative does not reveal any facts about Susan's commitment to farming or temperance, the intervention in the tribal council meeting demonstrated independence and her ability to make men do her bidding. It also demonstrated other qualities that the Meekers held dear: elocution, women's rights, and standing up for one's beliefs. In the years leading up to the Civil War, Nathan Meeker had been a vocal abolitionist. As an author of a large volume of short stories and a journalist, Nathan would have respect for an "eloquent and convincing speech." His daughters were vocal supporters of women's suffrage and the education of women. The image of Susan, an elegantly dressed woman who speaks on behalf of the vulnerable and oppressed, reminds one of East Coast women who fought for abolition, temperance, and suffrage.

Finally, what cultural work does the description of Susan as having a kind, Christian disposition do? First, an examination of what it does not do. This description does not give voice to Ute concerns about loss of land or rights, or to the cultural transformation the Utes experienced as Coloradoans restricted their movements. It also does not give an accurate or useful description of Ute religious practices or the experiences of Ute women. The description of Susan as having a noble, tender disposition demonstrates three things. By highlighting the role of religious identity in Anglo-American imagination of Native Americans, the description of Susan's disposition complicates racial categories. Second, just as the question of origin compelled Latter-Day Saints to send missionaries to Native Americans, the religious description of Susan's disposition was a call to action for readers. Finally, this use of religious identity to explain why some Utes were helpful and others not masks the complexities of the circumstances surrounding the Meeker Massacre.

Written just on the cusp of the formalization of the reservation system, the reimagining of Susan as a Christian advocate of white women was an attempt to sway public opinion toward the efforts of the assimilation movement, while still supporting the firm regulation of Indian Affairs by the War Department. The tension between turning all the affairs to the War Department and the support of the assimilation movement in the conclusion of the narrative reveals a seemingly complicated picture of racial categories. Rather than stereotyping all Native Americans as savages, readers are encouraged to use discretion in their wrath against the Utes, to not be like the Indians and "visit anger and punishment indiscriminately." Instead, readers are asked to think about their conceptions of a civilized person and to include a Ute woman among them. In this instance, race and barbarity are not naturally intertwined.

Second, Susan's religious disposition provided the means for a limited call to action. "Remembering" is not a concrete rallying platform, though it could be a weak appeal for the continuation of civilizing programs. Through a complication of stereotypical notions of civilization and Native American, readers must sort through the complex issue of Native American and U.S. governmental relations. The framework of a kind, Christian disposition provided a bridge between the war advocates and the peace advocates; perhaps, as the narrative states, there are some "bad" Indians who should be killed, but maybe there are "good" Indians that are worth saving because of their natural inclinations toward Christianity. The mixed messages of the narrative reflect the varied attempts by western Native Americans and the U.S. government to find an acceptable solution to the Anglo-American settlement of western lands and Native Americans' shrinking hunting grounds. The efforts of the government to turn Native Americans into Christian farmers were popular with some Anglo-American advocates. Proponents of this policy believed that education and integration were the only effective defense against Native American raids on western settlers. Others advocated more extreme policies, such as Pitkin's extermination plan. The captivity narrative walks a fine line between these two positions.

However, despite the apparent complexities in the captivity narrative regarding race and action, the narrative glosses over the complexities that led up to the Meeker Massacre. The religious identity of Susan's disposition played a significant role in this masking. Stated another way, religion is used to negotiate and simplify complex political situations, in this case, as a way to mask the complexities of U.S. expansion into Indian lands. Instead of situating the Meeker Massacre within the framework of miner and rancher intrusions onto reservation lands, or as Ute frustration with the lack of food supplies at the agency, or as the result of U.S. government intrusion into the private affairs of livelihood, the captivity narrative is framed as a justification for military regulation of Native Americans, tempered only by a call to remember the few Indians who have a tender, noble, Christian disposition. Like black and white hats in cowboy movies, religious identity served as a way to quickly identify the Utes who are on the side of the Anglo-Americans and those who are not.

Sydney Ahlstrom (2004), a historian of American religions, insisted that one could not understand religion without also understanding the social and historical contexts in which the religion thrived (p. xxii). One might also argue that nineteenth-century colonial contact between Euro-Americans and Native Americans cannot be fully understood without addressing the religious aspects of that contact. One localized example of colonial contact revealed a complex entanglement of economics, military engagements, farming practices, and religious ideals. In the case of representations of the Meeker outbreak, religious frameworks provided a means to simplify the complexities of contact between Anglo-Americans and Native Americans, masking the intricacies and moral dilemmas of expansion into Native American land.

Note

1. Meeker is located in northwestern Colorado, in the White River Valley and near the Flat Top Mountains.

Chapter 9

Visual Representation as a Method of Discourse on Captivity, Focused on Cynthia Ann Parker

Lin Holdridge

> *Our own existence cannot be separated from the accounts we give of ourselves. It is in telling our own stories that we give ourselves an identity. We recognize ourselves in the stories that we tell about ourselves. It makes very little difference whether these stories are true or false; fiction as well as verifiable history provides us with an identity*—Paul Ricoeur.
> —Ebersole 1995 p. 190

The burgeoning field of captivity narrative studies has produced many dynamic and diverse analyses, from historians, literary critics, and feminist writers to ethno-historians, anthropologists, archaeologists, and theologians. This rich seam of scholarship has highlighted multiple meanings and issues such as racial imperialism, gender, stereotyping, miscegenation, expansion, and nationalism, which have become enmeshed in the colonial discourses of power between Europeans and American Indians. The illustrations within the narratives, mostly consisting of woodcut engravings, are an obvious source of material for visual analysis, but the wider field of American art also provides appropriate and relevant works to study, from history painting and sculpture to landscapes. The artistic genres used to represent captive subjects and their captors provide useful information on differing stylistic depictions, particularly when those involved were white European females and Indian males, and how such visual constructs inform the overall written history (Truettner 1991).

Although the number of white captives reputedly taken is relatively small in relation to the overall American war story tradition (e.g., an estimated 1,641 were taken in New England between 1675 and

1763; Namias 1993, p. 7), captivity narratives flourished and grew in popularity over three and a half centuries and have been credited with being one of the main founding forces of America's literary history. The narratives began with Mary Rowlandson's account in the seventeenth century titled *A True History of the Captivity and Restoration of Mrs Mary Rowlandson,* published in Boston and London in 1682, and continued through to the captivity romances and dime novels of the eighteenth, nineteenth, and twentieth centuries and indeed, to the present day. The tradition also flourished in the Western film genre, playing out in such seminal films as *The Searchers* (1956), *Two Rode Together* (1961), *Little Big Man* (1970), *A Man Called Horse* (1970), *Dances with Wolves* (1990), and *Last of the Mohicans* (1992).

The scope of this chapter is not to produce a geographical or even a historical survey of such captivity narratives, but to contribute an art historical focus to the implications of the story and images relating to the captivity of Cynthia Ann Parker and the public perception of her life over the period following her initial capture. This will be contextualized by discussing stereotypical depictions of white female captives from the narratives, and images of other significant female "white Indians" who remained with their tribes for many years. Their stories are not generally written in the first person and are few in number, but the reception of their histories creates an interesting counterpoint to the clichéd tropes presented through the captivity narratives.

One of the earliest significant images published is a crude woodcut supposedly depicting a scene from Rowlandson's capture (see Boyle (1773) edition of the story or Kephart's (2005), front cover).[1] Mary Rowlandson, dressed in frontier dress, stands outside her house in a determined pose, aiming a musket at three vicious-looking Indians, wielding guns and tomahawks. The image of a woman with a musket had been an accepted and known symbol of patriotic women during the revolutionary era and this image is displaced here onto Rowlandson for effect, rather than as an illustration of what actually occurred (for interpretations of Rowlandson, see Ebersole 1995; Faery 1999; Slotkin 1973; Turner Strong 1999). The counterpart in the later editions, the woodcut of the patriotic mother, pairs with the fighting image to provide a good propaganda device for urging traditional women to take up arms, as if the use of violence would complement rather than compromise femininity and domesticity. The depiction of the Indians is lumpen, wooden, and poorly executed, with no attempt to delineate features or authenticate dress. The very crudeness of their depiction serves to authenticate the sense of menace. Neither the Rowlandson Indians nor the later images in the captivity narratives bear any resemblance to the pedigree of Indian representations first drawn by John White during his initial voyage to America in 1585 (Sloan 2007) and subsequently reinterpreted and engraved by Theodor de Bry for Thomas Harriot's publication *A briefe and true report of the new found land of Virginia* (1590). De Bry's images became widely used templates for depiction of the Indian "other" and were in part based upon the European Renaissance drawing tradition (Pratt 2005, plate14 and figure 5.1, p. 116).

The portrayal of the overt brutality of the Indian male toward European women in literature and imagery, starting with Rowlandson, heightened proportionately as tensions over wars and possession of land increased, from the mid-eighteenth century onward. The contrapuntal representation of the pure and fragile white woman, kidnapped and allegedly abused by the rapacious, bestial, dark-skinned savage became a putative and powerful norm in captivity narratives. This was often conflated with the image of the maternal woman, attempting to protect her young; for example, in an illustration from the *Narrative of the Captivity and Extreme Suffering of Mrs. Clarissa Plummer* (1838) (Namias 1993 p. 40). In this story, we see an image of Clarissa, wearing a long, short-sleeved dress, with her hair flowing free. She has been dragged out of her house and is kneeling on the ground in tears, her bare arms clutching her small child. A tall, dark-skinned Indian looms over them, grabbing the hair of the infant with one hand, while the other wields a tomahawk. The intent is obvious. In the background is a gruesome scene that shows Clarissa's husband being burnt alive while their captors lock hands and dance around the bonfire.

The widespread fear that white women captives would automatically be raped was initially predicated on the religious binary of the degenerate primitive and the vulnerable Christian female, prey to the "seductions of savagery" (Turner Strong 1999, p. 145). Rowlandson's text speaks of her captors in inhuman terms, describing them variously as "hell hounds...black creatures in the night...a lively resemblance of hell" (p. 99). By the mid-nineteenth century, well-known artists were also depicting the generic white female captive, unutterably at the mercy of the Indian savage and frequently imaged in a flowing white dress as in *The Capture of Daniel Boone's Daughter, Jemima,* an oil painting by Charles Wimar, *ca.* 1850. Here we see Jemima, snatched up by an Indian warrior, and placed in front of him, on his horse, as they gallop away (Namias 1993, p. 106; Slotkin 1973,

p. 352). Influenced by Romanticism in European culture, Jemima's drooping posture and bound hands denote her passivity and fragility, and the close, physical juxtaposition of the two figures serves to emphasize a similar binary as before, denoting the white maiden of sensibility who represents the values of civilization and the raw, brute force of the wild, untamed, and uncivilized other. This binary however, now secularized, reflects the high cultural and moral value placed on female sexual purity and also stands for the justification of manifest destiny and westward expansion. These attitudes are thus part of much broader tropes of gender relations, power, and patriarchal constructs (Ebersole 1995, p. 231).

Although the sexual use and abuse of Indian women by white men was commonplace throughout the colonial period, the actual instances of white women raped by Indians was less of a documented fact than a prurient fantasy of displaced male fears of the potency and attraction of the male sexual other. Among the New England Indians in particular, rape was not considered. Their strict warrior societies practiced continence, and aesthetically, black was esteemed as the color of beauty, not white. Women were frequently captured for adoption, and this was consistent during the colonial period. No Indian, therefore, would violate such women due to strong incest taboos (see Axtell 1975, p. 67). Many other scholars reinforce the lack of evidence of rape among the Indians of the East, although the same claims cannot necessarily be made for the Western tribes during the later phase of expansionism (see Castiglia 1996, p. 211; Faery 1999, p. 46; Slotkin 1973, p. 357; Turner Strong 1999, p. 187).

Stories of white women who had been captured, acculturated, and chose to stay with their Indian husbands and families presented the greatest threat of all—that of miscegenation. Once this boundary had been crossed, political, ideological, and cultural boundaries had also been breached, putting America's expansion mission at risk. The retrieval or at least discovery of these women, many of whom had been captured as children and therefore had been absent for long durations, occasioned a sense of relief that white society could at least reclaim them in some way and perhaps echo the redemptive and didactic quality of the earlier Puritan story. Although in many cases, their experience among the Indians was perceived to have been a singular life of hardship, abuse, and suffering, regardless of the actual facts, such women would often be seen as tainted and degenerate: not only by association with the "savage," but also by the assumption that they may well have had intimate relations with Indian men. How to perceive these women created a great degree of confusion as relatives were confronted with the reality of family members who had lived most of their lives with Indians and had little or no memory of white society, customs, or morés, nor much willingness to reembrace white culture. An example of a "white" Indian is shown in figure 9.1. Frances Slocum was captured in 1780 when she was five years old and raised by the Delawares. She later married a Delaware and when he deserted her, she subsequently married a Miami war chief, by whom she had two sons who died early, and two daughters. She was discovered by her Pennsylvanian relatives sixty-one years after she had been captured, whereupon they commissioned this portrait to be painted. In this depiction of Frances, the artist has made no attempt to show signs of her whiteness. Her skin appears dark as is her hair, and she displays no perceptible white traits. She sits stoically, with her hands crossed, her

Figure 9.1 Frances Slocum with her two daughters, George Winter, watercolor 1841. Courtesy of Tippecanoe County Historical Association, Lafayette, Indiana.

shoulders hunched, and averts her gaze in Indian fashion. One of her daughters turns her back to the artist in the belief that he would steal her soul. The other daughter too averts her eyes. The background of the image does not ground the sitters, but heightens their strangeness by leaving them hovering ambiguously in a pale blue ether.

In contrast, another portrait, painted by Jenni Brownscombe around the same time, shows Slocum's white lineage more clearly in the tone of her skin and the cast of her features. Her dress appears to be westernized Indian. She is alone, and seated on a chair within a log cabin, akin to those of the pioneers, which suggests a permanent dwelling. Her powerful gaze stares straight out of the canvas, as if to defend her own hybrid identity.

Frances Slocum chose not to return to her family and lived out the rest of her life in the Indian style, alone with her daughters. The portraits, however, indicate some degree of the confusion her discovery caused: should she be treated as white or Indian? Her story became known as that of *The Lost Sister of Wyoming*, and John Meginness's version, printed in 1891 by Heller Bros, includes a biblical quote on the title page: "I am become a stranger unto my brethren / And an alien unto my mother's children" (Psalms, lxix–8). Meginness reinforces this quote by voicing the difficulties Slocum would face, if she returned to white society (Ebersole 1995, p. 229).

The captive Mary Jemison, taken in 1758 at the age of fifteen years, chose to remain with the Senecas and wrote in her memoirs of her wonderful life with them and her fifty years of happy marriage to a Seneca man. During reprints of her story (the first account was told to and written by James E. Seaver in 1824), her husband is reinvented by subsequent hands as a brutal murderer (Namias 1993 p. 98).

> Although discovery would always be a cause for celebration tinged with horror and sympathy for a life perceived by white society to have been lived under such terrible duress for so long, the fact that she chose not to be redeemed, is actually romanticised by an inscription at the base of a statue of her (*Statue of Mary Jemison* H.K. Bush-Brown bronze, Letchworth State Park, New York). The statue, made in 1910, many years after Jemison's death, portrays her as hybridized; her dress is the rather pristine and beautiful garb of the generic Indian maiden, yet her features are distinctly white. The inscription reads: To the Memory of Mary Jemison.
>
> Whose home during more than 70 years of a life of strange vicissitude was among the Senecas upon the banks of this river; and whose history, inseparably connected with that of this valley, has caused her to be known as...The White Woman of the Genesee.

In this case, her refusal to reenter white society gained her some distance from the inevitable backlash suffered by the reclaimed "victim" and instead allowed her to become mythologized. Far from the earlier perception of such women as unredeemed captives (i.e., Eunice Williams), a new term was coined: white *squaw* (Turner Strong 1999, p. 145).

The story of Cynthia Ann Parker can be used as a model to which we may apply Spivak's theory of the doubly oppressed subaltern woman (Spivak in Ashcroft, Griffiths, and Tiffin 1997). Her first experience of oppression came as a child of nine when captured by the Comanche in an attack on Fort Parker, Texas, in 1836. Forced to live in an alien culture and environment, she was initially physically and mentally abused and unable to communicate until she mastered the Comanche language. Twenty-five years later, this process was then reversed and virtually repeated through her recapture (along with her two-year-old daughter) by Captain Sul Ross and his army. Cynthia Ann had by then completely acculturated within the tribe and was a respected member, wife, and mother of three children. Snatched from her Indian family and adoptive culture, she was bullied and interrogated by the soldiers before her uncle Isaac Parker came to claim her and take her home. Upon reaching Fort Worth along the way, all the students were let out of school so that they could see the captives. A first-hand account describes Cynthia Ann:

> She stood on a large wooden box, she was bound with rope, she was not dressed in Indian costume, but wore a torn calico dress. Her face was tanned, and she made a pathetic figure as she stood there, viewing the crowds that swarmed about her. The tears were streaming down her face, and she was muttering in the Indian language. The principal asked the children what she was saying, and he told them that she was asking to be taken back to her people. (Exley 2001, p.171)

This second capture rendered her mute once more, her native tongue long forgotten. She was reduced to silence, held against her will, alienated from a language she did not speak and a culture she did not comprehend; violently dislocated once more from her own history and identity. Furthermore, her return was celebrated throughout Texas as a politicized victory and a vindication of white settlement. Cynthia Ann's fame, or rather, notoriety, spread throughout the state and people traveled miles to see her.

Did she acclimatize? To the extent that she eventually learned English and was able to communicate verbally, maybe the answer is "yes." Superficially, in terms of having to adapt to the dress and social codes of white culture, perhaps. Her long years lived among the Indians and her complete acculturation meant she was unable to readapt successfully to her originating society. Two major factors played a dominant role here: first, she mourned in perpetuity for her husband and sons, and a way of life lost to her. Second, she was not encouraged to speak publicly of her Indian life. It was widely believed that she had suffered greatly among the Comanche, and her so-called redemption from such barbaric ways was seen as a triumph. In all the accounts, her longing for her Indian family and life was painfully palpable, and yet her personal story was never told. Her subjectivity was erased and relegated to the realms of subjugated knowledge.

The celebrated mythology of her return to white society overrode the personal, but despite the cheers and publicity, Cynthia Ann remained an uneasy and deeply unhappy hybrid, effectively silenced by white colonial discourse. Her recapture ironically replicates the silenced Native women's experience when captured by white colonialists. As Spivak poignantly posits, those such as Cynthia Ann Parker fall into the abyss of the "other as the self's Shadow." Her position as a hybridized woman is untenable: "As object of colonialist historiography and as subject of insurgency, the ideological construction of gender keeps the male dominant. If, in the context of colonial production, the subaltern has no history and cannot speak, the subaltern as female is even more deeply in shadow..." (Spivak in Ashcroft, Griffiths, and Tiffin 1997, p. 28). Cynthia Ann's uncle James Parker writes at length of his eventful and perilous years of searching for his captured relatives. His daughter, Rachel Plummer, recovered after many months with the Comanche, also writes of her experience, recounting some details of her abuse and suffering at their hands. Her individual voice is heard most strongly, however, when she describes many fascinating insights into Comanche culture in her narrative.

Subsequent to the recapture of Cynthia Ann, the real person is subsumed into Texan myth; the Parker clan was one of the foremost families in Texas. Both James and his brother Isaac were friends of General Sam Houston. James petitioned the government for years in his attempts to reclaim his missing relatives and Isaac stood as senator in the Texan government. Cynthia Ann was one of the first female children in that area of Texas to be captured and the last to be released. Her story was well known and her life became deconstructed and resurrected in order to vindicate the success of western expansionism. "It is not a coincidence that...much was made of her return on the eve of the Civil War, when Texas, then part of the

Confederacy, was preparing to participate in a conflict grounded in large part in the issue of race" (Faery 1999, p. 23). Parker and her story also became legendary as a prototype of its time, illustrating the dangers to white society and its values that intimate connection with Native people presumably presented. The fact that she had endured captivity twice and only wished to return to her Comanche family was neither understood nor countenanced. She was seen as a tragic figure, but only because she was perceived as wild and untameable; a degenerate version of the woman she might otherwise have become.

Cynthia Ann's eldest son by her Indian husband, Peta Nocona, was Quanah Parker. He would have been about eleven years of age at the time of his mother's recapture in 1861 and he did not learn of her whereabouts among her white family until a much later date. Though historical facts are uncertain as to the date of actual death of his father, it is certain that his immediate family group was broken up by the capture of his mother. His sister had also been abducted and his younger brother was to die shortly afterward. Lacking kin among the Comanche on his mother's side, it appears that his treatment by the tribe was harsh (traditionally because he was an orphan and probably also on account of his mixed blood). He therefore grew up on the outer edge of the Comanche kinship system, moving on to join other bands as a young warrior, notably the fierce Quahadas. He was to achieve notoriety in his own right as the last Comanche chief to practice sustained opposition to white occupation of Indian lands. Recognizing eventually that their only hope of survival was to negotiate with the government, Quanah finally led his people on to the reservation at Fort Sill in 1875.

It was then that he commenced a search for his mother, in order to reclaim her and his young sister and to recreate that strong sense of Comanche kinship that had been denied him. The story of his search is well-documented (DeShields 1886, preface, pp. 73, 76; Exley 2001, pp. 260, 263; Neeley 1995, pp. 148, 200, 230, 233–5; Selden 2006, pp. 3–10, 209–22, 237–52). The fact that he could not trace Cynthia Ann until long after her death only sustained her silence. Her status as the mother of an Indian chief was tacitly allowed within the mythological narrative, because Quanah acculturated very successfully to white politics and culture, acquiring wealth, land, fame, and the friendship of politicians such as President Roosevelt. He publicly declared himself to be both Indian and Texan and helped create yet another chapter of the pioneering Parker family, who eventually accepted him as kin. The link continues to this day in terms of the closeness of the two branches of the family, both white and Indian (Selden 2006, pp. 253–85). Quanah Parker represents one of the success stories of postwar Texan integration, for he was able to critically engage with the "other," which was crucial to the transforming process of cultural integration. Like his mother though, Quanah too is a hybrid; in his case, of mixed race birth, rather than the dual culturalism of Cynthia Ann's life. They both remain inextricably locked into Texan mythology, symbolically caught within the binary perception of hero and victim; Cynthia Ann, the white rose of Texas and the abused captive; Quanah, the noble savage and Texan businessman. The Cynthia Ann Parker as synonymously "white Indian" and "Texan heroine" has been the subject of an opera, a play, many novels, and biographies; the namesake of a college, a park; and the inspiration for a highly successful Hollywood western "The Searchers," among others. The reality of Cynthia Ann's actual life is subsumed into these mythological markers, which have come to stand for historical authenticity. Two further studies on Cynthia Ann and the Parkers have been published during the last decade (Exley 2001; Selden 2006).

In the 1930s, Julia Smith composed her opera *Cynthia Parker*. She had wished to write an opera based on a Texan story, to be included in the Texan centennial celebrations of independence in 1936. The work was not finished in time, and was first performed at the Texan State Teacher's College in Denton, in 1939. The structure of the work uses forms common to the operatic genre: an overture, arias, recitation, and dance sets. However, Smith attempted to address two of the main representational issues when composing an opera for the American public: accessibility, involving entertainment and participation as elements to appeal to a wide audience; and authenticity, which demanded a performance in keeping with the original spirit of the story. By using cowboy songs, Native American music, and stereotypical images and costume, Smith not only entertained, but also appealed to the audience to authenticate the opera as an historical account of their common past. Cynthia Ann's story was dramatically adapted and altered to fit the operatic needs, and to resolve Smith's concern that the original story did not have sufficient dramatic resolution. Hence, Cynthia's daughter Prairie Flower does not die, but is rescued and reunited with her brother, Quanah Parker, after an Indian raid on the homestead, in which Cynthia is accidentally shot and killed. The Indian outfit created for Leonora Corona, the well-known opera singer who portrayed Cynthia Ann, was a hackneyed "squaw" costume consisting of a beaded headband with feather, dark wig with plaits, a long, buckskin beaded dress and moccasins, none of which have any specific or particular reference to Comanche culture.

Similarly, Smith appropriated songs from *The Indian Book* (Natalie Curtis, in Buehner 2007, p. 38) and used stereotypical musical references known as "Indianisms," themes, and aural clues that signify certain characters or characteristics. Cynthia Ann's dichotomy as both a Parker and a Comanche are emphasized by two separate musical themes, both of which portray her as the doomed, tragic white/ Indian heroine. Cynthia's mournful aria expresses her sorrow at her recapture:

> It is true I was born of the white race Yet raised in the Indian lodges I was bride of a great chief, I bore three children for him—I rode with him into battle—I saw him fall in battle, Now, I am a captive here In the house of my white people's father—Aiee—Aiee—Aiee—Aiee. (Selden 2006, p. 264)

The Indianist noises and shrieks such as "Ai-eee," which reference Cynthia, identify her not only as a Comanche, but also as barbaric, less than civilized, and unable to convey her grief in intelligible words. However, the barbarian inference is also accompanied in the opera by its binary opposite—the noble savage—as evinced through the text as Cynthia speaks: "my heart is as light as an eagle's wing and strong as an eagle's tendons; my feet are young and brave and free and eager to be running" (Buehner 2007, p. 28).

The opera reinforces the stereotypical imaging of Cynthia Ann. It was performed in 1939 and received much attention and acclaim. The opera was again performed in 1985, although critical reception this time found the libretto and music dated and the story lacking veracity.

From the early to mid-twentieth century and onward, the same captivity topos was being played out on the celluloid screen. *The Searchers* (John Ford 1956) is loosely based on the book by Alan LeMay, which is again loosely based on the captivity story of Cynthia Ann Parker. This is a Western in the classic mode, containing all the prerequisite elements: good versus evil, conflicting gender roles, racism, and a horror of miscegenation. Although Ford goes some way to attempt to redress the balance on these issues, in particular, the public's view of white Indians by the close of the film, it still contains many moments that are directly linked to earlier attitudes as portrayed in the captivity narratives. Ethan Edwards, the main character (the lone white hero), is portrayed as a virulent Indian hater, and makes especial reference during the main body of the film to the effects of rape or of sexual congress between white women and Indians. The implication is that any white woman who has sexual relations with an Indian (whether against her will or not) becomes a dirty savage herself. This attitude applies to his niece Debbie, who was captured by the Comanche several years prior. *"Living with Comanche ain't bein' alive,"* he asserts (Ebersole 1995, p. 245). Many scholarly treatises have been written on this film, in particular, *The Searchers. Essays and Reflections on John Ford's Classic Western* (Eckstein and Lehman 2004), which offers a series of fascinating viewpoints. However, Gary Ebersole's (1995) comments seem not only pertinent, but to also reflect the long history of continuity of the captivity literature and its associated imagery:

> There is no serious attempt [here] to understand Indian culture...The Indian functions as a cardboard villain in the heroic saga of the white settling of the West and the civilizing process, as well as an excuse for a sustained diatribe against miscegenation. Yet the audience is left with the feeling that everything will be alright...And if the rape of the white woman was an inevitable, if unfortunate, fact of life on the frontier, perhaps it too contributed to the civilizing process by provoking the righteous and purifying violence of the white male directed against the Indians. (p. 245)

I have related here just a few examples of how images have been the hall of mirrors to the history of narratives, reinforcing the message of expansionism and miscegenation within the texts concerning white captives. Most of the individuals concerned spent a relatively short while in captivity. A crucial figure to emerge from the histories has been the white Indian, frequently captured as a child and absorbed into the tribe. Situated in the unarticulated space between two cultures, the concept and reality of the white Indian seems to embody the existential questions discussed by Gary Ebersole, which arise out of the conflict and chaos of settling America: "Could one lose one's identity?...was it possible to transform one's self fundamentally and thus escape from the bounded nature of a given sociohistorical identity? Was the vaunted distinction between 'civilized' and 'primitive' real?" (p. 190).

Two photographs, both of Cynthia Ann (figures 9.2 and 9.3), resist the stereotypical narrative illustration and also reflect upon Ebersole's quote and the seeming impossibility of a definitive answer to the questions posed. Photography has made powerful contributions to the field of imaging whites and Indians, and it is interesting to reflect whether this medium refutes or further mythologizes the stereotypes of race and gender as evidenced in the texts and subtexts of the captivity narratives. We need to take into consideration how

Figure 9.2 Cynthia Ann Parker, A. F. Corning, 1860 [Hacker]. Courtesy of Denver Public Library, Western History Collection, call no. X-32238.

Figure 9.3 Cynthia Ann Parker, photograph by William W. Bridgers. Courtesy of Degolyer Library, Southern Methodist University, Dallas, Texas Ag.2008.0005.

much such photographs are posed and constructed, with how much or little regard is given for the actual persona or situation of the individual and also, to distinguish the different genres and reasons for recording the subject.

Figure 9.2, a haunting photograph of Cynthia Ann, was taken at Fort Worth by A. F. Corning in 1860, on the way to Isaac Parker's home. She is breastfeeding her daughter Topsannah, and wears her hair short, possibly as a Comanche sign of mourning for her husband and two sons.

The formalist qualities of the image are striking, particularly the homespun blouse and kerchief, which neither denote the kind of western dress a female member of the well-known Parker family would wear, nor the buckskins to which Cynthia Ann had been accustomed. The hauntingly sad expression in her eyes is remarkable—all the more so for the fact that she looks straight into the camera and not to the side, as is usual with full frontal portraits of Indians. She does not however, engage with the photographer; the eyes are slightly unfocused and suggest a deeply distressed internalization. The hands also hold a great deal of tension, as they encircle and tightly hold her child to her breast.

The rhetoric of the image raises many questions as to its meaning. Such a photograph of a woman breastfeeding would normally be taken as a native field study for anthropology and classification of tribe and type. This is a white woman and it is also a studio photograph. It is reminiscent of the kind of government photographs taken of Indians, both full frontal and side on, as with the identification photographs taken of criminals within our own justice system; they are not posed, as for a representational portrait, but taken more as a literal record. So what is the photographer's intent and how does he view the woman he is photographing? He would have been aware of her history and fame. She is white, and yet the signifier of the baby at the breast indicates she is being perceived predominantly as Indian. The image has the curious taint of the freak and the sexually contaminated woman; the "white Indian" captured not only by the army, but also here by the white voyeur.

The image also operates on a symbolic level. Here is the mythic Cynthia Ann Parker, the stuff of legend for more than twenty years. The photograph, by presenting her in this specific way, mythologizes her story even further. The symbolic connotation of Madonna and child here is obvious, but also perverted, for we are presented with the fruits of miscegenation; the white woman with her Indian child. She is highly hybridized, engendered by her external and internal *distanciation* from both cultures, and the messages are uneasy and mixed. Who is the photograph for? What is its role? Who will the reader be? There is no overt evidence that the photograph was initially widely circulated although it was reproduced in the first account of her history (DeShields 1886). We do know, however, that Quanah Parker eventually obtained a copy and kept it in his room (p. 73).

There is only one other portrait of Cynthia Ann, taken several months later, on a visit to the secession conventions in Austin (figure 9.3). Taken there and dressed up by her neighbors in an attempt to "civilize" her, Cynthia Ann is once more captured in this photograph. She sits uneasily, with eyes averted, her hair caught in a netted snood, and wearing a cloak. The braided lapels, collar, and brooch fastening suggest strangely regal connotations and seem at odds with her body language. Her pose is stiff and awkward, her shoulders hunched, and we can read a range of emotions into her expression. Here again is that same unfocused and internalized gaze, although here it is averted to the side. Her expression suggests sadness, bewilderment, and fear, and evinces a feeling of alienation. Using Roland Barthes's (2000) theory of the *studium* and *punctum* to read this photograph (p. 25), we look at the image of a white woman, dressed in the conventions of her time, possibly in her best outfit, and sitting composed, for a formal portrait (the overall field of the photograph, the *studium*). However, on close examination, what disrupts and disturbs that general impression is the punctum—the little "sting" or focus that belies the whole and by focusing on the shock of a detail, changes the reading. In this case, it is twofold—the tight, down set of the mouth and the overly large, work-roughened hands, which are clasped tightly over her body. Together these two signs overwhelm the portrait and suggest a resistance—a resistance to this particular circumstance, the taking of the photograph, but also a resistance to the outfit she is clothed in, to white society and by implication, a resistance to colonization.

During the eighteenth century, as the numbers of white Indians increased and chose not to return, it became apparent that conversely, few Indians had or wished to become white (Axtell 1975, p. 56). This was in direct conflict with the perceived theology of the day, and the notion of white colonization with its intentions to convert and civilize the indigenous population. While the presence of these white Indians opened up new possibilities for changing one's cultural identity, this did not actually happen, and the narratives, novels, and images were used as a weapon to maintain the ideological white status quo of supremacy and order as the expansionist program rolled on. However, to return to the opening quote of Ricoeur: it is in the telling of our stories that we give ourselves an identity...it makes very little difference whether these stories are true or false...(Ebersole 1995, p. 190).

As with her Indian captors, who subsequently became her friends and family, Cynthia Ann was unable to tell her own story. The proliferation of material written about her and inspired by her have to some extent perpetuated and reinforced the mythology of western expansionism, but the powerful images we have of her intervene and mitigate by showing the real confusion and plight of this woman who could only exist in the liminal interstices between two cultures. Her story is of particular interest in that she was captured, enslaved, and subsequently adopted by the Comanche, then recaptured by the whites, and in a sense, "adopted" by them too. Such terms are difficult to unravel, but the visual history of Cynthia Ann Parker in distancing itself from the commonplace narrative illustrations helped to reinforce how interpretations of the word *captive* became blurred and interchangeable between white and Indian communities.

Note

1. The original account was printed in 1682, but woodcuts were not included until the editions printed from the 1770s onward.

Epilogue

Reflections and Refractions from the Southwest Borderlands

James F. Brooks

Some nine miles downstream from where I write in Santa Fe, New Mexico, there thrives a "living history" museum known as El Rancho de Las Golondrinas (The Ranch of the Swallows). Its core buildings date from 1710, when the *rancho* served as a *paraje*, or resting place, along *el camino real de tierra adentro* (the royal road of the interior lands) that connected Mexico City to its far distant colonial settlements in the province of *Nuevo Mexico*. Established by Miguel Vega y Coca, the rancho flourished and grew with the increase in trade through the era of the Bourbon Reforms and, especially, after the 1821 opening of the St. Louis to Chihuahua "Santa Fe Trail" that linked American and Mexican producers and consumers in a vibrant international trade.

Those familiar with the architecture of the Southwest might see echoes of the Spanish and North African countryside in the rancho today, a complex covering more than 160 acres and featuring a fortified, adobe *placita* (compound residence), complete with defensive tower; a nineteenth-century home and all of its outbuildings, a molasses mill, a threshing ground, several primitive water mills, a blacksmith shop, a wheelwright shop, a winery, and extensive vineyards (figure E.1). Many of the essential elements of Spanish and Mexican lifeways may be seen reenacted on the museum's programs, from sheep shearing to wool weaving, from corn and wheat fields to grain milling, from Catholic blessings of the *acequias* (irrigation ditches) in the spring to autumn harvest festivals replete with burrows grinding sorghum into molasses.

But one aspect of southwestern life is not relived for the visiting public, although gestured within the fortified compound. In one

Figure E.1 Reconstructed eighteenth-century fortified *placita* at Rancho de las Golondrinas, image courtesy of author.

corner of the placita, well secured by a heavy wooden door is the *cuarto de cautivos* (captives' room), wherein, according to the interpretive materials, lived Indian captives seized in warfare and housed at the rancho, either as laborers or awaiting purchase and "adoption" by other Spanish colonial families (figure E.2). The interpretive staff of Golondrinas deserves credit for noting the existence of the room and its occupants, but—like the furor surrounding the proposed depiction of African slavery at living museums such as Colonial Williamsburg and Jamestown—the lingering sensitivity among indigenous peoples in New Mexico, and awkwardness among the descendants of Spanish colonists, has prevented any attempt to portray Indian slavery at public events[1] (Gable and Handler 1993, 1994, 1997; Gable, Handler, and Lawson 1992).

Doing so would not be impossible, however. Throughout the lands formerly within the embrace of New Spain there exists a rich panoply of folk performance that grew from the practice. A staple of Christmas and New Year's ceremonies is the Matachines Dance, "the beautiful dance of subjugation" that portrays the conquest, courtship, and "marriage" of Cortez's consort La Malinche or Malantzín

Figure E.2 *Cuarto de Cautivos* at Rancho de las Golondrinas. Image courtesy of author.

during the Spanish conquest of Tenochtítlan. Like the Matachines Dance, which evolved from medieval Iberian *romances fronterizos* (frontier ballads) that wove both violence and romance into narratives of reconquest, the southwestern custom of *Los Comanches* (Comanche dances) reenacts the reciprocal capture and adoption of girls between Indian and Spanish colonial families, a theme seen often in this volume. Less well-known but more widespread are the dozens of *inditas* ("little Indian" songs or girls) that usually combine Spanish and Indian words in tender, sometimes humorous, lyrics implying a kinship (albeit covert and informal) between Spaniards and their Indian neighbors:

Indita, indita, indita	*Indita, indita, indita*
Indita de Cochití	*indita* from Cochití
No le hace que seiga indita	it doesn't matter that you are Indian
Sí al cabo no soy pa'ti	if in the end I'm not for you

Despite these elaborate folk traditions—Hispano and Native American—that commemorate the practice of intercultural slavery, few among the general public are aware of the phenomenon. Those who are aware of the hidden history often hew to the folk interpretation offered by one singer of an *indita*:

> In New Mexico, there never really was any *real* slavery. While there may have been some isolated cases of abuse or mistreatment (always repugnant), *inditas* or *inditos* were seen with favor and treated kindly, with love and decorum. They nearly always married into the family where they grew up. Poets chose to dedicate their songs to these adopted Natives—the highest compliment they could give—a beautiful way to honor these orphans, indeed.

As former New Mexico State historian Estévan Rael-Gálvez has commented, "being *like* family" is a far cry—legally, socially, and emotionally—from "being family," and served as a subterfuge for human bondage among his kinsmen (both Hispano and Indian) for centuries. Dr. Rael-Gálvez's courage in pushing the topic onto the edges of public consciousness has opened a space for knowledge once hidden with family memories to cautiously circulate in public forums. He has also opened the window for some to explore the rather provocative notion that captures and enslavements may have *predated* Spanish colonialism in the region (Barry in Loeffler, Loeffler and Lamadrid 1991, p. 39; Brooks 2002; Cameron 2008; Loeffler, Loeffler, and Lamadrid 1999; Rael-Gálvez 2002; Rodriguez 2009; Santos-Granero 2009).

Some seventy-five miles north of Rancho de las Golondrinas is another "living history" museum, the Martínez Hacienda on the lower reaches of the river that passes through Taos Pueblo and the more recent Euroamerican village of San Fernando de Taos (figure E.3). Even more fortress-like than Golondrinas, the Martínez family built its massive adobe room-blocks in the early nineteenth century to expand their mercantile trade business, especially that with neighboring *indios barbaros* such as Utes, Jicarilla Apaches, and Comanches. No small part of that trade involved the purchase of Indian children and women garnered in raids into the Great Basin, where the non-equestrian Paiutes were vulnerable to mounted indigenous raiders. And at the hacienda, too, one can find a corner room described as the *cuarto de cautivos*, with again a glancing and tantalizingly opaque reference to a system of slavery that long prevailed in the Southwest (Blackhawk 2006; Weber and Richardson 1996).

Equally intriguing, given the aspirations of this volume, is a plexiglass vitrine inside the *cuarto* that holds a small ceramic vessel (figure E.4). This bowl, dating to the fifteenth century and of the type known as "Potsui'i Incised," hints at a deeper history involving

Figure E.3 Martínez Hacienda, *cuarto de cautivos* in far corner of courtyard. Image courtesy of author.

Figure E.4 Potsui'i Incised Jar from Puye village, New Mexico, *ca.* 1425–1525, courtesy New Mexico Laboratory of Anthropology, collection no. 20852/11. Puye LA47 Museum of Indian Arts and Culture/Laboratory of Anthropology, Department of Cultural Affairs. www.miaclab.org. Photography by David McNeece.

the incorporation—coerced or voluntary—of outsiders in the pre-Hispanic period. The clay vessel features the incised designs associated with Plains villagers far to the east, not the painted geometrics common along the Chama river valley and the Pajarito Plateau whence the atypical Potsui'i Incised is found. Its maker crafted it not with the "paddle-and-anvil" techniques of Plains villagers but with the traditional coils of all southwestern Pueblo pottery. The interpreters at the Martínez Hacienda use the bowl to confirm some aspects of human exchange between indigenous societies, and hint that the practices of human bondage evident in the *cuarto de cautivos* may have begun much earlier, with the capture and integration of Plains village women into Pueblo society (Habichte-Mauche in Cameron 2008, pp. 181–204; Martin pp. 159–180).

How do these historic sites, far from the mainstream of narratives about slavery in Early America, through their folk interpretation and their material representations communicate with the wider meanings and contexts of North American Indian captivity, adoption, and slavery discussed in this volume? Perhaps productively.

Over the last decade or so I have argued that in the Southwest borderlands indigenous and colonial practices of capture, adoption, and enslavement merged over time to form a "slave system" in which victims symbolized social wealth, performed services for their masters, and produced material goods under the threat of violence. Although captives often assimilated through institutions of kinship, they seldom shed completely their alien stigma, and even then their numbers were regularly renewed through capture or purchase, thereby reinvigorating the servile classes. Grounded in conflict, the pattern developed through interaction into a unifying web of intellectual, material, and emotional exchange within which Native and Euroamerican men fought and traded to exploit and bind to themselves women and children of other peoples. As these "captives" became "cousins" through Native American and Spanish New Mexican kinship structures, they too became agents of conflict, conciliation, and cultural redefinition.

This regional pattern is born out and vigorously elaborated in rich detail in the essays collected in this volume. Unlike African chattel slavery in the British colonial (and later U.S. national) North America, the cases addressing the Native American experience with slavery (either as victims or as perpetrators, often both) show that this history of human bondage—in its many and diverse forms—found affinity with kin-based systems motivated less by a demand for units of labor than their desire for prestigious social symbols and the necessity of rebuilding populations shattered by disease and warfare. The kin-embedded structures of Native American slave holders created vastly different gender and class realities than those experienced by Native Americans in labor-oriented chattel slaveries. Because the captive women and children in this system often found themselves integrated within the host community through kinship systems—adoption and marriage in the indigenous cases, *compadrazgo* (godparenthood) and concubinage in the French and Spanish colonial cases, and biological reproduction through sexual violence in many British colonial examples—they participated in the gradual transformation of the host society. Most such slaves became members of the capturing society, often in marginal categories but in ways that allowed them to bring useful cultural repertoires and mediation to their new kinspeople. The ties between gender and power in the Southwest take more fertile meaning from the fact that the hapless women and children who became slaves also became the main negotiators of cultural, economic, and political exchange between groups.

As volume editors Pratt and Carocci make clear in their introduction, the colonial North American ethnic landscape can now be understood as "the product of an intermingling of peoples that has its roots in slaving, captivity, barter, exchange, ransom and other forms of human incorporation that frequently brought together peoples from very distant areas." The precise social mechanisms by which new peoples were broken and bound into these social formations occupies the center of several of the essays, as does the complicated and often confused perception of the practices as viewed by European and American observers, then and now.

The very early—even precolonial—roots of this alternating dynamic of inclusion through violence and exclusion through social boundary making is seen in Marvin Jeter's essay, in which he suggests that in the Southeast and Lower Mississippi valley "long-lived, indeed institutionalized and ritualized traditions of intersocietal conflict 'pre-adapted' the Native Americans for exploitation by European colonialists using divide-and-conquer strategies and tactics." He might well have extended this insight to the precolonial Southwest, where still little understood crises in the thirteenth and fourteenth centuries severely reduced Puebloan populations and redrew the settlement landscape from thousands of scattered farming hamlets to a few dozen aggregated, defensive towns, often barely able to sustain themselves from the surrounding agricultural and hunting resources. When Spaniards first ventured into the region in the sixteenth century, they found not only large masonry-and-adobe "cities" but also evidence of intertribal conflict and emerging violence from newly arrived Athapaskan "Teyas" who raided granaries each harvest season and engaged in a reciprocal capturing economy. Thus the arrival of Spanish slaving parties apparently supercharged a preexisting network of human trafficking (Brooks 2002, pp. 1–83; Lauber 1913, pp. 48–61; LeBlanc 1999).

Robbie Ethridge's essay on the "Mississippian shatter zone" focuses on the postcontact "region of instability in eastern North America that...was created by the combined conditions of the destablization of Native polities by their engagements with Spanish conquistadors; the internal political weaknesses of Native polities; the introduction of Old World pathogens; and the inauguration of a nascent capitalist economic system by Europeans through a commercial trade in Indian slaves." Her very important macroperspective on the centrality of slaving economies to colonial era Native American politics and history is substantiated in Eric Bowne's more narrowly focused examination of the political evolution among southeastern peoples, in which he finds "four 'types' of Native polities" that may help us to understand "the historical reality of the early colonial South: (1) Neotraditional polities, (2) militaristic slaving polities, (3) Euro-dependent polities, and (4) confederated polities." Over the course of a single generation in the late seventeenth and early eighteenth centuries, we see vanish from the region identities such as Guale, Mocama, Timucua, Calusa, Hitchitis, Alabamas, Okmulgees, Esaws, Waterees, and Congarees—either annihilated (?) or ceased to exist as distinct ethnic groups or were absorbed into new confederations such as the Catawbas and Creeks. Archaeological and historical research in the Southwest is beginning to show a similar thinning out and packing down of earlier identities under the hammer of that region's "shatter zone" (Carter 2009; Ethridge and Shuck-Hall 2009).

Following these essential framing essays we have a series of studies that move us in new disciplinary directions, as well as dialing in an even closer focus on colonial Louisiana, Virginia, the Cherokee Backcountry, western Oregon, and the *Comanchería* of the Southern Plains.

Dayna Bowker Lee shows that although the French first attempted to prohibit Indian slaving, within months the new settlements at New Orleans and in the hinterlands were thoroughly enmeshed in the trade and would become in its social and phenotypic composition archetypical for a New World slave society. As Bowker Lee points out, few Creoles who celebrate their partial Indian ancestry know (or will admit they know) that those progenitors served their role in creolization as victims of slavery—an awkward silence (or self-silencing) toward which I signaled earlier. In the Southwest, we're seeing the rebirth of a *genízaro* (auxiliary Indian warrior-slaves, attached to the Spanish colony) identity, as contemporary descendants of that caste reclaim—simultaneously—Indian and slave progenitors. The "cultural capital" currently attached to Indianness seems to outweigh the emotional deficit of slave descent, at least for the historical moment[2] (Gandert et al. 2000).

Pratt's fine grained art historical approach to the handful of images produced around John Smith's "captivity" among the Powhatans offers us the fascinating insight that "in the presentation of Smith's captivity we also see, perhaps, the origin of all those later accounts of hapless white victims surrounded by violent savages undertaking alien rituals." Compared to the very ambiguous (and real) experience of Pocahontas's captivity and the reality of African enslavement in the Atlantic world, the idealized victimization of Smith's fictional suffering among the Powhatans made easy viewing for consumers in the early modern Atlantic world (for comparative treatment, see Voigt 2009).

Castillo Street picks up Smith's story and extends key themes to the experience of African slaves and slave descendants such as Olaudah Equiano and John Marrant. Focusing on language and rhetoric, she shows "the ways in which these three individuals articulated their own experience of captivity and of contact with a culture very different to their own." She finds that extended residence and acquisition of Native languages brought more sympathetic (although never equalitarian) perceptions, which pushed uncomfortably against some of the more distancing notions of civilization embedded in their Christian faith. Similar slippage in faith and piety accompanied Christian missionary activity in the American Southwest, as non-Indian reformers found their own devotion to Christian "uplift" of Native peoples confounded by the deeply numinous perspectives of those they purported to civilize (Jacobson 1999).

Patrick Minges endeavors a more extended and detailed analysis of the Marrant tale, while offering a critique of its conventional representation as a "captivity narrative." Marrant's stay of several months among the Cherokee feels different to Minges than traditional stories of captivity: "What the very persons themselves may describe as 'captivity' for their kin, community, and avid audiences may not have been captivity at all but something more akin to adoption or, as in Marrant's case, absorption or a communal embrace." Minges's review of early colonial Cherokee cases of ambiguous ties between Tsalagi and external "others" is a useful caution that "the tentative nature" of ideas such as captivity, adoption, and slavery depend upon "the subtle contexts from which these descriptions arise, the profound nature of power relationships entailed in any cultural encounter, and the challenge of distance both temporal and intellectual." His cautions certainly pertain here in the Southwest, where the term *criada/o* (lit. "one raised up/adopted") has long served to hide the seamier side of being *como familiar* (like family) for Indians and their offspring in Hispano households.

Moving west geographically and forward in time, Brandi Denison and Lin Holdridge bring the sensibilities of a scholar of religion and art historian, respectively, to the interpretive challenges of seeking meaning from tales of capture and assimilation, or escape and redemption.

In her graceful discourse on the Meeker massacre and captivity narrative, Brandi Denison suggests "captivity narrative scholars often ignore the religious language in nineteen-century captivity narratives, suggesting that after the Puritan era, captivity narrative authors aimed to spread anti-Native American propaganda rather than express religious experiences." Countering this tendency, Denison lifts up the description of Chief Ouray's sister, "Susan," as having a "kind, noble, Christian disposition" that prompts her to save the Meeker women from certain death at the hands of their captors.

Placing the narrative in the context of an emerging reformist movement toward assimilation of Native Americans, the casting of Susan as a Christian in heart, if not in name, "was an attempt to sway public opinion" toward a new, if less than successful, Indian policy. Presbyterian missions into New Mexico and Arizona in the late nineteenth and early decades of the twentieth centuries sought similar policy outcomes, cloaked in the artifice of the Lord's work. But in the Southwest (with the important exception of the Hopis, where Protestant denominations flourish), missionaries ran into a solidly entrenched Catholic Church among the Pueblos, which then forced a double movement to characterize both indigenous spiritual practices and the Catholic faith as dangerously retrograde and a barrier to self-improvement.

This problem of voice and representation becomes even more profound in Lin Holdridge's exploration of the Cynthia Ann Parker experience. "As with her Indian captors, who subsequently became her friends and family," writes Holdridge, "Cynthia Ann was unable to tell her own story. The proliferation of material written about her and inspired by her have to some extent perpetuated and reinforced the mythology of western expansionism, but the powerful images we have of her intervene and mitigate by showing the real confusion and plight of this woman who could only exist in the liminal interstices between two cultures." Tracing the history of women's victimization narratives from the early colonial period through Hollywood westerns, Holdridge shows in Parker's case, a "double captivity"—first among the Comanches, and then among her white redeemers—that posed an insurmountable emotional hurdle for the woman, while providing rich grist for cinematic commentary of American's fears of miscegenation. And yet even in the Hollywood version of events, we may see cultural commentaries on captivity and adoption subtly buried in cinematic bluster, especially in the case of John Ford's *The Searchers* (Brooks pp. 265—84 in Eckstein and Lehman 2004).

Someday, perhaps, school kids visiting el Rancho de Las Golondrinas or the Martínez Hacienda will see some version of what these fine essays attempt to discern, deployed in a sensitive and compelling performance. If nothing else, the bonds made herein, and broken throughout, are nothing less than the underweave of colonialism, where women and children, and the families they composed, were central participants rather than bit actors. I applaud Stephanie Pratt and Max Carocci for gathering us all in London over those two brisk and bright winter days in 2008, and salute my colleagues for their deep engagement with questions both heartbreaking and transformative.

Notes

1. For debates about public interpretation of slavery at public sites and monuments, see citations listed, as well as the following websites:

    http://www.washingtonpost.com/wp-srv/local/daily/july99/williamsburg7.htm;

    http://www.history.org/almanack/places/hb/hbgrthopes.cfm;
    http://www.common-place.org/vol-03/no-04/lessons/;
    http://www.common-place.org/vol-01/no-04/slavery/white.shtml.

2. In 2007, the New Mexico State Legislature extended formal recognition to the *genízaro* descendants as an indigenous group (see House Memorial 40 and Senate Memorial 59, 2007), which did not carry legal standing; see also Malcom Ebright, *Genízaros*, webpage of the Office of the State Historian, New Mexico, http://www.newmexicohistory.org/filedetails.php?fileID=4836.

Notes on Contributors

Eric E. Bowne received his PhD in anthropology from the University of Georgia in 2003. He is the author of *The Westo Indians* published by the University of Alabama Press in 2005. His work has appeared in a number of volumes including most recently *Mapping the Mississippian Shatter Zone*, edited by Robbie Ethridge and Sheri Shuck-Hall. Bowne is currently working on a guidebook to public archaeology sites of the Mississippian period to be published by the University of Georgia Press and is preparing a book-length manuscript on the life of Henry Woodward.

James F. Brooks, SAR president and an interdisciplinary scholar of the indigenous and colonial past, has held professorial appointments at the University of Maryland, UC Santa Barbara, and UC Berkeley, as well as fellowships at the Institute for Advanced Study in Princeton and at the SAR itself during 2000–2001. The recipient of more than a dozen national awards for scholarly excellence, his 2002 book *Captives & Cousins: Slavery, Kinship and Community in the Southwest Borderlands* focused on the traffic in women and children across the region as expressions of intercultural violence and accommodation. He extends these questions most recently through an essay on the eighteenth- and nineteenth-century Pampas borderlands of Argentina in his coedited advanced seminar volume *Small Worlds: Method, Meaning, and Narrative in Microhistory* from SAR Press.

Max Carocci (PhD social anthropology, University of London, 2005) has been teaching indigenous arts of the Americas at the University of London since 2002. He started research with Native Americans in 1989 producing and directing several short anthropological films. He has published extensively on Native North American anthropology, art, history, and material culture. In 2011 he edited the proceedings of the conference *Turquoise, Henry Christy and European Collections* with Jonathan King and Colin McEwan. Among his latest publications is *Warriors of the Plains: The Arts of Plains Indian Warfare* (British Museum Press, 2012). He has recently curated an exhibition on Plains Indian art for the British Museum, and is currently working on an exhibition on the Native American photographic collections of the Royal Anthropological Institute of Great Britain and Ireland.

Susan Castillo Street is Harriet Beecher Stowe Professor of American literature at King's College London. She is the author of three monographs, *Notes from the Periphery*, *Colonial Encounters 1500–1768: Performing America*, and *American Literature in Context to 1865*, coeditor (with Ivy Schweitzer) of *The Literatures of Colonial America: An Anthology*, and editor of several essay collections. She has published extensively on Native American writing, early American writing, and the American South. She is also a published poet and literary translator.

Brandi Denison is assistant professor in the Department of Philosophy and the Program of Religious Studies at the University of North Florida. She is the editor for the Religion in the American West blog, sponsored through the American Academy of Religion. She teaches courses on American religious history, religion and race, and religion and nature.

Robbie Ethridge is professor of anthropology at the University of Mississippi. In addition to writing several articles and book chapters on the ethnohistory of the Indians of the American South, she is the author of *Creek Country: The Creek Country and Their World, 1796–1816* (University of North Carolina Press, 2003), and she is the coeditor, along with Charles Hudson, of the volume *The Transformation of the Southeastern Indians, 1540–1760*, published by the University Press of Mississippi (2002). She also coedited, with Thomas J. Pluckhahn, *Light on the Path: The Anthropology and History of the Southeastern Indians* (2006) published by the University of Alabama Press. Her latest coedited volume is *Mapping the Mississippian Shatter Zone: The Colonial Indian Slave Trade and Regional Instability in the American South* (2009), with Sherri Shuck-Hall, published by the University of Nebraska Press. Her latest monograph is entitled *From Chicaza to Chickasaw: The European Invasion and the Transformation of the Mississippian World, 1540–1715* (2010) published by the University of North Carolina Press.

Lin Holdridge has been a researcher at the University of Plymouth for over sixteen years and has published primarily in the fields of art history and fine art. Among her latest publications is the Routledge

Companion to Research in the Arts (eds. Michael Biggs and Henrik Karlsson; 2010). She currently works as the visual resources officer for the Faculty of Arts and is involved in various creative projects. She is also an independent art history lecturer and researcher, and is particularly interested in the visual cultures connected with Native American studies.

Marvin D. Jeter (PhD, Arizona State University, 1977) has been the UAM Research Station archeologist for the Arkansas Archeological Survey (AAS) for over twenty-five years. He has also worked in Alabama, Louisiana, Mississippi, and Tennessee in the U.S. Southeast, Illinois in the Midwest, and the mountains and deserts of Arizona in the Southwest. His major interests are the late prehistoric, protohistoric, and early historic Native American cultures of the Lower Mississippi Valley, and the history of archeology. His publications include: an archeological and bioanthropological overview of Arkansas, Louisiana, and western Mississippi (AAS, 1989); the award-winning *Edward Palmer's Arkansaw Mounds* (University of Arkansas Press, 1990; reprinted by University of Alabama Press, 2010); and since 2000, several book chapters and articles about late prehistoric to early historic cultural continuity, change, disruption, and possible connections of archeological sites and cultures with ethnohistorically documented tribal and linguistic groups. He has also authored a number of reviews of Southeastern and Southwestern archeological publications

Dayna Bowker Lee holds an MA in history and a PhD in anthropology. She served as assistant professor and director of the Louisiana Regional Folklife Program at Northwestern State University of Louisiana, where she continues to serve as adjunct faculty. Her research interests include Native Americans in the American Southeast, creolization, and French colonial Louisiana. Dr. Lee is currently the lead ethnographer and tribal liaison in a project to document traditional cultural properties along the Gulf coast between Louisiana and the Florida panhandle.

Patrick Minges is an independent scholar who specializes in the social and cultural interactions between African Americans and Native Americans in the Old South and in the Indian Territory. He has published three books on slavery, *Slavery in the Cherokee Nation* (2003), *Black Indian Slave Narratives* (2004), and *Far More Terrible for Women* (2006). He holds a PhD in religious history from Union Theological Seminary in the City of New York and an educational specialist degree in digital history and scholarly technology from the University of Virginia. He and his wife currently live in Quaker Gap, N.C. where he works for the New Schools Project of the State Department of Public Instruction and Stokes County Schools.

Stephanie Pratt is a member of the Dakota (Sioux) Nation and Associate Professor (Reader) in art history at the University of Plymouth in the United Kingdom. She has published widely on the visual representation of Native Americans in European art from the 1580s to the 1870s. Her recent book *American Indians in British Art, 1700–1840* (Oklahoma University Press, 2005) explored the complex workings behind the construction of an Indian image in the colonial and postcolonial periods. She was one of the curators of the exhibition *Between Worlds, Voyagers to Britain, 1700–1850* at the National Portrait Gallery in 2007 and is currently developing another exhibition on the "Indian Gallery" paintings of the American artist George Catlin, also for the National Portrait Gallery, London, opening in 2013.

Bibliography

Ahlstrom, Sydney. 2004. *A Religious History of the American People* (2nd ed.). Yale University Press.

Alchon, S. A. 2003. *A Pest in the Land: New World Epidemics in a Global Perspective*. Albuquerque: University of New Mexico Press.

Alexander, Michael, ed. 1976. *Discovering the New World Based on the Works of Theodore de Bry* London: London Editions.

Allain, Mathé. 1988. *"Not Worth a Straw": French Colonial Policy and the Early Years of Louisiana*. Lafayette: University of Southwestern Louisiana.

Alvord, Clarence W., and Lee Bidgood, eds. 1912. *The First Explorations of the Trans-Alleghany Region by Virginians 1650–1674* Cleveland: Arthur H. Clark Company.

Anderson, David G. 1994. *The Savannah River Chiefdoms: Political Change in the Late Prehistoric Southeast*. Tuscaloosa: University of Alabama Press.

———. 1996a. "Chiefly Cycling Behavior and Large-Scale Abandonment as Viewed from the Savannah River Basin," in J. F. Scarry (ed.), *Political Structure and Change in the Prehistoric Southeastern United States*, pp. 150–91. Gainesville: University Press of Florida.

———. 1996b. "Fluctuations Between Simple and Complex Chiefdoms: Cycling in the Late Prehistoric Southeast," in J. F. Scarry (ed.), *Political Structure and Change in the Prehistoric Southeastern United States*, pp. 231–52. Gainesville: University Press of Florida.

———. 1997. "The Role of Cahokia in the Evolution of Southeastern Mississippian Society," in T. R. Pauketat and T. E. Emerson (eds), *Cahokia: Domination and Ideology in the Mississippian World*, pp. 248–68. Lincoln: University of Nebraska Press.

———. 1999. "Examining Chiefdoms in the Southeast: an Application of Multiscalar Analysis," in J. E. Neitzel (ed.), *Great towns and Regional Polities in the American Southwest and Southeast*, pp. 215–42. Albuquerque: University of New Mexico Press.

Anderson, David G., and Kenneth E. Sassaman, eds. 1996. *The Paleoindian and Early Archaic Southeast*. Tuscaloosa: University of Alabama Press.

Anderson, David G., and Robert C. Mainfort, Jr, eds. 2002. *The Woodland Southeast*. Tuscaloosa: University of Alabama Press.
Anon. "Access Genealogy" (n.d.). *Nancy Ward*. Retrieved July 17, 2008, from Genealogy of the Cherokee Indians: http://www.accessgenealogy.com/scripts/data/database.cgi?ArticleID=0008950andfile=Dataandreport=SingleArticle.
Anon. "Carolina, S. O." (n.d.). *Early History of North Carolina*. Retrieved March 7, 2008, from NCInformation: http://www.ncinformation.com/History.htm.
Anon. n.d. "About the Choctaw-Apache Tribe of Ebarb" [cited at CATE, available at Choctaw Apache Tribe of Ebarb: http://www.choctaw-apache.org/ (accessed January 31, 2011).
Aptheker, H. 1963. *American Negro Slave Revolts*. New York: International Publishers.
Aranguiz y Cotes, Don Alonso de 1659 Letter to the Crown, 11-9-1659. Audiencia of Santo Domingo 839.
Archives des Colonies, Séries C11, Correspondence l'arrivée, Canada, Archives Nationales, Centre des Archives de Outre Mer, Aix-en-Provence, France.
Archives des Colonies, Séries C13, Louisiane, Archives Nationales, Centre des Archives de Outre Mer, Aix-en-Provence, France.
Arkush, Elizabeth. 2008. "Warfare and Violence in the Americas" (book review essay), *American Antiquity* (73): 560–75.
Arkush, Elizabeth, and Mark Allen, eds. 2006. *The Archaeology of Warfare: Prehistories of Raiding and Conquest*. Gainesville: University Press of Florida.
"Arrival of the Meeker Family at the Los Pinos Agency," *Denver Daily News*, October 29, 1879.
Ashcroft, Bill, Gareth Griffiths, and Helen Tiffin, eds. 1997. *The Post-Colonial Studies Reader*. London and New York: Routledge.
Atkinson, J. R. 2004. *Splendid Land, Splendid People: The Chickasaw Indians to Removal*. Tuscaloosa: University of Alabama Press.
Avery, George. 1999. *Annual Report for the Los Adaes Station Archaeology Program*. Los Adaes Station Archaeology Program, Department of Social Sciences, Northwestern State University, Natchitoches, Louisiana.
Axtell, James. January 1975. In "The White Indians of Colonial America *William and Mary Quarterly*," 3rd series, vol. 32, no. 1, pp. 55–88.
———. 1985. *The Invasion Within: The Contest of Cultures in Colonial North America*. Oxford: Oxford University Press.
———. 1990. *After Columbus: Essays in the Ethnohistory of Colonial North America*. Oxford: Oxford University Press.
———. 1992. *Beyond 1492, Encounters in Colonial North America*. Oxford: Oxford University Press.
———. 1994. *The European and the Indian Essays in the Ethnohistory of Colonial and North America*. Oxford: Oxford University Press.

———. 1997. *The Indians' New South: Cultural Change in the Colonial Southeast*. Baton Rouge and London: Louisiana State University Press.

Baker, B. J., and L. Kealhofer. 1996. *Bioarchaeology of Native American Adaptation in the Spanish Borderlands*. Gainesville: University Press of Florida.

Bamforth, Douglas. 1993. "Stone Tools, Steel Tools: Contact Period Household Technology at Helo," in J. D. Rogers and S. M. Wilson (eds), *Ethnohistory and Archaeology: Approaches to Postcontact Change in the Americas*, pp. 49–72. New York: Plenum Press.

Banerjee, Pompa. 2005. "The White Othello: Turkey and Virginia in John Smith's *True Travels*," in Robert Appelbaum and John Wood Sweet (eds), *Envisioning an English Empire. Jamestown and the Making of the North Atlantic World*, pp. 135–51. Philadelphia: University of Pennsylvania Press.

Barbour, Philip L. *Pocahontas and her world: A chronicle of America's first settlement in which is related the story of the Indians and the Englishmen, particularly Captain John Smith, Captain Samuel Argall, and Master John Rolfe*, Boston: Houghton Mifflin, 1970 [ca. 1969]

———, ed. 1986. *The Complete Works of Captain John Smith, 1580–1631*. Chapel Hill: University of North Carolina Press.

Bareis, Charles J., and James W. Porter, eds. 1984. *American Bottom Archaeology*. Urbana and Chicago: University of Illinois Press.

Barnett, James F. Jr. 2007. *The Natchez Indians: A History to 1735*. Jackson: University Press of Mississippi.

Barr, Juliana. 2005. "From Captives to Slaves: Commodifying Indian Women in the Borderlands." *Journal of American History* 92(1): 19–46.

———. 2007. *Peace Came in the Form of a Woman: Indians and Spaniards in the Texas Borderlands*. Chapel Hill: University of North Carolina Press.

Barthes, Roland. 2000. *Camera Lucida Reflections on Photography* [Richard Howard trans.]. London: Vintage Press.

Baum, Rosalie M. (Summer). 1994. "Early-American Literature: Reassessing the Black Contribution." *Eighteenth-Century Studies* (African American Culture in the Eighteenth-Century) 27(4): 533–49.

Beauchamp, William M. 1975 [1906]. "Civil, Religious and Mourning Councils and Ceremonies of Adoption of the New York Indians." *New York State Museum Bulletin*, 113 [reprint], Albany: University of the State of New York.

Beck, R. 2009. "Catawba Coalescence and the Shattering of the Carolina Piedmont, 1540–1675," in R. Ethridge and S. M. Shuck-Hall (eds), *Mapping the Mississippian Shatter Zone: The Colonial Indian Slave Trade and Regional Instability in the American South*, pp. 115–41. Lincoln: University of Nebraska Press.

Benson, Larry V., Timothy R. Pauketat, and Edward R. Cook. 2009. "Cahokia's Boom and Bust in the Context of Climate Change." *American Antiquity* (74): 467–83.

Bickham, Troy O. 2005. *Savages Within the Empire: Representations of American Indians in Eighteenth-Century Britain*. Oxford: Clarendon Press.

Biedma, L. H. de. 1993. "Relation of the Island of Florida," in L. A. Clayton, V. J. Knight Jr., and E. C. Moore (eds), *The De Soto Chronicles: The Expedition of Hernando de Soto to North America in 1539–1543* [J. Robertson trans.], pp. 221–46. Tuscaloosa: University of Alabama Press.

Blackhawk, Ned. 2006. *Violence over the Land: Indians and Empires in the Early American West*. Cambridge: Harvard University Press.

Blitz, John H. 1999. "Mississippian Chiefdoms and the Fission-fusion Process." *American Antiquity* (64): 577–92.

Blitz, John H., and Karl G. Lorenz. 2006. *The Chattahoochee Chiefdoms*. Tuscaloosa: University of Alabama Press.

Boissevain, Ethel. 1981. "Whatever Happened of the New England Indian Shipped to Bermuda to Be Sold as Slaves?" *Man in the Northeast* (21): 103–14.

Bolton, Herbert Eugene. 1914. *Athanase de Mézières and the Louisiana-Texas Frontier, 1768–1780*, 2 vols. Cleveland, Ohio: Arthur H. Clark Co.

Bourdieu, Pierre. 1977. *Outline of a Theory of Practice* (Richard Nice trans.). Cambridge, England: Cambridge University Press.

Bourne, Edward Gaylord, ed. 1904. *Narratives of the Career of Hernando de Soto in the Conquest of Florida as told by a Knight of Elvas*. New York: A.S. Barnes and Company.

Bowden, Henry. 1981. *American Indians and Christian Missions: Studies in Cultural Conflict*. Chicago: University of Chicago Press.

Bowne, Eric E. 2000. :The Rise and Fall of the Westo Indians: An Evaluation of the Documentary Evidence." *Early Georgia* 28(1): 56–78.

———. 2005. *The Westo Indians: Slave Traders of the Early Colonial South*. Tuscaloosa: University of Alabama Press.

———. 2009. "'Caryinge Awaye their Corne and Children': The Effects of Westo Slave Raids on the Indians of the Lower South," in R. Ethridge and S. M. Shuck-Hall (eds), *Mapping the Mississippian Shatter Zone: The Colonial Indian Slave Trade and Regional Instability in the American South*, pp. 104–14. Lincoln: University of Nebraska Press.

Boxer, Charles R. 1965. *The Dutch Seaborne Empire, 1600–1800*. New York: Alfred A. Knopf.

Boyd, Mark F., ed. and trans. 1936. "Expedition of Marcos Delgado from Apalachee to the Upper Creek Country in 1686." *Florida Historical Quarterly* (16): 1–32.

———. 1949. "Diego Peña's Expedition to Apalachee and Apalachicola in 1716." *Florida Historical Quarterly* (28): 3–48.

Boyd, Mark F., Hale G. Smith, and John W. Griffin. 1951. *Here They Once Stood: The Tragic End of the Apalachee Missions*. Gainesville: University Press of Florida.

Brain, J. 1978. "Late Prehistoric Settlement Patterning in the Yazoo Basin and Natchez Bluffs Region of the Lower Mississippi Valley," in B. D. Smith (ed.), *Mississippian Settlement Patterns*, pp. 331–368. New York: Academic Press.

Brain, Jeffrey P. 1988. "Tunica Archaeology" Cambridge, Massachusetts: *Papers of the Peabody Museum, Harvard University*, 78.

———. 1989. "Winterville: Late Prehistoric Culture Contact in the Lower Mississippi Valley." Jackson: *Mississippi Department of Archives and History Archaeological Reports*, 23.

———. 2008. Review of Adam King (Ed.). *Southeastern Ceremonial Complex: Chronology, Content, Context Southeastern Archaeology* (27): 158–61.

Brain, Jeffrey P., and Philip Phillips. 1996. *Shell Gorgets: Styles of the Late Prehistoric and Protohistoric Southeast*. Cambridge, Massachusetts: Harvard University Press.

Braund, Kathryn E. Holland. 1993. *Deerskins and Duffels: Creek Indian Trade with Anglo-America, 1685–1815*. Lincoln: University of Nebraska Press.

Bridges, Katherine, and Winston De Ville. 1967. "Natchitoches and the Trail to the Rio Grande: Two Eighteenth-Century Accounts by the Sieur Derbanne." *Louisiana History* (8): 239–359.

Brookes, Samuel O. 2003 "Discussant Comments," in C. H. McNutt, S. Williams, and M. D. Jeter (eds), "Woodland-Mississippian Transition in the Mid-South: Proceedings of the 22nd Mid-South Archaeological Conference, June 2–3, 2001," pp. 7–8, 92–5. Memphis: *University of Memphis Anthropological Research Center Occasional Papers*, 25.

Brooks, J. 2003. *American Lazarus: Religion and the Rise of African-American and Native American Literatures*. Oxford: Oxford University Press.

Brooks, James F. 1996 "'This Evil Extends Especially…to the Feminine Sex': Negotiating Captivity in the New Mexico Borderlands." *Feminist Studies* 22(2): 279–309.

———. 2002. *Captives and Cousins: Slavery, Kinship and Community in the Southwest Borderlands*. Chapel Hill: University of North Carolina Press.

———. 2004. "'That Don't Make you Kin': Borderlands History and Culture in *The Searchers*," in Eckstein and Lehman (eds), *The Searchers: Essays and Reflections on John Ford's Classic Western*, pp. 265–84. Detroit: Wayne State University Press.

Brown, Donald E. 1991. *Human Universals*. New York: McGraw-Hill.

Brown, Ian W. 1982. "An Archaeological Study of Culture Contact and Change in the Natchez Bluffs Region," in P. K. Galloway (ed.), *La Salle and His Legacy: Frenchmen and Indians in the Lower Mississippi Valley*, pp. 176–93. Jackson: University Press of Mississippi.

———. 1985. "Natchez Indian Archaeology: Culture Change and Stability in the Lower Mississippi Valley." Jackson: *Mississippi Department of Archives and History Archaeological Reports*, 15.

Brown, Ian W. 1991. "Historic Indians of the Lower Mississippi Valley: An Archaeologist's View," in D. Dye and C. Cox (eds), *Tuscaloosa Towns and Temples Along the Mississippi*, pp. 227–38. Tuscaloosa: University of Alabama Press.

Brown, James A. 1984. "Arkansas Valley Caddoan: The Spiro Phase," in R. E. Bell (ed.), *Prehistory of Oklahoma*, pp. 241–63. New York: Academic Press.

———. 1996. "The Spiro Ceremonial Center: The Archaeology of Arkansas Valley Caddoan Culture in Eastern Oklahoma," volumes 1 and 2. Ann Arbor: *Memoirs of the Museum of Anthropology, University of Michigan*, 29.

———. 2002. "Forty Years of the Southeastern Ceremonial Complex," in S. Tushingham, J. Hill, and C. H. McNutt (eds), *Histories of Southeastern Archaeology*, pp. 26–34. Tuscaloosa: University of Alabama Press.

———. 2007a. "On the Identity of the Birdman within Mississippian Period Art and Iconography," in F. K. Reilly III and J. F. Garber (eds), *Ancient Objects and Sacred Realms: Interpretations of Mississippian Iconography*, pp. 56–106. Austin: University of Texas Press.

———. 2007b. "Chronological Implications of the Bellows-shaped Apron," in A. King (ed.), *Southeastern Ceremonial Complex: Chronology, Content, Context*, pp. 213–45. Tuscaloosa: University of Alabama Press.

———. 2007c. "Sequencing the Braden Style within Mississippian Period Art and Iconography," in F. K. Reilly III and J. F. Garber (eds), *Ancient Objects and Sacred Realms: Interpretations of Mississippian Iconography*, pp. 213–45. Austin: University of Texas Press.

Brown, James A., and David H. Dye. 2007. "Severed Heads and Sacred Scalplocks: Mississippian Iconographic Trophies," in R. J. Chacon and D. H. Dye (eds), *The Taking and Displaying of Human Body Parts as Trophies by Amerindians*, pp. 278–98. New York: Springer.

Bucher, Bernadette. 1981. *Icon and Conquest: A Structural Analysis of the Illustrations of de Bry's Great Voyages* (Basia Miller Gulati trans.). Chicago: University of Chicago Press.

Buehner, Katie R. *Accessibility and Authenticity in Julia Smith's CYNTHIA PARKER* thesis for master's degree of music, University of N. Texas, December 2007: http://digital.library.unt.edu/permalink/meta-dc-5197:1 (accessed November 16, 2008).

Burk, John. 1805. *The History of Virginia from Its First Settlement to the Present Day*, vol. 2. Petersburg, Virginia.

Bushnell, Amy Turner. 1989. "Ruling 'the Republic of Indians' in Seventeenth-Century Florida," in P. Wood, G. Waselkov, and T. Hatley (eds), *Powhatan's Mantle: Indians in the Colonial South*, pp. 134–50. Lincoln: University of Nebraska Press.

Bushnell, David I. 1908. "The Account of Lamhatty." *American Anthropologist* 10(4): 568–74.

Butler, Brian M. 1991. "Kincaid Revisited: The Mississippian Sequence in the Lower Ohio Valley," in T. E. Emerson and R. Barry Lewis (eds),

Cahokia and the Hinterlands: Middle Mississippian Cultures of the Midwest, pp. 264–73. Urbana and Chicago: University of Illinois Press.

Butler, Jon. 1990. *Awash in a Sea of Faith: Christianizing the American People*. Cambridge, Mass: Harvard University Press.

Calloway, Colin G. 1992. *North Country Captives Selected Narratives of Indian Captivity from Vermont to New Hampshire*. Hanover and London: University Press of New England.

Cameron, Catherine M., ed. 2008. *Invisible Citizens: Captives and their Consequences*. Salt Lake City: University of Utah Press.

Carney, V. 2001. "'Woman is the Mother of All': Nanyehi and Kitteuha: War Women of the Cherokees," in B. A. Mann (ed.), *Native American Speakers of the Eastern Woodlands:Selected Speeches and Critical Analyses*, pp. 123–43. Westport (CT): Greenwood Publishing.

Carocci, Massimiliano. 1999. "Women, Temporary Liminality and Two-Spirits: The Staging of Community in Plains Indian Scalp Dance's Masquerade." *Journal of Ritual Studies* 13(2): 12–25.

Carocci, Max. Forthcoming 2012. *Warriors of the Plains: The Arts of Plains Indian Warfare*. London: British Museum Press.

Carroll, Lorraine. 2007. *Rhetorical Drag Gender Impersonation, Captivity, and the Writing of History*. Kent (OH): Kent State University Press.

Carter, William B. 2009. *Indian Alliances and the Spanish in the Southwest, AD 750–1750*. Norman: University of Oklahoma Press.

Castiglia, Christopher. 1996. *Bound and Determined Captivity, Culture-Crossing and White Womanhood from Mary Rowlandson to Patty Hearst*. Chicago and London: University of Chicago Press.

Cengage Learning (n.d.). *Nancy Ward*. Retrieved July 17, 2008, from Women's History: http://www.gale.cengage.com/free_resources/whm/bio/ward_n.htm.

Chacon, Richard J., and David H. Dye, eds. 2007. *The Taking and Displaying of Human Body Parts as Trophies by Amerindians*. New York: Springer.

Chacon, Richard J., and Rubén G. Mendoza, eds. 2005. *North American Indigenous Warfare and Ritual Violence*. Tucson: University of Arizona Press.

Chaplin, Joyce E. 2005. "Enslavement of Indians in Early America. Captivity Without a Narrative," in E. Mancke and C. Shammans (eds), *The Creation of the British Atlantic World*, pp. 45–70. Baltimore and London: John Hopkins University Press.

Chaudhuri, Jean, and Chaudhuri, Joyotpaul. 2001. *A Sacred Path: The Way of the Muscogee Creeks*. Los Angeles: UCLA American Indian Studies Center.

Cherry, James F. 2009. *The Headpots of Northeast Arkansas and Southern Pemiscot County, Missouri*. Fayetteville: University of Arkansas Press.

Cheves, Langdon, ed. 1897. "The Shaftesbury Papers and Other Records Relating to Carolina and the First Settlement on the Ashley River Prior to the Year 1676." *Collections of the South Carolina Historical Society* 5.

Claassen, Cheryl. 2005. "An Expanded View of Archaic Violent Death Burials," Paper presented at the 64th Annual Meeting of the Southeastern Archaeological Conference, Knoxville, Tennessee.

Clayton, Lawrence A., Vernon James Knight, Jr., and Edward C. Moore, eds. 1993. *The De Soto Chronicles: The Expedition of Hernando de Soto to North America in 1539–1543*. 2 vols. Tuscaloosa: University of Alabama Press.

Cobb, Charles R., and Brian M. Butler. 2002. "The Vacant Quarter Revisited: Late Mississippian Abandonment of the Lower Ohio Valley." *American Antiquity* (67): 625–41.

Colley, L. 2000. "Going Native, Telling Tales: Captivity, Collaborations, and Empire." *Past and Present* (168): 170–93.

Colley, Linda. 2003. *Captives Britain, Empire and the World 1600–1850*. London: Pimlico.

Coneah, Fred A. 1982. *A History of the Northern Ute People*. Salt Lake City, Utah: University of Utah.

110th CONGRESS 2008 *H. R. 2824*. Washington, D.C.: United States of America.

Congressional Record, 46th Congress, 2nd sess., 1880.

Connaway, John M. 2003. "Discussant Comments," in C. H. McNutt, S. Williams, and M. D. Jeter (eds), "Woodland-Mississippian transition in the Mid-South: proceedings of the 22nd Mid-South Archaeological Conference, June 2–3, 2001," pp. 24–8. Memphis: *University of Memphis Anthropological Research Center Occasional Papers*, No. 25.

——, ed. (In press). "The Oliver Site (22-CO-503), Coahoma County, Mississippi: A Late Woodland through Protohistoric Mound Complex in the Northern Yazoo Basin." Jackson: *Mississippi Department of Archives and History Archaeological Papers*, 34.

Conrad, Lawrence A. 1991. "The Middle Mississippian Cultures of the Central Illinois Valley," in T. E. Emerson and R. Barry Lewis (eds), *Cahokia and the Hinterlands: Middle Mississippian Cultures of the Midwest*, pp. 119–56. Urbana and Chicago: University of Illinois Press.

Cotter, John L. 1952. "The Mangum Plate." *American Antiquity* (17): 65–8.

Covington, James W. 1967. "Some Observations Concerning the Florida-Carolina Indian Slave-Trade." *The Florida Anthropologist* 20(1–2): 10–18.

Crane, Verner W. 1919. "The Southern Frontier in Queen Anne's War." *American Historical Review* 24 (April): 379–95.

——. 1929. *The Southern Frontier 1670–1732*. Ann Arbor: University of Michigan Press.

——. 2004. *The Southern Frontier, 1670–1732* [reprint]. Tuscaloosa: University of Alabama Press.

Cuello, José. 1988. "The Persistence of Indian Slavery and Encomienda in the Northeast of Colonial Mexico, 1577–1723." *Journal of Social History* 21(4): 683–700.

Danforth, E. H. 1879. "Letter from E.H. Danforth to E.A. Hayt," February 22, NA, RG 75, M234, R 208.

Dart, Henry Plauche, trans. 1921. "Records of the Superior Council of Louisiana." *Louisiana Historical Quarterly* 4(3): 324–60.

Davis, David Brion. 2006. *Inhuman Bondage: The Rise and Fall of Slavery in the New World*. Oxford: Oxford University Press.

Davis, R. P. Stephen. 2002. "The Cultural Landscape of the North Carolina Piedmont at Contact," in R. Ethridge and C. Hudson (eds), *The Transformation of the Southeastern Indians, 1540–1760*, pp. 135–54. Jackson: University of Mississippi Press.

De Batz. 1735. *Drawings by A. De Batz in Louisiana, 1732–1735* (David I. Bushnell ed.). Washington, D.C.: Smithsonian Miscellaneous Collections 80(5).

De La Porte, Abbe Joseph. 1774. *Le Voyageur François, ou Le Connoissance de L'ancien et du Nouveau Monde, mis au jour par M. l' Abbe Delaporte*, Vol. 10. Paris: L. Cellot.

De Vorsey, Louis J. 1971. *John Gerar William De Brahm's Report of the General Survey in the Southern District of North America*. Columbia: University of South Carolina Press.

Dearborn, Mary V. 1988. *Pocahontas's Daughters: Gender and Ethnicity in American Culture*. Oxford: Oxford University Press.

Decker, Peter R. 2004. *The Utes Must Go!: American Expansion and the Removal of a People*. Boulder (CO): Fulcrum Publishing.

Deloria, Vine. 1995. *Red Earth, White Lies: Native Americans and the Myth of Scientific Fact*. New York: Scribner.

DeMallie, Raymond J. 2004. "Tutelo and Neighboring Groups," in R. D. Fogelson (ed.), *Southeast, Handbook of North American Indians*, Vol. 14, pp. 286–300. Washington D.C.: Smithsonian Institution Press.

Demos, John. 1994. *The Unredeemed Captive*. London: Papermac.

Derounian-Stodola, Kathryn Zabelle. 1998. *Women's Indian Captivity Narratives*. New York: Penguin Books.

Derounian-Stodola, Kathryn Zabelle, and James Levernier. 1993. *The Indian Captivity Narrative, 1550–1900*. New York: Maxwell MacMillan International.

DeShields, James T. 2007. *Cynthia Ann Parker: The Story of Her Capture at the Massacre of the Inmates of Parkers Fort; Of Her Quarter of a Century Spent Among the Comanches (1886)*. USA: Kessinger Publishing.

Diamond, Jared M. 1997. *Guns, Germs, and Steel: The Fates of Human Societies*. New York: W. W. Norton.

Donald, Leland. 1985. "Captives or Slaves? A Comparison of Northeastern and Northwestern North America by Means of Captivity Narratives." *Culture* (5): 17–23.

———. 1997. *Aboriginal Slavery on the Northwest Coast of North America*. Berkeley: University of California Press.

Dowling, Lee. 1997. "*La Florida del Inca*: Garcilaso's Literary Sources," in P. Galloway (ed.), *The Hernando de Soto Expedition: History, Historiography,* and "Discovery" in the Southeast, pp. 98–154. Lincoln: University of Nebraska Press.

Drimmer, Frederick, ed. 1961. *Captured by the Indians 15 Firsthand Accounts, 1750–1870.* New York: Dover Publications Inc.

Drooker, Penelope Ballard. 1997. "The View from Madisonville: Protohistoric Western Fort Ancient Interaction Patterns," Ann Arbor: *Memoirs of the Museum of Anthropology, University of Michigan,* 31.

———. 2002. "The Ohio Valley, 1550–1750: Patterns of Sociopolitical Coalescence and Dispersal," in C. Hudson and R. Ethridge (eds), *The Transformation of the Southeastern Indians, 1540–1760,* pp. 115–34. Jackson: University Presses of Mississippi.

Dunn, William D. 1911. "Apache Relations in Texas, 1718–1750." *Southwestern Historical Quarterly* XIV(3): 198–274.

———. 1914. "The Apache Mission of the San Saba River: Its Founding and Failure." *Southwestern Historical Quarterly* XVII(4): 379–414.

Du Pratz, A. S. le P. 1947. *The History of Louisiana* [reprint]. New Orleans: Pelican Press.

Duval, K. 2003. "'A Good Relationship and Commerce': The Native political Economy of the Arkansas River Valley." *Early American Studies* (Spring): 67–8.

DuVal, Kathleen. 2006. *The Native Ground: Indians and Colonists in the Heart of the Continent.* Philadelphia: University of Pennsylvania Press.

Dye, David H. 1986. "Introduction," in D. H. Dye and R. C. Brister (eds), "The Protohistoric Period in the Mid-South: 1500–1700," pp. xi–xiv. Jackson: *Mississippi Department of Archives and History Archaeological Reports,* 18.

———. 2004. "Art, Ritual, and Chiefly Warfare in the Mississippian World," in R. V. Sharp (ed.), *Hero, Hawk, and Open Hand: American Indian Art of the Ancient Midwest and South,* pp. 190–205. New Haven, Connecticut: The Art Institute of Chicago and Yale University Press.

———. 2007. "Ritual, Medicine, and the War Trophy Iconographic Theme in the Mississippian Southeast," in F. K. Reilly III and J. F. Garber (eds), *Ancient Objects and Sacred Realms: Interpretations of Mississippian Iconography,* pp. 152–73. Austin: University of Texas Press.

Dye, David H., and Adam King. 2006, "Desecrating the Sacred Ancestor Temples: Chiefly Conflict and Violence in the American Southeast," in R. J. Chacon and R. G. Mendoza (eds), *North American Indigenous Warfare and Ritual Violence,* pp. 160–81. Tucson: University of Arizona Press.

Dye, David H., and C. A. Cox, eds. 1990. *Towns and Temples along the Mississippi.* Tuscaloosa: University of Alabama Press.

Early, A. M. 2000. "The Caddos of the Trans-Mississippi South," in B. G. McEwan (ed.), *Indians of the Greater Southeast: Historical Archaeology and Ethnohistory,* pp. 123–33. Gainesville: University Presses of Florida Press.

Easery, D. 2007. "Colonialism Before Contact," PhD fourth semester paper, Department of Anthropology. Chapel Hill: University of North Carolina.

Ebersole, Gary L. 1995. *Captured by Texts Puritan to Post-modern Images of Indian Captivity.* USA: University Press of Virginia.

Eckstein, Arthur M., and Peter Lehman, eds. 2004. *The Searchers Essays and Reflections on John Ford's Classic Western.* Detroit: Wayne State University Press.

Ekberg, Carl J. 2007. *Stealing Indian Women: Indian Slavery in the Illinois Country.* Urbana and Chicago: University of Illinois Press.

Elliott, Emory, ed., and Davidson, Cathy N. assoc. ed. *Columbia History of the American Novel.* New York: Columbia University Press, 1991.

Elliott, John Huxtable. 2006. *Empires of the Atlantic World: Britain and Spain in America 1492–1830.* New Haven and London: Yale University Press.

Eltis, Davis, Frank D. Lewis, and Kenneth L. Sokoloff, eds. 2004. *Slavery in the Development of the Americas.* Cambridge: Cambridge University Press.

Elvas, Gentleman of. 1993. "True Relation of the Vicissitudes that Attended the Governor Don Hernando de Soto and Some Nobles of Portugal in the Discovery of the Provence of Florida," in L. A. Clayton, V. J. Knight Jr., and E. C. Moore (eds), *The De Soto Chronicles: The Expedition of Hernando de Soto to North America in 1539–1543* [J. Robertson trans.], pp. 25–219. Tuscaloosa: University of Alabama Press.

Emerson, Thomas E. 2002. "An Introduction to Cahokia 2002: Diversity, Complexity, and History." *Midcontinental Journal of Archaeology* (27): 127–48.

———. 2007. "Cahokia and the Evidence for Late Pre-Columbian War in the North American Mid-continent," in R. J. Chacon and R. G. Mendoza (eds), *North American Indigenous Warfare and Ritual Violence,* pp. 129–48. Tucson: University of Arizona Press.

Emerson, Thomas E., and Jeffrey S. Girard. 2004. "Dating Gahagan and its Implications for Understanding Cahokia-Caddo Interactions." *Southeastern Archaeology* (23): 57–64.

Emerson, Thomas E., and Timothy R. Pauketat, eds. 2002. "Cahokia 2002: Diversity, Complexity, and History." *Midcontinental Journal of Archaeology* [special issue] 27(2):127–48.

Emerson, Thomas E., Randall E. Hughes, Mary R. Hynes, and Sarah U. Wisseman. 2002. "Implications of Sourcing Cahokia-style Flint Clay Figurines in the American Bottom and the Upper Mississippi River Valley." *Midcontinental Journal of Archaeology* (27): 309–38.

Emmitt, Robert. 2000. *The Last War Trail: The Utes and the Settlement of Colorado.* Boulder, CO: University Press of Colorado.

Ennis, D. J. 2002. *Enter the Press-gang: Naval Impressment in Eighteenth-century British Literature.* Newark (DE): University of Delaware Press.

Equiano, Olaudah (Gustavus Vassa). 2001. *The Interesting Narrative of the Life of Olaudah Equiano, or Gustavus Vassa, the African, Written by Himself* (Werner Sollors ed.). New York: Norton.

Esarey, Duane. 2003. "The 17th Century Midwestern Slave Trade in Colonial Context," Paper presented at the Midwest Archaeological Conference, South Bend, Indiana.

Essenpreis, Patricia S. 1978. "Fort Ancient Settlement: Differential Response at a Mississippian—Late Woodland Interface," in B. D. Smith (ed.), *Mississippian Settlement Patterns*, pp. 141–67. New York: Academic Press.

Ethridge, Robbie. 2006. "Creating the Shatter Zone," in T. J. Pluckhahn and R. Ethridge (eds), *Light on the Path: The History and Anthropology of the Southeastern Indians*, pp. 207–18. Tuscaloosa: University of Alabama Press.

———. 2009a. "Introduction: Mapping the Mississippian Shatter Zone," in R. Ethridge and S. M. Shuck-Hall (eds), *Mapping the Mississippian Shatter Zone: The Colonial Indian Slave Trade and Regional Instability in the American South*, pp. 1–62. Lincoln: University of Nebraska Press.

———. 2009b. "The Making of a Militaristic Slaving Society: The Chickasaws and the Colonial Indian Slave Trade," in A. Gallay (ed.), *Indian Slavery in Colonial America*, pp. 251–76. Lincoln: University of Nebraska Press.

———. 2009c. "Afterword: Some Thoughts on Further Work," in R. Ethridge and S. M. Shuck-Hall (eds), *Mapping the Mississippian Shatter Zone: The Colonial Indian Slave Trade and Regional Instability in the American South*, pp. 418–24. Lincoln: University of Nebraska Press.

———. 2010. *From Chicaza to Chickasaw: The European Invasion and the Transformation of the Mississippian World, 1540–1715*. Chapel Hill: University of North Carolina Press.

Ethridge, Robbie, and Charles Hudson, eds. 2002. *The Transformation of the Southeastern Indians, 1540–1760*. Jackson: University Press of Mississippi.

Ethridge, Robbie, and Sheri M. Shuck-Hall, eds. 2009. *Mapping the Mississippian Shatter Zone: The Colonial Indian Slave Trade and Regional Instability in the American South*. Lincoln: University of Nebraska Press.

Everett, C. S. 2009. "'They Shalbe Slaves for their Lives': Indian Slavery in Colonial Virginia," in A. Gallay (ed.), *Indian Slavery in Colonial America*, pp. 67–108. Lincoln: University of Nebraska Press.

Exley, Jo Ella Powell. 2001. *Frontier Blood: The Saga of the Parker Family*. Texas A & M University Press.

Faery, Rebecca Blevins. 1999. *Cartographies of Desire Captivity Race and Sex in the Shaping of an American Nation*, Norman: University of Oklahoma Press.

Fausz, J. Frederick. 1984. "Present at Creation: The Chesapeake World that Greeted the Maryland Colonists," *Maryland Historical Magazine* (79): 7–20.

Feest, Christian F. 1967. "The Virginia Indian in Pictures, 1612–1624." *The Smithsonian Journal of History* 2(1): 1–30.
Fehrenbach, T. R. 2007. *Comanches: The History of a People*. London: Vintage Press.
Ferguson, B. R., and N. L. Whitehead. 1999. "The Violent Edge of Empire," in R. B. Ferguson and N. L. Whitehead (eds), *War in the Tribal Zone: Expanding States and Indigenous Warfare* (2nd ed.), pp. 18–28. Santa Fe: School of American Research.
Fickes, Michael L. 2000. "'They Could not Endure that Yoke': The Captivity of Pequot Women and Children after the War of 1637." *The New England Quarterly* 73(1): 58–81.
Field, Eugene "Chipeta." 1911. In Eleanor H. Caldwell, ed., *Entertainer and Entertained*, pp. 22–3. Mayhew Publishing.
Fiske, J. 1892. *The Discovery of America* (Vol. III). Boston: Houghton and Mifflin.
Fitts, Mary Elizabeth, and Charles L. Heath. 2009. "'Indians Refusing to Carry Burdens': Understanding the Success of Catawba Political, Military, and Settlement Strategies in Colonial Carolina," in R. Ethridge and S. M. Shuck-Hall (eds), *Mapping the Mississippian Shatter Zone: The Colonial Indian Slave Trade and Regional Instability in the American South*, pp. 142–62. Lincoln: University of Nebraska Press.
Fitzpatrick, Tara. 1991. "The Figure of Captivity: The Cultural Work of the Puritan Captivity Narrative." *American Literary History* 3(1, Spring): 1–26.
Forbes, Jack D. 1983. "Mustees, Half-Breeds and Zambos in Anglo North America: Aspects of Black-Indian Relations." *American Indian Quarterly* 7(1): 57–83.
———. 1993. *Africans and Native Americans: The Language of Race and the Evolution of Red-Black Peoples*. Urbana and Chicago: University of Illinois Press.
Foreman, Carolyn T. 1943. *Indians Abroad, 1433–1938*. Norman: Oklahoma University Press.
Fortier, Andrew C., and Dale L. McElrath. 2002. "Deconstructing the Emergent Mississippian Concept: The Case for the Terminal Late Woodland in the American Bottom." *Midcontinental Journal of Archaeology* (27): 171–215.
Fortier, Andrew C., Thomas E. Emerson, and Dale L. McElrath. 2006. "Calibrating and Reassessing American Bottom Culture History." *Southeastern Archaeology* (25): 170–211.
Foster, H. Thomas, Mary Theresa Bonhage-Freund, and Lisa O'Steen. 2007. *Archaeology of the Lower Muskogee Creek Indians, 1715–1836*. Tuscaloosa: University of Alabama Press.
Fowler, Melvin L. 1974. "Cahokia: Ancient Capital of the Midwest," Menlo Park, California: Cummings Publishing Company, *Addison-Wesley Modules in Anthropology*, 48.

———. 1975. "A Pre-Columbian Urban Center on the Mississippi." *Scientific American* 233(2): 92–101.
Fowler, Melvin L., Jerome C. Rose, B. V. Leest, and Steven R. Ahler. 1999. "The Mound 72 Area: Dedicated and Sacred Space in Early Cahokia." Springfield: *Illinois State Museum Reports of Investigations*, 54.
Fox, William A. 2009. "Events as Seen from the North: The Iroquois and Colonial Slavery," in R. Ethridge and S. Shuck-Hall (eds), *Mapping the Mississippian Shatter Zone: The Colonial Indian Slave Trade and Regional Instability in the American South*, pp. 63–80. Lincoln: University of Nebraska Press.
Fried, M. H. 1967. *The Evolution of Political Society*. New York: McGraw-Hill.
Gable, Eric, and Richard Handler. October 1993. "Colonialist Anthropology at Colonial Williamsburg." *Museum Anthropology* 17: 26–31.
———. June 1994. "The Authority of Documents at Some American History Museums." *Journal of American History* 81: 119–36.
Gable, Eric, Richard Handler, and Anna Lawson. 1992. "On the Uses of Relativism: Fact, Conjecture, and Black and White Histories at Colonial Williamsburg." *American Ethnologist* 19, 4: 791–805.
Gallay, Alan. 2002. *The Indian Slave Trade: The Rise of the English Empire in the American South, 1670–1717*. New Haven and London: Yale University Press.
Galloway, Patricia K. 1983. "Henri de Tonti du Village des Chacta, 1702: The Beginning of the French Alliance," in P. K. Galloway (ed.), *La Salle and His Legacy: Frenchmen and Indians in the Lower Mississippi Valley*, pp. 146–75. Jackson: University Press of Mississippi.
———, ed. 1989. *The Southeastern Ceremonial Complex: Artifacts and Analysis*. Lincoln: University of Nebraska Press.
———. 1995. *Choctaw Genesis 1500–1700*. Lincoln: University of Nebraska Press.
———, ed. 1997. *The Hernando de Soto Expedition: History, Historiography, and 'Discovery' in the Southeast*. Lincoln: University of Nebraska Press.
———. 2002. "Colonial Period Transformations in the Mississippi Valley: Dis-integration, Alliance, Confederation, Playoff," in C. Hudson and R. Ethridge (eds), *The Transformation of the Southeastern Indians, 15401760*, pp. 225–47. Jackson: University Presses of Mississippi.
Galloway, Patricia, and Jason Baird Jackson. 2004. "Natchez and Neighboring Groups," in R. D. Fogelson (ed.), *Southeast, Handbook of North American Indians*, Vol. 14, pp. 598–615. Washington, D.C.: Smithsonian Institution Press.
Gandert, Miguel et al. 2000. *Nuevo Mexico Profundo: Rituals of an Indo-Hispano Homeland*. Albuquerque: University of New Mexico Press.
Ganoe, John T. 1938. "The Beginnings of Irrigation in the United States." *The Mississippi Valley Historical Review* 25(1): 59–78.
Gates, H. L. 1989. *The Signifying Monkey: A Theory of African-American Literary Criticism*. Cambridge: Oxford University Press.

Gaudio, Michael. 2008. *Engraving the Savage: The New World and Techniques of Civilization*. Minneapolis: University of Minnesota Press.
Gayarré, Charles. 1903. *History of Louisiana*, 4 vols. New Orleans, F.F. Hansell and Bro. Ltd.
Gibson, A. N. 1971. *The Chickasaws*. Norman: University of Oklahoma Press.
Giraud, Marcel. 1958. *Histoire de La Louisiane Française: Années de Transition, 1715–1717*. Paris: Presses Universitaires de France.
Gleach, Frederic W. 1997. *Powhatan's World and Colonial Virginia: A Conflict of Cultures*. Lincoln: University of Nebraska Press.
Gnecco, Cristóbal, and Carolina Hernández. 2008. "History and its Discontents: Stone Statues, Native Histories, and Archaeologists." *Current Anthropology* (49): 439–66.
Goddard, Ives, Patricia Galloway, Marvin Jeter, Gregory Waselkov, and John Worth. 2004. "Small Tribes of the Western Southeast," in R. D. Fogelson (ed.), *Southeast, Handbook of North American Indians*, Vol. 14, pp. 174–90. Washington, D.C.: Smithsonian Institution Press.
Goldstein, Lynne G., and John D. Richards. 1991. "Ancient Aztalan: The Cultural and Ecological Context of a Late Prehistoric Site in the Midwest," in T. E. Emerson and R. Barry Lewis (eds), *Cahokia and the Hinterlands: Middle Mississippian Cultures of the Midwest*, pp. 193–206. Urbana and Chicago: University of Illinois Press.
Gordon, Richard. 2006. "Following Estevanico: The Influential Presence of an African Slave in Sixteenth-century New World Historiography." *Colonial Latin American Review* 15(2): 183–206.
Gould, Philip. 2000. "Free Carpenter, Venture Capitalist: Reading the Lives of the Early Black Atlantic." *American Literary History* 12(4): 659–84.
"Grateful Susan," *Chicago Tribune*, October 30, 1879.
The Greeley Tribune
Green, William, ed. 1995. "Oneota Archaeology: Past, Present, and Future," Iowa City: *Office of the State Archaeologist, University of Iowa, Report* 20.
Green, William. 1998. 'The Erie/Westo Connection: Possible Evidence of Long Distance Migration in the Eastern Woodlands During the 16th and 17th Centuries, Paper presented at the Southeastern Archaeological Conference, Greenville, SC.
Green, William. 2001. "Chiwere Sociopolitical Complexity? Reconciling Mythology and Archaeology," Paper presented at the Midwest Archaeological Conference, LaCrosse, Wisconsin.
Greenblatt, Stephen. 1991. *Marvellous Possessions. The Wonder of the New World*. Chicago: University of Chicago Press.
Griffin, James B. 1937. "The Archaeological Remains of the Chiwere Sioux."*American Antiquity* (2): 180–1.
———. 1943. *The Fort Ancient Aspect: its Cultural and Chronological Position in Mississippi Valley Archaeology*. Ann Arbor: University of Michigan Press (reissued in 1966 as *University of Michigan Museum of Anthropology Anthropological Papers*, 28).

Griffin, James B. 1960. "A Hypothesis for the Prehistory of the Winnebago," in S. Diamond (ed.), *Culture in History,* pp. 809–65. New York: Columbia University Press.

Habib, Imtiaz. 2008. *Black Lives in the English Archives, 1500–1677: Imprints of the Invisible.* Ashgate.

Habicht-Mauche, Judith. 2008. "Captive Wives? The Role and Status of Nonlocal Women on the Protohistoric Southern High Plains," in Cameron (ed.), *Invisible Citizens,* pp. 181–204. Salt Lake City, UT: University of Utah Press.

Hacker, Margaret Schmidt. 1990. *Cynthia Ann Parker the Life and Legend.* El Paso: Texan Western Press, University of Texas at El Paso.

Hahn, Steven Christopher. 1995. *A Miniature Arms Race: The Role of the Flintlock in Initiating Indian Dependency in the Colonial Southeastern United States 1656–1730.* Unpublished master's thesis, Department of History, University of Georgia, Athens.

———. 2004. *The Invention of the Creek Nation, 1670–1763.* Lincoln: University of Nebraska Press.

Hajda, Yvonne. 2005. "Slavery in the Greater Lower Columbia Region." *Ethnohistory* 52(3): 563–88.

Hall, David, ed. 1997. *Lived Religion in America: Toward a History of Practice.* Princeton: Princeton University Press.

Hall, Gwendolyn Midlo. 1992. *Africans in Colonial Louisiana: The Development of Afro-Creole Culture in the Eighteenth Century.* Baton Rouge: Louisiana State University Press.

Hall, Joseph M. 2009a. *Zamumo's Gifts: Indian-European Exchange in the Colonial Southeast.* Philadelphia: University of Pennsylvania Press.

———. 2009b. "Anxious Alliances: Apalachicola Efforts to Survive the Slave Trade, 1638–1705," in A. Gallay (ed.), *Indian Slavery in Colonial America,* pp. 147–84. Lincoln: University of Nebraska Press.

Hall, Robert L. 1989. "The Cultural Background of Mississippian Symbolism," in P. K. Galloway (ed.) *The Southeastern Ceremonial Complex: Artifacts and Analysis,* pp. 239–78. Lincoln: University of Nebraska Press.

———. 1991. "Cahokia Identity and Interaction Models of Cahokia Mississippian," in T. E. Emerson and R. Barry Lewis (eds), *Cahokia and the Hinterlands: Middle Mississippian Cultures of the Midwest,* pp. 30–4. Urbana and Chicago: University of Illinois Press.

———. 2004. "The Cahokia Site and its People," in R. V. Sharp (ed.), *Hero, Hawk, and Open Hand: American Indian Art of the Ancient Midwest and South,* pp. 93–103. New Haven, Connecticut: The Art Institute of Chicago and Yale University Press.

Hally, D. J., M. T. Smith, and J. B. Langford Jr. 1990. "The Archaeological Reality of De Soto's Coosa," in D. Hurst Thomas (ed.), *Columbian Consequences* Vol. 2, *Archaeological and Historical Perspectives on the Spanish Borderlands East,* pp. 121–38. Washington: Smithsonian Institution Press.

Hally, David J., and Mark Williams. 1994. "Macon Plateau Site Community Pattern," in David J. Hally (ed.), *Ocmulgee Archaeology, 1936–1986*, pp. 84–95. Athens: University of Georgia Press.

Hamalainen, Pekka. 2008. *The Comanche Empire*. New Haven, Connecticut: Yale University Press.

Hamilton, Henry W. 1952. "The Spiro Mound." *Missouri Archaeologist* (14): 1–276.

Hamilton, Peter J. 1897. *Colonial Mobile*. Boston and New York: Houghton, Mifflin and Co.

Hammond, George P. 1956. "The Search for the Fabulous in the Settlement of the Southwest." *Utah Historical Quarterly* (24): 1–19.

Handler, Richard, and Eric Gable. 1997. *The New History in an Old Museum: Creating the Past at Colonial Williamsburg*. Durham: Duke University Press.

Hann, John H. 1988. *Apalachee: The Land between the Rivers*. Gainesville: University of Florida Press.

———. 1994. "The Apalachee of the Historic Era," in C. Hudson and C. Chaves Tesser (eds), *The Forgotten Centuries: Indians and Europeans in the American South, 1521–1704*, pp. 327–54. Athens: University of Georgia Press.

Hanson, Lee H. Jr. 1966. *The Hardin Village Site*. Lexington: University of Kentucky Press.

———. 1975. "The Buffalo Site: A Late 17th Century Indian Village Site (46Pu31) in Putnam County, West Virginia," *West Virginia Geological and Economic Survey Reports of Archaeological Investigations* 5.

Hariot, Thomas *A briefe and true report of the new found land of Virginia* [fascim. Reproduction of the 1590 Theodor de Bry Latin edition accompanied by the modernized English text], Charlottesville: Published for the Library of the Mariners' Museum by the University of Virginia Press, 2007.

Harris, Marvin. 1979 *Cultural Materialism: The Struggle for a Science of Culture*. New York: Random House.

Haskell, Thomas Nelson. 1889. *The Indian Question: Young Konkaput, the King of Utes, A Legend of Twin Lakes and Other Occasional Poems*. Denver (CO): Collier and Cleveland Publishing Company.

Haynes, Gary. 2002. *The Early Settlement of North America: The Clovis Era*. Cambridge, England: Cambridge University Press.

Heizer, Robert F., ed. 1974. "Indenture, Kidnapping and Sale of Indians," in R. F. Heizer (ed.), *The Destruction of California Indians*, pp. 219–41. Santa Barbara and Salt Lake City: Peregrine Smith Inc.

———. 1988. "Indian Servitude in California," in W. Washburn (ed.), *History of Indian-White Relations, Handbook of North American Indians*, Vol. 4, pp. 414–16. Washington D.C.: Smithsonian Institution Press.

Henige, David. 1997. "'So Unbelievable it has to be True': Inca Garcilaso in Two Worlds," in P. K. Galloway (ed.), *The Hernando de Soto Expedition: History, Historiography, and "Discovery" in the Southeast*, pp. 155–77. Lincoln: University of Nebraska Press.

Herndon, Ruth Wallis, and Ella Wilcox Sekatau. 1997. "The Right to Name: The Narragansett People and Rhode Island Officials in the Revolutionary Era," in C. G. Calloway (ed.), *After King Philip's War: Presence and Persistence in Indian New England*, pp. 114–43. Hanover and London: University Press of New England.

———. 2003. "Pauper Apprenticeship in Narragansett Country: A Different Name for Slavery in Early New England," in *Slavery and Antislavery in New England. The Dublin Seminar for New England Folklife Annual Proceedings*, pp. 56–70.

Hess, Ralph H. 1912. "The Beginnings of Irrigation in the United States." *The Journal of Political Economy* 20(8): 807–33.

Heuman, Gad, and James Walkin, eds. 2003. *The Slavery Reader*. London: Routledge.

Hickerson, D. A. 1997. "Historical Processes, Epidemic Disease, and the Formation of the Hasinai Confederacy." *Ethnohistory* 44(1): 31–52.

Higginbotham, Jay. 1977. *Old Mobile: Ft. Louis de la Louisiane*. Museum of the City of Mobile, Mobile, Alabama (83): 206–207.

Hilgeman, Sherri L. 2000. *Pottery and Chronology at Angel*. Tuscaloosa: University of Alabama Press.

Hills, Patricia. 1973. *The American Frontier: Images and Myths*. New York: Whitney Museum of American Art.

Hinsley, Curtis M. 1981. *Savages and Scientists: The Smithsonian Institution and the Development of American Anthropology, 1846–1910* (reprinted in 1994 as *The Smithsonian and the American Indian: Making a Moral Anthropology in Victorian America*). Washington, D.C.: Smithsonian Institution Press.

Hoig, Stanley. 1998. *The Cherokee and their Chiefs: In the Wake of Empire*. Fayetteville: University of Arkansas Press.

Hoffman, Bernard G. 1964. "Observations on Certain Ancient Tribes of the Northern Appalachian Province," Smithsonian Institution Bureau of American Ethnology, pp. 195–245. *Bulletin* 191 Washington, D.C.

Hoffman, M. P. 1990. "The Terminal Mississippian in the Arkansas River Valley and Quapaw Ethnogenesis," in D. H. Dye and C. A. Cox (eds), *Towns and Temples Along the Mississippi*, pp. 208–26. Tuscaloosa: University of Alabama Press.

Hoffman, Paul E. 1994. "Narvaez and Cabeza de Vaca in Florida," in C. Hudson and C. Chaves Tesser (eds), *The Forgotten Centuries: Indians and Europeans in the American South, 1521–1704*, pp. 50–73. Athens: University of Georgia Press.

———. 1997. "Did Coosa Decline Between 1541 and 1560?" *The Florida Anthropologist* 50(1): 25–9.

Holmes, William F. S. 1994. *Hardin Village: A Northern Kentucky Late Fort Ancient Site's Mortuary Patterns and Social Organization*. Lexington, MA thesis, Department of Anthropology, University of Kentucky.

Honour, Hugh. 1975. *The New Golden Land. European Images of America from the Discoveries to the Present Times*. New York: Harper and Row.

House, John H. 2002. "Wallace Bottom: A Colonial-era Archaeological Site in the Menard Locality, Eastern Arkansas," *Southeastern Archaeology* (21): 257–68.

Howard, James H. 1968. "The Southeastern Ceremonial Complex," Columbia, Missouri: *Memoirs of the Missouri Archaeological Society*, 6.

Howard, Sarah Elizabeth. 1902. *Pen Pictures of the Plains*. Denver, CO: The Reed Publishing Company.

Hoxie, Frederick E. 2001. *A Final Promise: The Campaign to Assimilate the Indians, 1880–1920*. Lincoln: University of Nebraska Press.

Hudson, Charles. 1976. *The Southeastern Indians* (2nd ed.). Knoxville: University of Tennessee Press.

———. 1984. "De Soto in Arkansas: A Brief Synopsis," Fayetteville: *Arkansas Archeological Society Field Notes* (205): 3–12.

———. 1987. "Juan Pardo's Expedition beyond Chiaha." *Tennessee Anthropologist* (12): 74–87.

———. 1990. *The Juan Pardo Expeditions: Spanish Explorers and the Indians of the Carolinas and Tennessee, 1566–1568*. Washington, D.C.: Smithsonian Institution Press.

———. 1993. "Reconstructing the de Soto Route West of the Mississippi: Summary and Comments," in G. A. Young and M. P. Hoffman (eds), *The Expedition of Hernando de Soto West of the Mississippi, 1541–1543*, pp. 143–54. Fayetteville: University of Arkansas Press.

———. 1994. "The Hernando de Soto Expedition, 1539–43," in Hudson and Chaves Tesser (eds), *The Forgotten Centuries*, pp. 74–10.

———. 1997. *Knights of Spain, Warriors of the Sun: Hernando de Soto and the South's Ancient Chiefdoms*. Athens: University of Georgia Press.

———. 2002. "Introduction," in R. Ethridge and C. Hudson (eds), *The Transformation of the Southeastern Indians, 1540–1760*, pp. xxii–xxxvi. Jackson: University Press of Mississippi.

———. 2005. *The Juan Pardo Expeditions: Exploration of the Carolinas and Tennessee, 1566–1568* (2nd ed.). Tuscaloosa: University of Alabama Press.

Hudson, Charles, and C. Chaves Tesser, eds. 1994. *The Forgotten Centuries: Indians and Europeans in the American South, 1521–1704*. Athens: University of Georgia Press.

Hudson, Charles, J. E. Worth, and C. DePratter. 1990. "Refinements in Hernando de Soto's Route through Georgia and South Carolina," in D. H. Thomas (ed.), *Columbian Consequences*, vol. 2, *Archaeological and Historical Perspectives on the Spanish Borderlands East*, pp. 107–19. Washington D.C.: Smithsonian Institution Press.

Hudson, Charles, M. T. Smith, and C. DePratter. 1984. "The Hernando de Soto Expedition: From Apalachee to Chiaha." *Southeastern Archaeology* (3): 65–77.

———. 1990. "The Hernando de Soto Expedition: From Mabila to the Mississippi River," in D. H. Dye and C. A. Cox (eds), *Towns and Temples along the Mississippi*, pp. 181–207. Tuscaloosa: University of Alabama Press.

Hudson, Charles, M. T. Smith, C. DePratter, and E. Kelley. 1989. "The Tristan de Luna Expedition, 1559–1561." *Southeastern Archaeology* (8): 31–45.

Hudson, Charles, R. A. Beck Jr., C. DePratter, R. Ethridge, and J. E. Worth. 2008. "On Interpreting Cofitachequi." *Ethnohistory* 55(3): 465–90.

Hulton, Paul. 1984. *America 1585: The Complete Drawings of John White.* Chapel Hill: University of North Carolina Press; London: British Museum Publications.

Hutchinson, D. L. 2006. *Tatham Mounds and the Bioarchaeology of European Contact: Disease and Depopulation in the Central Gulf Coast Florida.* Gainesville: University Press of Florida.

d'Iberville, P. le M. 1981. *Iberville's Gulf Journals* (1699–1702). (Richebourg Gaillard McWilliams trans.). Tuscaloosa: University of Alabama Press.

Iseminger, William R., George R. Holley et al. 1990. "The Archaeology of the Cahokia Palisade," Springfield: *Illinois Historic Preservation Agency, Cultural Resources Studies*, 14.

Jacobi, Keith P. 2007. "Disabling the Dead: Human Trophy Taking in the Prehistoric Southeast," in R.J. Chacon and D. H. Dye (eds), *The Taking and Displaying of Human Body Parts as Trophies by Amerindians,* pp. 299–338. New York: Springer.

Jacobson, Margaret. 1999. *Engendered Encounters: Feminism and Pueblo Cultures, 1879–1934.* Lincoln: University of Nebraska Press.

Jameson, J. F. 1907. *Original Narratives of Early American History: Spanish Explorers in the Southern United States.* New York: Charles Scribner's Sons.

Jefferson, James et al. 1972. *The Southern Utes: A Tribal History.* Southern Ute Tribe.

Jenkins, Ned J. 2009. "Tracing the Origins of the Early Creeks, 1050–1700 C.E.," in R. Ethridge and S. Shuck-Hall (eds), *Mapping the Mississippian Shatter Zone: The Colonial Indian Slave Trade and Regional Instability in the American South,* pp. 188–249. Lincoln: University of Nebraska Press.

Jennings, Matthew H. 2009. "Violence in a Shattered World," in R. Ethridge and S. M. Shuck-Hall (eds), *Mapping the Mississippian Shatter Zone: The Colonial Indian Slave Trade and Regional Instability in the American South,* pp. 272–94. Lincoln: University of Nebraska Press.

Jeter, Marvin D. 1977. "Archaeology in Copper Basin, Yavapai County, Arizona: Model Building for the Prehistory of the Prescott Region" Tempe: *Arizona State University Anthropological Research Papers*, 11.

———. 1986. "Tunicans West of the Mississippi: A Summary of Early Historic and Archaeological Evidence," in D. H. Dye and R. C. Brister (eds), *The Protohistoric period in the Mid-South: 1500–1700,* pp. 38–63. Jackson: *Mississippi Department of Archives and History Archaeological Reports*, 18.

———. 2002. "From Prehistory through Protohistory to Ethnohistory in and Near the Northern Lower Mississippi Valley," in R. Ethridge and

C. Hudson (eds), *The Transformation of the Southeastern Indians, 1540–1760*, pp. 177–223 and (endnotes) 301–13. Jackson: University Press of Mississippi.

———. 2003a. "Discussant Comments," in C. H. McNutt, S. Williams, and M. D. Jeter (eds), "Woodland-Mississippian Transition in the Mid-South: Proceedings of the 22nd Mid-South Archaeological Conference, June 2–3, 2001," pp. 73–6, 182–9. Memphis: *University of Memphis Anthropological Research Center Occasional Papers*, 25.

———. 2003b. "Review," Jill E. Neitzel (ed.), *Great Towns and Regional Polities in the American Southwest and Southeast Southeastern Archaeology* (22): 113–16.

———. 2007. "The Outer Limits of Plaquemine Culture: A View from the Northerly Borderlands," in M. A. Rees and P. C. Livingood (eds), *Plaquemine Archaeology*, pp. 161–95. Tuscaloosa: University of Alabama Press.

———. 2009. "Shatter Zone Shock Waves along the Lower Mississippi," in R. Ethridge and S. Shuck-Hall (eds), *Mapping the Mississippian Shatter Zone: The Colonial Indian Slave Trade and Regional Instability in the American South*, pp. 365–87. Lincoln: University of Nebraska Press.

Jeter, Marvin D., and Robert J. Scott Jr. 2008. "*Keo*, Quartz Crystals, Carets, et cetera: Southerly Plum Bayou vs. Northerly Coles Creek Cultural Elements." *The Arkansas Archeologist* (47): 43–82.

Jeter, Marvin D., Jerome C. Rose, G. Ishmael Williams, and Anna M. Harmon. 1989. "Archeology and Bioarcheology of the Lower Mississippi Valley and Trans-Mississippi South in Arkansas and Louisiana," Fayetteville: *Arkansas Archeological Survey Research Series*, 37.

Jeter, Marvin D., Kathleen H. Cande, and John J. Mintz. 1990. "Goldsmith Oliver 2 (3PU306): A Protohistoric Archeological Site Near Little Rock, Arkansas," Fayetteville: Report submitted to the Federal Aviation Administration by Arkansas Archeological Survey.

John, Elizabeth A. H. 1975. *Storms Brewed in Other Men's Worlds: The Confrontation of Indians, Spanish, and French in the Southwest, 1540–1795*. College Station: Texas A and M University Press.

Johnson, Jay K., John W. O'Hear, Robbie Ethridge, Brad R. Leib, Susan L. Scott, and H. Edwin Jackson. 2008. "Measuring Chickasaw Adaptation on the Western Frontier of the Colonial South: A Consideration of Documentary and Archaeological Data." *Southeastern Archaeology* (27): 1–30.

Jolliett, L., and J. Marquette. 1917. "The Mississippi Voyage of Jolliett and Marquette, 1673," in L. P. Kellog (ed.), *Early Narratives of the Northwest, 1634–1699*, pp. 227–57. New York: Charles Scribner's Sons.

Jones, B. Calvin. 1982. "Southern Cult Manifestations at the Lake Jackson Site, Leon County, Florida: Salvage Excavation of Mound 3." *Midcontinental Journal of Archaeology* (7): 3–44.

Joutel, H. 1846. "Joutel's Historical Journal of Monsieur de la Salle's Last Voyage to Discover the River Mississippi," in B. F. French (ed.), *Historical Collections of Louisiana* Vol. 1 (reprint), pp. 85–193. New York: Wiley and Putnam.

Joutel, H. 1998. *The La Salle Expedition to Texas: The Journal of Henri Joutel* (William C. Foster ed. and Johanna S. Warren trans.) Austin: Texas State Historical Association.

Kathryn, Zabelle, ed. 1998. *Women's Indian Captivity Narratives*. London: Penguin.

Keeley, Lawrence H. 1996. *War before Civilization*. Oxford: Oxford University Press.

Kehoe, Alice. 1998. *The Land of Prehistory*. New York: Routledge.

———. 2007. "Osage Texts and Cahokia Data," in F. K. Reilly III and J. F. Garber (eds), *Ancient Objects and Sacred Realms: Interpretations of Mississippian Iconography*, pp. 246–61. Austin: University of Texas Press.

Keller, Robert H. 1983. *American Protestantism and United States Indian Policy, 1869–1882*. Lincoln: University of Nebraska Press.

Kelly, John E. 1991. "Cahokia and its Role as a Gateway Center in Interregional Exchange," in T. E. Emerson and R. Barry Lewis (eds), *Cahokia and the Hinterlands: Middle Mississippian Cultures of the Midwest*, pp. 61–80. Urbana and Chicago: University of Illinois Press.

Kelly, John E., James A. Brown, Jenna M. Hamlin, Lucretia S. Kelly, Laura Kozuch, Kathryn Parker, and Julieann Van Nest. 2007. "Mound 34: The Context for the Early Evidence of the Southeastern Ceremonial Complex at Cahokia," in A. King (ed.), *Southeastern Ceremonial Complex: Chronology, Content, Context*, pp. 57–87. Tuscaloosa: University of Alabama Press.

Kelly, John E., Steven J. Ozuk, Douglas K. Jackson, Dale L. McElrath, Fred A. Finney, and Duane Esarey. 1984. "Emergent Mississippian Period," in C. J. Bareis and J. W. Porter (eds), *American Bottom Archaeology*, pp. 128–57. Urbana and Chicago: University of Illinois Press.

Kelton, Paul. 2007. *Epidemics and Enslavement: Biological Catastrophe in the Native Southeast*. Lincoln: University of Nebraska Press.

———. 2009. "Shattered and Infected: Epidemics and the Origins of the Yamasee War, 1696–1715," in R. Ethridge and S. M. Shuck-Hall (eds), *Mapping the Mississippian Shatter Zone: The Colonial Indian Slave Trade and Regional Instability in the American South*, pp. 312–32. Lincoln: University of Nebraska Press.

Kephart, Horace, ed. 2005. *The Account of Mary Rowlandson and Other Indian Captivity Narratives*. New York: Dover Publications Inc.

Kicza, John E 2002 "First Contacts," in Deloria and Salisbury (eds), *A Companion to American Indian History*, pp. 35–8. Oxford: Blackwell.

Kidder, Tristram R. 2007. "Contemplating Plaquemine Culture," in M. A. Rees and P. C. Livingood (eds), *Plaquemine Archaeology*, pp. 196–205. Tuscaloosa: University of Alabama Press.

Kidwell, Clara Sue. 1992. "Indian Women as Cultural Mediators." *Ethnohistory* 39(2): 97–107.

Kidwell, Clara Sue, and Alan Velie. 2005. *Native American Studies*. Edinburgh: Edinburgh University Press.

King, Adam. 2003. *Etowah: The Political History of a Chiefdom Capital.* Tuscaloosa: University of Alabama Press.

———. 2006. "The Historic Period Transformation of Mississippian Societies," in T. J. Pluckhahn and R. Ethridge (eds), *Light on the Path: The Anthropology and History of the Southeastern Indians,* pp. 179–95. Tuscaloosa: University of Alabama Press.

———. 2007a. "The Southeastern Ceremonial Complex: From Cult to Complex," in A. King (ed.), *Southeastern Ceremonial Complex: Chronology, Content, Context,* pp. 1–14. Tuscaloosa: University of Alabama Press.

———. 2007b. "Mound C and the Southeastern Ceremonial Complex in the History of the Etowah Site," in A. King (ed.), *Southeastern Ceremonial Complex: Chronology, Content, Context,* pp. 107–33. Tuscaloosa: University of Alabama Press.

Kingsbury, S. M. (n.d.). *The Thomas Jefferson Papers Series 8. Virginia Records Manuscripts. 1606–1737.* Retrieved March 13, 2008, from Library of Congress American MemoryProject: http://memory.loc.gov/cgi-bin/ampage?collId=mtj8andfileName=mtj8pagevc03.dbandrecNum=266.

Kinnaird, Lawrence. 1945–1949. *Spain in the Mississippi Valley: 1765–1794,* 4 vols. Annual Report of the American Historical Association for 1945 Washington, D.C.: U. S. Government Printing Office.

Klier, Betje Black. 2000. *Pavie in the Borderlands: The Journal of Théodore Pavie to Louisiana and Texas, 1829–1830.* Baton Rouge: Louisiana State University Press.

Knight, Vernon James Jr. 1994. "The Formation of the Creeks," in C. H. Hudson and C. C. Tesser (eds), *The Forgotten Centuries: Indians and Europeans in the American South 1521–1704,* pp. 373–92. Athens: University of Georgia Press.

Knight, Vernon James Jr., and Vinca P. Steponaitis. 1998. *Archaeology of the Moundville Chiefdom.* Washington: Smithsonian Institution Press.

Knight, Vernon James Jr., James A. Brown, and George E. Lankford. 2001. "On the Subject Matter of Southeastern Ceremonial Complex Art." *Southeastern Archaeology* (20): 129–53.

Kolodny, Annette. 1984. *The Land Before Her: Fantasy and Experience of the American Frontiers 1630–1860.* University of North Carolina Press.

Kopytoff, Igor. 1982. "Slavery." *Annual Review of Anthropology* 11: 207–30.

Kowalewski, Stephen A. 2006. "Coalescent Societies," in T. J. Pluckhahn and R. Ethridge (eds), *Light on the Path: The Anthropology and History of the Southeastern Indians,* pp. 94–122. Tuscaloosa: University of Alabama Press.

Kroeber, Alfred L. 1939. "Cultural and Natural Areas of Native North America." *University of California Publications in American Archaeology and Ethnology,* 38.

Kulla, Anthony. 2007. "Friendship Display at Reconnection Festival in Bermuda." *Pequot Times* July: A1.

Kupperman, Karen. 2000. *Indians & English. Facing Off in Early America*. Ithaca and London: Cornell University Press.
———. 2007. *The Jamestown Project*. Boston: Harvard University Press.
La Harpe, Jean-Baptiste Bénard de. 1971. *The Historical Journal of the Establishment of the French in Louisiana* (Joan Cain and Virginia Koenig trans.). Lafayette: University of Southwestern Louisiana Press.
La Salle, N. de. 2003. *The La Salle Expedition on the Mississippi River: A Lost Manuscript of Nicolas de la Salle, 1682* (W.C. Foster ed. and J. S. Warren trans.). Austin: Texas State Historical Association.
Lafitau, Joseph Francois. 1724. *Customs of the American Indians Compared with the Customs of Primitive Times* (William N. Fenton and Elizabeth L. Moore ed. and trans.) 1974–1977. Toronto: Champlain Society.
Lahontan [Baron de], Louis Armand de Lom D'Arce. 1703. *New Voyages to North-America. Containing an Account of the Several Nations of that Vast Continent*. London: Printed for H. Bonwicke.
Lankford, George E. 2007a. "Some Cosmological Motifs in the Southeastern Ceremonial Complex," in F. K. Reilly III and J. F. Garber (eds), *Ancient Objects and Sacred Realms: Interpretations of Mississippian Iconography*, pp. 8–38. Austin: University of Texas Press.
———. 2007b. "The 'Path of Souls': Some Death Imagery in the Southeastern Ceremonial Complex," in F. K. Reilly III and J. F. Garber (eds), *Ancient Objects and Sacred Realms: Interpretations of Mississippian Iconography*, pp. 174–212. Austin: University of Texas Press.
Lapham, H. 2005. *Hunting for Hides: Deerskins, Status, and Cultural Change in the Protohistoric Appalachians*. Tuscaloosa: University of Alabama Press.
Lauber, Almon Wheeler. 1979 [1913]. *Indian Slavery in Colonial Times within the Present Limits of the United States*. Williamstown, Massachusetts: Corner House Publishers.
———. 2002. *Indian Slavery in Colonial Times within the Present Limits of the United States* (reprint). Honolulu (HI): University Press of the Pacific.
Lawson, John. 1967. *A New Voyage to Carolina*. Chapel Hill: University of North Carolina Press.
Le Page du Pratz. 1757–1758. *Histoire de la Louisiane*. Paris.
LeBlanc, Steven A. 1999. *Prehistoric Warfare in the American Southwest*. Salt Lake City: University of Utah Press.
Lederer, John. 1958. *The Discoveries of John Lederer* (William P. Cumming ed.). Charlottesville: University of Virginia Press.
Lee, Aubra Lane. 1989. "Fusils, Paint, and Pelts: an Examination of Natchitoches-based Indian Trade in the Spanish Period, 1766–1791" Unpublished master's thesis, Natchitoches: Northwestern State University.
Lee, Dayna Bowker. 1989. "Indian Slavery in Lower Louisiana During the Colonial Period, 1699–1803," Unpublished master's thesis, Natchitoches: Northwestern State University.

Lekson, Stephen H. 2002. "War in the Southwest, War in the World." *American Antiquity* (67): 607–24.

———, ed. 2006. *The Archaeology of Chaco Canyon: an Eleventh-century Pueblo Regional Center*. Santa Fe: School of American Research Press.

Lemay, J. A. Leo. 1992. *Did Pocahontas Save Captain John Smith?* Athens, GA; London: University of Georgia Press.

Lemée, Patricia R. 2003. "Ambivalent Successes and Successful Failures: St. Denis, Aguayo, and Juan Rodríguez," in François Lagarde (ed.), *The French in Texas: History, Migration, Culture*, pp. 35–45. Austin: University of Texas Press.

Leoffler, Jack, Katherine Loeffler, and Enrique de Lamadrid. 1999. "La música de los viejitos," in *Hispano Folk Music of the Río Grande del Norte*, pp. 25–47, stanza p. 33. Albuquerque: UNM Press. "Letter from Settlers of Snake and Bear River Valleys to Reverend Rush Shippen," 1879, NA, RG 75, M234, R 208.

Levenier, James A. 1975 "Indian Captivity Narratives: Their Functions and Forms," Unpublished PhD Dissertation, University of Pennsylvania.

Levernier, James, and Cohen, Hennig, eds. 1977. *The Indians and their Captives*, [Contributions in American Studies no. 31]. Westport, Conn; London: Greenwood Press.

Lewis, David Rich. 1984. *Neither Wolf nor Dog: Indian Americans, Environment, and Agrarian Change*. Oxford Press.

L'Isle, Guillaume de. 1718. *Carte de la Louisiane et du Cours du Mississipi*, Digital map image, U.S. Library of Congress.

Logan, R. W. 1940. "Estevanico, Negro Discoverer of the Southwest: A Critical Reexamination." *Phylon (1940–1956)* 1(4): 305–14.

Lopinot, Neal H. 1997. "Cahokian Food Production Reconsidered," in T. R. Pauketat and T. E. Emerson (eds), *Cahokia: Domination and Ideology in the Mississippian World*, pp. 52–6. Lincoln: University of Nebraska Press.

———. 2003. "Lifeways: An Archaeobotanical Perspective on the Transition," in C. H. McNutt, S. Williams, and M. D. Jeter (eds), "Woodland-Mississippian Transition in the Mid-South: Proceedings of the 22nd Mid-South Archaeological Conference, June 2–3, 2001," pp. 142–4. Memphis: *University of Memphis Anthropological Research Center Occasional Papers*, 25.

Lorenz, Karl G. 2000. "The Natchez of Southwest Mississippi," in B. G. McEwan (ed.), *Indians of the Greater Southeast: Historical Archaeology and Ethnohistory*, pp. 142–77. Gainesville: University Press of Florida.

MacNeil, Denise. 2005. "Mary Rowlandson and the Foundational Mythology of the American Frontier Hero." *Women's Studies: An Interdisciplinary Journal* 34(8): 625–53.

Magnaghi, Russell M. 1981. "Changing Material Culture and the Hasinai of East Texas." *Southern Studies* 20(4): 412–26.

———. 1998. *Indian Slavery, Labor, Evangelization and Captivity in the Americas: an Annotated Bibliography*. Lanham, Maryland and London: The Scarecrow Press Inc.

Mainfort, R. C., Jr. 2001. "The Late Prehistoric and Protohistoric Periods in the Central Mississippi Valley," in D. S. Brose, C. W. Cowan, and R. C. Mainfort Jr. (eds), *Societies in Eclipse: Archaeology of the Eastern Woodlands Indians,* pp. 173–90. Washington: Smithsonian Institution Press.

Mann, Michael. 1992. *The Last of the Mohicans,* feature film, Morgan Creek Productions, Morgan Creek International distributors.

Marceaux, Shawn, and David H. Dye. 2007. "Hightower Anthropomorphic Marine Shell Gorgets and Duck River Sword-form Flint Bifaces: Middle Mississippian Ritual Regalia in the Southern Appalachians," in A. King (ed.), *Southeastern Ceremonial Complex: Chronology, Content, Context,* pp. 165–84. Tuscaloosa: University of Alabama Press.

Margry, Pierre, ed. 1876–1886. *Découvertes et Etablissements des Francais dans L'Ouest et dans Le Sud 1886 de L'Amérique Septentrionale,* 6 vols. Paris: Imprimérie D. Jouaust.

Marrant, J. 1785. *A Narrative of the Lord's Wonderful Dealings with John Marrant, a Black, Fourth Edition, Enlarged by Mr. Marrant, and Printed (with Permission) for his Sole Benefit, with Notes Explanatory.* Spitalfields: R. Hawes.

———. 1789. *A Sermon Preached on the 24th Day of June 1789, Being the Festival of St. John the Baptist, At the Request of the Right Worshipful the Grand Master Prince Hall, and the Rest of the Brethren of the African Lodge of the Honourable Society of Free and Accepted.* Boston: Bible and Heart.

———. (n.d.). *Narrative of John Marrant.* Retrieved February 17, 2008, from Black Loyalists:OurHistoryOurPeople: http://www.blackloyalist.com/canadiandigitalcollection/documents/diaries/marrant_narrative.htm.

Marren, Susan. 1993. "Between Slavery and Freedom: The Transgressive Self in Olaudah Equiano's Autobiography.'" *PMLA* 108(1): 91–108.

Marrinan, Rochelle A., and Nancy Marie White. 2007. "Modeling Fort Walton Culture in Northwest Florida." *Southeastern Archaeology* (26): 292–318.

Martin, Deborah L. 2008. "Ripped Flesh and Torn Souls: Skeletal Evidence for Captivity and Slavery from the La Plata Valley, New Mexico, AD 1100–1300," in Cameron (ed.), *Invisible Citizens,* pp. 159–180. Salt Lake City, UT: University of Utah Press.

Martin, Joel W. 1994. "Southeastern Indians and the English Trade in Skins and Slaves," in C. Hudson and C. Chaves Tesser (eds), *The Forgotten Centuries: Indians and Europeans in the American South, 1521–1704,* pp. 304–24. Athens and London: University of Georgia Press.

Martin, Scott W. J. 2008. "Languages Past and Present: Archaeological Approaches to the Appearance of Northern Iroquoian Speakers in the Lower Great Lakes Region of North America." *American Antiquity* (73): 441–63.

Mason, van Wyck. 1937. "Bermuda's Pequots." *Harvard Alumni Bulletin* (39): 616–20.
Maxcy, T. S. 1999. *Chickasaw Ethnohistory 1721–1740: The Journal of the Council and Council in Assembly, South Carolina Sessional Papers.* M.A. Oxford: University of Mississippi.
May, Cedrick. Winter 2004. "John Marrant and the Narrative Construction of an Early Black Methodist Evangelical." *African American Review* 38(4):553–70.
Mazrim, R., and D. Esarey. 2007. "Rethinking the Dawn of History: The Schedule, Signature, and Agency of European Goods in Protohistoic Illinois." *Midcontinental Journal of Archaeology* 32(2): 145–200.
McDonald, W. 1914. *Selected Charters and other Documents Illustrative of American History (1606–1775).* London: MacMillan and Co.
McDowell, W. L., Jr. 1992. *Journals of the Commissioners of the Indian Trade, September 20, 1710–29 August 1718* (reprint). Columbia: South Carolina Department of History and Archives.
McEwan, Bonnie G., ed. 1993. *The Spanish Missions of La Florida.* Gainesville: University Press of Florida.
———. 2000a. *Indians of the Greater Southeast: Historical Archaeology and Ethnohistory.* Gainesville: University Press of Florida.
McEwan, Bonnie G. 2000b. "The Apalachee Indians of Northwest Florida," in McEwan (ed.), *Indians of the Greater Southeast*, pp. 57–84.
———. 2004. "Apalachee and Neighboring Groups," in B. McEwan (ed.) *Southeast, Handbook of North American Indians*, Vol. 14, pp. 669–76. Washington, D.C.: Smithsonian Institution Press.
McGhee, Robert. 2008. "Aboriginalism and the Problems of Indigenous Archaeology." *American Antiquity* (73): 579–97.
McLoughlin, William G. 1994. "Christianity and Racism: Cherokee Responses to the Debate over Indian Origins, 1760–1860," in W. H. Conser Jr. (ed.), *The Cherokees and Christianity, 1794–1870: Essays in Acculturation and Cultural Persistence*, pp. 145–7. Athens: University Georgia Press.
McWilliams, Richebourg G., ed. and trans. 1981. *Iberville's Gulf Journals.* Tuscaloosa: University of Alabama Press.
Means, Russell, and Marvin J. Wolf. 1995. *Where White Me Fear to Tread: The Autobiography of Russell Means.* New York: St. Martin's Press.
Meeker, Arvilla. 1879. "Mrs. Meeker's Story" November 12, *Greeley Tribune,*
———. 1897. "Letter to Children," March 5, Nathan C. Meeker papers, WH1680, Western History Collection, The Denver Public Library.
———. 1897. Diary, 1846, Nathan C. Meeker Papers, Colorado Historical Society.
Meeker, Josephine. 1976. *The Ute Massacre: Brave Miss Meeker's Captivity, Her Own Account of it: also the Narratives of Her Mother and Mrs. Price, to which is Added further Thrilling and Intensely Interesting Details, Not*

Hitherto Published, of the Bravery and the Frightful Sufferings Endured by Mrs. Meeker, Mrs. Price, and Her Two Children, and by Miss Josephine Meeker, The Garland Library of Narrative of North American Indian Captivities; v. 93. New York: Garland Publishing.

Meeker, Nathan C. 1878. "Letter to Senator Teller," May 27, Nathan C. Meeker papers, WH1680, Western History Collection, The Denver Public Library.

———. 1879. "Nathan Meeker to E.J. Carver," July 10, Nathan C. Meeker papers, WH1680, Western History Collection, The Denver Public Library.

———. 1879. "The Utes of Colorado," *The American Antiquarian* (4): 224–6.

———. 1879 "Will Indians Work?" 2 April, *Greeley Tribune*, pg. 1

———. 1878. "Letter to Senator Teller," May 27, Nathan C. Meeker papers, WH1680, Western History Collection, The Denver Public Library.

———. 1879. "Nathan Meeker to E.J. Carver," May 19, Nathan C. Meeker papers, WH1680, Western History Collection, The Denver Public Library.

———. 1878. "Woman, the Natural Savage," December 11, *Greeley Tribune*.

———. 1879. "Letter to Arvilla Meeker." July 1, Nathan C. Meeker papers, WH1680, Western History Collection, The Denver Public Library.

———. 1879. "Letter to the Commissioner of Indian Affairs," September 10, NA RG 75, GR, White River, LR.

———. 1879. "Letter to Commission of Indian Affairs," September 8, NA RG 75, GR, White River, LR.

———. n.d. "A New Spiritual World," unpublished manuscript, Nathan C. Meeker Papers, Colorado Historical Society.

Merrell, James. 1989. *The "Indians" New World: Catawbas and Their Neighbors from European Contact Through the Era of Removal*. Chapel Hill: University of North Carolina Press.

Meyers, Maureen. 2009. "From Refugees to Slave-Traders: The Transformation of the Westo Indians," in R. Ethridge and S. M. Shuck-Hall (eds), *Mapping the Mississippian Shatter Zone: The Colonial Indian Slave Trade and Regional Instability in the American South*, pp. 81–103. Lincoln: University of Nebraska Press.

Milanich, Jerald T. 1999. *Laboring in the Fields of the Lord: Spanish Missions and Southeastern Indians*. Washington, D.C.: Smithsonian Institution Press.

Milanich, Jerald T., and Charles Hudson. 1993. *Hernando de Soto and the Indians of Florida*. Gainesville: University Press of Florida.

Mills, Elizabeth Shown. 1977. *Natchitoches 1729–1803: Abstracts of the Catholic Church Registers of the French and Spanish Post of St. Jean Baptiste des Natchitoches in Louisiana*. New Orleans: Polyanthos.

———. 1981. *Natchitoches Colonials: Censuses, Military Rolls, and Tax Lists, 1722–1803*. Chicago: Adams Press.

———. 1985. "(De) Mézières-Trichel-Grappe: A Study of a Tri-caste Lineage in the Old South." *The Genealogist* 6 (Spring): 4–84.
Mills, Gary B. 1977. *The Forgotten People: Cane River's Creoles of Color.* Baton Rouge: Louisiana State University Press.
Mills, Gary B., and E. S. Mills. 1977. "Louise Marguerite: St. Denis' Other Daughter." *Southern Studies* XVI (3): 321–8.
Milne, George Edward. 2009. "Picking Up the Pieces: Natchez Coalescence in the Shatter Zone," in R. Ethridge and S. M. Shuck-Hall (eds), *Mapping the Mississippian Shatter Zone: The Colonial Indian Slave Trade and Regional Instability in the American South*, pp. 388–417. Lincoln: University of Nebraska Press.
Milner, George R. 1980. "Epidemic Disease in the Post Contact Southeast: A Reappraisal." *Midcontinental Journal of Archaeology* (5): 39–6.
———. 1998. *The Cahokia Chiefdom: The Archaeology of a Mississippian Society.* Washington, D.C.: Smithsonian Institution Press.
———. 1999. "Warfare in Prehistoric and Early Historic Eastern North America." *Journal of Archaeological Research* (7): 105–151.
———. 2002. *The Moundbuilders: Ancient Peoples of Eastern North America.* London: Thames and Hudson.
———. 2007. "Warfare, Population, and Food Production in Prehistoric Eastern North America," in R. J. Chacon and R. G. Mendoza (eds), *North American Indigenous Warfare and Ritual Violence*, pp. 182–201. Tucson: University of Arizona Press.
Milner, George R., and Virginia G. Smith. 1990. "Oneota Human Skeletal Remains," in S. K. Santure, A. D. Harn, and D. Esarey (eds), "Archaeological Investigations at the Morton Village and Norris Farms 36 Cemetery," pp. 111–48. Springfield: *Illinois State Museum Reports of Investigations*, 45.
Milner, George R., Eve Anderson, and Virginia G. Smith. 1991. "Warfare in Late Prehistoric West-central Illinois." *American Antiquity* (56): 581–603.
Minet, January Baptiste. 1987. "Voyage Made from Canada inland Going Southward During the Year 1682," in R. S. Weddle (ed.), *La Salle, the Mississippi, and the Gulf: Three Primary Documents* (Ann Linda Bell trans.), pp. 29–70. College Station: Texas A and M University Press.
Minges, Patrick. 2004. *Black Indian Slave Narratives.* Winston-Salem, NC: John F. Blair Publisher.
Mitchell, Donald. 1984. "Predatory Warfare, Social Status, and the North Pacific Slave Trade." *Ethnology* 23(1): 39–48.
Mochon, Marion Johnson. 1972. "Language, History, and Prehistory: Mississippian Lexico-reconstruction." *American Antiquity* (37): 478–503.
Monsforth, Robert P. 2007. "Human Trophy Taking in Eastern North America During the Archaic Period: The Relationship to Warfare and Social Complexity," in R. J. Chacon and D. H. Dye (eds), *The Taking and Displaying of Human Body Parts as Trophies by Amerindians*, pp. 222–7. New York: Springer.

Montgomery, Benilde. 1993. "Recapturing John Marrant," in Frank Shuffleton (ed.), *A Mixed Race:Ethnicity in Early America*. Oxford: Oxford University Press.

Mooney, James. 1900. *Myths of the Cherokees*. Bureau of American Ethnology: Government Printing Office Washington, D.C: Smithsonian Institution.

Moore, David. 2002. *Catawba Valley Mississippian: Ceramics, Chronology, and Catawba*. Tuscaloosa: University of Alabama Press.

Morgan, D. W. 1997. "The Earliest Historic Chickasaw Horse Raids into Caddoan Territory." *Southern Studies* 8(3 and 4): 93–118.

Morgan, E. 1975. *American Slavery American Freedom: The Ordeal of Colonial Virginia*. New York: W.W. Norton and Company.

Morgan, Gwenda. 1984. "Sold into Slavery in Retribution against the Nanziattico Indians." *Virginia Cavalcade* 33(4): 168–73.

Morse, Dan F., and Phyllis A. Morse. 1983. *Archaeology of the Central Mississippi Valley*. New York: Academic Press.

Mossiker, Frances. 1976, 1996. *Pocahontas: The Life and Legend*. New York: Da Capo Press.

Mrozowski, Stephen A. 2010. "Creole Materialities: Archaeological Exploration of Hybridized Realities on a North American Plantation." *Journal of Historical Sociology* 23(1): 16–39.

Muller, Jon. 1966. "An Experimental Theory of Stylistic Analysis," Cambridge, Massachusetts: PhD dissertation, Department of Anthropology, Harvard University.

———. 1986. *Archaeology of the lower Ohio River Valley*. New York: Academic Press.

———. 1989. "The Southern Cult," in P. K. Galloway (ed.), *The Southeastern Ceremonial Complex: Artifacts and Analysis*, pp. 11–26. Lincoln: University of Nebraska Press.

———. 1997. *Mississippian Political Economy*. New York: Plenum Press.

———. 2007. "Prolegomena for the Analysis of the Southeastern Ceremonial Complex," in A. King (ed.), *Southeastern Ceremonial Complex: Chronology, Content, Context*, pp. 15–37. Tuscaloosa: University of Alabama Press.

Nairne, Thomas. 1988. *Nairne's Muskhogean Journals: The 1708 Expedition to the Mississippi River* (Alexander Moore ed.). Jackson: University of Mississippi Press.

Namias, June. 1993. *White Captives: Gender and Ethnicity on the American Frontier*. Chapel Hill: University of North Carolina Press.

Nash, Gary B. 1974. *Red, White, and Black: The Peoples of Early America*. Englewood Cliff, NJ: Prentice Hall.

Nassaney, Michael S., and Kendra Pyle. 1999. "The Adoption of the Bow and Arrow in Eastern North America." *American Antiquity* (64): 243–63.

Nathan C. Meeker papers, WH1680, Western History Collection, The Denver Public Library.

Nathan C. Meeker Papers, Colorado Historical Society.

Neeley, Bill. 1995. *The Last Comanche Chief The Life and Times of Quanah Parker*. New York & Toronto: John Wiley & Sons, Inc.

Neitzel, Jill E., ed. 1999. *Great Towns and Regional Polities in the American Southwest and Southeast*. Albuquerque: University of New Mexico Press.

Neitzel, Robert S. 1983. *The Grand Village of the Natchez Revisited*, Archaeological Report no. 12. Jackson: Mississippi Department of Archives and History.

———. 1997. *Archaeology of the Fatherland Site: The Grand Village of the Natchez*, Archaeological Report no. 28. Jackson: Mississippi Department of Archives and History.

Oatis, Steven J. 2004. *A Colonial Complex: South Carolina's Frontiers in the Era of the Yamasee War 1680–1730*. Lincoln University of Nebraska Press.

O'Brien, Patricia J. 1991. "Early State Economics: Cahokia, Capital of the Ramey State," in H. J. M. Claessen and P. van de Velde (eds), *Early State Economics*, pp. 143–75. London: Transaction Publishers.

Osburn, Katherine M. B. 1998. *Southern Ute Women: Autonomy and Assimilation on the Reservation, 1887–1934*. Albuquerque: University of New Mexico.

Pauketat, Timothy R. 1997. "Cahokian Political Economy," in T. R. Pauketat and T. E. Emerson (eds), *Cahokia: Domination and Ideology in the Mississippian World*, pp. 30–51. Lincoln: University of Nebraska Press.

———. 2002. "A Fourth-generation Synthesis of Cahokia and Mississippianization." *Midcontinental Journal of Archaeology* (27): 149–70.

———. 2003. "Resettled Farmers and the Making of a Mississippian Polity." *American Antiquity* (68): 39–66.

———. 2004. *Ancient Cahokia and the Mississippians*. Cambridge, England: Cambridge University Press.

———. 2007. *Chiefdoms and Other Archaeological Delusions*. Lanham, Maryland: Altamira Press.

Pauketat, Timothy R., and Thomas E. Emerson, eds. 1997. *Cahokia: Domination and Ideology in the Mississippian World*. Lincoln: University of Nebraska Press.

Pearce, Roy Harvey. 1947. "The Significances of the Captivity Narrative." *American Literature* (19): 1–20.

———. 1967. *Savagism and Civilization: A Study of the Indian and the American Mind*. Baltimore: John Hopkins University Press.

Perdue, Theda. 1979. *Slavery and the Evolution of Cherokee Society: 1540–1866*. Knoxville: University of Tennessee Press.

———. 1998. *Cherokee Women: Gender and Culture Change, 1700–1835*. Lincoln: University of Nebraska Press.

Perttula, T. 1992. *The Caddo Nation: Archaeological and Ethnohistoric Perspectives*. Austin: University of Texas Press.

———. 2002. "Social Changes among the Caddo Indians in the 16th and 17th Centuries," in C. Hudson and R. Ethridge (eds), *The Transformation of the Southeastern Indians, 1540–1760*, pp. 249–70. Jackson: University Presses of Mississippi.

Peyser, Joseph L. 1989/1990. "The Fate of the Fox Survivors: A Dark Chapter in the History of the French in the Upper Country, 1726–1737." *Wisconsin Magazine of History* 73(2): 83–110.

Phillips, Philip. 1970. "Archaeological Survey in the Lower Yazoo Basin, Mississippi, 1949–1955." Cambridge, Massachusetts: *Papers of the Peabody Museum, Harvard University*, 60, Parts 1 and 2.

Phillips, Philip, and James A. Brown. 1978. *Pre-Columbian Shell Engravings from the Craig Mound at Spiro, Oklahoma*. Cambridge, Massachusetts: Peabody Museum Press, Harvard University.

Philips, Philip, James A. Ford, and James B. Griffin. 1951. "Archaeological Survey in the Lower Mississippi Alluvial Valley, 1940–1947," Cambridge, Massachusetts: *Papers of the Peabody Museum, Harvard University*, 25.

Plog, Fred T., 1974. *The Study of Prehistoric Change*. New York: Academic Press.

Pluckhahn, Thomas J., and Robbie Ethridge, eds. 2006. *Light on the Path: The Anthropology and History of the Southeastern Indians*. Tuscaloosa: University of Alabama Press.

Podruchny, C. 2006. *Making the Voyageur World: Travelers and Traders in the North American Fur Trade*. Lincoln: University of Nebraska Press.

Poehls, Robert L. 1944. "Kingston Lake Site Burials." *Journal of the Illinois State Archaeological Society* 1 (April): 36–8.

Pollack, D. 2004. *Caborn-Welborn: Constructing a New Society after the Angel Chiefdom Collapse*. Tuscaloosa: University of Alabama Press.

Porter, Kenneth W. 1932. "Association as Fellow Slaves." *Journal of Negro History* 17(3): 294–7.

Pratt, Mary Louise. 1992. *Imperial Eyes, Travel Writing and Transculturation*. New York and London: Routledge.

Pratt-Smiles, Stephanie. 1992. "Native American in Stone: the Simcoe Memorial in Exeter Cathedral," in Mick Gidley (ed.), *Representing Others: White Views of Indigenous Peoples*, pp. 14–24. Exeter: University of Exeter Press.

Pratt, Stephanie. 2005. *American Indians in British Art, 1700–1840* Norman: Oklahoma University Press.

———. 2009. "Truth and Artifice in the Visualization of Native Peoples: from the time of John White to the beginning of the eighteenth century,," in Kim Sloan (ed.), *European Visions: American Voices*, British Museum Research Publications 172, London: British Museum Press: 33–40. Online access: http://www.britishmuseum.org/pdf/1-Pratt-Truth%20and%20Artifice.pdf.

Price, T. Douglas, James H. Burton, and James B. Stoltman. 2007. "Place of Origin of Prehistoric Inhabitants of Aztalan, Jefferson Co., Wisconsin." *American Antiquity* (72): 524–38.

Priestly, H. I., ed. and trans. 1928. *The Luna Papers: Documents Relating to the Expedition of Don Tristán de Luna y Arellano for the Conquest of La Florida in 1559–1561*. 2 Vols. Deland: The Florida State Historical Society.

Prince Hall and Peter Bess et al. 1947. "To the Honorable Council and House of Representatives for the State of Massachusetts Bay, in General Court assembled, January 13, 1777," p. 22 in J. A. G. Clark *Clark's History of Prince Hall Freemasonry 1775–1945* Des Moines, IA: United Grand Lodge of Iowa, F. and A.M.

Prucha, Francis Paul. 1984. *The Great Father: The United States Government and the American Indians* [abridged ed.]. Lincoln: University of Nebraska Press.

Quintana, Frances Leon. 2004. *Ordeal of Change: The Southern Utes and Their Neighbors.* New York: Altamira Press.

Rael-Gálvez, Estévan. 2002. "Identifying Captivity and Capturing Identity: Narratives of American Indian Slavery in Colorado and New Mexico, 1776–1934," Ph . dissertation, University of Michigan.

Ramenofsky, A. 1987. *Vectors of Death: The Archaeology of European Contact.* Albuquerque: University of New Mexico Press.

Ramenofsky, A., and Patricia Galloway. 1997. "Disease and the Soto Entrada," in P. Galloway (ed.), *The Hernando De Soto Expedition: History, Historiography, and "Discovery" in the Southeast* [new ed.], pp. 259–82. Lincoln: University of Nebraska Press.

Rangel, R. 1993 "Account of the Northern Conquest and Discovery of Hernando de Soto," in L. A. Clayton, V. J. Knight, Jr., E. C. Moore (eds), *The De Soto Chronicles: The Expedition of Hernando de Soto to North America in 1539–1543* [J. Robertson trans.], pp. 246–306. Tuscaloosa: University of Alabama Press.

Rankin, Robert L. 1993. "Language Affiliations of Some de Soto Place Names in Arkansas," in G. A. Young and M. P. Hoffman (eds), *The Expedition of Hernando de Soto West of the Mississippi, 1541–1543,* pp. 210–21. Fayetteville: University of Arkansas Press.

Ravesloot, John C., and Patricia M. Spoerl. 1989. "The Role of Warfare in the Development of Status Hierarchies at Casas Grandes, Chihuahua, Mexico," in D. C. Tkaczak and B. C. Vivian (eds), "Cultures in Conflict: Current Archaeological Perspectives, pp. 130–7. University of Calgary, Alberta, Canada: *Proceedings of the 20th Annual Chacmool Conference.*

Rawley, James A. 2005. *The Transatlantic Slave Trade: A History* [revised ed.]. Lincoln: University of Nebraska Press.

Rees, Mark A., and Patrick C. Livingood, eds. 2007. *Plaquemine Archaeology.* Tuscaloosa: University of Alabama Press.

Regnier, A. 2001. *A Stylistic Analysis of Burial Urns from the Protohistoric Period in Central Alabama.* M.A. Tuscaloosa: University of Alabama.

Reid, John Phillip. 1970. *A Law of Blood: The Primitive Law of the Cherokee Nation.* New York: New York University Press.

Reilly, F. Kent III. 2004. "People of Earth, People of Sky: Visualizing the Sacred in Native American Art of the Mississippian Period," in R. V. Sharp (ed.), *Hero, Hawk, and Open Hand: American Indian Art of the Ancient Midwest and South,* pp. 124–37. New Haven, Connecticut: The Art Institute of Chicago and Yale University Press.

———. 2007. "The Petaloid Motif: A Celestial Symbolic Locative in the Shell art of Spiro," in F. Kent Reilly III and James F. Garber (eds), *Ancient Objects and Sacred Realms: Interpretations of Mississippian Iconography*, pp. 39–55. Austin: University of Texas Press.

Renfrew, Colin 1974. "Beyond a Subsistence Economy: The Evolution of Social Organization in Prehistoric Europe," in C. B. Moore (ed.) "Reconstructing Complex Societies: an Archaeological Colloquium," pp. 69–95. Chicago: *Bulletin of the American School of Oriental Research*, 20.

Rennie, Neil. 2007. *Pocahontas, Little Wanton: Myth, Life and Afterlife*. London: Bernard Quaritch Ltd.

Reséndez, Andrés. 2007. *A Land So Strange: The Epic Journey of Cabeza de Vaca*. New York: Basic Books.

"The Return of the Meeker Family at Los Pinos," *Chicago Tribune*, October 29, 1879, p. 1.

Rice, Glen E., and Steven A. LeBlanc, eds. 2001. *Deadly Landscapes: Case Studies in Prehistoric Southwestern Warfare*. Salt Lake City: University of Utah Press.

Richter, Daniel K. 1992. *The Ordeal of the Longhouse: The Peoples of the Iroquois League in the Era of European Colonization*. Chapel Hill: University of North Carolina Press.

———. 2001. *Facing East from Indian Country, A Native History of Early America*. Cambridge, Mass and London: Harvard University Press.

Riggs, B. (Forthcoming.) "Reinterpreting the Chestowee Raid of 1713."

Rodriguez, Sylvia. 2009. *The Matachines Dance: A Ritual Dance of the Indian Pueblos and Mexicano/Hispano Communities*. Santa Fe, NM: Sunstone Press.

Rolingson, Martha Ann. 1998. "Toltec Mounds and Plum Bayou Culture: Mound D Excavations." Fayetteville: *Arkansas Archeological Survey Research Series*, 54.

Ross-Stallings, Nancy A. 2007. "Trophy Taking in the Central and Lower Mississippi Valley," in R. J. Chacon and D. H. Dye (eds), *The Taking and Displaying of Human Body Parts as Trophies by Amerindians*, pp. 339–76. New York: Springer.

Rountree, Helen C. 1990. *Pocahontas's People: The Powhatan Indians of Virginia Through Four Centuries*. Norman: University of Oklahoma Press.

———. 1993. "Who Were the Powhatans and Did They Have a Unified 'Foreign Policy'?" in Helen C. Rountree (ed.), *Powhatan Foreign Relations, 1500–1722*, pp. 1–19. Charlottesville and London: University Press of Virginia.

Rowland, Dunbar, and Albert Godfrey Sanders, eds. and trans. 1927–1932. *Mississippi Provincial Archives 1704–1743: French Dominion*, 3 vols. Jackson: Mississippi Department of Archives and History.

Rowlandson, Mary. 1682. *A true history of the captivity & restoration of Mrs. Mary Rowlandson, a minister's wife in New-England: Wherein is set forth the cruel and inhumane usage she underwent amongst the heathens, for eleven weeks' time: and her deliverance from them*. London: Printed first at New-England, and re-printed at London and sold by Joseph Poole, at the Blue Bowl in the Long-Walk, by Christs-Church Hospital.

Rudes, Blair A., Thomas J. Blumer, and J. Alan May. 2004. "Catawba and Neighboring Groups," in R. D. Fogelson (ed.), *Southeast, Handbook of North American Indians*, Vol. 14, pp. 301–18. Washington, D.C.: Smithsonian Institution Press.

Rushforth, Brett. 2003. "'A Little Flesh We Offer You': The Origins of Indian Slavery in New France." *William and Mary Quarterly* 3d Series, 60(4): 777–808.

Russell, Elizabeth Abigail Dillard. 2001. "The Princess and the Prostitute: A Study of Eighteenth-Century Representations of Native American Women," MA/PhD needed, Dissertation Auburn University.

Sabo, G. 2000. "The Quapaw Indians," in B. G. McEwan (ed.), *Indians of the Greater Southeast: Historical Archaeology and Ethnohistory*, pp. 178–203. Gainesville: University Presses of Florida Press.

Said, Edward. 1978. *Orientalism*. New York: Vintage Press.

Saillant, J. 1999. "Dress, Power, and Crossing (the Atlantic): Figuring the Black Exodus to Sierra Leone in the Late Eighteenth Century," in J. Munns and P. E. Richards (eds), *The Clothes that Wear Us: Essays on Dressing and Transgressing in Eighteenth-century Culture*, pp. 301–19. Newark (DE) and London: University of Delaware Press and Associated University Presses.

———. n.d. *Journal Of Millennial Studies* [online]. Retrieved January 17, 2008, from "Wipe Away All Tears from Their Eyes": John Marrant's Theology in the Black Atlantic, 1785–1808: http://www.mille.org/publications/winter98/saillant.PDF.

Sainsbury John A. 1975. "Indian Labor in Early Rhode Island." *The New England Quarterly* 48(3): 378–93.

Salley, Alexander S., ed. 1911. *Narratives of Early Carolina 1650–1674*. New York: Charles Scribner's Sons.

———. 1928. *Records in the British Public Records Office Relating to South Carolina*, 2 volumes. Atlanta: Foote and Davis Company.

Santos-Granero, Fernando. 2009. *Vital Enemies: Slavery, Predation, and the Amerindian Political Economy of Life*. Austin: University of Texas Press.

Santure, Sharron K., Alan D. Harn, and Duane Esarey. 1990. "Archaeological Investigations at the Morton Village and Norris Farms 36 Cemetery." Springfield: *Illinois State Museum Reports of Investigations*, 45.

Saunders, Rebecca. 2000. "The Guale Indians of the Lower Atlantic Coast: Change and Continuity," in Bonnie G. McEwan (ed.), *Indians of the Greater Southeast: Historical Archaeology and Ethnohistory*, pp. 26–56. Gainesville: University Press of Florida.

Saucier, Roger T. 1974. "Quaternary Geology of the Lower Mississippi Valley." Fayetteville: *Arkansas Archeological Survey Research Series*, 6.

Sayers, Daniel O., P. Brendan Burke, and Aaron M. Henry. 2007. "The Political Economy of Exile in the Great Dismal Swamp." *International Journal of Historical Archaeology* 11(1): 60–97.

Scarry, John F. 1994. "The Apalachee Chiefdom: A Mississippian Society on the Fringe of the Mississippian World," in C. Hudson and C. Chaves Tesser (eds), *Athens: The Forgotten Centuries: Indians and Europeans in the American South, 1521–1704*, pp. 156–78. University of Georgia Press.

———. 1996. "Stability and Change in the Apalachee Chiefdom," in J. F. Scarry (ed.), *Political Structure and Change in the Prehistoric Southeastern United States*, pp. 192–227. Gainesville: University Press of Florida.

———. 2007. "Connections between the Etowah and Lake Jackson Chiefdoms: Patterns in the Iconographic and Material Evidence," in A. King (ed.), *Southeastern Ceremonial Complex: Chronology, Content, Context*, pp. 134–50. Tuscaloosa: University of Alabama Press.

Schaafsma, Polly. 2007a. "Documenting Conflict in the Prehistoric Pueblo Southwest," in R. J. Chacon and R. G. Mendoza (eds), *North American Indigenous Warfare and Ritual Violence*, pp. 114–28. Tucson: University of Arizona Press.

———. 2007b. "Head Trophies and Scalping in Southwestern Rock Art," in Richard J. Chacon and David H. Dye (eds), *The Taking and Displaying of Human Body Parts as Trophies by Amerindians*, pp. 90–123. New York: Springer.

Schambach, Frank F. 1993, "Some New Interpretations of Spiroan Culture History," in J. B. Stoltman (ed.), "Archaeology of Eastern North America: Papers in Honor of Stephen Williams," pp. 187–230. Jackson: *Mississippi Department of Archives and History Archaeological Reports*, 25.

———. 1996. "Mounds, Embankments, and Ceremonialism in the Trans-Mississippi South," in R. C. Mainfort Jr. and R. Walling (eds), "Mounds, Embankments, and Ceremonialism in the Midsouth," pp. 36–43. Fayetteville: *Arkansas Archeological Survey Research Series*, 46.

———. 1999. "Spiro and the Tunica: A New Interpretation of the Role of the Tunica in the Culture History of the Southeast and Southern Plains, A.D. 1100–1750," in R. C. Mainfort Jr. and M. D. Jeter (eds), *Arkansas Archaeology: Essays in Honor of Dan and Phyllis Morse*, pp. 169–224. Fayetteville: University of Arkansas Press.

Schimmel, Julie. 1991. "Inventing 'the Indian,'" in W. H. Truettner (ed.), *The West as America: Reinterpreting Images of the Frontier, 1820–1920*, pp. 149–89. Washington, D.C.: Smithsonian Institution Press.

Schroedl, G. 2000. "Cherokee Ethnohistory," in B. G. McEwan (ed.), *Indians of the Greater Southeast: Historical Archaeology and Ethnohistory*, pp. 204–41. Gainesville: University Presses of Florida Press.

Seeman, Mark F. 2007. "Predatory War and Hopewell Trophies," in R. J. Chacon and D. H. Dye (eds), *The Taking and Displaying of Human Body Parts as Trophies by Amerindians*, pp. 167–89. New York: Springer.

Selden, Jack R. 2006. *The Parker Story.* Palestine, Texas: Clacton Press.
Service, E. R. 1931. *Primitive Social Organization.* New York: Random House.
Shelby, Charmion Clair. 1923. "St. Denis's Declaration Concerning Texas in 1717." *Southwestern Historical Quarterly* 26(3): 165–83.
Shuck-Hall, Sheri. M. 2009. "Alabama and Coushatta Diaspora and Coalescence in the Mississippian Shatter Zone," in R. Ethridge and S. M. Shuck-Hall (eds), *Mapping the Mississippian Shatter Zone: The Colonial Indian Slave Trade and Regional Instability in the American South,* pp. 250–71. Lincoln: University of Nebraska Press.
Sibley, John 1832. "Historical Sketches of the Several Indian Tribes in Louisiana." *American State Papers, Class II, Indian Affairs* vol. I, pp. 721–5. Gales and Seaton: Washington, D. C.
Silliman, Stephen. 2010. "Indigenous Traces in Colonial Spaces: Archaeologies of Ambiguity, Origin, and Practice." *Journal of Social Archaeology* 10(1): 28–58.
Silverman, David J. 2001 "The Impact of Indentured Servitude on the Society and Culture of Southern New England Indians, 1680–1810." *The New England Quarterly* 74(4): 622–66.
Skinner, Alanson. 1915. "Iowa Societies," in Clark Wissler (ed.), "Societies of the Plains Indians," *Anthropological Papers of the American Museum of Natural History* (11) 1912–1916, pp. 679–740. New York: American Museum of Natural History.
Sloan, Kim, ed. 2007. *A New World England's First View of America.* London: The British Museum Press.
Slotkin, Richard. 1973. *Regeneration through Violence: The Mythology of the American Frontier, 1600–1860.* Connecticut: Wesleyan University Press.
Smith, Bruce D. 1986 "The Archaeology of the Southeastern United States: from Dalton to De Soto" *Advances in World Archaeology* (5): 1–92
———. 2007. *Rivers of Change: Essays on Early Agriculture in Eastern North America* [revised ed.]. Tuscaloosa: University of Alabama Press.
Smith, John. 1608. *A True Relation of Such Occurences and Accidents of Note, as Hath Hapned in Virginia.*
———. 1612. *A Map of Virginia,* Amsterdam: Theatrum Orbis Terrarum; New York: Da Capo Press, 1973 (a facsimile. Made from the British Museum copy G.7120).
———. 1624. *The generall historie of Virginia, New-England, and the Summer Isles: with the names of the adventurers, planters, and governours from their first beginning. Ano: 1584. to this present 1624. With the procedings of those severall colonies and the accidents that befell them in all their journyes and discoveries.* London: 1624.
Smith, Maria O. 1997. "Osteological Indications of Warfare in the Archaic Period of the Western Tennessee Valley," in D. L. Martin and D. W. Frayer (eds), *Troubled Times: Violence and Warfare in the Past,* pp. 241–65. New York: Gordon and Breach.

Smith, Marvin T. 1987. *Archaeology of Aboriginal Culture Change in the Interior Southeast: Depopulation during the Early Historic Period.* University Press of Florida.
———. 1990. "Glass Beads from the Goldsmith Oliver 2 Site," in M. D. Jeter, K. H. Cande, and J. J. Mintz Goldsmith (eds), "Oliver 2 (3PU306): A Protohistoric Archeological Site near Little Rock, Arkansas," pp. 217–22. Fayetteville: Report submitted to the Federal Aviation Administration by Arkansas Archeological Survey.
———. 2000. *Coosa: The Rise and Fall of a Mississippian Chiefdom.* Gainesville: University Presses of Florida.
———. 2002. "Aboriginal Population Movements in the Postcontact Southeast," in C. Hudson and R. Ethridge (eds), *The Transformation of the Southeastern Indians, 1540–1760*, pp. 3–20. Jackson: University Presses of Mississippi.
Snow, Dean R. 2007. "Iroquois-Huron Warfare," in R. J. Chacon and R. G. Mendoza (eds), *North American Indigenous Warfare and Ritual Violence*, pp. 149–59. Tucson: University of Arizona Press.
Snow, Dean R., and K. M. Lamphear. 1988. "European Contact and Indian Depopulation in the Northeast: The Timing of the First Epidemics." *Ethnohistory* (35): 15–33.
Speck, Frank G. 1942. *The Tutelo Spirit Adoption Ceremony. Reclothing the Living in the Name of the Dead.* Harrisburg: Pennsylvania Historical Commission.
Sprague, Marshall. 1954. *Massacre: The Tragedy at White River.* Boston: Little Brown and Company.
Staden, Hans. 1557 [1592]. *Americae tertia pars memorabile provinciae Brasiliae historiam contine[n]s, germanico primùm sermone scriptam à Ioan[n]e Stadio..., nunc autem latinitate donatam à Teucrio Annaeo Priuato Colchanthe [i.e., J. A. Lonicer]...Addita est narratio profectionis Ioannis Lerij in eamdem provinciam, qua[m] ille initio gallicè conscripsit, postea verò Latinam fecit. His accessit descriptio morum and ferocitas incolarum illius regionis, atque colloquium ipsorum idiomate conscriptum...Omnia recens evulgata and eiconibus in aes incisa ad vivum expressis illustrata...studio and diligentia Theodori de Bry... MDXCII*, Latio donata a C. C. A. [C. Clusius]. [by Bry, Theodor de]. (1592).
Starkey, Armstrong. 1998. *European and Native American Warfare, 167 1815.* Norman: Oklahoma University Press.
Starna, William. 1991. "Seventeenth Century Dutch-Indian Trade: A Perspective from Iroquoia," in N. A. McClure Zeller (ed.), *A Beautiful and Fruitful Place: Selected Rensselaerswijck Seminar Papers*, pp. 243–50. New York: New Netherland Publishing.
Starna, William A., and Ralph Watkins. 1991. "Northern Iroquoian Slavery." *Ethnohistory* 38(1): 34–57.
Stedman, Raymond William. 1982. *Shadows of the Indian. Stereotypes in American Culture.* Norman: Oklahoma University Press.

Stelle Lenville J. 2008. *Inoca Ethnohistory Project: Eye Witness Descriptions of the Contact Generation, 1673–1700*. Center For Social Research, Parkland College: http://virtual.parkland.edu/lstelle1/len/center_for_social_research/inoca_ethnohistory_project/inoca_ethnohistory.htm (13/10/08; visitor 07200)

Stephanson, Anders. 1995. *Manifest Destiny: American Expansionism and the Empire of Right*. New York: Hill and Wang.

Stephens, Alan. 1976. *White River Poems: Conversations, Pronouncements, Testimony, Recollections, and Meditations on the Subject of the White River Massacre Sept, 29, 1879*. Chicago: The Swallow Press.

Stephenson, Scott. 2007. "The Decorative Art of Securing Captives in the Eastern Woodlands," in J. C. H. King and C. F. Feest (eds), *Three Centuries of Woodlands Indian Art*, pp. 55–66. Altenstadt: ZKF Publishers.

Steponaitis, Vincas P. 1978. "Location Theory and Complex Chiefdoms: A Mississippian Example," in B. Smith (ed.), *Mississippian Settlement Patterns*, pp. 417–53. New York: Academic Press.

———. 1983. *Ceramics, Chronology, and Community Patterns: An Archaeological Study at Moundville*. New York: Academic Press.

———. 1986. "Prehistoric Archaeology in the Southeastern United States, 1970–1985." *Annual Review of Anthropology* (15): 363–404.

Stojanowski, C. 2004. "Population History of Native Groups in Pre and Post Contact Spanish Florida." *American Journal of Physical Anthropology* 123(4): 316–32.

Stratton R. B. 1983. *Captivity of the Oatman Girls*. Lincoln and London: University of Nebraska Press.

Strezewski, Michael. 2006. "Patterns of Interpersonal Violence at the Fisher Site." *Midcontinental Journal of Archaeology* (31): 249–79.

Stubbs, J. D. Jr. 1982. "The Chickasaw Contact with the La Salle Expedition in 1682," in P. K. Galloway (ed.), *La Salle and His Legacy: Frenchmen and Indians in the Lower Mississippi Valley*, pp. 49–59. Jackson: University Press of Mississippi.

Sturm, Circe. 2002. *Blood Politics: Race, Culture, and Identity in the Cherokee Nation of Oklahoma*. Berkeley: University of California Press.

Sturtevant, William C. 1976. "First Visual Images of Native America," in F. Chiapelli (ed.), *First Images of America: The Impact of the New World on the Old*, pp. 417–54. Los Angeles: University of California Press.

———., ed. 1978. *Northeast, Handbook of North American Indians*, Vol. 15. Washington, D.C.: Smithsonian Institution Press.

Sturtevant, William C. 1993. "The First American Discoverers of Europe." *European Review of Native American Studies* 7(2): 23–9.

Surrey, N. M. Miller. 1916. *The Commerce of Louisiana During the French Regime, 1699–1763*. New York: Columbia University.

"Susan, Agent Meeker," *Macon Weekly Telegraph*, November 11, 1879.

Swanton, John. R. 1911. *Indian Tribes of the Lower Mississippi Valley and Adjacent Coast of the Gulf of Mexico*. Bureau of American Ethnology, Bulletin No. 43. Washington: Government Printing Office.

Swanton, John. R. 1929. "The Tawasa Language." *American Anthropologist*, n.s. 31(3): 435–53.

———. 1939. "Final Report of the United States De Soto Expedition Commission." Washington, D.C.: 76th Congress, 2nd Session, House Documents, 71.

Takaki, Ronald. 2000. *Iron Cages: Race and Culture in 19th Century America.* Oxford: Oxford University Press.

Tanner, H. H. 1989. "The Land and Water Communication Systems of the Southeastern Indians," in P. H. Wood, G. A. Waselkov, and T. H. Hatley (eds), *Powhatan's Mantle: Indians in the Colonial Southeast,* pp. 6–20. Lincoln: University of Nebraska Press.

———. 2002. "Hypothesis: Consequences of Indian Long Distance Travel," Paper presented at the Annual Meeting of the American Society for Ethnohistory, Quebec City, Quebec, October 16–20, 2005.

Theler, James L., and Robert F. Boszhardt. 2006. "Collapse of Crucial Resources and Culture Change: A Model for the Woodland to Oneota Transformation in the Upper Midwest." *American Antiquity* (71): 433–72.

Thornton, Russell. 1987. *American Indian Holocaust and Survival: A Population History since 1492.* Norman: University of Oklahoma Press.

Thorowgood, Thomas. 2003. *Jews in America, or Probabilities that the Americans are of that Race.* Kessinger Publishing

Thwaites, Reuben G., ed. 1896–1901. *The Jesuit Relations and Allied Documents: Travel and Explorations of the Jesuit Missionaries in New France, 1610–1791.* 73 vols. Cleveland: Burrows Brothers.

Tilton, Robert S. 1994. *Pocahontas: evolution of an American narrative* [Cambridge Studies in American Literature and Culture, no. 83]. Cambridge: Cambridge University Press.

Todd, V. H. 1973. *Christoph von G.s Account of the Founding of New Bern, hg. von V.H. Todd, 1920* (Neudr. 1973, Enthäldt. und Franz. Versionen).

Tomalin, Claire. 2002. *Samuel Pepys: The Unequalled Self.* London: Viking, and New York: Knopf-Random House.

Tonti, H. de. 1702. "Extrait d'une lettre de M. de Tonty á M. d'Iberville du village des Chacta, le 23 Fev. 1702 et Extrait d'autre lettre du meme au meme, des Chacta, le 14 mars 1702, " Archives National de France, Archives du Ministére de la Marine, Section Modernne, Série JJ Archives du Service Hydrographique, Sous-série 2 JJ 56, Manuscrits de M. Delisle, Amérique Septentrionale, no. 20.

———. 1983. "Extract from a Letter from M. de Tonti to M. d'Iberville, from the Village of the Chacta, February 23, 1702 and Extract from another letter from the same to the same, From the Chacta, March 14, 1702," in Patricia K. Galloway (ed.), *La Salle and His Legacy: Frenchmen and Indians in the Lower Mississippi Valley* (Patricia K. Galloway trans.), pp. 166–73. Jackson: University Press of Mississippi.

Tonty [Tonti] H. 1846a. "Memoir by the Sieur de la Tonty. Memoir Sent in 1693, on the Discovery of the Mississippi and the Neighboring Nations by M. de la Salle, from the Year 1678 to the Time of his Death, and by the

Sieur de Tonti to the Year 1691" in B. F. French (ed.) *Historical Collections of Louisiana* Vol. 1, pp. 52–78. New York: Wiley and Putnam.
Tonty [Tonti], H. de. 1898. "Relation of Henri de Tonty Concerning the Explorations of La Salle, 1678–1683" (Melville B. Anderson trans.). Chicago: The Caxton Club.
Traphagan, John W. 2008. "Embodiment, Ritual Incorporation, and Cannibalism among the Iroquoians after 1300 C.E." *Journal of Ritual Studies* 19(2): 99–113.
Trigger, Bruce G. 1978. "Early Iroquoian Contacts with Europeans," in B. G. Trigger (ed.), *Northeast, Handbook of North American Indians,* Vol. 15, pp. 344–56. Washington, D.C.: Smithsonian Institution Press.
———. 1990. *The Huron: Farmers of the North* [2nd ed.]. Fort Worth, TX: Holt, Rinehart, and Winston.
Trubitt, Mary Beth. 2003. "Mississippian Period Warfare and Palisade Construction at Cahokia," in R. J. Jeske and D. K. Charles (eds), *Theory, Method, and Practice in Modern Archaeology,* pp. 148–62. Westport, Connecticut: Praeger.
Truettner, William H. 1991. *The West as America Reinterpreting Images of the Frontier, 1820–1920.* Washington and London: Smithsonian Institution Press.
Turner Strong, Pauline. 1999. *Captivating Selves, Captivating Others The Politics and Poetics of Colonial American Captivity Narratives.* Boulder, Colorado: Westview Press.
———. 2002. "Transforming Outsiders: Captivity, Adoption, and Slavery Reconsidered," in P. J. Deloria and N. Salisbury (eds), *A Companion to American Indian History,* pp. 339–56. Oxford: Blackwell.
———. 2008. "Representational Practices," in T. Biolsi (ed.), *A Companion to the Anthropology of American Indians,* pp. 341–59. Oxford: Blackwell.
Usner, Daniel H. Jr. 1989. "American Indians in Colonial New Orleans," in P. Wood, G. Waselkov, and T.H. Hatley (eds), *Powhatan's Mantle: Indians in the Colonial Southeast,* pp. 104–27. Lincoln and London: University of Nebraska Press.
———. 1992. *Indians, Settlers, and Slaves in a Frontier Exchange Economy: The Lower Mississippi Valley Before 1783.* Chapel Hill: University of North Carolina Press.
———. 1995. "Indian-Black relations in Antebellum Louisiana," in S. Palmié (ed.), *Slave Cultures and the Cultures of Slavery,* pp. 145–61. Knoxville: University of Tennessee Press.
———. 2003. *American Indians in the Lower Mississippi Valley: Social and Economic Histories.* Lincoln: University of Nebraska Press.
"Ute Squaw," *Miners Register,* July 7, 1863, p. 3. C.1.
"Ute Squaw escaped from Arapaho's," *Dolores News,* May 15, 1880.
VanDerBeets, Richard. 1973. *Held Captive by Indians: Selected Narratives, 1642–1836* [1st ed.]. Knoxville: University of Tennessee Press.
———. 1984. *The Indian Captivity Narrative: An American Genre.* Lanham, MD: University Press of America.

VanDerBeets, Richard. 1984. "Mary Rowlandson," vol. 245, E. Elliot (ed.), *Dictionary of Literary Biography: American Colonial Writers 1606–1734*. Michigan: Bruccoli Clark Book.
Vaughan, Alden T. 1983. *Narratives of North American Indian Captivity: A Selective Bibliography*. New York: Garland Publishing.
———. 2006. *Transatlantic Encounters; American Indians in Britain, 1500–1776*. Cambridge and New York: Cambridge University Press.
Vehik, Susan C. 2002. "Conflict, Trade, and Political Development on the Southern Plains." *American Antiquity* (67): 37–64.
———. 2006. "Wichita Ethnohistory," in R. J. Hoard and W. E. Banks (eds),, *Kansas Archaeology*, pp. 206–18. Lawrence: University Press of Kansas
Vogel, Dan. 1986. *Indian Origins and the Book of Mormon: Religious Solutions from Columbus to Joseph Smith*. Salt Lake City: Signature Books.
Vogel, Robert C. 1976. "The Bayou Pierre Settlements." *North Louisiana Historical Association Journal* 8(3): 110–11.
Voigt, Lisa. 2009. *Writing Captivity in the Early Modern Atlantic: Citations of Knowledge and Authority in the Iberian and English Imperial Worlds*. Chapel Hill: University of North Carolina Press.
Von Graffenried, Christoph/Michel Franz Louis. 1711. *Pen Drawing of the Captivity of Baron Christoph von Graffenried and Surveyor General John Lawson* (Mss.Muel.466). Bern, Switzerland: Burgerbibliothek.
Wagner, Peter. 1995. *Reading Iconotexts: From Swift to the French Revolution*. London: Reaktion Books.
Wallace, Henry D., and William H. Doelle. 2001. "Classic Period Warfare in Southern Arizona," in G. E. Rice and S. A. LeBlanc (eds), *Deadly Landscapes: Case Studies in Prehistoric Southwestern Warfare*, pp. 239–87. Salt Lake City: University of Utah Press.
Warburton, Miranda, and Richard M. Begay. 2005. "An Exploration of Navajo-Anasazi Relationships." *Ethnohistory* (52): 533–61.
Ward, T., and R. P. S. Davis, Jr. 1993. *Indian Communities on the North Carolina Piedmont A.D. 1000 to 1700*. Chapel Hill: University of North Carolina Press.
Waring, Antonio J., Jr., and Preston Holder. 1945. "A Prehistoric Ceremonial Complex in the Southeastern United States." *American Anthropologist* (47): 1–34.
Waselkov, G. A. 1988. "Lamhatty's Map: How Indians Viewed the South 300 Years Ago." *Southern Exposure* 16(2): 23–9.
———. 1989a. "Seventeenth-Century Trade in the Colonial Southeast." *Southeastern Archaeology* 8(2): 117–33.
———. 1989b. "Indian Maps of the Colonial Southeast," in P. H. Wood, G. A. Waselkov, and T. H. Hatley (eds), *Powhatan's Mantle: Indians in the Colonial Southeast*, pp. 292–343. Lincoln: University of Nebraska Press.
———. 1994. "The Macon Trading House and Early European-Indian Contact in the Colonial Southeast," in D. J. Hally (ed.), *Ocmulgee Archaeology, 1936–1986*, pp. 190–5. Athens: University of Georgia Press.

Waselkov, G. A., and M. T. Smith. 2000. "Upper Creek Archaeology," in B. G. McEwan (ed.), *Indians of the Greater Southeast: Historical Archaeology and Ethnohistory*, pp. 242–64. Gainesville: University Presses of Florida Press.

Weber, David J., and Anthony Richardson. 1996. *On the Edge of Empire: The Taos Hacienda of Los Martinez*. Santa Fe: Museum of New Mexico Press.

Webre, Stephen. 1984. "The Problem of Indian Slavery in Spanish Louisiana, 1769–1803." *Louisiana History* 25(2): 117–35.

Wedel, Mildred Mott. 1973. "The Identity of La Salle's Pana Slave." *Plains Anthropologist* 18(61): 203–17.

Weinberg, Albert K. 1963. *Manifest Destiny: A Study of Nationalist Expansion in American History*. Chicago: Quadrangle Books.

Wells, Douglas C., and Richard A. Weinstein. 2007. "Extraregional Contact and Cultural Interaction at the Coles Creek—Plaquemine Transition: Recent Data from the Lake Providence Mounds, East Carroll Parish, Louisiana," in M. A. Rees and P. C. Livingood (eds), *Plaquemine Archaeology*, pp. 38–65. Tuscaloosa: University of Alabama Press.

Werner, Fred H. 1985. *Meeker: The Story of the Meeker Massacre and the Thornburgh Battle*. Greeley (CO): Werner Publications.

Weslager, Clinton. 1961. *Dutch Explorers, Traders, and Settlers in the Delaware Valley, 1609–1664*. Philadelphia: University of Pennsylvania Press.

Wesson, C. B. 2008 *Households and Hegemony: Early Creek Symbolic Capital, Prestige Goods, and Social Power* Lincoln: University of Nebraska Press

——. 2002. "Prestige Goods, Symbolic Capital, and Social Power in the Protohistoric Southeast," in C. B. Wesson and M. A. Rees (eds), *Between Contacts and Colonies: Archaeological Perspectives on the Protohistoric Southeast*, pp. 110–2. Tuscaloosa: University of Alabama Press, 5.

Weyanoke Association. n.d. *Red and Black: The Legacy of Native and African Peoples in Charles City County*. Retrieved March 13, 2008, from Weyanoke Association: http://www.weyanoke.org/symposium.html.

White, Richard. 1991. *The Middle Ground: Indians, Empires, and Republics in the Great Lakes Region, 1650–1815*. Cambridge: Cambridge University Press.

Whitely, Simeon. 1879. "Letter to Arvilla Meeker," November 10, Nathan C. Meeker papers, WH1680, Western History Collection, The Denver Public Library.

Whyte, Thomas R. 2007. "Proto-Iroquoian Divergence in the Late Archaic—Early Woodland Period Transition of the Appalachian Highlands." *Southeastern Archaeology* (26): 134–44.

Wiegers, Robert P. 1988. "A Proposal for Indian Slave Trading in the Mississippian Valley and its Impact on the Osage." *Plains Anthropologist* 33(180): 187–202.

Wilcox, David R., Gerald Robertson Jr., and J. Scott Wood. 2001. "Organized for War: The Perry Mesa Settlement System and its Central Arizona

Neighbors," in G. E. Rice and S. A. LeBlanc (eds), *Deadly Landscapes: Case Studies in Prehistoric Southwestern Warfare*, pp. 141–94. Salt Lake City: University of Utah Press.

Williams, M. 1994. "Growth and Decline of the Oconee Province," in C. Hudson and C. Chaves Tesser (eds), *The Forgotten Centuries: Indians and Europeans in the American South, 1521–1704*, pp. 179–96. Athens: University of Georgia Press.

Williams, Samuel Cole, ed. 1948. *Lieutenant Henry Timberlake's Memoirs, 1756–1765*. Marietta: GA: Continental Book Company.

Williams, Stephen. 1990. "The Vacant Quarter and Other Late Events in the Lower Valley," in D. H. Dye and C. Ann Cox (eds), *Towns and Temples along the Mississippi*, pp. 170–80. Tuscaloosa: University of Alabama Press.

Williams, Stephen, and Jeffrey P. Brain. 1983. "Excavations at the Lake George site, Yazoo County, Mississippi, 1958–1960." *Papers of the Peabody Museum, Harvard University*, 74.

Williamson, Ron. 2007. "Otinontskiaj ondaon" ("the house of cut-off heads"): The History and Archaeology of Northern Iroquois Trophy Taking," in R. J. Chacon and D. H. Dye (eds), *The Taking and Displaying of Human Body Parts as Trophies by Amerindians*, pp. 190–221. New York: Springer.

Wilson, S. M., and J. D. Rogers. 1993. "Historical Dynamics in the Contact Era," in J. D. Rogers and S. M. Wilson (eds), *Ethnohistory and Archaeology: Approaches to Postcontact Change in the Americas*, pp. 3–18. New York: Plenum Press.

Wolf, Eric R. 1982. *Europe and the People without History*. Berkeley: University of California Press.

Wood, P. 1974. *Black Majority: Negroes in Colonial South Carolina from 1670 through the Stono Rebellion*. New York: W. W. Norton Company.

Wood, Peter H. 1988. "Indian Servitude in the Southeast," in W. Washburn (ed.), *History of Indian-White Relations, Handbook of North American Indians*, Vol. 4, pp. 407–40. Washington D.C.: Smithsonian Institution Press.

Woods, P. D. 1980. *French Indian Relations on the Southern Frontier, 1699–1762*. Ann Arbor: UMI Research Press.

Woodward, H. 1911. "Woodward"s Faithfull Relation of My Westoe Voiage Was Written in December 1674," in A. S. Salley (ed.), *Narratives of Early Carolina, 1650–1708*, pp. 125–34. New York: Charles Scribner's Sons.

Worth, John E. 1995. *The Struggle for the Georgia Coast: An Eighteenth Century Retrospective on Guale and Mocama*, Anthropological Papers of the American Museum of Natural History 75. New York: American Museum of Natural History.

———. 1998. *The Timucuan Chiefdoms of Spanish Florida*, 2 Vols. Gainesville: University Press of Florida.

———. 2000. "The Lower Creeks: Origins and Early History," in B. G. McEwan (ed.), *Indians of the Greater Southeast: Historical Archaeology and Ethnohistory*, pp. 265–98. Gainesville: University Presses of Florida Press.

———. 2002. "Spanish Missions and the Persistence of Chiefly Power," in R. Ethridge and C. Hudson (eds), *The Transformation of the Southeastern Indians, 1540–1760*, pp. 39–64. Jackson: University of Mississippi Press.

———. 2004. "Yamasee," in R. D. Fogelson (ed.), *Southeast, Handbook of North American Indians*, Vol. 14, pp. 245–53. Washington, D.C.: Smithsonian Institution Press.

———. 2006. "Bridging Prehistory and History in the Southeast: Evaluating the Utility of the Acculturation Concept," in T. J. Pluckhahn and R. Ethridge (eds), *Light on the Path: The Anthropology and History of the Southeastern Indians*, pp. 196–206. Tuscaloosa: University of Alabama Press.

———. 2007. *The Struggle for the Georgia Coast: An Eighteenth-Century Spanish Retrospective on Guale and Mocama*, Anthropological Papers of the American Museum of Natural History, No. 75. [Reprint] Tuscaloosa: University of Alabama Press.

———. 2009. "Razing Florida: The Indian Slave Trade and the Devastation of Spanish Florida, 1659–1715," in R. Ethridge and S. M. Shuck-Hall (eds), *Mapping the Mississippian Shatter Zone: The Colonial Indian Slave Trade and Regional Instability in the American South*, pp. 295–311. Lincoln: University of Nebraska Press.

Wright, Leitch Jr. 1981. *The Only Land They Knew: The Tragic Story of the Indians in the Old South*. New York: Free Press.

Young, Gloria A., and Michael P. Hoffman, eds. 1993. *The Expedition of Hernando de Soto West of the Mississippi*. Fayetteville: University of Arkansas Press.

Zafar, Rafia. 1991. "Capturing the Captivity: African Americans among the Puritans." *MELUS* 17(2): 19–35.

Index

Abihkas, 60, 70
   Coosa's fusion with, 50
   Upper Creeks and, 76
   Woodward and, 59
abolition movement, 15
   Equiano and, 124, 126
   Meeker and, 153, 164
Acolapissa, St. Denis and, 80
Adair, James, 162
Adam, Robert, 16
Adams, Charles, 148, 158
adoption
   Cahokian-Mississippian ideology and, 36–37
   between Indian and Spanish families, 187–188
   indigenous forms of, 9
   Lauber's semantic analysis and, 9
   of white women captives, 170
"Adoption, Captivity, and Slavery: Changing Meanings in Colonial North America," 1
adoption/captivity/slavery;
   see also captivity; slavery
   archeological, ethnohistorical, and anthropological evidence of, 19
   fluid definitions of, 133–134, 139–140, 144
   framing, 8–11
   imagery of, 11–14
   indigenous perspectives on, 5
   intermingling resulting from, 5–6
   macro- and microlevels of analysis of, 14–17
   meanings attributed to, 4–5
   misconceptions about, 117
   in Southwest borderlands, 190–195
      affinity with kin-based systems, 190–191
   visual and textual representations of, 19
   visual representations of,
      see imagery; visual representations
African Americans, Native ancestry of, 138
African slave trade
   historical emphasis of, 1–2
   labor demand and, 17
   in Louisiana, 81–82
African slaves, 193
   depiction at living museums, 186
   manumission of, 88
   refuge with Seminole, 140
   settlement among Cofitachequi Indians, 135–136
African women, marriageable status of, 84
Africans
   Cherokee and, 145–146
   indentured servant status of, 137–138
   interactions with Native Americans, 20
   Sandys's school and, 138–139

INDEX

agricultural economy
  in southern LMV, 33
  Ute transition to, 150–151
  violence and warfare and, 26, 32
Ahlstrom, Sydney, 165–166
Alabamas, 50–51
  demise of, 192
  movements of, 70
  survival through confederations, 78
  Upper Creeks and, 76
  Woodward and, 59
Aldridge, W. A., 128
Algonquians
  Cahokians and, 45n14
  positive imagery of, 110
Algonquin language, Smith's knowledge of, 120
Alimamos, 136–137
Altamaha, de Soto and, 70
American Indians, *see* Native Americans; *specific groups*
American West, imaging of, 12
Aminoya, 52
Angel site, palisades in, 30
Angélique, 90
Anlico, 52–53
  Spanish military assaults and, 50
Apache; see also *Canneci* (Lipan Apache); Lipan Apache
  Spanish expeditions against, 91
Apacheans, 38
Apafalaya, 50
Apalachee
  dissolution of, 15
  as neotraditional polity, 68
Apalachicolas, 51–52, 70
  and Lower Creeks, 76
  Woodward and, 59
Aptheker, Herbert, 135–136
Archaic groups, violence and, 25
Argall, Samuel, 102
assimilation policies, 43
  Hayes administration and, 152
  Meeker captivity narrative and, 164–165

versus removal/extermination, 149
shift away from, 157
Attakullakulla, 140
Axtell, James, 148
"Aztalan" site, 29

Bacon's Rebellion, 78
Bacon's Rebellion
  Occaneechis and, 56
Balthazar, 93
Barnum, P. T., 153–154
Barr, Juliana, 11
Barthes, Roland, 182
Battle of Taliwa, 140
Battle of the Little Bighorn, 160
Baudouin, François, 93
Baum, Rosalie Murphy, 144
Bean, Lydia Russell, 141
Beaver Wars, 72
beloved women; *see also* Cofitachequi, Queen of
  of Cherokee, 141
Bienville, Jean-Baptiste Le Moyne de, 80, 82–83
Billouart, Louis, 89
black, Native American classification as, 6–7
black Indians, nonrecognition of, 5
Blair, James, 138
Bloch, Marc, social historical approach of, 66
bondage; *see also* slavery
  forms of, 9–10
  religious/social/gendered aspects of, 10
Boone, Daniel, 169–170
Boone, Jemima, 169–170
bow and arrow, adoption of, 25–26
Bowne, Eric, 19, 192
Braden style, 34, 35
Brain, Jeffrey, 45n10
Braudel, Fernand, social historical approach of, 66
Brooks, James, 11, 19–20, 21, 145
Brown, James A., 34–35

Brownscombe, Jenni, 172
Buisson de Saint Cosmé, Jean-François, 80
bureaucratic genocide, 7
burial customs
  at Cahokia, 27–28
  at Fisher site, 30
  Mississippian culture and, 29
  mound *versus* nonmound, 33
  Oneota, 30
  during Woodland periods, 26
Butler, Jon, 149

Cabeza de Vaca, Alvar Nuñez, 37–38
Caddo
  Chickasaws and, 57, 59
  in Louisiana slave trade, 89
  Osage and, 87–88
  St. Denis's alliance with, 83–84
Caddo confederacies
  Chickasaw slaving and, 61
  in new South, 62
Caddoan chiefdoms, 26
  Chickasaw chiefdoms and, 61
Caddoan Crenshaw site, evidence of violence at, 31
Cadillac, Antoine Laumet de la Mothe, 81
Cahokia
  abandonment of, 37
  "Big Bang" of development at, 28, 44n6
  colonies of, 29
  controversy over, 28
  cultural expansion by, 31
  development and demise of, 27–28
  and evidence of hierarchy and violence, 27
  and Pax Cahokiana, 44n8
  peaceable relationships of, 30
  Southeast-Southwest parallels to, 44n5
Calusa, demise of, 78, 192
Canneci (Lipan Apache), enslavement of, 85, 90, 93, 94

Canneci women, enslavement of, 87
capitalist economic system
  and demise of Mississippian chiefdoms, 53
  and destabilization of Native polities, 47, 49
  in Mississippian shatter zone, 192
  in transformation of southeastern Indian polities, 66
captive children, integration into Southwest kinship systems, 191
captive Indian women;
  see also Indian women
  integration into Southwest kinship systems, 191
captive Native Americans;
  see also Indian slaves
  lack of study of, 99
captives
  as active agents, 18
  Nan'yehi and, 141
  role in political negotiation, 150
  without clans, 141
  women's role in fate of, 144, 161
captive-taking
  Comanche, 43
  between Indian and Spanish colonial families, 187–188
  in Louisiana, 82–83
  by militaristic slaving societies, 71–73, *see also* militaristic slaving societies
  precontact, 188
  social/political functions of, 81
  17th-century practices of, 23–24
captivity
  among Europeans and Eastern/Middle Eastern empires, 99
  defined, 117
  Equiano's perspective on, 123
  power relations and, 134
  as quintessential colonial experience, 98

captivity—*Continued*
  visual representation as method of discourse on, 167–183, *see also* Parker, Cynthia Ann
  in western states, 19
  without narrative, 1–2
captivity narratives, 131–146; *see also* Equiano, Olaudah; Marrant, John; Meeker captivity narrative; Parker, Cynthia Ann; Smith's capture by Powhatan Indians
  art historical focus on, 167–183
  Eurocentric lens of, 117
  in film, 168
  imagery accompanying, 12, *see also* imagery; visual representations
  language and, 118
  and number of whites captured, 167–168
  religious language in, 148–149
  stereotyping in, 8
  Street's analysis of, 20
captivity of colonial newcomers
  as framing device, 99
  images of American Indians and, 98–99
Capture of Daniel Boone's Daughter, Jemima, The, 169–170
Caribbean islands
  Indian forced exodus to, 16
  slave trade in, 15
Caribbean peoples, indigenous ancestry of, 5–6
Carocci, Max, 43, 195
Carondelet, Francisco Luis, 94
Carson, Kit, 150
Casas Grandes, 44n5
Casqui, 52, 53
Catawba, 47
  chiefdoms coalescing with, 55
  Cofitachequi and, 76
  confederacy of, 75
  in new South, 62

Catawba Confederacy, 192
  slave raids and, 76
Catholicism
  required Indian education in, 91
  in Southwest, 194
Cecile, 93
Chakchiuma, slave trade and, 60
Chaplin, Joyce, 2
Charles Town, founding of, 41
Charles V, Indian slavery banned by, 16
Chattahoochee migration, phases of, 63n3
chattel model of slavery, 6
Chaudhuri, Jean, 145
Cherokee, 47
  bondage forms of, 10
  Fort Watauga attacked by, 141
  Marrant's adoption by, 128, 193
  mixed Native/African identity of, 145
  in new South, 62
  slaving by, 56
  war with Myskoke, 140
Cherokee Freedmen, 146
Cherokee language, Marrant's acquisition of, 127–128, 132–133
Cherokee Nation, H.R. 2824 and, 146
Cherokee-speaking polities, migration of, 55
Cheyenne, Susan's capture by, 159
Chicasa, dissolution of, 15
Chickasaw, 47
  Choctaws and, 64n10
  contact with Europeans, 56–57
  English arming of, 41
  English slave trade and, 42
  European trade and, 56–58
  Marrant and, 128
  in new South, 62
  retaliation against, 61
  slave raids on Natchez, 69
  slave trade and, 19, 56–61, 81
Chickasaw women, enslaved, 82
chiefdoms; *see also specific chiefdoms*
  controversy over term, 43n2

INDEX

decline of, matrilineal clans and, 67
group-oriented *versus* individualizing, 33
Mississippian, 26, 37, 47
non-Mississippian, 26
southeastern development of, 32
child captives
of Chickasaws, 61
in Southwest kinship system, 191
Chipeta, 158
Chiscas, militaristic slaving practices of, 73
Chitimacha
French and, 80–81
in Louisiana Indian slave trade, 89
peace with France, 86
Chitimacha women, enslaved, 82, 92
Chiwere-Siouans
ethnohistory of, 36
Oneota culture and, 37
Choctaw, 47
Chickasaw raids on, 59–60, 62
Chickasaw war with, 64n10
Marrant and, 128
in new South, 62
Christian missionaries, 193
Christian reform movements
U. S. Native American policy and, 151
vis á vis manifest destiny, 149
Christianity
Native American conversion to, 148
propagation of, 138–139, 154–155
clans, strengthening of, by slaving threat, 75
Classic Hohokam sites, 44n5
Clouseau, François, 91
coastal Indians; see also *petites nations;* settlement Indians
kidnaping and enslavement of, 16
Westo and Occaneechi predations and, 54–55
Code Noir, 83, 88

Cofitachequi
African slave refugees and, 135–136
dissolution of, 15
Queen of, 18, 70, 136, 144
slave trade influence and, 76
Cofitachequi chiefdom
de Soto and, 70
disappearance of, 55
European disease and, 76
Coles Creek culture, equivocal evidence of violence in, 32–33
College of William and Mary, 138
Colley, Linda, 99, 134
colonial exploitation, and Indian traditions of violence and enmity, *see* Indian traditions of violence and enmity
colonial oppression; *see also* English; French; Spanish
and demise of Mississippian chiefdoms, 53
colonizing strategies
militaristic slaving societies and, 71–73
types of, 66
Comanche
"empire" of, 42–43
in Louisiana slave trade, 89
Parker's capture by, 20–21, 173, *see also* Parker, Cynthia Ann
Rachel Plummer's capture by, 174
Spanish expeditions against, 91
Comanche dances, 187
Comanche women, enslaved, 82
compadrazgo (godparenthood), 191
concubinage, 10, 82, 191
confederated polities, 75–78, 192
Congarees
demise of, 192
survival through confederations, 78
Connaway, John, 45n15
Coosa
de Soto's encounter with, 49–50
dissolution of, 15, 63n2

INDEX

Coosa chiefdom
  demise of, 67
  movements of, 70
Coosada chiefdom, dissolution of, 55
corn mother, stories of, 145
Corning, A. F., 180
Corona, Leonora, 176
Coronado, Francisco Vázquez de, 38
coureurs de bois, Chickasaw and, 57
Coweta, 51
  Woodward and, 59
Craig Mound, 34
Creek Confederacy, 75–76, 192
  formation of, 51–52
  in new South, 62
Creeks
  Lower, *see* Lower Creeks
  Upper, *see* Upper Creeks
Creole blacks, nonrecognition of, 5
Creole population, Indian ancestry of, 95–96, 192–193
cuarto de cautivos (captives' room), 186
  at Martínez Hacienda, 188, 189f
  slavery evidence in, 190
cultural practices, colonial impacts on, 14–15
Cussetah, 51
Cussetas, Woodward and, 59
Cynthia Parker (Smith), 176–177

Dances with Wolves, 168
Danforth, E. H., 152, 154
d'Anghiera, Pietro Martire, 3
D'artaguiette d'Iron, Jean Baptiste-Martin, 81
de Batz, Alexander, 14
de Bry, Johann Theodore, 108
de Bry, Mattaeus Merian, 108
de Bry, Theodore, 11, 13, 97, 108, 110–111
  depictions of Smith's capture, 112, 113f
  engraving by, 107, 107f, 109f
  Indian images by, 169

de Bry family
  images of Pocahontas, 103
  images published by, 105
de Luna, Tristán, 50, 65
De Mézières, Athanase, 90, 91–92
de Soto, Hernando, 27, 65
  Apalachee and, 68
  chiefdoms encountered by, 70
  Cofitachequi and, 55, 136
  impact on Mississippian chiefdoms, 51–52
  impact on Mississippian cultures, 50–51
  and Mississippian chiefdom alliances, 52–53
  and narratives of Mississippian culture, 49
  Natchez Indians and, 69
  Southeast *entrada* of, 38–40
Delawares, Slocum's adoption by, 171–172
Denison, Brandi, 19, 20, 194
Derbanne, François Guyon des Prés, 84
Description of New England (Smith), 104
destabilization, in transformation of southeastern Indian polities, 66
Dhegiha Sioux, 54
  migration of, 45n18
d'Iberville, Pierre Le Moyne, 58, 59
Dodsworth, Anthony, 59
Dolet, Pierre, 92–93
Du Tisne, Claude-Charles, 85
Duchene, Augustin, 93
Dupre, Jean Baptiste, 93
Dutch
  Caribbean slaving by, 16
  domestic wars and colonial exploits, 42
  and introduction of capitalist economy, 53
  Iroquois armed by, 40
  wars of, 42

INDEX

Ebersole, Gary, 178
Ebert Canebrake site, 51
ecological factors, in peaceable cultures, 33
Edwards, Jonathan, 133
Eiakintomino, 12
Emry, Thomas, 119
English
  Caribbean slaving by, 16
  first contact with Powhatans, 97
  Indian slave trade and, 42, 68
  and introduction of capitalist economy, 53
  Natchez relationship with, 69
English-Powhatan encounter, visual imaginings of, 97–115, *see also* Hamor, Ralph; Pocahontas (Matoaka); Powhatans; Smith, John
enslavement, *see* slaves; *specific groups*
Equiano, Olaudah, 20, 117, 123–127, 193
  abolitionist activities of, 124, 126
  attitudes toward captors, 129
  background of, 124
  Christian ideology and, 129
  English acculturation of, 125–127
  English language and, 125–126
  and reversal of Eurocentric racial stereotypes, 124–125
Erie people, Iroquois defeat of, 40–41
Eries, 72, *see also* Westos
  transition into Westo, 41
Esaws
  demise of, 192
  survival through confederations, 78
Estavanico, 134–135
Esteban, 38
ethnic groups, rethinking extinction of, 7
ethnic identity, interethnic relations and, 7
Ethridge, Robbie, 19, 66, 70–71, 78, 192

Etowah, 32
  and trade with Apalachee, 68
Euro-dependent polities, 73–75, 192
  advantages of, 75
  factors in dissolution of, 77–8
European colonization, Native responses to, 65
European trade
  Chickasaws and, 56–58, 64n7
  intra-Indian competition for, 53
evangelism; *see also* Catholicism; Spanish mission system
  coercion and, 10
  enslavement and, 139
exchange networks, during Woodland periods, 25

Feest, Christian, 97, 112
Féliciane, 86, 88
Felix, 93
film, captivity narratives in, 168, 177–178
firearms
  confederated polities and, 78
  Natchez acquisition of, 69
  Native acquisition of, 71–75
  Yamasee acquisition of, 77
Fisher site, 30
Fivekiller, 140
Flour Chief, 86
Fort Ancient culture, 30, 37
  proto-Dhegiha Siouans and, 41
Francisco de Chicora, 3
Françoise, 90
Frederic, François, 93
Freedmen
  Cherokee, 146
  paradox of, 140
French
  and agitation of tribal rivalries, 83
  Caribbean slaving by, 16
  claims on Mississippi Valley, 79–80
  Indian alliances of, 79–80
  and introduction of capitalist economy, 53

French—*Continued*
  and Louisiana Indian slave trade, 89
  in Lower Mississippi Valley, 52
  Natchez and, 69, 86–87
  peace with Chitimacha, 86
  in Protohistoric Period, 37
  war with Chitimacha, 81
  westward-tending influence of, 42–43
fur trade
  slave trade and, 57–58
  in transformation of southeastern Indian societies, 66

Gagnard, Pierre, 93
Gallay, Alan, 53, 56, 58, 64n10
Gates, Henry Louis, 131–132, 144–145
gender, mythology of, 178, 180
gender roles, 18
Generall Historie of Virginia, New England, and the Summer Isles (Smith), 103–104, 119
  and images of Smith's captivity, 112
  and promotion of settlement, 122
Geneviève, 91
genízaro, 193
  recognition of descendents of, 195n2
genocide, bureaucratic, 7
Girard, Pierre, 90
Gleach, Frederic, 123
Goldsmith Oliver site, 40, 45n16, 45n17
Goncalvez, Vasco, 136
Goose Creek men, war with Westos, 77–78
Gordon, Richard, 135
Gottfriedt, Johann Ludwig, 113f
Gould, Philip, 133
Grand Voyages (de Bry), 108, 110–111
Grande Terre, Jeanne de la, 84
Grande Terre, Marie Thérèse de la, 84, 92
Grant, Ulysses S., 151

Grappe, Alexis, 92
Grappe, Louise Marguerite Guedon, 92
Greeley, Horace, 153, 163
Greenblatt, Stephen, 117–118
Guachoya, 52–53
Guale, demise of, 78, 192
Guale chiefdom, Westo and Occaneechi predations and, 54–55
Guatari chiefdom, 55

Hall, Prince, 144–145
Hamor, Ralph, 100
  depiction of Pocahontas, 108–110, 109f, 113
  publications of, 103
Hariot, Thomas, 107–108, 169
Harpe, Bénard de la, 85
Hayes, Rutherford B., 152
Hector, 93
Hitchitis
  demise of, 192
  survival through confederations, 78
Hitichi language, 51
Hodenosaunee, *see* Iroquois
Hoffman, Paul, 63n2
Holdridge, Lin, 19, 20, 194–195
Hole, William, 104
  image of Smith captivity, 106, 108
"Hopewellian" cultures, 25
Houston, Sam, 174
Huberdeaux, Silvie, 92, 93
Hudson, Charles, 38, 65–66
Huntingdon, Countess of, 128
Huron people, Iroquois defeat of, 40–41

Iapassus, 108–110, 109f
  perjorative/diabolical depictions of, 109–110, 110f, 113, 113f
Iberville, Pierre Le Moyne d'
  and occupation of lower Louisiana, 79
  peace efforts of, 80

INDEX

Ichisi, de Soto and, 70
iconography, 35–36, *see also* imagery; visual representations
　determining meaning of, 35–36
iconotext, 104, 111
identity
　mixed Native/African, 145
　re-creation of, 7
　as social/political construction, 145–146
　stories and, 167
identity formation, indigenous perspectives and, 5
Illinois
　Iroquois slaving campaigns and, 54
　as slavers of Plains Indians, 45n14
　visual representations of, 14
imagery; *see also* iconography; visual representations
　of adoption/captivity/slavery, 11–14
　of American Indians and European captives, 98–99
　in captivity narratives, 12
　in *Grand Voyages* (de Bry), 108
　of Indians in Rowlandson capture, 168–169
　pejorative/diabolical, 108, 109–110, 110f, 113, 113f, 114, 121, 123
　photographic, 178, 179f, 180–181, 180f
　of Plummer capture, 169
　positive, of Algonquians, 110
　in promotion of Jamestown colony, 113
　reconfiguration from peaceful to pejorative, 110–111
　of Rowlandson's capture, 168–169
　of scalping, 8, 34–35, 35f
　of Smith's capture by Powhatan Indians, 100, 193
　in Smith's publications, 104–105, 105f
　Southern Cult, 33–36, 35f
　of white women captives, 168, 176–178

indentured servants, African, 137–138
Indian captives, transport across Atlantic, 16
Indian children, purchase of, in Southwest, 188
Indian confederacies, *see* confederated polities; *specific confederacies*
Indian polities; *see also specific groups*
　context of, 67
　types of, 66, *see also* confederated polities; Euro-dependent polities; neotraditional polities
Indian slave holders, kinship structures of, 191
Indian slave trade; *see also* militaristic slaving societies
　Catawba Confederacy and, 76
　Chickasaws and, 56–61, 58–59
　Cofitachequi and, 76
　commercialization of, 49
　Creek Confederacy and, 76
　and demise of Mississippian chiefdoms, 53
　English and, 42
　Iroquois and, 54
　in Louisiana, 81–96, 83–84
　militaristic slaving societies and, 71–73
　in Mississippian shatter zone, 192
　Natchez Indians and, 69
　Natchitoches as center of, 89
　Occaneechi and, 54–55
　official "end" of, 17
　tradition of, 60–61
　traditions of violence and enmity and, *see* Indian traditions of violence and enmity
　Westos and, 54–55
　women's role in, 141
　Yamasee Confederacy and, 76–77
Indian slaves
　Africans outnumbered by, 17
　baptism of, 87–88, 95

Indian slaves—*Continued*
  in Caribbean islands, 6
  classification as black/mulatto, 94
  cuartos de cautivos and, 186, 188, 189f, 190
  European fears of, 17
  Lauber's linguistic analysis and, 8–9
  lawsuits for freedom, 93–94
  manumission of, 88
  missing historical coverage of, 1–2
  population in 18th century, 17
  price of, 64n9
  racial laws/census miscounting and, 6
  registration of, 89–91, 95
Indian trade networks, 57–58
  in transformation of southeastern Indian societies, 66
Indian traditions of violence and enmity
  agricultural development and, 26
  Cahokia site and, 27
  colonial divide-and-conquer strategies and, 23, 191–192
  Indian slave trade and, 23–46
  and northward and eastward expansion of Mississippian culture, 28–31
  in precontact times, 24–25
  sociopolitical complexity and, 26–27
  terminal prehistoric and protohistoric developments and, 37–40
  during Woodland periods, 25–26
Indian warrior slaves, 193
Indian women
  enslaved, 81–82, 90–91
  marriageable status of, 84
  purchase of, in Southwest, 188
  sexual use and abuse of, 170
Indians, southern, *see* southern Indian groups
indigenous narratives, lack of, 3

indigenous perspectives, historical and contemporary implications of, 5
inditas, 187
infectious disease, *see* Old World disease
Inoca, *see* Illinois
insurrection, Sancousy and, 17
Iroquois, 42
  alliances of, 42
  bondage forms of, 10
  captive taking by, 42
  Dutch arming of, 40–41, 42
  Lafitau's account of, 13–14
  as militaristic slaving society, 54
  retreat of, 56
  slaving campaigns of, 54
  Tuscaroras and, 63n6
Israel, lost tribes of, Native Americans and, 161–162

Jamestown Colony, 100
  charter and beginnings of, 118–119
Jemison, Mary, 132, 172–173
  reinvention of husband of, 172–173
Jeter, Marvin, 19, 191–192
Joara chiefdom, 55
Julie, 93
Julien, 86

Keller, Georg, 100, 108
Kelton, Paul, 62
Kidwell, Clara Sue, 123
Kincaid site, palisades in, 30
King Carlos III, 91
King James, 104, 118
King Williams's War, 79
kinship, slavery and, 11
Kit Carson treaty, 150–151
Kiwasa, 107, 107f
Kowalewski, Steve, 67
Kroeber, Alfred, 24
Kupperman, Karen, 123

INDEX

La Grande Terre, Jean de, 18
La Salle, Nicolas, 82
La Salle, René-Robert Cavalier de
  Chickasaw encounter with,
    56–57
  Mississippi Valley claims of, 79
  Natchezans and, 41
labor, forced, 10
Lafitau, Father Joseph Francois,
  13–14
Lake Jackson site, 34
Lamhatty, 3, 58
language
  in colonial descriptions of Native
    customs, 3
  Equiano and, 125–126
  Indo-European, cultural
    interpretations with, 8–9
  Native, Euro-American
    inexperience with, 71
language as mediator
  in captivity narratives, 118, 120,
    193
  in Marrant's narrative, 127–128
Last of the Mohicans, The (Mann),
  99, 168
Late Mississippian South, Hudson's
  social geography of, 66
Latter-day Saints, beliefs about Native American origins, 162
Lauber, Almon Wheeler, 8–9, 58
Le Comte, Thérèse, 94
Le Maire, François, 82
Lee, Dayna Bowker, 19
LeMay, Alan, 177
linguistic groups, southeastern,
  39–40
Lipan Apache
  enslaved, 91
  in Louisiana, 89, 95
  Spanish warfare with, 86
Lords Proprietors
  slave trade monopoly of, 73
  and wars over Indian trade,
    77–78

Lost Sister of Wyoming, The, 172
Louis XV, antislavery edict of, 83
Louisiana
  African slavery in, 81–82
  attempted slavery ban in, 80
  Indian slave trade in, 81–96,
    192–193
  Indian *versus* African slaves in, 87, 87t
  as slave sorting point, 19
  social identities on, 79–96
Lower Creeks, 51–52, 59, 75–76
  Apalachicola and, 76
  groups comprising, 59
Lower Mississippi Valley
  archaeological studies in, 23
  culture-historical overview of,
    25–27
  defined, 44n3
  French *versus* Spanish accounts of
    Indian groups in, 38–39
  Mississippian cultural expansion
    into, 31–32
  peaceful tendencies in, 32–33
  terminal prehistoric and
    protohistoric developments
    in, 37–40

Mabila
  battle of, 63
  dissolution of, 15, 47
  Spanish military assaults and,
    50–51
MacNeil, Denise, 131
Macon Plateau, 32
Magnaghi, Russell, bibliography of,
  9–10
Malinche, La (Malintzín), 186–187
Man Called Horse, A, 168
Mangum site, 34
manifest destiny, vis à vis Christian
  reform movements, 149
Mann, Michael, 99
Map of Virginia, A (Smith),
  102–104
  illustration in, 104–105, 105f

Marcos de Niza, Fray, 38
Marianne, 92
Marie Louise, 87
Marie-Anne, 91
Marksville culture, 25
Marquette, Père, Quapaw and, 41
Marrant, John, 20, 115n3, 117, 127–129, 193
   abolitionist activities of, 143–144
   African Lodge #459 and, 143–144
   British capture of, 143
   as captive *versus* adoptee, 133–134
   captivity narrative paradigm and, 133
   Cherokee capture and adoption of, 128
   Cherokee language and, 118, 132–133
   Christian ideology and, 129
   Gates's interpretation of, 131–132
   school of, 142–143
   transformed identity of, 141–142
Marren, Susan, 125
marriage
   forced, 10
   Native women with Europeans, 19, 82
Martínez Hacienda, 195
   cuarto de cautivos of, 188, 189f
   Potsui'i incised jar at, 188, 189f, 190
Matachines Dance, 186–187
Matahan, 112
material culture
   Cahokian, 31
   infrastructures of, 43n1
   Native-produced, 12
Matoaka, *see* Pocahontas (Matoaka)
matrilineal clans, chiefdom decline and, 67
May, Cedrick, 133
Meeker, Arvilla, 147, 148, 153, 154, 157, 158, 162–163
Meeker, Flora, 158
Meeker, Josephine, 147, 154, 157, 158

Meeker, Nathan, 147, 152, 162
   abolition activities of, 164
   appointment to White River Agency, 153–154
   attitudes toward Utes, 155
   and "Christianizing" of Utes, 154–155
   and idea of religious community, 163
   religious idealism of, 149
   views of women, 163
   worldview of, 163–164
Meeker, Ralph, 157, 161
Meeker captivity narrative, 147–166, 194
   captive release in, 148
   compiler of, 161
   19th-century religious fervor and, 162
   and omission of Ute concerns/religious practices, 164
   as propaganda, 149, 160, 164–165
   publication of stories of, 157–158
   religion in masking of political issues in, 165–166
   southwest captivity economy and, 150
   Susan's role in, 148–149, 158–165
Meeker Massacre, 20, 164–165, 194
Meginness, John, 172
métis children, 84, 88
   liberation of, 94–95
métis people, Canadian recognition of, 5
Metoyer, Louis, 94–95
Middle Passage, 2
   Equiano's experience of, 124
   in reverse, 6
Miles, Tiya, 145
militaristic slaving societies, 53–54, 63n5, 70–73, 192, *see also* Indian slave trade
   and access to firearms, 71–72
   captive-taking by, 71–73
   demise of, 78

diminished influence of, 56
Euro-American inexperience with Native languages and, 71
Euro-American wars with, 77–78
impact on chiefdoms, 54–56
second generation of, 56–57
military losses, in transformation of southeastern Indian polities, 66
Minges, Patrick, 20, 193
Miro, Esteban, 93
miscegenation
 fears of, 170
 and images of white women captives, 178
missionaries, *see* Spanish mission system
missions, evangelization and, 10
Mississippian chiefdoms, 26, 37, 47
 alliances of, 52–53
 characteristics of, 49
 collapse of, 52–53
 de Soto's impact on, 51–52
 demise of classic traits of, 67
 dissolution of, 15
 Iroquois slaving campaigns and, 54
 lost, 52
Mississippian culture, 26, 47
 characteristics of, 49
 controversy over terminology for, 43n2
 expansion into LMV and southeast, 31–32
 northward and eastward expansion of, 28–31
 transformation of, 47,
  see also Mississippian shatter zone
Mississippian period, literature on, 63n1
Mississippian polities, de Soto's impact on, 49–50
Mississippian shatter zone, 47–64
 factors creating, 192
 new South and, 62–63
 slaving and disease and, 62

Mobila women, enslaved, 82
Mocama, demise of, 78, 192
Mocama chiefdom, Westo and Occaneechi predations and, 54–55
Modoc War, 160
Monet, Dorothée, 94
Monet, Louis, 94
Monteche, Dominique, 87
Montesino, Antonio, 135
Montgomery, Benilde, 133
Morgan, David W., 57
Mormons, beliefs about Native American origins, 162
Morvan, François, 90–91
Moundville, 32, 49
Moytoy I, 140
Muller, Jon, 34
Muskhogean language, 51
Muskogeans, 37
Myskoke
 corn mother story of, 145
 war with Cherokee, 140
mythology
 iconography interpretations based on, 36–37, 45n12
 of Pochahontas-John Smith encounter, 100
 of race and gender, impacts of photography, 178, 180
 of western expansionism, 195

Nairne, Thomas, 60, 61
Namias, June, 158
Nan'yehi (Nancy Ward), 140–141, 144–145
Napituca, Spanish military assaults and, 50
Narrative of the Captivity and Extreme Suffering of Mrs. Clarissa Plummer, 169
Natchez Indians, 39–40, 52
 dissolution of, 15
 French and, 86–87
 in Louisiana Indian slave trade, 89
 as neotraditional polity, 68–69

Natchez Indians—*Continued*
Northern
migration of, 41
Tunicans and, 45n18
relationships with French and English, 69
Natchitoches, French post at, 84–95
Native American agencies
establishment and administration of, 151
government control of, 152
Grant's "Peace Policy" and, 151
Indian removal to, 43
Native American groups;
see also entries under Indian; *specific groups*
nonfederally recognized, 5
Native American policy
assimilation *versus* removal/extermination approaches to, 149
19th-century debate over, 149
religious reformers and, 151
Native American writers, revisionist, 25
Native Americans; *see also entries under* Indian; *specific groups*
attempted conversion of, 138–139
captive, 99
classification as blacks, 6–7
depictions of, *see* imagery; visual representations
"diaspora" of, 6
interactions with Africans, 20
precontact, "superhumanizing" of, 25
religious explanations of origins of, 161–162
stereotyping of, 8
as victims/perpetrators of slaving practices, 2
Native languages, Euro-American inexperience with, 71
Native polities, factors in destabilization of, 47, 49
Navajo, origin stories of, 45n13

Naylor, Celia, 145
neotraditional polities, 67–70, 192
cultural, social, and political continuity and, 67–68
nonaggression pacts of, 76
Neutrals people, Iroquois defeat of, 40–41
Nocona, Peta, 175
Norris Farms site, 30
North America, culture-historical overview of, 25–27
North American newcomers, literature on, 98–99

Occaneechi
Bacon's Rebellion and, 56
impact on Native Southern peoples, 54–55
militaristic slaving practices of, 73
as militaristic slaving society, 54
slave trade activities of, 19
Ocute, de Soto and, 70
Ocute chiefdom, dissolution of, 55
Okmulgees
demise of, 192
survival through confederations, 78
Olamico chiefdom, 55
Old World diseases
Apalachee and, 68
coastal groups and, 77
Coosa decline and, 50
and demise of Mississippian chiefdoms, 53
and destabilization of Native polities, 47
impact on eastern U. S. peoples, 15
in Mississippian shatter zone, 192
southern slave trade and, 62
in transformation of Southeastern Indian polities, 66
Omaha people, migration of, 41
Oñate, Don Juan de, 45n16
Oneota
chiefdoms of, 26
Chiwere Siouans and, 37
Woodland society evolution into, 30

Opechancanough, 100, 122
Opitchapam, 122
O'Reilly, Alejandro, 89–90, 93
Orendorf excavation, 29
origin stories, Navajo, 45n13
Osage, 46n20
　in Louisiana Indian slave trade, 89
　"shatter zone" and, 42–43
Osage women, enslaved, 87–88
Otari chiefdom, 55
Ouray, 148, 158, 159, 194

Pacaha, 52, 53
palisaded villages
　at Cahokia, 28
　Mississippian cultures and, 29
　in Ohio Valley, 30–31
Pamphilo de Narvaez, 134
Pamunkey, Smith's capture by, 100–101, see also Smith's capture by Powhatan Indians
Pana, 3
Panis, John, 16
Paquimé, 44n5
Pardo, Juan, 55, 65
Parker, Cynthia Ann, 18, 167–183, 179f, 180f
　and blurring of term *captive*, 183
　capture and adoption of, 20
　double captivity of, 194–195
　as doubly oppressed subaltern, 173
　first-hand account of, 173
　mythologizing of, 176
　opera based on story of, 176–177
　political uses of captive narrative of, 174–175
　public perception of, 168
　white family's recapture of, 173–174
Parker, Isaac, 173, 174, 180
Parker, James, 174
Parker, Quanah, 181
　mythologizing of, 176
　postwar Texan integration and, 176
　role in Comanche society, 175
　search for mother, 175–176
Pax Cahokiana, 44n8

peace
　archaeology of, 32–33
　state-imposed *versus* egalitarian coexistence, 44n8
peace ceremonies, calumet-like, 33
peaceable cultures, cultural-ecological factors in, 33
Pepys, Samuel, 42
petites nations, 52, 55, 73–75
photographs
　impacts on mythologizing stereotypes, 178, 180
　of Parker, 179f, 180–182, 180f
Pitkin, Frederick, 154, 157, 161, 165
Plains women, capture and integration into Pueblo society, 190
plantation system, in transformation of southeastern Indian societies, 66
Plaquemine culture
　equivocal evidence of violence in, 33
　Southern Cult artifacts and, 34
Plum Bayou culture, equivocal evidence of violence in, 32–33
Plum Bayou-Coles Creek-Plaquemine peoples, chiefdoms of, 26
Plummer, Clarissa, images of capture of, 169
Plummer, Rachel, 174
Pocahontas (Matoaka)
　captivity of, 112–113
　capture and forced acculturation of, 100, 102, 193
　de Bry's images of, 103, 112
　death of, 102
　in Hamor's account, 108–110, 109f
　omitted from Smith's accounts, 102–103
　reception by Queen Anne, 104
　as savior *versus* captive, 114
　Smith's depiction of, 123
　in Smith's *Generall Historie*, 103–104
　visual accounts of, 20

political alliances, European, 16–17
polity; *see also* Indian polities; southeastern Indian polities
versus culture/society, 66
Potsui'i incised jar, 188, 189f, 190
pottery, Cahokian, 30, 31
power relations, captivity and, 134
Powhatan (Wahunsenacock/Wahunsenacawh), 100–101
   de Bry's images of, 112
   Hole's imagining of, 106
   Smith associations of diabolical with, 108
   Smith's first meeting with, 119–120
Powhatan Confederation, Sandys's school and, 138
Powhatans
   first contact with English, 97
   Smith's capture by, 193
Powhatan's meeting house, 105–108, 105f, 110
Prairie Flower, 176
Pratt, Stephanie, 20, 193, 195
Present State of Virginia (Hamor), 100
Price, Flora, 147, 157
prostitution, 10
Protohistoric Dark Ages, 39
Protohistoric Period, of LMV, 37
proto-Iroquoian culture, development of, 31
Pueblo society, capture and integration of Plains women into, 190

Quahadas, 175
Quapaw, 39, 40, 46n20, 54
   migration of, 40–41
   settlement in LMV, 52
   slaving "shatter zone" and, 40–41
Queen Anne, and reception of Pocahontas, 104
Quigualtam, 52
Quivira-Wichita, 38, 46n20
Quizquiz, 52

race, mythology of, 178, 180
racial laws, in Virginia, 6

Rael-Gálvez, Estévan, 188
Raimond, Pierre, 90
Raleigh, Sir Walter, 9
Ramenofsky, Ann, 53
Ramey Incised pottery, 30, 31
Rancho de Las Golondrinas, El, 185, 186f, 195
rape by Indian men
   fears of, 169
   lack of evidence for, 170
   recorded evidence, 5
religious language, in captivity narratives, 148–149
religious organizations, reservation supervision by, 151–152
Renfrew, Colin, 33
repartimientos, 10
Richahecrians; *see also* Westos
   raids of, 72–73
Riche, Jean, 88
Ricoeur, Paul, 167
Ridde, Jacque, 90
Riggs, Brett, 56
ritual
   Smith's description of, 101–102, 121–122
   torture and, 24
Roanoke Voyages, 97–98
Robinson, Jehu, 119
Rolfe, John, 102, 112, 137
Ross, Sul, 173
Roulleau, Jacques, 90
Rountree, Helen, 101–102
Rousseau, Pierre, 92–93
Rowlandson, Mary, 99
   as cultural hero, 131
   popularity of, 168

Saillant, John, 142
St. Augustine, missionary establishment in, 15–16
St. Denis, Louis Juchereau de, 80, 83–84
   appointment at Natchitoches, 84–85

INDEX

Indian slave trade and, 84–87
   marriage and children, 84
St. Denis, Louise Marguerite
   Juchereau de, 84, 88
St. Denis, Marie Pétronille de, 90
San Fernando de Taos, 188
Sánchez Navarro y Gomes
   Mascorro, Manuela, 84
Sancousy, insurrection led by, 17
Sandys, Edwin, 137–138, 144
Santo de Silva, Fray, 91
Saunt, Claudio, 145
scalping, images of, 8, 34–35, 35f
Schurz, Carl, 152
Searchers, The, 168, 195
   Parker narrative and, 177–178
   scholarly treatises on, 178
Seaver, James E., 172
Seminole
   enslaved, runaway Africans
      and, 140
   removal to Indian Territory, 140
Seneca, Jemison's adoption by, 172
settlement Indians, 52, 55
   Euro-dependency of, 73–75
sexual purity, female, 170
sexual servitude, of Indian women,
   10, 82, 191
shatter zone
   Ethridge's concept of, 70–71
   Mississippian, 47–64, 192
   Northeastern/Eastern Seaboard,
      40–41
   Osage and, 42–43
   Quapaw and, 40–41
   southeastern, 192
   Wichita and, 42–43
shatter zone effect, 99
Shawnee, European traders and, 58
Shawnee mercenaries, 56
Shuck-Hall, Sheri, 54
Sibley, John, 95
Siouans
   bondage forms of, 10
   Cahokian connections of, 36
   Dhegiha, 37, 45n18

proto-Dhegiha, 41
Sandys's school and, 138
slave trade
   British abolition of, 1
   pre-African origins of, 2
   U. S. abolition of, 15
slavery
   among Southwest societies, 188,
      190–195
   Anglo-American and indigenous
      context for, 1
   chattel model of, *see* chattel model
      of slavery
   complexity of term, 2–3
   evangelism and, 139
   indigenous forms of, 60–61
   intercultural, in Southwest,
      187–188
   interpretation at public sites, 186,
      195n1
   kinship and, 11
   Lauber's definition of, 9
   Native American, *see* Indian slaves
   precontact, in Southwest,
      191–192
   predating Spanish
      colonialism, 188
   shifting definitions of, 3–4
slaves; *see also* African slaves; Indian
   slaves
   flight to Indian communities, 137
   "white," 99
slaving campaigns, British, 2
slaving networks, North American
   extent of, 15
slaving societies, militaristic,
   see militaristic slaving
   societies
Slocum, Frances, Delaware adoption
   of, 171–172, 171f
Smith, John, 115n3
   on acts of Indian kindness,
      120–121
   attitude toward Indian culture,
      128–129
   background of, 118

Smith, John—*Continued*
  capture by Powhatan Indians, 98,
    see also Smith's capture by
    Powhatan Indians
  first meeting with Powhatan,
    119–120
  illustrations in narratives of, 13
  knowledge of Algonquin
    language, 120
  narrative of, 98–99
  pejorative/diabolical images of
    Powhatans, 128–129
  Powhatan's adoption of, 123
  published writings of, 102–105,
    115n2
  references to Powhatan, 108
  return to England, 102
  Virginia Company expedition
    and, 118–119
  visual accounts of, 20
Smith, Julia, 176
Smith, Marvin, 70
Smith's capture by Powhatan
  Indians, 98, 117–123, 193
  accounts of, 100–102
  de Bry's images of, 112
  description of, 121–122
  Hole's imagining of, 106
  images of, 100, 110–111, 111f
  as mythoprosaic representation, 131
  ritualized social incorporation
    and, 101–102
  rituals involved in, 121–122
social incorporation, 117,
    see also adoption/captivity/
    slavery
  contrasting perspectives on, 14–15
  forms of, 99–100
  gendered aspect of, 18
  interpretations of, 2–3
  meanings attributed to, 4–5
  Native American practices of,
    10–11
  ritualized, Smith's capture and,
    101–102
  techniques and function, 99

sociopolitical organization
  Mississippian, 31
  relationship to escalating
    violence, 26–27
Sorel *dit* Marly, Pierre, 93
"Southeastern Ceremonial Complex",
    see "Southern Cult"
Southeastern Indian polities
  analytical vocabulary for, 65–78
  disappearance of, 192
  factors shaping in
    18th century, 66
  in historic *versus* prehistoric
    periods, 66
  transformation of, 48f
  types of, 192
"Southern Cult," violence and
    warfare and, 33–37, 35f
Southern Indian groups;
    see also *specific groups*
  French *versus* Spanish accounts
    of, 38–39
  transformation of, 24f
Southwest
  captive-taking between Indian
    and Spanish families in,
    187–188, 194
  captivity economy in, 150
  Catholicism in, 194
  Spanish arrival in, 150
Southwest borderlands
  adoption/capture/slavery in,
    190–195
  precontact intertribal conflict in,
    191–192
  reflections from, 185–195
Spain, and Louisiana Indian slave
    trade, 89–90
Spanish
  Apalachee and, 68
  and destabilization of Native
    polities, 47
  flight from Florida, 16
  in Protohistoric Period, 37
  in Southwest, 150
  Wichita treaties with, 91

Spanish conquistadors, routes of, 65–66
Spanish mission system, 15–16, 53
  as forced labor, 16
  slave raiders and, 62
  in transformation of southeastern Indian societies, 66
Spiro site, as Mississippian outpost, 32
Spotswood, Alexander, 138–139
Staden, Hans, 12–13
stereotyping
  in captivity narratives, 8
  photography and, 178, 180
  racial, 124–125
  of women captives, 168
Stewart, John, 59
Street, Susan Castillo, 20
Sturm, Circe, 145
subaltern, doubly oppressed, Parker as, 173
Susan (sister of Ouray)
  Cheyenne capture of, 159
  "Christian disposition" of, 148, 149
  explanations of intervention by, 149, 159, 161–162, 164–165, 194
  Meeker captive release and, 148
  role in Meeker captivity narrative, 158–165
  role in 19th-century propaganda, 148–149
Susquehannocks, Erie Indian trade with, 72
Swanton, John, 38

Taensa
  Louisiana site of, 46n19
  migration of, 41
Taensa women, enslaved, 82
Talisi, de Soto's impact on, 51
Taliwa, Battle of, 140
Tallapoosa, 51, 70
  Upper Creeks and, 76
  Woodward and, 59
Tame Deer, 140

Tascalusa, Spanish military assaults and, 50
Tawakoni, enslaved, 91
technological superiority, trope of, 119–120
Tenochtítlan, Spanish conquest of, 187
Texas, St. Denis's trade with, 85–86
Thibault, Nicolas, 90
Thorowgood, Thomas, 161–162
Timucua, demise of, 78, 192
Tisquantum, 3
Tomahitans, militaristic slaving practices of, 73
"Tombe of the Weroans," 105–106, 106f
Tonti, Henri de, 57, 60, 61, 64n8
Topsannah, 179f, 180
torture, ritualized, 24
Towasa Indians, 58–59
trade, *see* African slave trade; European trade; Indian slave trade; slave trade
trade relationships, Spiro-Caddoan-Plains tribes, 32
Troyville culture, 26
True Discourse of the Present Estate of Virginia, A (Hamor), 103
True History of the Captivity and Restoration of Mrs. Mary Rowlandson, 168
True Relation of Such Occurrences and Accidents of Note (Smith), 102–103, 104, 119
Tsalagi, 140
  corn mother story of, 140
  and Nan'yehi's rescue of captive, 141
Tunicas, 39, 40, 52
  Chickasaw slaving and, 61
  Natchezans and, 45n18
  Quapaw defeat of, 41
Tupi peoples, 13
Turner Strong, Pauline, 10, 11, 117
Tuscarora War, 78

Tuscaroras
  coerced education of, 138–139
  defeat of, 63n6
  as middlemen, 56
Two Rode Together, 168

Union Colony, 153, 155, 163
U. S. Native American policy, assimilation *versus* removal approaches to, 157
Upper Creeks, 51, 75–76
  Woodward and, 59
Ute Indians
  and attack on Meeker family, 147
  horses and, 150, 156–157
  Meeker captive release and, 148
  Meeker Massacre and, 20, 164–165, 194
  perspective on whites, 155–156
  resources on reservation of, 160
  as slave trade victims, 150
  transition to agricultural economy, 150–151
  U. S. treaties with, 150–152
Utiangue, 52

"Vacant Quarter," 37
Vasconcelos, Andre de, 136
Vasquez de Ayllón, Lucas, 135
Vaughan, Robert, 110–111, 112
Vega, Garcilaso de la, 40
Vega y Coca, Miguel, 185
Viard, François, 87–88
Villiers, François de, 92
violence
  agricultural economies and, 32
  cultures tending away from, 32–33
  evidence from La Salle's expedition, 41
  Fisher site evidence, 30
  male, as cultural universal, 25
  Mississippian culture and, 31
  Mississippian evidence of, 29
  in pre-Columbian North America, 99
  "southern cult" and, 33–37
  Southern Cult imagery and, 34
  traditions of, *see* Indian traditions of violence and enmity
  visual representations of, 12, 13–14
Virginia, racial laws in, 6
Virginia Company, and propagation of Christianity, 138
Virginia narratives, *see* Hamor, Ralph; Pocahontas (Matoaka); Powhatans; Smith, John
visual evidence, 5
visual field, framing, 11–14
visual representations;
  see also iconography; imagery
  as evidence, 12
  neglect of, 12
  objects depicted in, 13
  studies of, 11–14

Wagner, Mark, 104
Ward, Nancy (Nan'yehi), 140–141, 144–145
warfare
  as cultural universal, 25
  and demise of Mississippian chiefdoms, 53
  indigenous slavery and, 60–61
  Mississippian, 19
  Southern Cult imagery and, 34
  in Southwest areas, 44n5
Waterees
  demise of, 192
  survival through confederations, 78
weaponry; *see also* firearms
  Southern Cult imagery and, 34
Welch, James, 64n8
Welch, Thomas, 59, 64n8
Werowocomoco, 100, 101
West Indies, and middle passage in reverse, 6

Westos, 7
  aggression against settlement Indians, 74
  dissolution of, 56
  English slave trade and, 42
  Erie evolution into, 41
  Euro-American wars with, 77–78
  European colonizing strategies and, 72–73
  impact on Native Southern peoples, 54–55
  as militaristic slaving society, 54
  slave trade and, 19, 59
Weyanoke people, 137
White, John, 20, 105–106, 106f, 110, 169
white captives, numbers of, *versus* number of captivity narratives, 167–168
white Indians, 178
  and choice to remain with "captors," 182
White River Ute Agency, 147, 150–151, 152
  Meeker's appointment to, 153
"white" slaves, 99
white women captives, 168, 195
  adoption of, 170
  and choice to stay with captors, 170–171
  and fears of rape, 169
  film images of, 177–178
  and portrayal of male Indian brutality, 169
  stage images of, 176–177
  white attitudes toward, 170–171, 178
Whitefield, George, 133
Whitely, Simeon, 159
Wichita
  in Louisiana slave trade, 89
  "shatter zone" and, 42–43
  Spanish expeditions against, 91
  treaties with Spain, 91
William and Mary College, 144

Williams, Roger, 133
Williamson, Peter, 132
Wimar, Charles, 169–170
women; *see also* Indian women; white women captives; *specific Indian groups*
  African, marriageable status of, 84
  role in indigenous slavery, 141
women captives; *see also* Indian women, enslaved; Meeker captivity narrative; Parker, Cynthia Ann; Pocahontas (Matoaka); Rowlandson, Mary
  of Chickasaws, 61
  stereotypical depictions of, 168
  white, *see* white women captives
Wood, Peter, 135
Woodland peoples
  evolution into Oneota culture, 30
  Mississippian culture and, 29
Woodland periods
  controversy over terminology for, 43n2
  culture-historical overview of, 25–26
  violence during, 25–26
Woodward, Henry, 55, 59
  Cofitachequi and, 70, 76
Woolman, John, 133
Wyandots, 54

Yamasee Confederacy, 75
  firearms acquired by, 77
  slave raids and, 76–77
Yamasee War, European trade and, 62
Yamasees
  Ocute coalescence with, 55
  slaving by, 56
Yeardley, George, 137, 138
Yssa chiefdom, 55
Yuchis, slaving by, 56

Zafar, Rafia, 128

GPSR Compliance

The European Union's (EU) General Product Safety Regulation (GPSR) is a set of rules that requires consumer products to be safe and our obligations to ensure this.

If you have any concerns about our products, you can contact us on

ProductSafety@springernature.com

In case Publisher is established outside the EU, the EU authorized representative is:

Springer Nature Customer Service Center GmbH
Europaplatz 3
69115 Heidelberg, Germany

www.ingramcontent.com/pod-product-compliance
Lightning Source LLC
LaVergne TN
LVHW051914060526
838200LV00004B/136